D0142415

JANÁČEK AND HIS WORLD

JANÁČEK

AND HIS WORLD

EDITED BY MICHAEL BECKERMAN

PRINCETON UNIVERSITY PRESS
PRINCETON AND OXFORD

Published by Princeton University Press, 41 William Street,
Princeton, New Jersey 08540
In the United Kingdom: Princeton University Press,
3 Market Place, Woodstock, Oxfordshire OX20 1SY

Library of Congress Control Number 2003105438

ISBN 0-691-11675-X (cloth)
ISBN 0-691-11676-8 (paperback)

British Library Cataloging-in-Publication Data is available

This publication has been produced by the Bard College Publications Office:

Ginger Shore, Director

Mary Smith, Art Director

Composed in Baskerville by Natalie Kelly

Text edited by Paul De Angelis

Music typeset by Don Giller

Printed on acid-free paper. ∞

www.pupress.princeton.edu

Printed in the United States of America

1 3 5 7 9 10 8 6 4 2

In memory of my recently departed friends:

Robert Freeman
Professor
Brilliant archivist, wonderful colleague, courageous soul

Yasunari Takahashi
Shakespeare translator & educator
The leading English language scholar in Japan. Witness to the
first of my many animated discussions about Janáček

Jaromil Jireš
Film director
I never knew a warmer, sweeter man, nor one that
loved Janáček's music more

Jiří Fukač
Creator of crazy paradigms

May they live on through their families, through their work,
and in the thoughts of those that loved them

Contents

Acknowledgments

To all my wonderful colleagues at UC Santa Barbara for their encouragement over the years and especially Paul Berkowitz, William Prizer, Alejandro Planchart, Pieter van den Toorn, and Dolores Hsu. To Lee Rothfarb for his friendship and encouragement. Thanks also to the marvelous Judy Klinge, Sandy Cummings, Elizabeth Guerrero, Jan Nisen, Shelly Vizzolini, Marcia Campbell, and Mark Summerfield.

Special thanks to John Tyrrell for making valuable suggestions about which documents to include and sending me material, and of course, for his splendid contribution to this volume.

Thanks to Jiří Fukač, Miloš Štědroň, Joe Auner, Diane Paige, Judith Mabary, Derek Katz, Geoffrey Chew, Alena Němcová, and Paul Wingfield for their help and wonderful work.

Special thanks to Anne Swartz, Jarmila Gabrielová, Hugh Macdonald, and Lizette Reyes.

Thanks to Ginger Shore, Diane Rosasco, Erin Clermont, Don Giller, and Natalie Kelly for their splendid work. Special thanks to Paul De Angelis for his wonderful editing, encouragement, and valuable suggestions at all stages of the project, especially the late ones where it really mattered.

Thanks to Véronique and Tatiana Firkušný for their painstaking work with these difficult translations.

Thanks and expressions of warmth and admiration to Leon Botstein, Irene Zedlacher, Mark Loftin, Robert Martin, and Susan Gillespie of Bard College for their ongoing devotion to the marvelous Bard Music Festival, and a special thanks to Chris Gibbs for his many important contributions to the whole project. Also a big thanks to Dr. Helena Gibbsova for her critical and diacritical contribution. Warm thanks to Jonathan Levi for being a wonderful model in so many ways.

Warmest thanks to Chris and Julia Shaida, and Isabel and Jack who gave us a home when we had none. Special thanks to Gloria Beckerman and Jeremiah Stamler. Thanks also to Erdman "Pal" Palmore for his always stimulating comments on my work.

Sincere thanks to Pauline Lum and Rena Mueller of New York University for their help in many ways, and to Gage Averill who makes all things possible. Thanks also to my dear friend Laverne Lunde who put up with me and put me up for years, and to Francine, Jackie, and Harriet, and especially to Joe at Silver Wings.

Thanks to Richard Taruskin for his support, and for his performance of Janáček's *Capriccio* which I still remember fondly.

To Tetsuo Kishi and Oleg Podgorný for inspiring me.

To my family Charles, Bernard, Anna and Karen for surviving our move to New York.

Inevitably in any project there are some people who deserve the greater parts of the author's thanks. In this case the most heartfelt thanks must go to Dr. Eva Drlíková who has edited the visionary journal *Opus Musicum* through good times and bad, and is administrator of the Janáček Center in Brno. Thoughout this process she happily answered innumerable e-mails, sent photographs and articles, responded to queries from me and a host of others, and has been in general everything to everyone. Without her this book would have been far less.

Finally, warm thanks to Alan Ross who first introduced me to Janáček, and John Wehle who gave me his father's books.

JANÁČEK AND HIS WORLD

Introduction:

Janáček and Our World

MICHAEL BECKERMAN

In the 1970s and '80s in Brno, we Janáček scholars had a marvelous and well kept secret. There, in this provincial capital, *enormous* conference/festivals took place that were entirely dedicated to our man. Indeed, one cannot imagine how in the so-called "dark days" they managed so many concerts in such a short time: more than forty in a week, including five or six operas. A full day of musicological conferencing would be followed by a concert of Bulgarian contemporary music at 4 P.M., selected Janáček chamber compositions at 6 P.M., *Makropulos* at 8 P.M., and a recital of Janáček's folk song settings at 10 P.M., maybe with original costumes.

In a great tribute to my ignorance—or at least complete lack of mathematical skills—I had arrived in Brno in the fall of 1978 as a graduate student, not realizing that my year-long tenure in Czechoslovakia would embrace the fiftieth anniversary of the composer's death and in 1979, the 125th jubilee of his birth. It seemed that there was hardly a week that went by without a festival of some kind! And the hero of all these celebrations was essentially all *ours*: our own, almost undiscovered genius. I returned to the United States, where I finished my dissertation, continuing to study Janáček and his music until the late 1980s.

Returning to Janáček and his world after fifteen years is akin to entering a different universe. First, of course, there is no more Czechoslovakia, Communist or otherwise, and that tinge of a Le Carré novel no longer clings to research trips abroad. In the old days "Czech Music" itself seemed an exotic Other, needing to be nurtured and rescued, while today one can hardly see any putative *us* for all the mustered Others. Too, Janáček in those days seemed a cause worth fighting for. He was in a continual state of being discovered, but never seemed to have it completely made—either in the concert hall or the academy. As a graduate student and again in my first teaching position, I was sometimes taken to task for "spending time on a third-rate composer."

But there is more. In those days we hoped against hope that somehow Janáček would become part of the great canon of Western music and take his place with the good Germans at the center and the more or less welcomed semi-ethnic guests such as Chopin, Liszt, Verdi, and a few others. It turns out that there were (and are) two basic ways to get your subject into the canon. First, you can argue that they are simply better than people think they are. Arguments based on quality are difficult to sustain, however, especially since they depend on what people think of those who are doing the arguing. So, hedging our bets, many of us also resorted to a particular kind of canon tweaking to center our candidate. I specialized in the covert nationalist argument: the canon is Germanocentric and ill-judges all those who are not German. (Here was one bite out of the canon.) Several went further and trotted out the Teutonic Aesthetic Argument: not only is the canon German, but it has a fundamental aesthetic bias about how artworks should unfold that stems from the fact that it was most notably circumscribed by German-speaking scholars. Therefore the entire aesthetic must be tinkered with to accommodate Janáček's style. (Another bite.) Meanwhile, all over the academic map, people were taking well-meaning, logical, and only mildly self-serving nibbles out of the canon, just like I was—feminist bites, Latino bites, jazz bites, and bites for the sake of biting.

While it is perfectly clear that in the process of dethroning the authors from their sanctified perches, critics have tried to hijack some of their "aura," they did make profound observations. How can you have Masters if there is no Master Narrative? Besides, if the great sweep of history has led to, in our case, a Fast Food Fat Nation more anxious to emulate Rome than Greece, we would do well to doubt the charismatic saint-building that has led us to this point.

So here we are. Janáček's works are performed in the premiere opera houses throughout the world, every serious string quartet plays his works in that genre, and his piano compositions are featured on countless recitals. Janáček is ready to step into the Hall of Fame—but he is more like "One in the Pantheon That Vanished," or as children used to say, "Look Ma, No Canon!"

Of course, friends have tried to console me. One said, "Look, don't feel bad. That stuff is only for the academy. Outside, in the real world, the canon still lives. We're slow on the uptake." That gives me pause.

***

Whether or not one believes a canon exists, the question of how Janáček might have crawled back into it from the edge of oblivion is compelling. There are several explanations; each has adherents:

1. There was an opening for a "jagged ethnic seeker of truth" in the ecosystem of the operatic repertoire.
2. He's a goddamn great composer.
3. Janáček essentially mastered the vocabulary of his time and shifted it slightly to make it seem exotic.
4. Janáček offered music accessible enough to satisfy the conservatives and prickly enough to satisfy the modernists, thus avoiding the kind of lethal criticism that could have stopped his forward progress at any time. In order to be making it so long after his death, Janáček had to, in effect, please almost everyone in a manner inconsistent with historical reception for *any* figure.
5. Stuff happens in history and we do not know why.

To these I will add my own suggestion: Janáček was able to thrive decades after his death because he had figured out what drama was, how it worked, and how to ever tighten the noose of tension on stage and off. He understood, more than almost any of his contemporaries, that a certain kind of drama consisted of "duels" between evenly matched protagonists. Often his operas proceed as a carefully drawn sequence of such encounters: think only of *Jenůfa*, Act 2, which unfolds as a series of contests or duels between:

Introduction:
Jenůfa-Kostelnička: struggle over Jenůfa's baby

Buildup:
Kostelnička-Števa: Kostelnička scares Števa, but is powerless to get him to marry Jenůfa
Kostelnička-Laca: Laca admits his love for Jenůfa, but is horrified that she has a child

Double Climax:
Kostelnička against herself: Her "Co chvíla" (In a moment); her "To be or not to be" decision to murder Jenůfa's baby
Jenůfa against herself: Jenůfa masters her fears and sings the "Ave Maria"

Winding Down:
Kostelnička and Jenůfa: Jenůfa finds out about the death of her baby
Jenůfa and Laca: The two reconcile and agree to marry

This is quintessential Janáček. And it is the only reason we have heard of him today. Janáček was a "boiler down to basic elements" kind of composer, musically and dramatically, whether he wanted to be or not. In his hands the symphony becomes a sinfonietta, the concerto a concertino; the operas are spare, or as one British horn player said to me about *The Cunning Little Vixen*: "How can you not like an opera that has you in the pub by 9:30?"

***

Fine as far as it goes, but how did Janáček become Janáček? That spark plug of Russian national music, Mily Balakirev, believed, with a confidence bordering on fanaticism, that traditional conservatory teaching would rob composers of their individuality. Musorgsky may be considered either the vindication or the ruinous result of that approach. This delicate dance between genius and training has been going on for at least the last century, along with a similar dialogue between the mainstream and the periphery. Janáček spent just enough time in various conservatories to discover what he did not want, and danced between the provincial and the center even within his own country. Conventional pedagogy was not for him, as his *Complete Theory of Harmony* makes quite clear. Prague also was ultimately not for him, and while Brno was no Esterháza, Janáček figured out what technical resources he needed to compose with the most minimal drag on his originality.

Of course coming to a full understanding of this process is problematic, primarily because the musical work often hides the very things it appears to reveal. Despite our attempts to have authority over it, at bottom music is neither "of this world" nor in a pure realm of "musical space," but rather is in a continual mode of participating in and escaping both—always becoming something other than what it is, forever going beyond the "mere" intention of its creator.

Pygmalion, the Golem, Frankenstein's monster: We cannot predict what we create even if we are mediocre. There is a wonderful paradox about musical composition: one would think that those who excel in it should be able to proscribe and determine the way an audience will react to their works. But something strange happens: the more powerful the imagination of the composer, and the more the composer tries to control it, the *less* predictable it is and the more it travels down its own overgrown path.

***

In choosing the essays for this collection I have tried to be comprehensive, including scholars from diverse backgrounds and orientations.

The first essay, by Leon Botstein, is an important first step in the recuperation of a significant critic and translator. When I first went to Czechoslovakia I spent a good deal of time at both the "Old New" Synagogue and the Jewish Town Hall with its kosher cafeteria. As I sipped my watery chicken soup one of the servers, a member of the local community, stopped a little longer than usual at my table. This was only to whisper, with a wispy urgency: "If you're really here to do research on Janáček, don't let them forget *Max Brod!*"

Max Brod? As a young Janáček scholar I knew who he was, but no one was talking about him at all. Not only was he Jewish, but a Zionist as well, and in an age of Soviet domination, he had disappeared completely from Janáček studies. Brod's fate recalls a moment around the same time when one of the inspectors (censors) of a new Janáček exhibition stopped dangerously before Janáček's descriptive line about *From the House of the Dead* which read: "In every human being a spark of God."

I am somewhat ashamed to say that I did not heed the call to remember Max Brod at that time, somewhat lazily falling into the trap of considering him to have unacceptably tampered with Janáček's works in translation. As the years have passed though, I have gradually come to acknowledge him as perhaps the single most important catalyst to Janáček's international success. While I cannot claim myself to have fulfilled the mandate of the kosher waitress, Leon Botstein's powerful essay on the subject would have satisfied her, and so many others whose contributions were systematically minimized for political reasons. The essay is rounded out with appendices containing articles on Janáček's operas by Max Brod and Theodor Adorno.

Although we scholars tend to drastically overemphasize our roles in determining musical tastes and hierarchies in concert music, in the arena of Janáček studies and performance it is impossible to overestimate the impact of John Tyrrell's oeuvre. Not only has he done critical work editing scores in collaboration with Sir Charles Mackerras, but he has published no less than five volumes dealing with various aspects of Janáček, making available many documents in English or any language for the first time. He is currently working on a major biography of Janáček and in the second essay of this volume tells us, quite simply and elegantly, "How Janáček Composed Operas."

The third essay brings to mind the most notable conservatory in Moravia, known as JAMU, short for Janáčkova akademie múzických umění. "Múzických umění" does *not* translate as "Musical Arts" but rather "Arts of the Muses," or "Musial Arts," as they might say in St. Louis. What a fitting name for an institution associated with Janáček! While we may always question the impact of biographical events on musical composition, it is difficult to imagine how Janáček's later career would have proceeded had he not fallen in love with Kamila Stösslová. Diane Paige, who wrote a dissertation on the subject of women in Janáček's operas, looks into the new sub-science of Muse-ology in trying to determine the how and why of Kamila's influence.

It is hard to imagine a work in the operatic firmament more peculiar than Janáček's *Osud*. Taking place in a spa, we have a composer writing an opera about a composer (or is that a composer writing an opera about another composer writing an opera?) and the work features everything from death by staircase to attack by thunderstorm. *Osud* followed directly on the heels of *Jenůfa*. Though critics have always acknowledged the glory of the music they have invariably disparaged the plot, which does in some ways make the libretto of *The Magic Flute* seem coherent by comparison. In his contribution to this volume, Geoffrey Chew does a valuable service for this opera by putting it into the context of similar works written in the decadent turn-of-the-century style in the Czech Lands. If, in the end, we still find *Osud* a one of a kind work, Chew's study shows how many of its concerns were widely shared by writers of the time.

While one could always argue that problems with *Osud* stem from the fact that despite *Jenůfa*'s success Janáček was still inexperienced as an opera composer, the same excuse could hardly be made for *The Excursions of Mr. Brouček*, first performed in 1920. Yet audiences and directors have continued to struggle with a work that travels from contemporary Prague, to the moon, to the fifteenth century. Derek Katz has elsewhere convinced us that Janáček's success is at least in part dependent on his deep knowledge of contemporary opera. In his essay here he explores the problematics of national and international as well as periphery and center in determining both Janáček's personal success and the fate of this extraordinary opera.

Zdenka Janáček's memoirs reveal her husband to have been at best incredibly difficult and at worst, a sadistic brute. Many of us felt, after its publication, that we were in a new era of Janáček studies. How could anyone view as wholesome and intrepid the composer's search for artistic truth and his depiction of women if he was, at home, the most selfish possible human being? And of course, these revelations fit nicely into a certain discourse about patriarchies, dead white males, and all the doubts we have about the way our predecessors carried on in the past. Along comes Paul Wingfield to warn us of what we should have already known: autobiographies and memoirs always tell us more about their creators than their subjects. Turning the tables on the author, and biography in general, Wingfield performs an imaginary psychotherapy on Zdenka and her book and in the process defends Janáček and his work.

It has been said that if the earth were reduced to the size of a billiard ball, it would be smoother than a billiard ball. The reason this strikes us as potentially fascinating involves our resistance to it. Could things that loom so large to us be less than nothing in the grand scheme of things? To have Mt. Everest vanish is somewhat disconcerting. However, we may do the same thing with history. If, say, the "1890s in Brno" were reduced to a single day, the part about which we know something is less than a second. And that does not even include such data as the unknowable mental processes of those who lived at the time. How can we reconstruct the past when so much is missing? In the essay that closes Part I of this volume, I decided to start with one of Janáček's business cards that I recently purchased, throw in such things as history, internet auctions, beanie babies, and the notion of creative personality, and see how far I could get.

The second part of the volume, with its own introduction, consists of Janáček's writings previously unavailable in English.

***

Despite the diversity of the essays in this volume, readers may be surprised that there is no article by a Czech writer. Surely the intense tradition of Brno Janáček studies deserves to be represented by more than the two edited pieces by Miloš Štědroň and Eva Drlíková in Part II of the book! Of course, there *was* to be such a piece, and it was to have been written by Jiří Fukač. In an earlier collection, *Janáček and Czech Music*, Fukač had written a wonderful article titled "Janáček and the Dance of the Categories," based on the paper he had delivered in 1988. Coming at the subject from a critical perspective, rare in the field, he argued that:

> Musicologists sometimes claim to have recognized authentic biographical reality, but actually they are taken in tow by the suggestively self-stylizing musicians they explore.

He posed the question of the ways in which our view of the composer was "stigmatized" and inflected by a range of approaches from the hagiographical to the ideological and made a point of focussing on Janáček's upbringing in the context of the "dialectics of castle and sub-castle life." Looking at the music itself, he concluded that "Janáček's music acquires its great fascination by challenging you to take an active part in the building and rebuilding of the meaning."

About a year ago I asked him to update the conclusions he had come to fifteen years earlier and offer a new view of Janáček. I felt that there was no one more apt than Fukač to write such a piece. In the long Brno chain from the dean of Janáček studies, Vladimír Helfert, through Jan Racek and Bohumír Štědroň, to Jiří Vysloužil and finally Fukač, he was the one with the liveliest intellect, the most brilliant sense of engagement and irony. He had survived the Good Old Bad Old Days as a prime organizer and the right hand man of Jiří Vysloužil, Professor of Musicology in Brno. After the revolution, he took over the reshaping of Czech musicology and spent an incredible amount of time creating the *Dictionary of Czech Musical Culture*, published in 1997. He seemed to understand intuitively the connection between contemporary Brno and Janáček's time, its bullheaded, powerful combination of world class originality and provincial insecurity, and he seemed, with his sometimes opaque writing and powerful intellect, to embody those same tendencies.

As the months passed I began to get reports that Fukač was not well, indeed that he was seriously ill. Several e-mails were answered with the usual merriment, but he did add that "Just now, I am in the middle of my radiotherapy, which means that I am more and more tired. I hope that the situation will change in some weeks." Things improved for a while and he began working on this, and other pieces. I still expected something, but on November 17 I received a note from his assistant, Jiří Zahrádka, that he was seriously ill and in the hospital. I wrote back the following:

Dear Mr. Zahrádka:
    I would be grateful for any information about Prof. Fukač. He is a dear old friend of mine. Please let me know if there is anything I can do. I once again send him my warmest wishes, best hopes for health, and of course he is a member of the Holy Order: Sons and Daughters of Bebin. [a long-standing Brno in-joke]
Best wishes,
Michael Beckerman

A week later, on November 25, the following message arrived:

Dear Prof. Beckerman,
    I have very sad news for you. Prof. Fukač died on Friday evening. But before he asked me to send you a reply to your last e-mail. His

reply is as follows: "I will try to create gradually a very crazzy account about Janáček paradigma. But wait, I need some weeks."
Yours sincerely
Jiří

I wept of course. And laughed too. What would this crazy paradigm be, coming from the next world or the great beyond? Would he have found in just a few words, without jargon or obfuscation, without self-serving theoretical "apparatus," some explanation for how the music of this strange man has survived and endured in the broader world? How his music has come to stand for dramatic directness and expressive power?

Would he have noted that each year the "His" in the Bard Festival "_____and HIS World" sounds louder and more problematic, and offered an essay on "Janáček and *Her* World? Or Fukač might have explored a neo-Freudian paradigm, equating the power of the composer's work not merely with its avowed or self-conscious goals, but with the interaction between these and the necessarily hidden and unknowable sides of its character. Musicology and Theory seem to proceed under the assumption that a great work is somehow the sum total of the composer's intentions. And yet how could that be? Since there is no proof that we have privileged access to our own thoughts, it stands to reason that we do not always know what we think. Therefore our creations will be composed of intention *and* everything that eludes our grasp.

Fukač might have described Janáček as a brilliantly creative personality disorder, or as the concrete manifestation of Zdeněk Nejedlý's worst nightmare, or, a passionate lexicographer, he might have compiled Janáček as a series of dictionary definitions.

Of course we do not know, and cannot know what undoubtedly original paradigm Fukač might have created. Hopefully though, it may be a spur to us on our journey, both here, and in coming years. For Janáček studies will surely be making a bold transition between the kind of scholarship that tries to shed light on a particular figure, to the kind that uses the scholarship and the figure to shed light on the rest of the world.

And as for Janáček and the canon? A prickly figure who spent his life prolonging the fitful tension between center and periphery, Janáček might have found enshrinement somewhat stultifying. Groucho-like, this insider's outsider wouldn't have wanted to belong to any canon that would have him for a member.

A Note on Titles and Terms

To some extent Janáček titles are standardized, but there are persistent problems. The original title for *Jenůfa* is the much better and more accurate (though slightly confusing) *Její Pastorkyňa* (Her stepdaughter). *Příhody lišky Bystroušky* means literally "The Adventures of Sharp Ears the Fox," or "The Adventures of the Vixen Bystrouška." It has become known as "The Cunning Little Vixen" in most English productions, after Brod's German translation. Our various authors use different versions of this, and I have left them the way they are. The same is true for *Věc Makropulos*. While it literally means "Thing Makropulos," it cleverly refers both to the court case that animates the opera (hence "The Makropolus *Case*") and to the entire unfolding of events surrounding it ("The Makropolus *Affair*)." I prefer just *Makropulos*, but again, our authors have their own preferences. Finally, *Zápisník zmizelého* has been rendered as "The Diary of One Who Vanished," or "Diary of One Who Disappeared."

PART I

ESSAYS

The Cultural Politics of Language and Music: Max Brod and Leoš Janáček

In Memoriam Rudolf Firkušný

There are people who have not genius so much as a certain talent for anticipating the wishes of a century, or even a decade, before these have ever been expressed.

He who understands the wise is himself wise.
— Georg Christoph Lichtenberg, *Notebooks*

I

History is rarely kind to personalities in literature and music with talent, industry, influence, and visibility whose achievements seem, posthumously, to lack some lasting quality of genius or originality. The result is that our sense of the past becomes distorted. Aesthetic judgments interfere with the task of historical interpretation and reconstruction. We often recall only the names of such individuals rather than their work. Consider the composers John Field, Joachim Raff, and Roy Harris, or writers as nominally famous as Lord Byron and George Sand. Despite repeated efforts at revival and critical revisionism, what we remember are fragments of once widely disseminated work or merely the manner in which they lived and interacted with others. Their historical significance is diminished. Harris has receded from view and remains in the shadow of Copland. Field is recalled in the context of Chopin, as is Sand, who is also remembered mostly for her legendary style and influence on novelists, particularly Tolstoy. Byron is not read much, but referenced alongside Keats and Shelley. Raff, once a prominent, prolific, and respected composer and writer, is memorable now mostly for his link to Liszt.

Max Brod is an intriguing example of such a personality. He was exceptionally brilliant, precocious, multifaceted, and energetic. Throughout his life he displayed an enviable facility. He was tireless and astonishingly prolific. He wrote poetry, fiction, plays, criticism, and music. He was widely read. Born in 1884 in Prague, Brod died eighty-four years later, in 1968 in Tel Aviv. He left behind twenty novels, of which only one is now even remotely referred to, the 1916 *Tycho Brahes Weg zu Gott*.[1] Brod wrote one of the most influential twentieth-century books on Heine.[2] His literary and musical activities ran parallel to his engagement with politics, including Zionism, pacifism, and Czech nationalism. He dabbled in philosophy. He was, by all accounts, charismatic and generous (despite a falling out with Franz Werfel, whose career he helped launch).[3] After emigrating to Palestine in 1939 he became a key advisor to the Habimah Theatre Company. He was active in the World Center for Jewish Music in Palestine, contributed to *Musica Hebraica* and wrote "the first comprehensive study of music in Israel, *Die Musik Israels* (1951; rev. 1976)."[4]

But Brod's permanent place in history is linked with his uncanny and pathbreaking advocacy of three contemporaries, whose work is now deemed central to the twentieth century, if not characteristic of that century's aesthetic achievement: Franz Kafka, Leoš Janáček, and Jaroslav Hašek. Brod had the ambivalent fortune to live into old age. At the end of his life, having seen his own work largely forgotten, he knew that his role championing the work of others would be his claim to immortality. He enlarged the range of his talent for discovery to include Carl Nielsen and two Czech composers whose work, despite Brod's praise and loyalty, has remained obscure: Adolf Schreiber (Brod's teacher), and Ladislav Vycpálek.[5]

Brod not only reviewed Hašek's *The Good Soldier Švejk*, which appeared first between 1921 and 1923, but turned it into a play in 1928 (with Hans Reiman). The play was enormously successful and was subsequently adapted by Erwin Piscator. Brod's version has been revived periodically and made into film.[6] Hašek characterized Brod's generous behavior eloquently: "He loved his creative neighbors as he loved himself, and by so doing sacrificed a substantial part of his own creative mission."[7] Indeed, Brod's strategy was to avoid "gratuitous criticism." He saw himself as a kindred soul, a creative artist capable of advocacy, rather than a "noncreative" critic. Critics and biographers who were themselves not artists tended to be envious and inclined to write dry, resentful accounts debunking the greatness of others. As an artist Brod believed he could fearlessly express the kind of wonderment that placed shortcomings and doubts well into the background and permitted one to recognize overarching uniqueness and greatness. As Brod once put it, "My principle of criticism is to remain empathetic with the virtues of a creative artist as a means of enlarging the scope of my own spiritual realm and to take into account shortcomings only when absolutely necessary. The negative never comes into play. It needs only to be inferred if something interferes with a positive response."[8]

Brod was Kafka's closest friend and confidant. Whatever skepticism exists about his role in editing, completing, and promoting Kafka, it is reasonable to suggest that, without Brod, Kafka's place as one of the seminal figures of the twentieth century might not have been secured. For that reason alone a sympathetic approach to Brod is called for, even if Brod's own work, particularly the somewhat self-serving post-World War II writings, make him easy to dismiss. Brod knew that he himself was no Kafka. But he was at the same time a formidable intellect. His advocacy of Kafka was successful in part because in his lifetime, particularly before 1939, his voice as a writer possessed a wide resonance.

If many critics are ambivalent about Brod's role in Kafka's success, they have maintained a bland but mostly empathetic attitude toward Brod's relationship with Leoš Janáček. As Janáček's pupil and protégé, the great pianist Rudolf Firkušný observed, "without Max Brod, Leoš Janáček's world reputation would not have arrived for many more years."[9] Given that when Brod encountered Janáček, the composer was over sixty and lived in relative obscurity in Brno, one is tempted to speculate that without Brod, Janáček might never have achieved, in his lifetime or posthumously, the centrality in the repertory his music now possesses. As Alma Mahler-Werfel put it, without Brod Janáček would have remained "a nothing, someone who even in the boundaries of his homeland would have remained unappreciated."[10] In 1953 Brod proudly quoted Janáček's own unpublished encomium, "Just at the right time he came, like a messenger from heaven. And he was himself a poet. I was afraid to read his words of enthusiasm to the end. I might have become too proud."[11]

Brod did for Janáček what Brahms had done for Dvořák: he found a way to take an artist from the so-called periphery into the mainstream, which in the European context for music meant German-speaking Europe. Brahms legitimated Dvořák's artistic achievement as more than exotic. Brod was one of the eulogists at Janáček's funeral. He was the only one to speak in German. He spoke on behalf of "the tens of thousands who have had the joy of experiencing your art in German opera houses."[12]

Brod's impact on Janáček, however, went further than that of Brahms on Dvořák. Brahms commented on Dvořák's work, helped advance his career, and offered to copyedit proofs for Simrock prior to publication.

Brod, in contrast, not only succeeded in bringing Janáček to prominence even in Prague and certainly the world outside of the Czech lands, but he became integral to the composer's capacity during the last twelve years of his life to write his best music.[13] He was crucial to Janáček's astonishing "Indian Summer" of compositional productivity, working as collaborator and translator on nearly all the operas that are now performed, the works that make Janáček the only twentieth-century rival to Puccini and Richard Strauss as a successful writer of operas.[14]

The close collaboration between Brod and Janáček has been well documented.[15] Nonetheless, Brod's advocacy of Janáček has been questioned, distorted, and trivialized by some, most notably and recently by Milan Kundera. Kundera's essentially false claim is that Brod failed to understand Janáček and his music and to place Janáček "in a *large context*, the cosmopolitan context of European music." Such criticism suggests that it may be timely to take a closer look at what compelled Brod to champion Janáček and his music.[16]

As with Kafka, an explanation initially seems superfluous; after all, the works of Kafka and Janáček possess self-evident genius and originality. Discovering them might seem analogous to uncovering some sort of treasure, whose worth, like the contents of a pharaoh's tomb, is priceless. But simply to claim that *Jenůfa*—or as Brod first saw it in Prague in 1916, *Her Stepdaughter*—was so self-evidently great that the reasons for its advocacy are obvious, won't do. Unlike the circumstances surrounding Kafka, Brod was not the very first, or one of the first, to see the work. Unlike Kafka, Janáček was neither from Prague nor a contemporary writer or German-speaking Jew of the same generation. Janáček was not unknown in Czech musical circles. *Jenůfa* had been considered and passed over for a production in Prague before 1916. It was the composer Josef Suk, Dvořák's son-in-law and twenty years younger than Janáček, who urged Brod to see the work of a provincial composer.

Although the Brod–Janáček relationship has been explored from the vantage point of Janáček, it remains less well understood from Brod's point of view.[17] Brod, who played the piano well, also composed. He was active in writing music criticism for Prague's leading German newspapers, the *Prager Tagblatt* and *Abendblatt*. Music, particularly for the German-speaking Jewish intellectuals in Prague, was an art form that carried a multifaceted symbolic, political, and social significance. Franz Werfel, for example, made the tireless advocacy of Verdi over Wagner a lifelong project. Brod and Werfel shared, alongside Janáček, a self-conscious anti-Wagnerian sensibility, but in Brod's case, the attraction to Janáček's music drew from sources well beyond the reaction to Wagner. For Werfel to champion Verdi required no critical discernment; the Verdi–Wagner rivalry in the minds of the public for music was not new. Also Werfel, though his memory was prodigious and he could sing long stretches of the operas by heart, remained an enthusiastic amateur. Not so Brod. A well-trained musician, by 1916 Brod had already thought carefully about contemporary music, particularly by Czech composers. His embrace of Janáček drew on technical mastery and personal experience as a composer, which were well beyond anything of which Werfel or his other Prague literary contemporaries would have been capable. In this regard—as an observer of musical life writing in the German language—Brod can be properly compared with two contemporaries, Kurt Singer and Theodor W. Adorno.[18]

But Brod went further. He exploited his musical training and compositional ambitions in order to work successfully in a complex manner with Janáček as advisor, semi-muse, editor, and translator who was also quasi-librettist. Brod's own compositional output ultimately extended to only thirty-eight opus numbers. Like his teacher Schreiber, whose suicide Brod ascribed to a modern critical prejudice that prized command of an academic concept of compositional technique over the "pure, elegant, and truthful tone of the heart," Brod wrote mostly songs: music with texts.[19] Indeed, as Brod's service to Janáček initially as a critic and then collaborator indicated, it was Brod's capacity to use language with music and on behalf of music that made the difference. Brod's skepticism about the appeal to an evaluation of technique as a criterion of criticism was directed at the misuse of a normative notion of compositional craft. Criticism of so-called technique was applied rhetorically and routinely in German criticism as grounds for disparaging the music of many non-German composers, notably Janáček and Musorgsky.[20]

Brod's position was not defensive. His own compositions reveal familiarity if not facility with established conventions. The two Heine settings, opp. 1 and 1b from 1900 and 1901, demonstrate an awkward capacity to write late-Romantic harmony and produce musical impressions of texts. In op. 1, written when Brod was sixteen, the piano accompaniment is assured and supports a sentimental albeit uninspired melodic line whose pathos is unmistakable. Brod had clearly looked at Schubert, Schumann, Wolf, and, in terms of harmony, Wagner. Op. 1b is somewhat more interesting, utilizing rhythmic ingenuity, with moments of elegance and subtlety. Again, skill in the piano writing is evident. In op. 1b, one catches a glimmer of Brod's desire to extend the tonal palette toward a more Straussian model.[21]

This direction is particularly audible in settings of texts by Flaubert and Schiller that Brod wrote several years later. In two lieder, dating from 1908 and 1910, one senses the influence of Mahler. In a third song, a setting of Goethe's "Sankt Nepomunks Vorabend," written in 1916, the year Brod first heard *Jenůfa*, Mahlerian gestures, affected moments of simplicity, and attempts at musical drama all can be heard.[22] Brod's language remains tonal but is marked by an increasingly heavy and not altogether skilled reliance on chromaticism and overlapping tonalities. But the hint of conventional sentimentality is never lost, as the rhythmic figuration, line, and structure suggest. Only later—as in the 1921 setting of Psalm 126—does one encounter a sparser texture, attempts at abrupt shifts in tonality, and the use of dissonance. One finds also a self-conscious integration of a specifically Jewish cantorial element in the vocal line, a direction possibly inspired by Janáček's use of Czech speech melody as a basis for motivic construction. In the end Brod's musical setting is too obvious in its reliance on predictable gestures and transitions, despite the surface homage to a rhetoric of expressive intensity and a passing modernist flirtation with atonality.[23]

Equally revealing when we turn from Brod's own music to the music criticism he wrote during the period of his close association with Janáček is Brod's attitude to the music of Richard Strauss. Strauss was the contemporary composer from Germany who had been most influential on the cadre of younger composers in Eastern Europe in the early stages of their careers, including Karol Szymanowski, Béla Bartók, and Janáček himself. Yet of all living composers Strauss posed the greatest challenge to Brod the critic. In Strauss, the unbelievably great seemed forever tied to its opposite. Kitsch and inspired moments of the most imaginative modern music (the last act of *Der Rosenkavalier*, for example) existed, incomprehensibly, side by side. Even in *Elektra*, Strauss, with no evident demonstrative or ironic purpose, mixed up the *schmissig*, the fashionable, dashing, zippy, and cheaply attractive with the profound. Brod understood the extent to which Strauss, uniquely among contemporaries, commanded all the aspects of compositional craft, from melody and harmony to form and orchestration.[24] But when Brod compared Strauss's *Alpine Symphony* to Vítězslav Novák's *The Storm*, all he found in Strauss was virtuosity in technique and a "naked realism."[25] Unlike Berlioz's *Harold in Italy* or other great works that responded through music to landscape, all one encountered in Strauss was the "tourist." Strauss had to "have everything" and described all that he saw with perfection, but he failed to penetrate surface experience or express something more profound about being in the world. His realism demonstrated virtuosity without a soul.

Novák's work communicated that which Strauss's might have, and Berlioz's clearly did: a journey through music of an authentic spiritual character.[26] The greatness of Novák's musical transformation of the drama and the text of Stavopluk Čech lay in the composer's capacity to use music to transcend formal aesthetics, the representational and the illustrative.[27] Landscape—even of the Alps—natural events, like a storm, and words (particularly in what John Tyrrell has characterized as Čech's "undistinguished and unconsciously comic" text)[28] represented an external world that, as in the case of Strauss, could be brilliantly depicted and evoked in music. But music possessed a greater potential, which Novák displayed. Music could transform externality, so that a storm became "the storm of the soul." As Brod put it, "The composer made out of the purely aesthetic and pictorial *post hoc* the model of an ethical *propter hoc*."[29] Using the well-known logical fallacy, Brod sought to define the task of the composer. A technique sufficient to link music to its references (e.g. Strauss) did not imply, causally, the capacity to write music that realized the transcendent possibilities inherent in the aesthetics of musical perception and communication (e.g., Novák). Great music could realize the ethical potential of the aesthetic and reach beyond surface realism into the realm of human inwardness and truth.

The notion that music had the power to penetrate and transform reality and inspire humanity (listeners and participants) to a sensibility higher and nobler than mere perception provided Brod with the vocabulary with which to express his admiration for Josef Suk. In a short article praising the Violin Fantasy, op. 23, Brod described how a performance of the work succeeded in reviving the depressed, tired, and exhausted orchestra resigned to a mechanical routine. The work dispelled, for both the players and the audience, the sense of hopelessness created by the outbreak of the war in 1914 and rekindled the humanistic spirit of Beethoven's Ninth Symphony. Brod praised Suk as well for *Asrael*, the Fantastic Scherzo, op. 25, and the String Quartet, op. 31. Suk's works restored "desire and skin to my bones and filled me with the breath of life."[30]

It is easy to dismiss such hyperbole as sentimental and naive. Yet Brod's views reveal a conviction about the power of the aesthetic, and in particular music, in the context of the crises of modern existence and contemporary politics circa 1914. Brod expressed this conviction in a shockingly direct manner, but it was not exceptional. The dense philosophical apparatus of Theodor W. Adorno and the more sophisticated critical discourse of German and Viennese Jewish contemporaries (e.g., Paul Bekker, Adolf Weissmann, Paul Stefan, Max Graf, and even Julius Korngold) conceal a comparable belief in the political significance and ethical power of music as an art form.

Brod's most extensive statement on the link between aesthetics and politics in music, and the immanent ethical power of truly great music, was written a few years after World War II, in 1951. Brod argued that each nationality, including the Jews, could find in music a synthesis between the particular and the universal. Music as an art form was "universal" in its grammar and logic. But each nation—as had been so brilliantly demonstrated by the Czechs, from Smetana to Janáček—could lend universal music "a special coloring, a previously unheard nuance." "Every ethically based nationalism" in music "must be limited by an embracing universalist humanism" whose boundaries were defined by a shared commitment to universal rules of musical logic and criteria of judgment. By adhering to a shared aesthetic foundation, composers could reach listeners from disparate nations. Listeners, no matter their ethnicity or nationality, could share in the expression of a distinct national identity and derive universal human insights from the musical realization of national differentiation. Brod termed this ideal aesthetic achievement in music "national humanism."[31]

Brod used Smetana as the prime example of the achievement of a true and therefore ethical national humanism. Smetana integrated that which signified the ethnic and particularistic with a language of expression that reached beyond the local and national. The formal and technical structure of musical communication was transnational. A great national composer, Smetana used the universal dimensions of musical communication not to foreground the ethnic or denature the particular, but to integrate it—without camouflage, without compromise, but with transformation. The once foreign became an audible part of a universal discourse. Pride in the local, even assertiveness, was then utilized to expand the accumulated rhetoric and grammar of the universal.[32]

Brod's statements implied a progressive expansion of the universal over time. The particular and national contributed to this expansion of the universal (as the examples of Mahler and Janáček indicated). What was once national could be transformed, appropriated, and responded to, beyond the national boundaries of origin. In this process, however, the particular retained its integrity. Music then functioned as a nondivisive marker of a distinct identity. In Brod's view Tchaikovsky had also accomplished this goal, even though Tchaikovsky and Smetana were composers who had been wrongly accused by their countrymen of being insufficiently national and too accommodating to the universal. Brod extended the same ethical praise to Musorgsky, whose advocacy of the Slavic and Russian was more pronounced than Tchaikovsky's.[33] In Brod's view Tchaikovsky and Musorgsky, without apology and in different ways, used the national in the service of the universal. Music became at once a means of national cultural definition and a medium that underscored the sense of equality and commonality among all nations. That the "universal" was defined by deeming normative an essentially Austro-

German tradition of musical compositional practice was not a concern of Brod's.[34]

Brod's advocacy of a "liberal and human nationalism" in art that derived from and was contingent on a German cultural tradition of musical practice can be placed alongside not only his views on other matters, but the sensibilities of many of Brod's German-speaking Jewish contemporaries who lived in Prague. One of Brod's admirers has said that some synthesis of nationalism and humanism represented "the only possible approach for a cultured Jew in his relationship to other nations" in pre-1933 Europe.[35] And in fact this familiar conclusion about the lure of a culturally based response to or exit from the political predicaments of early twentieth-century nationalism with its attendant anti-Semitism has received substantial scholarly scrutiny. Nonetheless, the place of music in this dynamic has remained undeservedly peripheral.[36]

Brod's view of Smetana as a model national humanist, for example, is strikingly similar to that of Heinrich Schenker. Schenker (1868–1935), a Galician born Jew living in Vienna, was not a Zionist like Brod but a practicing Jew and member of the Vienna Kultusgemeinde. Schenker was overwhelmed with "wonderment" at Smetana's "genius" precisely because *The Bartered Bride* revealed, beneath a disarming simplicity and a "harmless" integration of local color, music that deserved comparison only with Mozart. According to Schenker, no one since Mozart had so commanded the "mysteries of motivic and thematic usage and the capacity to extend them and make them sustain function" or "rendered mood and character so brilliantly through the orchestra or through large gesture, sound color, rhythm, and modulation."[37] Considering that Schenker was radically conservative in his judgments, a theorist and critic for whom Beethoven and Brahms represented the pinnacle of achievement, this was indeed high praise. What appealed to both Brod and Schenker about Smetana was precisely the seamless if not brilliant integration of the national element consistent with the normative and formalist framework of aesthetic judgment.

The context for Brod and Schenker's enthusiasm for Smetana is crucial. The construction of identity and the violence in national movements circa 1900—particularly the Czech, German, and Polish—were at least off-putting if not dangerous to Jews living in the midst of Czechs, Germans, and Poles in the Habsburg monarchy. What Smetana demonstrated was the capacity to reconcile national sentiment with a neutral, shared language of art, thereby removing the sting from national solidarity. Smetana's art offered an alternative but forceful construct of national pride that united and did not exclude the Jews. The national inhabited the same aesthetic space as all great art. Brod recognized that pride in cultural and political identity, made possible for him by Zionism, was itself a universal aspiration. Nationalism could assume a superior ethical meaning when, through art, it became compatible with the universal. Through art, nationalism, inclusive of Zionism, could become tolerant in a manner that contemporary political Czech nationalism rarely was—with the exception of that of Masaryk, one of Brod's heroes.[38] Through art, Jews might with enthusiasm participate in "Czechness" without seeming to violate or deny their own distinction as Jews. When Max Brod compared Janáček to Smetana, he was continuing this line of reasoning. Kundera's view of Brod's attitude toward Janáček and his critique of Brod's comparison of Janáček to Smetana are therefore mistaken. Smetana's achievement for Brod was to have placed the Czech element within the "large context of European cosmopolitan musical culture," as the distinctly Czech successor to Mozart (having written, for Schenker, at least the best comic opera since *Figaro*). It was precisely this achievement which Janáček, in Brod's view, had matched and surpassed.[39]

Brod's implicit notion that there existed a neutral, universal aesthetic in music that could be adapted to or appropriated on behalf of the real, temporal, and local or the particularistic and differentiated in national character and experience, ran parallel to Schenker's claim that tonality, as a system, possessed objective legitimacy. For Schenker, the possibilities of tonality could never be exhausted and remained susceptible to adaptation and innovation. Schenker's tolerance for compositional modernist experimentation was notoriously low. Brod in contrast tried hard to embrace musical modernism, despite misgivings. Since his construct of normative musical aesthetics was vague, Brod could acknowledge that Schoenberg's ambition was not to destroy normative standards but to restore and advance them through radical change. Brod recognized that for Schoenberg, as for him, what was at stake was the cause of truth and ethics in musical aesthetics. Brod had read Schoenberg's *Harmonielehre*. Brod's review of *Pierrot Lunaire*, after a concert conducted by Schoenberg at a Verein für musikalische Privataufführungen event in Prague, as well as his analysis of *Gurrelieder*—all from the 1920s—reveal close familiarity with Schoenberg's oeuvre, including opp. 9, 11, and 19. Although resistant to the musical vocabulary, Brod praises the aesthetic and ethical authenticity of Schoenberg's project, which was closer to Kafka's in literature than Janáček's in music.

Brod recognized that critics attacked music they failed to grasp, whether that of Musorgsky, Janáček, or Schoenberg, by taking refuge behind the accusation of lack of technique. Thus in defending Schoenberg he stressed the enormity of Schoenberg's technical command of the elements of composition. For Brod, however, Schoenberg's capacity to influence the future of the normative universal dimension of musical communication went beyond technique. It was the result of Schoenberg's intense ethical and emotional engagement with the extra-musical. In Schoenberg's case, the real-life circumstances did not seem those of nationalism (since the German in music was assumed to be the template for the universal) but rather the conflicts of early twentieth-century modernity. Although Brod heard Schoenberg's aesthetic-ethical authenticity most clearly in his manipulations of late Wagnerianism in *Gurrelieder* and in his debt to Mahler's *Das Lied von der Erde* in *Pierrot*, the radical seemed justified by the crises of contemporary life.

Although Brod detected an Old Testament Jewish theological element in the text of *Gurrelieder*, he recognized that Schoenberg and Franz Schreker had as their project the search for an aesthetic means adequate to the specific conditions of modernity. Brod's position revealed a gap between the concerns of German-speaking Jews in Prague in the early 1920s and those of the Jews of Vienna and the German Reich. Outside of Prague, in German-Jewish circles unsympathetic to Zionism, the crisis of values associated with modernity—ethical, political, cultural, and aesthetic—took precedence. The object that the universal art of music had to confront was not so much nationalism as the intensity, confusion, and harshness of the concrete reality in which humans struggled after World War I. This external reality impelled an aesthetic transformation beyond post-Wagnerian romanticism.

Brod, as a Prague writer and musician, was more concerned with the Czech–German dynamic than modernity per se. Nonetheless, as his appreciation for Schoenberg and Schreker in the 1920s suggests, he shared a pessimistic view of the radical character of modernity. Complexity, instability, and impersonality in life (resulting in overtaxed nerves) characterized modern life. This was starkly in contrast with a simpler and idealized rural past. The use of a lush "overcomplicated" orchestral palette (by Schreker), or the opposite move, away from Wagnerian monumentalism to a leaner and more condensed means of expression (Schoenberg), both seemed appropriate responses.[40] It would be Janáček's special genius, however, to articulate the crises of modernity more simply and directly, using an original and affirmative Czech national sensibility. Like Schoenberg, Janáček created a new musical strategy that could take its place outside of the Czech context as an ethical musical response and antidote to the perils of modernity.

II

The investment in a concept of musical aesthetics as ethical in a dual sense—at once universal and at the same time uniquely capable of expressing or concretizing the particular—was cherished by German-speaking Jews in the decades surrounding World War I. Music did not assume merely a symbolic role in a larger construct of *Bildung*. Nor did it serve as an abstract medium of entertainment or an arena for expression of the nostalgic (or to some, regressive) taste and discernment of its middle-class adherents. Music was a social and public activity, political, and visibly demonstrative, notably in the opera theater. Music possessed parallels with language, particularly in its public function and communicative logic. Yet music seemed uniquely capable of managing a synthesis between universality (and by implication, the ethical and the good) and local human experience (including issues of identity and politics). Unlike language, music seemed to be able to communicate across the cultural and political barriers maintained by language. This thought held particular attraction for educated German-speaking Jews. Seemingly unbridgeable conflicts normally expressed in language—those linked to national identity and class—could be given a different voice through music and thus constructively transmuted into a universal discourse. Musical communication could then mediate among particularistic sensibilities, thereby deepening the recognition of a shared human condition.[41]

The more complicated the linguistic and thus cultural political environment, the more alluring the appeal of music as reaching beyond language. As Fritz Mauthner, the philosopher of language, recalled in his autobiography, Jewish children growing up in Prague had to negotiate German, Yiddish, Czech, and Hebrew, not to mention the regional dialects of all but Hebrew.[42] The Prague Jews of Brod's generation were largely German speaking and therefore tied to a distinct minority, particularly in the city. As ethnic Germans were drawn to an anti-Semitic as well as anti-Czech nationalism of their own, Prague Jews were increasingly marginalized as non-Germans within that German speaking minority, not only in Prague but throughout Bohemia. Caught between a Czech majority and a non-Jewish German minority in terms of language, Prague Jews were cut off from the ordinary linkages between language and political identity.[43] J. P. Stern observed that the German language that Prague Jews cultivated was sustained in such a radically isolated if not artificial context that it took on its own aspects of authentic classicism, purity, and superiority. Prague's literary German was aestheticized in a manner reminiscent of Brod's construct of music.

The German language used in Vienna, on the other hand, facilitated integration into the majority culture and politics of the city, even for Jews. Vienna, unlike Prague, was from 1867 to the early 1930s a polyglot city marked by immigration; the acquisition of German was an uncontested and indispensable common necessity. As Gustav Pick's wildly popular 1885 *Fiakerlied* suggests, language represented a plausible and well-trodden access point into the city's culture—as literary instrument, symbol of class and culture, and sign of place and particularity (e.g., the command of Viennese dialect).[44] Looking backwards from a post-1938 perspective, it is painful to confront the enormous premium placed on the German language by Jewish inhabitants in Prague and Vienna. Jews cultivated a self-consciously refined German marked by a sense of its superiority—a linguistic habit that anti-Semites later deemed little more than a sign of the recalcitrant artificiality of the Jew. This was ironic since language, particularly in Prague, was the necessary instrument for communication outside of the Jewish community, whether toward the Czech majority or the German minority. Not surprisingly, therefore, pride in proper linguistic usage and the notion of a normative ethical value sustained by protecting language from debasement, became widespread among Jewish writers at the turn of the century. In both cities, the centrality of language assumed a role among Jews that among non-Jews was usually reserved for politics. As the promise of genuine assimilation became increasingly remote, the question of language among Jews—German or Czech—could be transformed only by forging a national politics of their own, as a nation within Europe or through Zionism. The ambivalent fascination with Yiddish among Jewish writers in Vienna (negatively on the part of Karl Kraus) and Prague (including Kafka), and the revival of Hebrew in the years around World War I, reflect this reality.

The sense of power and effectiveness associated with language was at risk in a political climate characterized, particularly for Jews in Prague, by a multifaceted disenfranchisement. The German and Czech languages had become politicized. Music seemed more resistant. The romance with music deepened as the ethical potential of language diminished. The concern for the preservation of language, a belief in its ethical properties, and an attachment to language as potentially effective in human life—hallmarks of Jewish intellectuals at the fin de siècle (as the examples of Freud and Kafka suggest)—spilled over into musical aesthetics, which was influenced by this obsession with the linguistic. As language's ethical and practical prestige became threatened, the conception of the future of music bifurcated into radical conservatism and radical progressivism. Both among modernists and anti-modernists, music, construed as a language, was understood as requiring a defense against the debasement of modern politics, commerce, popular culture, philistine taste, and the lure of the so-called extra-musical. In this Schenker and Schoenberg were in agreement. After all, music, if protected, might function like an ideal universal language, as a surrogate antidote in a world marked by ethnic tension and national conflict.

By the early 1900s, Brod and his fellow educated German Jews found, as J. P. Stern put it, that the attempt to identify with the "deutscher Geist was spurned as infamous and ludicrous."[45] In politics Brod turned to Zionism. But in his construct of Zionism, he did not feel compelled to abandon German as his primary language and did not detach himself from loyalty to the Republic of Czechoslovakia after 1918, in which Jews attained official status as a minority nation. Zionism allowed Brod a political base within Prague from which to cultivate his enthusiasms for the German language and Czech music, all without having to substitute culture for politics. However, as the gulf widened between the German and the Jewish, Brod's self-conscious attention to the character of linguistic expression shifted from issues of purity (in the sense of Karl Kraus) to the status of language as medium of modern culture and the quotidian.

Aware of the limits of language, Brod turned away from new German music, with the exception of his enthusiasm for Max Reger.[46] He saw in the Czech musical revival more cause for optimism about the potential of positive multinational communication. Music became a model for language in the sense that in music an elevated universalist aesthetic aspiration could be reconciled with a stark realism. At the same time Brod, despite his technical training, increasingly construed music in terms of language. He became deeply invested in how words and music could function together, particularly during his collaboration with Janáček.[47] Within the context of Prague, however, there was skepticism about the analogy between music and language. Kafka and Fritz Mauthner, unlike Brod, resisted any facile linkage between language and music, particularly in modernity. Rather, they perceived the gulf between these two modes of human expression. Music could not, in human affairs, become a surrogate for language.

Kafka was quite conscious that he had difficulties with music. That fact, he once confessed, caused him to be overwhelmed with "a quiet bittersweet mourning." The feeling vanished quickly, Kafka reported, but the fleeting encounters with his personal distance from music left him with ever more clarity of "how endlessly distant the people closest to me are." Implicitly, music represented to him a potential source of connection to others and to humanity, one that remained inaccessible to him. Indeed, Kafka observed that "music is for me like the ocean. I am overpowered, and transported to a state of wonderment. I am enthusiastic but also anxious when faced with endlessness. I am, as is evident, a poor sailor. Max Brod is the exact opposite. He rushes head-long into the waves of sound. Now that's a champion swimmer."[48] Music—the ocean—is placed by Kafka in opposition to language, which by implication is land. Music is vast and endless but also strangely amorphous, without the firmness and contours of land. Music requires the particular special skills of sailing and swimming, which are optional in life, yet alluring. Courage is also required since the mass of water is dangerous and undifferentiated. It is a space in which the individual might easily drown.[49] The nature of music suggests attraction and fear; it is an arena in which one can disappear and become indistinct.

A different consequence of Kafka's view of music can be gleaned when one compares these observations by Kafka with his well-known 1917 "Report to an Academy," published in Martin Buber's periodical *Der Jude*, to which Brod was a frequent contributor. The image of Brod as champion swimmer can be set alongside the ape in Kafka's parable. The ape chooses a career as a performer in the musical theater. The fame Jews achieved through musical performance and composition utilizing a nonverbal virtuosity created the illusion of acceptance by the non-Jewish audience. The ape, through theatrical virtuosity, deludes himself as to his identity. Like the ape who believes he is human (but who is never seen as such), the Jew who immerses himself in the ocean of music—like Brod—uses the nondenotative, nonrepresentational yet human character of music to disappear as distinct, to merge with the rest of humanity. But this never really occurs, no matter how well one sails or swims. Indeed, as Brod himself discovered during the 1930s, the allure of music over language—the apparent ease with which a national humanistic synthesis could be achieved—did not succeed in generating a sense of universality. Kafka's image of music as an ocean underscored the popular illusion among many European Jews that with the requisite training music, rather than language, could become the form of life and culture through which it appeared more possible to lose pariah status.[50]

Kafka's distance from his friend's enthusiasm for the potential and nature of music in modernity can be compared with a more philosophical parallel in Mauthner. What is significant in Mauthner's sparse references to music in his extensive analysis of language is the extent to which he attached a mystical character to musical communication. Music, in its modern form, was emancipated from movement and language. It had achieved, albeit slowly, a status akin to mathematics.

Mathematics "is an endlessly more subtle instrument than language," Mauthner observed, but it does not contain, in its elements, that which can assist in the understanding of the interior of the human condition, which is why so many mathematicians, for Mauthner, were mystics. Likewise, no technical knowledge of the elements of music can even hint at the "powerful mystical effect of music." The secret of music's meaning among those exposed to it remains sealed off and protected from analysis or communication through language.[51] From Mauthner's point of view, Brod's ideal of an effective national humanism in music was implausible.

If Brod argued for a linkage between aesthetics and ethics in music—a position quite similar, in terms of the criteria of judgment, to that developed by Ludwig Wittgenstein—Mauthner came indirectly to a conclusion similar to Kafka's.[52] Mauthner stressed the mystical dimension of music as reflective of its resistance to a parallelism with language. For Mauthner, poetry and music had once been inextricably tied to everyday human physical activity, including work and dance. But over time music in Western culture had detached itself from its anthropological origins in human movement. Mauthner's speculations on the original musicality of speech and movement found unwitting echoes in Janáček's theories and Brod's enthusiasm for them. In modern history music, like poetry, had become separated from ordinary action and movement. Wagner's attempt to reconnect words and music into "the total work of art" was therefore a "gigantic misunderstanding." In Wagner's hands music as an art form had become even more removed from the quotidian. Nonetheless, music's emancipation from language and ordinary life—Mauthner's analysis of the history of modern art music—suggested a path quite divergent from Wagner.[53] If one could return to the quotidian, and concentrate on the speech rhythms in societies where movement, speech, and music had not been separated over the span of two hundred years of modern history, then a valid linkage between music and language in modernity could be forged. This was precisely what Brod understood Janáček to have achieved.[54]

It was not Mauthner's intent to denigrate the achievement of modernity in the creation of an abstract, self-referential aesthetic language of music. Mauthner's version of modernity as creating an emancipated musical logic, however, implied the possibility of a revival of music's origin in ordinary activity (speech and movement), a revival that could create a novel framework for the synthesis of the universal and particular sought by Brod. The direct engagement with the nineteenth-century formalist aesthetics of musical autonomy had led Brod to recognize the insufficiency of formalism on the one hand and, like Mauthner, the inadequacy of Wagner's solution. Within the unique linguistic context of the

Czech lands, where the capital of Prague did not, like Vienna or Budapest, entirely dominate the provinces linguistically or culturally, the possibilities of a different path had already been made apparent by Smetana and Dvořák. For Brod, music's universality and ethical power were not dependent, as in the case of Schenker, on maintaining "the rigid formalist integrity of an aesthetics of autonomy." As with Bartók, Janáček's forays into documenting folk materials and speech patterns represented the assertion of a preserved rural tradition against a progressive cosmopolitan urban culture. The past, sustained in the provincial present, held the key for modernity.

There was more parity between city and country in the Czech context, more comparability between Brno and Prague than in German Austria between, for example, Linz and Vienna. Furthermore, the Jews of Prague were not the only Jews in the Czech landscape. Jews therefore were not seen, as in Vienna, primarily as cosmopolitan. Rather, in the context of the rise of Czech nationalist culture Jews, linguistically German yet not German, could theoretically assume a role as mediators between the new Czech renaissance and the rest of Europe. Like Mauthner, Brod's instincts led away from Wagner and the artificiality of the leitmotif. Music, if reconnected to human life, could assume the role of a bridge between the German and the Czech, and the urban and the rural. The bridge could not, however, be constructed out of a romanticized primitivism. It had to be adequate to modernity. Mauthner, brought up in an earlier generation but within the same crucible as Brod, through his close and obsessive scrutiny of the connection between language and meaning, revealed a conceptual framework strikingly similar to that which Brod brought to bear in his encounter with Janáček's music. The difference lay in Brod's belief that the abstract musical discourse Mauthner described could be demystified and reconnected to life.

Modernity, for Brod, posed a daunting challenge to any strategy located merely in a nostalgia for a simpler premodern past. Brod shared the view of the contemporary world as particularly beset by egotism, aggression, incomprehension, mistrust, and above all violence among distinct cultures and nations. Modern language and literacy, as Karl Kraus and others were tireless in reminding their readers, failed as countervailing phenomena. Modern music and musical culture might possess a potential advantage in the cultural politics of modernity. It could transform the linguistic. If modern music could reconnect to speech and movement in modernity, without a regressive nostalgia, then music's narrative could be made accessible across divisions and underscore a common existential experience. Kurt Singer, like Brod a defender in principle of the possibilities of new music, wrote in 1929 from Berlin that under the right conditions music in the contemporary world "could once again become a religion espousing brotherhood among people and lead to the recognition of the highest aspirations of the will and creative ambition." Music could transform "the ordinary," place "excess" to the side, and alter the "everyday into a holiday, opportunity into necessity, and commerce into religion." Singer was looking for the great "transformation" that would grace humankind with "happiness." This would be achieved at the expense of extreme individualism, "egotism, hate, ignorance, and narrow-mindedness."[55] For this to happen a new idealism in music would have to reveal "truth, beauty, and interiority" as opposed to "the untruthful ugly business of music."[56] Using modernity, music in its public function could help lead the way out of the contemporary crisis, even if for Singer the prospects seemed dim and located exclusively within the realm of music defined as an aesthetic experience elevated beyond commerce and daily life.

It was precisely this search for an adequate modern music overtly outside of the post-Wagnerian tradition that led Brod to accept Suk's suggestion to hear *Jenůfa*. And in Janáček he found the ideal answer not only to possibilities of the uses of music within the cultural politics of the Czech lands, but a model for a true universal national humanism in modern music. Janáček, all on his own in Brno, had found the new path. He had restored music's links to basic human experience—hence its essential but ethical realism—without denying modernity. This realization explains the extraordinary amazement and intensity of Brod's response to *Jenůfa* in 1916. Here, from the first sounds, was music that was original, human, and modern. It was built on a deep connection between human behavior—speech and movement—and music. Through psychological insight and the truth-telling of music it transformed the real and particular into the universal, all without sacrifice to the evident Czech character of sound and story. And the technical command of the advanced uses of the elements of composition was evident. Brod would later ascribe the same virtues to Janáček's instrumental and choral music.

That the crisis of modernity was the frame for Brod's amazement can be gleaned from the opening lines of his 1916 account of *Jenůfa*. Brod was in search of an artistic response adequate to the catastrophe of war. Hearing Janáček's music restored his sense of hope and his love of life. The fact that Janáček was outside the establishment, wholly original, following his own "inner laws" uncorrupted by the modern commerce of music, was as significant as his authenticity as a Czech artist. *Jenůfa* was more truthful than "philosophical essays." His "divine music" said more about "the character of the nation and true nationalism than all theories." Yet it was the music that transformed what might at first be a romanticized "primitive" and "unenlightened" folk context into a parable of the human condition, exactly as Smetana had done in *The Bartered Bride*. As in Kafka, Janáček's economy of means and surface simplicity had initially concealed his capacity to confront the dilemmas of modernity. Out of so-called realism and what was on the surface a folk opera came "music of timelessness, of eternity and of an essential creativity" to be preserved in the "sanctity" of the human soul. It was "lifelike art" that relied on "unnaturalistic free forms of creation," much like Expressionism. The absolute and the real had been fused.[57]

Indeed, Brod understood from the start the stark difference between Janáček and Wagner. The link between music and text in Wagner was contrived when compared to Janáček, who displayed lyrical beauty and a nonmanipulative realism in the use of musical technique. Indeed, "local color, as well as impressionistic elements are merged with the purest strictures of form of so-called absolute music," wrote Brod. Furthermore, "the national and the universal-aesthetic are not merely tied together, but both streams rush forward together in the same blood vessel, and are rendered actual as sharing a unified and common impulse."[58] *Jenůfa* revealed purity of aesthetic form and all the virtues of an organic self-contained work of art. It manifested a local and universal contemporaneity suffused with ethical meaning, and yet it communicated with ease and with a musical originality rooted in speech. Immediately Brod compared Janáček to non-Czech composers: from the past, Bach; and from the present, Carl Nielsen. In referring to Janáček's technique as an artist, Brod placed him alongside the sculptor Auguste Rodin.[59]

When the two men met it was clear that Brod liked Janáček—well beyond any sense of Brod being flattered by Janáček or of idealizing him as some unspoiled exemplar of the essential Czech personality. Brod realized that Janáček was no provincial.[60] Janáček's intense and obsessive relationship with Kamila Stösslová later would offer Brod reassurance and comfort, in light of the potential of anti-Semitism coming from so committed a Slavophile—Kamila and her husband were both Jewish.[61] But the most astonishing confirmation of the significance of Janáček's originality and importance as signaling the possibilities of a universally valid modern music of genius came with the task of translating Janáček into German. Brod was initially resistant to the idea in view of Janáček's theories regarding the close connection between Czech speech and the musical material.[62] Brod realized that the music implied the possibilities of using a German diction that was not classically "operatic," but a "libretto prose that followed exactly the musical dynamic." The result Brod achieved in providing German texts to Janáček's music redeemed the possibility of translation. Music facilitated what seemed impossible in politics: the forging of communication between the Czech and the German. Music compensated for the limits of language. Janáček's music had made "humanism possible, not hate among nations. It is not easy," Brod observed, "to sustain in these insane times such self-evident principles."[63] Janáček was far more important than a Czech master. He took a place alongside Mahler as meeting headlong the paradox facing the modern artist: how to reconcile national identity, the terms of reality of contemporary existence, and universality through art. Janáček demonstrated that it could be done.

By the time Brod wrote his short biography of Janáček in 1925, they had been working together for nearly a decade, *Jenůfa* had become a success not only in Vienna but in Berlin, and Janáček was renowned throughout Europe in Brod's translation. Brod's other translations also took hold. In 1925 Brod stressed Janáček's relative simplicity, intense humanity, and truthful spirituality. What seemed "primitive" was actually an alternative to "barbarism" in modernity. Janáček brought beauty to the exceptional soul in a world characterized by unhappiness and chaos. Yet Janáček had developed a musical means to express "the endless empathy with suffering." His musical language was derivative of speech. Through the harmonic strategy of combining chords and accounting for their acoustic overhang in real time, and through the use of overlapping but interrelated rhythmic patterns, Janáček transcended the limits of both naturalism and expressionism. Brod took Janáček's theoretical writings seriously because there was a need for a theory that could serve as a model outside a Czech context. Janáček's analysis of speech pattern, intonation, rhythm, and harmony provided the technical apparatus that other cultures and nations could emulate to generate a music of modernity that, unlike that of Schoenberg, was tied directly to the psychology of human experience. Janáček developed a method to penetrate the soul of the individual and represent it to others, through music. He achieved in modernity what Wagner had failed to do: to reconnect music with its origins in speech and movement, to life as it was conducted.

Brod understood that Janáček's approach differed markedly from two rival strategies: those offered by Strauss and by the verismo style, particularly that of Mascagni and Puccini.[64] Although Strauss, particularly in his collaboration with Hofmannsthal, was profoundly concerned with the importance of speech and the comprehensibility of the text, he remained tied to a concept of poetic speech and its musical implications rather than to the musical content of speech. Poetry suggested musical equivalents not primarily in sound and pattern, but through meaning and reflection. Furthermore, harmonic color was suggested by ideas and events, not movement and speech. Lastly, the orchestra provided a restless, complex envelope into which the voice was integrated. Insofar as the voices in Strauss are foregrounded, the orchestra functions as a fundamental context, framing the evident artificiality of the stage and drama. This explains why Strauss's figurations and orchestrations are so intricate and dense. Long vocal lines are complicated by filigree, and voices merge with instrumental counterpoint into a tightly woven fabric that suggests the ongoing turmoil of real time. Strauss sought transparency in the relationship of voice and orchestra but rendered it hard to achieve by working against a sentimentalized simplicity in the overall musical texture.

The orchestra in Strauss relentlessly utilizes all the accumulated rhetoric of the history of music. With irony, Strauss reminds the listener of what Mauthner referred to as the two hundred years that had created an autonomous musical discourse. In the end, as Strauss's arrangements of operatic excerpts and his 1925 film setting of *Rosenkavalier* reveal, his integrated musical logic can work even when voices and words are removed (even if Strauss rightly considered the comprehensibility of the libretto crucial). Language provides the narrative framework that defines the possibilities for a parallel but engaging, self-consciously theatrical musical structure. There is little of Janáček's musical transformation of linguistic realism and narrative naturalism.

As for verismo style, Janáček's strategy was strikingly different when it came to the connection between language and music, even if he was influenced by contemporary Italians, particularly by *Cavalleria Rusticana*, *La Bohème*, and *Tosca* (for *The Makropulos Affair*). As Michele Girardi has observed, Puccini forced his texts to conform to musical ideas, particularly in the matter of meter and accent. Puccini had a "natural inclination to create a musical image of the plot and the setting." The inherited traditions of musical rhetoric, altered and adapted by the composer, subordinated the details of the text and of speech. Even meter in poetry had to bend to musical ideas.[65] What Janáček took from the Italians was not their use of language, but their skill in structuring musical drama and controlling large-scale musical time. Janáček admired the "newly acquired freedom in harmonic and tonal progressions" of his Italian contemporaries in the choice and construction of the implied harmonies of the motivic and melodic material.[66]

For Brod, Janáček stood apart most of all because of his use of speech. In this he went beyond pattern, timbre, and intonation to recognize in language usage psychological states capable of musical realization. The achievement of a compelling ethical musical experience that was truthful in Brod's terms derived from the source of Janáček's music—the quotidian response to life expressed through language. Janáček was a writer's composer. The musical within language expanded art's capacity to narrate and represent; music deepened and universalized language's communicative power in a fragmented world. There was, in the end, nothing reductively folklike, primitive, or even Czech in Janáček's approach. The realism of the music and the operas managed to transcend the artificiality of verismo, or the theatrical virtuosity of Strauss, through its authentic link to the expression of experience. Janáček was able to communicate a range of emotion and experience in music because his musical imagination was rooted in concrete human reflection and expression well beyond mere dependence on or representation of plot, actual speech, or melody. Inspired invention and transformation were Janáček's virtues. The artist was an individual, not as aesthete or egotist but as an original philosophical humanist psychologist rooted in an authentic connection to a national culture. This constituted Janáček's uniqueness.

It is instructive to compare Brod's tireless advocacy of Janáček with the relative lack of attention paid him by Theodor W. Adorno. Adorno wrote far more before 1939 about Bartók, with whom, after 1945, he linked Janáček in passing.[67] Adorno's evident Germanocentrism only partially explains this fact. (Despite the success of *Jenůfa* in Germany after 1924, Janáček did not merit the attention of Schoenberg either.) However, in the 1920s, when Adorno, himself in his twenties, was writing criticism in Frankfurt, he wrote several reviews, a 1924 one of *Jenůfa*, and two 1929 reviews of *The Makropulos Affair*.[68]

Adorno's response to *Jenůfa* was dismissive. He reduced Janáček's strategy to an "unreal" aesthetic "substrate." Adorno focused on the folk element and failed to see "a work of art." To Adorno, Janáček's music merely "speaks in dialect," and it required further transformation. Where Brod heard a work of art in the grand tradition that transcended the local, Adorno, despite his recognition of Janáček's basic compositional procedure, recognized mere honest simplicity and an admirable anti-Wagnerianism. Adorno was even skeptical about the authenticity of the "folk essence," which he regarded to be the "center of the theatrical and musical events" of *Jenůfa*. Adorno perceived nothing of Brod's claim of universality, psychological insight, and originality.

The situation changed for Adorno in 1929. Much of the reason for this was the libretto of *The Makropulos Affair*. It lacked the exotic surface of folk character. What attracted Adorno instead was the fragmentary nature of the score and story line; they seemed adequate to modernity and reminiscent of literary modernism. Kafka became the focus of comparison and contrast. The "normal" was exploited by the composer, not the fantastic (Schoenberg) or "the scary evocation of the past" (Stravinsky). Normality became, through Janáček's music, absurd. Yet in the end, despite the strong impression the work made on Adorno, the opera's music was deemed enigmatic and unique in a self-contained manner. The work was categorized as "one of a kind." Its place was not in the mainstream of opera, even modern opera, but on the margins, "on the experimental stage."[69]

In both reviews Adorno recognized Janáček's integrity. However, in stark contrast to Brod, he did not hear in Janáček anything approaching a model for contemporary music or opera. In contrast to Schoenberg or Berg, and even Stravinsky, there were no aesthetic and philosophical terms within the music to generalize from. The overall narrative effect implied at best a flattering comparison with a literary analogue, Kafka. But Adorno did not go so far as to hear in Janáček's music any parallel to Kafka's genius in the use of language. Where Brod recognized an original approach to the traditions of musical composition, a strategy of cross-national significance adequate to contemporary life and politics, Adorno saw something remarkable but idiosyncratic that offered neither a system nor a model. Although Adorno, like Brod, ascribed ethical significance to what was genuine and progressive in musical art, in Janáček he found no hint of world historical significance.

III

Janáček's worldwide prominence in the repertory since the late twentieth century holds every promise of continuing. The reasons for this closely resemble the grounds on which Max Brod championed Janáček's approach to writing music, not only in opera, but in the traditions of instrumental and choral music, where the "local" must be transformed without the evident help of the visual. Adorno's commitment to a different route for modern music, derived from Schoenberg and the Second Viennese School, has retained few followers, despite a sustained period of success in the mid-twentieth century. Although Brod commands little respect today as thinker and writer and Adorno continues to exert substantial influence in music scholarship and criticism in Germany, England, and America, Adorno's dismissal of Janáček as central to a contemporary construct of musical communication and composition—of Janáček's manner of connecting music and modern life—should give pause to those eager to adopt or imitate Adorno's analytical premises.

In 1925 at the ISCM Festival in Venice Janáček observed: "The virtues or inadequacies of the other works in the programmes arise from the fact that their composers either know or do not know (Igor Stravinsky, sonata) that the rules of composition are not exclusive, that they follow the rules of human thought as a whole."[70] Max Brod understood that this connection between human thought (i.e., expression through speech) and music underlay Janáček's achievement. Adorno did not. Despite the cloying sentimentality, egotism, and overheated moralism in some of his writing, Brod should receive the respect he deserves. There is after all, something ethically encouraging about Janáček's centrality to our contemporary cultural and musical landscape. Brod had the wisdom to recognize and understand it before anyone else.

Max Brod

APPENDIX A: MAX BROD ON LEOŠ JANÁČEK'S *JENŮFA*

TRANSLATED BY SUSAN H. GILLESPIE

Impoverished, how impoverished are the war years. Scarcely a bashful minute of warmth, of uplift! Then suddenly an artistic event of the greatest importance glows in my direction, glows through me . . . can I still blaze along with it, or will it just burn a black hole in me? An evening on which I once more tremble and weep, on which I give thanks to my God that he has let me come into the world to taste such a fullness of happiness, such a fullness of the most extreme tranquility of soul. . . . Yes, once upon a time it was otherwise. Such an evening impelled me upward, I floated on high, held myself blazing in a lighter air. Today I can no longer do that. "I am the man who has seen affliction," these words of Jeremiah's ring in my ears, and they don't go well with floating and blazing. I am confused, benumbed. It has been five weeks since that happy event came my way, and even today I do not feel sufficiently collected to speak of it in a considered way or rather hurl it joyfully into the world, as I ought. . . . Into this world it is perhaps no longer possible to hurl anything joyfully. . . .

This event was the performance of the new opera by Leoš Janáček: *Jenůfa (Její pastorkyňa)*.

Of the new opera? The oddity of the event begins here. The opera is already twelve years old, it gathered dust in various Czech theater bureaus, was performed in Brno many years ago without great success. Only its new staging, which was rejected by most, attracted a certain amount of attention.

Meanwhile, the composer of the opera, who lives in Brno and is described as a very original, stubborn character with an aversion to compromise of any kind, has turned sixty-two. In numbers: 62. And in his sixty-second year, the hale and healthy old man, surely one of the most significant individuals that the Czech people have ever produced, has the satisfaction of seeing his play on the boards of the Prague National Theatre, sees the smashing success of the work with the public and serious professional critics, sees innumerable performances to a sold-out house. Without any advertising, the difficult and tragic work gains acceptance, wins all hearts, simply through its inner power. And why only today? This fact of the twenty-years-delayed discovery of Janáček will remain for all times one of the oddest artifacts in the history of art. It indicates, at a minimum, that even such a numerically small, self-regarding people as the Czechs have not yet gained the inner

· 37 ·

strength to create order within itself, to sweep aside destructive cliquish-
ness and apply its creative powers in the right places—although this (in
my opinion) would be one of the most important national and political tasks, even more important than the world-shattering question of
mono- or bilingual street signs. If an oversight of this kind occurs in a
large organism, one is more readily inclined to excuse it on account of
the complexities, excessive diversity, and breadth of popular life. When
a people are few in number, and one would like to envision a close, famil-
ial concern for each of its members and for such irreplaceable building
blocks as great artists the most loving care and attention—then this
general disgrace of the human race, which does not know how to care
for what is best in itself, weighs even heavier on one's heart. How could
this possibly happen, one asks? And lays it alongside the other disap-
pointments and riddles.

But the work itself, regardless of the murkiness of its terrestrial fate,
regardless of the epoch into which it by chance first pours out its mystical light—the work itself shines with unaffected certainty, as powerful
as the days when the gods came down to dwell among the daughters
of men, yes, cloaked in the crimson of its simple, spotless purity, in the
inexpressible power of its perfect being—a Medusa before which the
vagaries of daily life turn to stone and vanish into nothing.

The libretto is quickly recounted. It stems from Gabriele Preiss, who
is an expert observer of Moravian peasant life, and is rich in fine details
of characterization, as well as interesting from a linguistic point of view,
in its mastery of the particular folk dialect.

Two brothers (stepbrothers) are wooing the beautiful Jenůfa. But
the reckless one, who is called Števa, no longer needs to woo. When the
curtain rises, he has long since had his way. The other one, Laca, the
most unique, and at the same time the most upright figure in the opera,
is abrupt and tender, serious and suffering. The lads in the village are
returning from the military recruiter's. Števa has not been recruited;
now he is supposed to marry. It is worth reflecting on the fact that the
fortunate lover enters singing a tearful folk song: He has been inducted,
the poor thing, and may not marry—although everyone knows how favor-
able his actual situation is. In short—he is drunk, he has had altogether
enough of the beautiful Jenůfa. He pulls her roughly into the dance.
Then Jenůfa's foster mother steps in. She is the secret mistress of the
village, above everyone else in intelligence and energy, a judge and a
prophetess. Without knowing of the pregnancy of her unhappy foster
daughter (a second Rose Bernd), she forbids the marriage.* The fol-

---

*Rose Bernd is the title character in a five-act play by Gerhard Hauptmann. —(Translator)

lowing two acts bring the denouement. The child, a small Steva, has been born. Still the faithless fiancé has not turned up. Jenůfa and her foster mother are facing their downfall, two proud, highly respected people of the region. Then, as Jenůfa lies in a feverish sleep, the foster mother seizes the child and shoves him beneath the ice of the mill brook. Jenůfa has no inkling of the disaster; resigned, she girds herself for marriage to the previously despised Laca. On the wedding day, the child's body is discovered. The foster mother surrenders to the assembled populace—a scene that is reminiscent of the end of Tolstoy's *The Power of Darkness*. But Jenůfa and Laca, who has unwaveringly and silently accompanied his dearly beloved through all the chaos, have elevated their love for each other, over corpses, into a realm of heavenly humanity. The noise of the trial has subsided. The two human beings stand face to face, free and great, surrounded by harps and the harmony of the wind choir. The concluding scene, by itself, with its tender and powerful melodies, its natural intensification, its closing melody with arms outstretched endlessly wide—this scene alone earns the work a place among the eternal creations. The realism of the peasant opera flows into the clear, simple symbol of two good, truly good souls. And strange— the music, until then stamped with an acutely national character (I like to call Janáček a Moravian-Slovakian Smetana, but with a darker, more passionate, as it were, southern hue); here the music becomes general, merely musical music; the intermediate stage of ethnography has emptied into the great ocean of humanity. And for the first time, after all the terrible scenes, we hear, in the last act of the libretto, the sublimity of the great name: "God." "O Laca, most beloved soul," sings Jenůfa, "O come, o come! Now I feel in my heart the love, the greater love that pleaseth God himself, the Lord." And the violins and trumpet fanfares rise *maestoso* in a double melody.

This very final scene, better than philosophical essays, takes us to the center of that love-blazing idea that shows pure humanity arising from a popular essence [*aus dem Volklichen*] that is intuited truly and without egoism; and this divine music says more to me about the essence of the nation and of true nationalism than any theory. Similarly, a very small, merely episodic scene at the beginning, which I would like to emphasize for this reason, shows that the true friend of the people and man of the people (Janáček is described as such, in a practical political sense, as well), drawing on his more profound knowledge of the people, frequently arrives at a concept that is far from stereotypical—a concept that runs in a direction diametrically opposite from the scurrilously self-evident concept of the people promoted by adherents of so-called Realpolitik, writers of lead articles, and feuilleton scribblers.

As Jenůfa longingly awaits her beloved, her young head already swimming with the cares of future motherhood, a shepherd boy runs onto the stage. He asks her to write a new page for him, he has already learned everything on the previous one. "Wait 'til I go to the city, I will bring you a primer, you will learn from it. And I will teach you to write, too, so you will become a better person." And the boy runs off yodeling. "Jenůfa has taught me to read," he cries joyfully to the woods that surround the mountain mill. Janáček constructs the entire scene on a soft, simple melody. How intuitively the poet and the composer have got it right! Yes, the people are not crude and dumb and muscle-bound, as superficial "folk poets" depict them. Something endlessly fine, distinguished seems to blossom forth on the ground of simple peasant souls. Nowadays we are accustomed to looking down on every striving for education as "clever" and "ambitious" and "rationalistic." In the very attempt to see the people as "unliterary," we have created an utterly literary concept of a "dull" spirit of the people. We make a bugaboo of "false Enlightenment" [Aufklärerei]. With what unspeakable grace and rightness, by contrast, this tiny scene brings to the stage the eternal, holy striving away from the animal and toward humanness. It is a scene of the highest virtue. "Jenůfa has taught me to read." This young herdsman, so different from all the Romantic shawm-playing shepherd boys who populate our stages, asks in all modesty, without knowing it, for eternal human rights in the form of a decent primary school. On cursory first sight, one could almost call him a Jewish shepherd boy. Perhaps this is why he pleases me so much. But in all seriousness—I feel the rightness, the eternal rightness in this brief figure and his melody, and, in his presence, I feel how windy and false it is simply to glorify the instincts. Precisely what at first blush appears improbable is the essential aspect of the scene. And it brings tears of affirmation to my eye, just like that unforgettable scene in *The Bartered Bride,* when the polka is played in the first scene. A folk dance—here some loveless popular musician would naturally barge in right away with rough chords. Not so the loving Smetana, who understood the soul of the people. "People"—this is something tender and noble at its most intimate, something honorable and elflike. Pianissimo and legato, soft as silk, Smetana begins the polka, then a delicate staccato. They do not dance any more politely in the most elegant salon than at Smetana's carnivals.

That, my friends, is the genius! The book-loving shepherd boy. The elflike village. Always otherwise than your school learning would have you imagine.

And this intimately popular character, never transformed into something crude, is expressed in every modulation, every motif of Janáček's.

In an essay—Janáček has published some remarkable theoretical articles, which have to be read with perpetual shaking of the head, they are so honest and yet paradoxical—he recounts that he gladly allows himself to be "drawn in" by the sound of spoken words. He secretly listens to the conversations of people walking by, reads their facial expression, observes every rise and fall of the speech melody, notates it, and discovers in it and its peculiar rhythm the entire world of the speaker, the time of day, the lighting, heat, warmth, society, mood of the moment. "I felt a quiet joy at the beauty of these speech melodies, their capacity for eloquence, the power of their expression."

The realism of this peculiar method might seem suspect. But here is where the genius comes into play. Not the speech melody, but inspiration, reformulation enters into the work of art. "A speech motif," says Janáček, "breathes with its own warmth, glows in its own light. I hone its melodic corners, its rhythmic surfaces—like a jewel." From this element he also derives the harmony. Similarly, the orchestra, which is treated in a unique manner, but simply, almost without any polyphony, is heard only as a means of underscoring the speech melodies. In this regard, he is probably the most diametrical opposite of Wagner that can be imagined. In Janáček, the main music is brought back up from the orchestra onto the stage. Quite often he leads the strings in unison with the singing. One hears cantilenas of a sort that have not been heard since Verdi.

I do not deny that this bizarre theory of speech melodies, if it had chanced to occur to a composer of lesser gifts, might have generated a disgusting potpourri in mosaic style. But Janáček is so strongly imbued with musical substance that he gives every turn of phrase a sufficiently powerful melodic line, never becomes fragmented or unsure. The reason for this lies deeper than his personal genius. Never has the blessing of an art that is rooted in the popular essence [*Volkstum*] been clearer to me than here. Janáček's speech melodies, namely, sound no different than pure abridged, half-suppressed, long-spun-out melodies of Moravian-Slovakian folk songs, genuine sounds of nature. The genius of the people speaks from every measure. In every recitative there are flashes, like heat lightning, of genuine popular tone. Hence the impression of a mosaic never arises, everything seems to flow from the same inexhaustible source, melody upon melody gushes forth with unforced lightness, ever new, the ear cannot hear enough of it. The doubter, who knows nothing but this report, and not the opera itself, might still be of the opinion that a strict classical form can never be preserved with this principle of melodies succeeding one another, no matter how unified the tone to which they are tuned. Here, Janáček utilizes a technique that is so simple and solves the problem so completely that one must regard this brilliant solution with awe. It is a familiar observation that people from rural areas tend to repeat individual words and sentences, listen to their own echo with a kind of amazed shaking of the head, and repeat it again and again and again. Janáček makes extraordinarily rich use of this realistic observation (precisely the repetitions have garnered him the greatest attacks—along with the simple orchestration, almost devoid of counterpoint). In this way, on the one hand, he accurately represents the natural forms of expression of his milieu. On the other, he simultaneously creates broad surfaces within the work, upon which he can spread out his motifs expansively, can stylize them according to their inner needs. May the theorist, drawing on what is perhaps a rather rare example, conclude from this that the truth of nature and the most strict stylization are not always and not necessarily the polar opposites as which academic art is accustomed to portraying them. Among the many insights I owe to this opera (the truly real, essential character of the work offers wisdom for researchers from the most diverse fields), I hold that this is the most valuable—that here we have an entirely lifelike art that nonetheless obeys none other than its own inner laws of unnaturalistically free-form creation, in other words, Expressionism. The oft-repeated word or phrase is good description, satisfies the Impressionist; but at the same time it is, in its repetition, something neutral, a mere vessel for overflowing musical inspiration, which proceeds in an entirely unprogrammatic way, the same way as absolute music, in the unprecedented liveliness of its variation, gradation, enlargement, above all its most delicate rhythmic transformation, in other words in the strictest style of a mass as it might be celebrated, say, in Baden. As there the frequently repeated "Kyrie Eleison" becomes merely material for a fugue, which expresses these two words purely musically, in the style of the new, wordless material, not through tone painting; so Janáček repeats his text without any constraint, for as long as the musical phrase requires it, and a dialogue passage, literally translated, assumes a form such as the following (I have selected the scene that immediately follows the above-mentioned episode with the shepherd boy):

Old woman: What desires you have, girl. You taught Barena to read, too. You have the understanding of a man, just like your foster mother. You should have been a teacher.
    Jenůfa (with a sigh): Ba, ba, my understanding, dear lady, has long ago fallen somewhere into the millstream. Ba, my understanding, lady, ba, my understanding has long since fallen

somewhere into the millstream—there somewhere into the mill-stream fallen—long since fallen into the millstream.

Within this strange form of the text, going well beyond the mere words, the autonomous melody unfolds; not illustrating each individual word through the use of motifs that resemble signals (as in Wagner in his weaker scenes), not inserting quotations into unrelated moods—no, [it unfolds] as if dreaming freely, at random, spinning itself out in a completely unearthly, nonmaterial medium, in the most purely musical form, exhausting and fully unfolding itself, so that each phrase repeated in this way represents a piece of music that is complete, unified, and inten-sified. This technique naturally appears in such an obvious form only at the formal climaxes of the work. But traces of it appear everywhere, imposing the Master's energetic will to form in an unforced way (this indeed is what gives it its genius—stylization that is unforced, close to realism, and yet musically immanent) breathing through even the finest bronchia of his creation.

If I am not much mistaken, Janáček has found the principle of form within which in the future every acceptable musical drama will have to move. Exemplary is the way in which he combines the most material local color (i.e. Impressionist elements) with the most purely formal strict-ness of abstract "music for its own sake" [*Musik an sich*]. But not in such a way that he combines elements of the national and the generally artis-tic after the fact—no, both currents flow together in the same bloodstream, have their effect as one and the same impulse. In this way, the splendid, all-human final scene of the work is implicitly preformed in every previous measure, is embedded in the whole design. The same inner transfusion of the great, general power of music that flows toward us from Bach (like Bach, Janáček is a master of the organ) and the par-ticular individuality of the nation is also a characteristic of Smetana, as it is of the much too little known Danish genius Carl Nielsen.

[from *Prager Sternenhimmel* (Vienna: Paul Zsolnay, 1966), pp. 17–30]

APPENDIX B: THEODOR W. ADORNO REVIEWS
JENŮFA AND *THE MAKROPULOS AFFAIR*

TRANSLATED BY SUSAN H. GILLESPIE

February 1924

Jenůfa, by Leoš Janáček. As the veristic *Cavalleria* once did, the twenty-year-old opera of the Czech composer undertakes to move *Volkheit*—folkishness—into the center of theatrical and musical events. It is that romantically intuited *Volkheit* that is unproblematically grounded in itself, in which word and tone rest undivided next to each other, concretely aimed at the same thing. If this *Volkheit* is already unreal the moment it offers itself up conclusively to free-roaming wishes, it is doubly unreal as an aesthetic substrate, since in truth the latter would have to give birth to the work of art and cannot be generated within it. While Leoncavallo and Mascagni ironically reveal the unreality of their subject by means of the drastic externality of the musical gestures and the obvious goings-on onstage, Janáček's radically consequential procedure deepens the questionable nature of his intent. This is demonstrated in exemplary fashion by the relationship of word and tone. The musical emphasis is moved up into the vocal line, which, supported by specially invented stylistic constructions, is related not to the *intent* of the words, but rather to their *sound*, in order to retain the unity of word and tone in a sensual blend. But this succeeds only apparently, for in the context of the psychologically developed action, the words and sentences do in fact acquire their own meaning, which the composer grasps only by means of the adoption of national form elements, which are meant to embrace both the poetry and the music. The same *Volkheit*, in other words, whose homogeneity was originally meant to guarantee the unity of word *sound* and music, is called upon after the fact to fuse word *meaning* and music. With this, the music is reduced to the measure of those abstractions that distilled their means from real folk music and is rewarded only by its vague convergence with the realm of literary subjects. The meaningful contents of the poetry remain unconnected, the music speaks in dialect.

Despite this fundamental insight, *Jenůfa* exhibits a purity of psychic type, a lyrical genuineness in its particles, which is rarely found in contemporary opera. Almost throughout, the ascetically and simply joined music remains free of bad pathos and sentimentality; Wagner's influence is avoided altogether. And in the romantically imagined form of the work something of genuine folk essence breaks through occasionally.

Jenůfa has turns of phrase whose Czech identity is unfalsified heritage, turns of phrase filled with wordless, devoted apathy.

The premiere at the Frankfurt Opera (under Ludwig Rottenberg) gave satisfaction. Frau Lauer-Kottlar achieved a performance that was musically and theatrically exceptional.

[*Zeitschrift für Musik* 91, vol. 2 (1924), p. 92ff.]

April 1929

Janáček, *The Makropulos Affair*. The only event at the opera this season: the German premiere of Janáček's *The Makropulos Affair*, but an event indeed. This work of a mature artist, which gets by technically with the debris of a folkloristically dissolved impressionism, but at the same time distinguishes itself definitively from folklorism—this work, despite its moderate elements, is revolutionary in the manner of its configuration. The impressionistic atoms, which at one time would have been meant, in their oscillation, to form the whole, here become means of creating a form whose power resides in the tiniest, invariant particle. It is an opera form crafted from conjoined fragments, of a type that can be created only by old age—an old age that has become thoroughly indifferent to the foregrounds of closed form. We know how the elderly Goethe joined the *Wanderjahre* together from novellas, fragments, plot particles, and finally tossed in aphorisms, which the improvised roof of the form was supposed to shelter. Without intending to compare them, [there is] something of that magnificent randomness, of that monad-like power, which so fills every fragment that the fragment means the whole and scarcely needs the whole anymore—the work has something of this kind of furrowed, significant old-age physiognomy. Death itself intrudes into the form and lets the individual element contrast with others, unconnected—the way an old man sometimes falls silent because the fullness of existence in between the sentences shatters the form of speech. This also explains the choice of material. No matter that the libretto ultimately behaves as if death were a blessing and life a curse; that it flattens the figure of the female lead with metaphorical symbolism, surrounds her with a fog of bad mysticism. In truth, here the absurd and enormous question being asked is whether it is possible to do away with death, since this question will have appeared to the old man suddenly, with the force of an explosive wish. True, the blessing presents itself as a curse. But this merely reflects in a confused and unrecognizable way what can be intended as the central meaning in truth—something that, by the way, is also unrecognizable in the libretto, which ultimately would like to reinstate the natural order against which its own intention and the music as a whole so forcefully rebel. This music is an illegible system of canals that crisscross the surface of the text; illegible, it is true, but nevertheless configured in such a way that in the end no doubt remains about the meaning. Above all, the second act, behind the scenes at the theater, with the horrifically normal operetta entry of the demystified buffo Hauk-Šendorf, is remarkable—characterized by an entirely new, quotidian demonic character who is not at all out of the ordinary, but has the chill of real existence. Only the final act, in deference to the text and following its dictates, veers back to the opera schema, brings about a transcendence whose content is much less clear than all the foregoing confusion. But even the conclusion is not able to draw the inconspicuous and alien face of the score seriously into the realm of the ordinary. There remains, in this opera, something that can very rarely be claimed, especially in music for the stage—a shock. The risk of performing [it] should be taken over and over again. The performance in Frankfurt is very creditable, conducted by Krips, with staging by Mutzenbecher. Marty was sung extraordinarily well by Frau Gentner-Fischer. Herr Vetra as Gregor deserves special mention.

[*Musikblätter des Anbruch* 11, no. 4 (1929), p. 167.]

April 1929

Janáček's *Makropulos Affair*, which was premiered in Frankfurt, may be a lost cause; in any case it is something noteworthy and, it seems to me, even great. Here the gamble of the absurd, as it is otherwise risked only by the young avant-garde, has come under the sway of a mature style that can bear up under the gamble because it is already above all prevailing consciousness—right up to death's doorstep—and its sparse clarity truly has a different power than when youth takes risks merely as a result of youthful drives. The wager begins with the extraordinary choice of text. This libretto, which contains within it much borrowing and a certain amount of mistily symbolic, questionable mysticism, is, centrally, the attempt to pose in a cool, sober way the problem of the physical immortality of human beings. The way this is done can be compared with no one but Kafka, in whose city Janáček lived [*sic*]. As one must accept, in Kafka, that a traveler wakes up and finds himself transformed into a bedbug, one must similarly accept that the singer Emilia Marty was born in the year 1586 and hence is 350 years old. As in Kafka, the metaphor—these travelers are all like bedbugs—suddenly, with a stroke of the wand, becomes real, nonsymbolic, and makes everyday life transparent in the glare of the absurd; similarly, the banal stage actors' metaphysics—the singer actually has all the characters she embodies within her—is rendered with seriousness. Thus, behind the scenes, she has once been—nonmetaphorically, and by no means interpretable as a symbol of psychological data—Eugenia Montez, Ellinor MacGregor, even Elsa Müller, all this utterly and completely. As ultimately in Kafka actual, nonmetaphorical reality, confronted with the empirical one, becomes senseless, torturous, difficult to traverse, and absurd, and only occasionally shines through—and then in the most unassuming passages—so the physically immortal woman comes, here and now, into the light of perfect ambiguity; and what is so powerful about her—that death is suspended—is hardly evident anymore, becomes confused in the mythical twilight, and finally appears as a curse. This, at any rate, is how the most profound intentions of the libretto may have been planned. The third act, however, thoroughly contradicts this, reinstates the shattered order of the natural, turns death into a blessing and life into a curse, and devalues what came before by installing it *post festum* as a mystical metaphor that attempts to prove with the pantheistic platitude that life and death are, once again, actually the same. The strongest argument for the music is that it fails to live up to this impoverished pseudo-philosophy and, as is ultimately unavoidable when it comes to pantheistic transcendences, falls into a fundamentally hollowed-out ecstasy. With this exception, however, it has followed the script with an economy that is unprecedented even for Janáček. It has followed it into secrets that the script, by itself, scarcely wants to reveal. Its absurdity is one of a kind. It is not that of explosive fantasy-construction, as in Schoenberg; nor is it the scary evocation of the past, as in Stravinsky. It is the absurdity of the normal, possessed. Ghosts of the ordinary appear in it—this, too, like Kafka's prose. It is as if the tiniest tonal flourishes, from whose unsystematic repetition the construction is joined together, are looked at so closely that they reveal their demonic origin; above all, one must think here of the scene with the old bon vivant Hauk-Šendorf, who, sixty years later, encounters his lover who hasn't changed—the demonic quality of the utterly inconspicuous. Throughout, the score achieves a splendid density; far from all psychology, even far from accompaniment, actually a difficult-to-traverse, dark system of shafts that cuts through the surface of the libretto with an unknown objective, characterized by a modesty in which horror dwells, shines through for seconds with a scarcely endurable brightness. It is a completely enigmatic music, which demands [something] of the hearer without the latter being able to understand in advance what it is actually demanding.

The work should be performed on an experimental stage; musical and theatrical interpretation should begin with the attempt to convey its meaning. In the normal business of opera, this is not conceivable. At any rate, the Frankfurt performance was at an astonishingly good level. The conducting of Krips, who holds the baton during the period of the opera's interregnum, advocated for the work with a beautiful fidelity; Mutzenbecher staged it with very good success. At the center of the evening stood Frau Gentner-Fischer as Emilia Marty. Her achievement was equally outstanding musically and theatrically. Considering that the current level of the German opera theater is utterly incomprehensible, it is incomprehensible that this extraordinary singer does not occupy a prominent place, but is forced to perform repertory. The young Maris Vetra made a fine introduction as Gregor.

[*Die Musik* 21, no. 7 (1929), p. 538f.]

NOTES

1. For a listing of Brod's work and a short biography (with interview material), see Berndt W. Wessling, *Max Brod: Ein Porträt* (Stuttgart: W. Kohlhammer, 1969), pp. 129–31. On Brod, see Margarita Pazi, *Max Brod: Leben und Persönlichkeit* (Bonn: Bouvier, 1970).

2. See Max Brod, *Heinrich Heine* (Amsterdam: Allert de Lange, 1934). It was revised and published in English as *Heinrich Heine: The Artist in Revolt* (London: Valentine, Mitchell, 1956). On Brod's Heine interpretation and its influence, see Margarita Pazi, "Max Brod's Presentation of Heinrich Heine," in *The Jewish Reception of Heinrich Heine,* ed. Mark H. Gelber (Tübingen: Max Niemeyer, 1992), pp. 173–84.

3. See Peter Stephan Jungk, *Franz Werfel: A Life in Prague, Vienna, and Hollywood* (New York: Grove Weidenfeld, 1990), pp. 19–20, 28; see also the account of the Brod–Werfel tension in Wessling, *Max Brod,* pp. 46–47. If one can accept the account in Mirka Zemanová's biography of Janáček, Brod was a considerable ladies' man. See Mirka Zemanová, *Janáček: A Composer's Life* (Boston: Northeastern University Press, 2002), pp. 136 and 233.

4. Philip V. Bohlman, *The World Center for Jewish Music in Palestine 1936–1940* (Oxford: Oxford University Press, 1992), p. 160. See also Yehuda Cohen, "Die Musik Max Brods," in *Max Brod 1884–1984: Untersuchungen zu Max Brods literarischen und philosophischen Schriften,* ed. Margarita Pazi (New York: Peter Lang, 1987), pp. 193–206. For a modern recording of Brod's music, from his early settings of Heine to the music of his later years, infused by a self-conscious Israeli orientalism, see Max Brod, *Tod und Paradies: Chamber Works* (Supraphon Records CD 1121882931 Prague, 1994).

5. Max Brod, *Streitbares Leben: Autobiographie* (Frankfurt am Main: Insel, 1979), pp. 259–78. The text of this edition follows the 1969 version that included material from Brod's intended revisions. Brod was also crucial to the careers of the composers Manfred Gurlitt and Jaromír Weinberger (the libretto of whose particularly successful 1926 opera *Švanda dudák* Brod translated into German). The cases of Schreiber and Vycpálek (1882–1969) are in fact ideal reflections of the several strands and patterns within Brod's history of critical advocacy. Both composers were contemporaries. Brod's dedication to Schreiber (1883–1920) was essentially personal and sentimental. Schreiber had studied with Dvořák and owing to lack of success committed suicide. Brod wrote a biography of Schreiber and defended the value of his music, particularly the songs. Although the two men were close and both Jewish, Brod was an early convert to Zionism while Schreiber was an enthusiastic Czech patriot. See Max Brod, *Der Prager Kreis* (Frankfurt: Suhrkamp, 1979), pp. 58–59 and *Prager Sternenhimmel* (Vienna: Paul Zsolnay, 1966), pp. 73–74. On the other hand, Vycpálek seems to have had no personal connection to Brod. His music is essentially unknown outside of the Czech lands. But as a student of literature Vycpálek was committed to Czech traditions. Like Brod he straddled music and literature until devoting himself to composition, studying with Vítězslav Novák, one of Dvořák's pupils and a major force in Czech music. Brod appreciated that Vycpálek was a committed craftsman of the highest order of skill and integrity, with links, like Janáček, to the struggle to articulate a distinctive Czech sensibility. Vycpálek did not thrive under the Communist regime, something Brod was keenly sympathetic to and aware of. Brod properly understood Vycpálek's compositional engagement with Bach and polyphony. See John Tyrrell's entry in *The New Grove,* vol. 26 (London: Macmillan, 2001), pp. 914–16.

6. See *Kindler's Literatur Lexikon,* vol. 5 (Zurich: Kindler, 1964), pp. 1156–68.

7. Quoted in Wessling, *Max Brod,* p. 24.

8. Brod, *Prager Sternenhimmel*, p. 105, see also pp. 9, 13–14. Brod's stance toward criticism is another reason Robert Weltsch may have been right when he suggested that in another era, Brod "might have become a rabbi." Weltsch had in mind a hundred years before Brod's birth. The insight might extend to a projection into the future, to the post–World War II pastoral rabbinate. See Weltsch's elegant essay, "Max Brod and His Age," *Leo Baeck Memorial Lecture No. 13* (New York: Leo Baeck Institute, 1970), p. 12.

9. Quoted in Charles Susskind, *Janáček and Brod* (New Haven: Yale University Press, 1985), p. 153.

10. Wessling, *Max Brod,* p. 35.

11. Max Brod, *Leoš Janáček* (Vienna: Universal, 1956), p. 68.

12. Ibid. This speech has been characterized in Janáček biographies somewhat differently than Brod himself recounted it in 1953, citing Brod's reference to the "hundreds of thousands of German-speaking listeners" who "enjoyed the works of Janáček's musical genius." See Jaroslav Vogel, *Leoš Janáček* (Prague: Academia, 1977), p. 379.

13. See Vilém Tausky, "Recollections of Leoš Janáček," in *Janáček: Leaves from His Life,* ed. Vilém Tausky and Margaret Tausky (London: Kahn and Averill, 1989), p. 9.

14. The one exception in the post-1916 work is *The Excursions of Mr. Brouček.* Brod was taken aback at what he regarded as a glorification of war in the work and declined to do the translation, something he regretted later in life. See Meinhard Saremba, *Leoš Janáček: Zeit, Leben, Werk, Wirkung* (Kassel: Bärenreiter, 2001), pp. 256–57.

15. The Brod–Janáček correspondence, with Brod writing in German and Janáček in Czech, has been published. See Jan Racek and Artuš Rektorys, eds., *Korespondence Leoše Janáčka s Maxem Brodem* (Prague: Státní nakladatelství krásné literatury, hudby a umění, 1953).

16. See Milan Kundera, *Testaments Betrayed: An Essay in Nine Parts,* trans. Linda Asher (New York: HarperCollins, 1995), pp. 252–55. Kundera's views on Brod are disarmingly scandalous in their prejudices. Using a kind of informality of style, Kundera trashes the facile image of Brod generated by many critics of Brod's approach to Kafka. Kundera betrays not the slightest familiarity with Brod's actual published views. It is as if Kundera is afraid that over time he, too, will be regarded as a figure more akin to Brod—a minor epigone—than as a successor to Kafka or Janáček. He therefore lets his readers know whose side he is on—that he is in a position to condescend to Brod and defend the greats against the Max Brods of this world. I want to thank Christopher Gibbs for bringing this text to my attention. It should be noted that Milan Kundera's father, Ludvík Kundera (1891–1971), was a musicologist and pianist and an admirer of Janáček's. Ludvík Kundera was born and worked in Brno where he headed the Conservatory right after the war. He also helped edit the critical edition of Janáček's works.

17. See the accounts in Susskind, *Janáček and Brod,* the best source on Brod and Janáček, and those in all the leading biographies of Janáček, including Vogel, Saremba (who comes closest to questioning the sources of Brod's enthusiasm), Zemanová—all op. cit. See also Hans Hollander, *Leoš Janáček: Leben und Werk* (Zurich: Atlantis, 1964), pp. 63–64, and Horst Richter, *Leoš Janáček* (Leipzig: VEB Breitkopf und Härtel, 1958), p. 57.

18. Kurt Singer (1885–1944) was a polymath like Brod. He was a physician, violinist, choral conductor, and, like Brod (although with different politics) active in Jewish affairs. Singer was a well-regarded critic and teacher in Berlin who in 1933 organized the Jüdischer Kulturbund. He died in Theresienstadt. On Singer, see Fred. K. Preiberg, *Musik im NS-Staat* (Cologne: Dittrich, 2000), p. 80; Michael H. Kater, *The Twisted Muse: Musicians and Their Music in the Third Reich* (New York: Oxford University Press, 1997), p. 97; and Jozǎ Karas, *Music in Terezín: 1941–1945* (New York: Beaufort Books, 1985), pp. 100–101. Adorno studied with Berg and composed and wrote on music. These activ-

ities would be dwarfed by his philosophical work. There is some irony in this comparison given the intellectual contempt Brod is held in and the elevated status Adorno retains today. Both, however, wrote about music from inside, so to speak. And both suffered from some hesitancy and unfulfilled ambition as composers; see in Adorno's case Sigfried Schibli, *Der Komponist Theodor W. Adorno* (Frankfurt: Impressum, 1988).

19. Brod, *Prager Sternenhimmel*, pp. 73–74.

20. See, for example, Brod's discussion of *Boris Godunov* in *Prager Sternenhimmel*, pp. 64–67.

21. Max Brod, "Mir träumte…" (Heine) and "Die Botschaft" (Heine), *Tod und Paradies* CD, tracks 1 and 2.

22. It should be noted that Brod possesses a notorious place in the literature on Gustav Mahler. As Brod's theory of national humanism in music suggests, Mahler was for Brod a distinctly "Jewish" composer in the most positive sense. Mahler is said to have drawn from Jewish sources in his musical materials, sources that express the Jewish diaspora soul. This point of view became increasingly strident after World War II, as can be discerned from Brod's discussion in *Die Musik Israels* (Tel Aviv: WIZO/Sefer Press, 1951), pp. 30–34. See also Max Brod, *Gustav Mahler: Beispiel einer deutsch-jüdischen Symbiose* (Frankfurt: Ner Tamid, 1961).

23. Max Brod, *Vier Lieder* (Vienna: Universal 8762). The Flaubert song is entitled "Die Königin von Saba singt," and the Schiller, "Die Grösse der Welt." See also Yehuda Cohen in Pazi, *Max Brod,* pp. 194–97.

24. Max Brod, "Richard Strauss Woche," in *Prager Sternenhimmel*, pp. 105–11.

25. Max Brod, "Über Vítězslav Novák's 'Sturm'" in *Prager Sternenhimmel*, p. 94. Novák's work, for solo voices, chorus, and orchestra was completed in 1910. Strauss's *Alpine Symphony* was begun in earnest in 1911 and was finished in 1915.

26. In this paraphrase, notions of soul and feeling (*geistig* and *Empfindung* in German), are in play. The issue is not that these words translate poorly but they suggest a vocabulary of assumptions quite typical of the period in talk about visual art, literature, and music. Brod's characterization of Strauss, for example, was quite widespread, particularly in regard to the *Alpine Symphony*. It needs to be said, albeit parenthetically, that a case for greatness and profundity that goes well beyond the evident skill and illustrative virtuosity of the work, can be made for the *Alpine Symphony* that challenges Brod's views, in Brod's own terms. The issue here is that Brod, and many of Strauss's contemporaries, did not choose to hear the work or things in the work, the way we might today. One can, for example, find distance, loss, intimacy, and irony beneath the brilliant surface of this work and a connection to Mahler that would have surprised Brod. Overcoming the legacy of an evaluative and descriptive consensus passed down in the language of criticism is not, however, so easy—which is why Brod's intervention and accomplishment vis-a-vis Janáček are so significant.

27. See the description of Novák's *The Storm* (Bouře), op. 42, in Mirko Očadlík, *Svět orchestru: Česká hudba* (Prague: Panton, 1961), pp. 333–36.

28. John Tyrrell, "Vítězslav Novák," in *The New Grove*, vol. 18, p. 213.

29. Brod, *Prager Sternenhimmel*, p. 96.

30. Brod, "Ein Wort für Meister Suk," in *Prager Sternenhimmel*, pp. 90, 93.

31. Max Brod, *Die Musik Israels*, p. 8.

32. Brod was conscious of the fact that, particularly in post-1945 Czechoslovakia, there was a politically charged critical discourse about nationalism that pitted Smetana against Dvořák. In his Janáček book, he therefore took pains to stress Janáček's allegiance to both composers. See Brod, *Janáček*, pp. 19–21. It must be noted that in Janáček's case, the connection between narrative, language, and musical form in instrumental music owes

much to Dvořák, particularly to his late tone poems, settings of the poetry of Erben—despite Hugh Macdonald's caveats. See Janáček's own commentaries, translated by Tatiana Firkušný in *Dvořák and His World*, ed. Michael Beckerman (Princeton: Princeton University Press, 1993), pp. 262–76; and Hugh Macdonald, "Narrative in Janáček's Symphonic Poems," in *Janáček Studies*, ed. Paul Wingfield (Cambridge: Cambridge University Press, 1999), pp. 36–55.

33. Like Janáček, Brod became an advocate for Musorgsky and a critic of those who questioned his technique and the quality of his work. See Max Brod, "Das verkannte Genie," in *Prager Sternenhimmel*, pp. 68–73.

34. Ibid., pp. 9–10. Clearly Brod's theory fit neatly with his Zionism and his efforts, after 1948, to generate an authentic Israeli musical idiom.

35. Robert Weltsch, "Max Brod and his Age," p. 10.

36. See two exceptional recent books on the subject in which Brod figures significantly: Scott Spector, *Prague Territories: National Conflict and Cultural Innovation in Franz Kafka's Fin de Siècle* (Berkeley: University of California Press, 2000); and Hillel J. Kieval, *Languages of Community: The Jewish Experience in the Czech Lands* (Berkeley: University of California Press, 2000).

37. Heinrich Schenker, "Friedrich Smetana," in *Die Zukunft* 4 (1893): 37–40, quoted in Helmut Federhofer, *Heinrich Schenker: Nach Tagebücher und Briefen* (Hildesheim: Olms, 1985), pp. 252–53. Max Brod's attachment to Smetana, and particularly *The Bartered Bride*, lasted his entire life. Brod's last book, published in 1962, sought to redeem the reputation of Karl Sabina (1813–1877), *The Bartered Bride's* librettist who was also a police spy for the Habsburg monarchy, determined to undermine the Czech national movement. Sabina's double life was exposed and he was ultimately imprisoned. He died in obscurity and extreme poverty. See Max Brod, *Die verkaufte Braut: Der abenteuerliche Lebensroman des Textdichters Karel Sabina* (Munich: Bechtle, 1962).

38. On Masaryk's crucial connection to the Jewish question, his resistance to anti-Semitism and his complex but admirable relationship to the Jewish question in Czech politics, see Kieval, op. cit., and, for a contemporary assessment, Ernst Rychnovsky, ed., *Masaryk und das Judentum* (Prague: Marsverlagsgesellschaft, 1931).

39. See Kundera, *Testaments Betrayed*, and Brod, *Leoš Janáček*, pp. 8–10.

40. Brod, *Prager Sternenhimmel*, pp. 77–89, 103–04, and *Leoš Janáček*, p. 5.

41. See Leon Botstein, *Judentum und Modernität* (Vienna: Böhlau,1991), pp. 44–54 and 126–48.

42. Fritz Mauthner, *Prager Jugendjahre* (Frankfurt: S. Fischer, 1969), pp. 30–34, and Botstein, *Judentum und Modernität*, pp. 55–72.

43. The most important scholarly literature on this vast subject is Hillel J. Kieval, *The Making of Czech Jewry: National Conflict and Jewish Society in Bohemia, 1870–1918* (New York: Oxford University Press, 1998), the already cited Kieval, *Language of Communities*, the book cited by Scott Spector, and Gary B. Cohen, *The Politics of Ethnic Survival: Germans in Prague 1861–1918* (Princeton: Princeton University Press, 1981).

44. Pick, a Jew, emigrated from the Hungarian border to Vienna and ended up writing the quintessential musical symbol of old Viennese traditions. See Botstein, "Sozialgeschichte und die Politik des Ästhetischen: Juden und Musik in Wien 1870–1938," in *Quasi una Fantasia: Juden und die Musikstadt Wien* (Wolke, forthcoming).

45. Stern's essays on these issues are indispensable. See "On Prague German Literature" and "Words Are Also Deeds," in J. P. Stern, *The Heart of Europe: Essays on Literature and Ideology* (Oxford: Blackwell, 1992), particularly pp. 50 and 66.

46. Brod's affection for Reger and his music is not surprising, considering Reger's prestige as a classicist and master of musical traditions, and as an alternative to Strauss's influence. See Brod, *Streitbares Leben*, pp. 253–59.

47. Brod's enthusiasm for Janáček's work and theories becomes more understandable in this context. The relationships among language, realism, and music, particularly vis-á-vis Janáček, are discussed in a somewhat parallel manner in Carl Dahlhaus, *Realism in Nineteenth-Century Music*, trans. Mary Whitall (Cambridge: Cambridge University Press, 1985), pp. 95–106.

48. Quoted in Jaroslav Procházka, "Brods Übersetzungen des Librettos der *Jenůfa* und die Korrekturen Kafkas," in *Leoš Janáček-Materialen*, ed. Jakob Knaus (Zurich: Leoš Janáček Gesellschaft, 1982), p. 30. This metaphor of music being like an ocean in which one swims is strikingly similar to that used by Nietzsche, particularly in his description of the impact of Wagner's music upon the soul, whether Kafka was aware of this or not. *Menschliches, Allzumenschliches*, vol. 2, Aphorism 134, in Friedrich Nietzsche, *Werke*, vol. 1 (Munich: Hanser, 1954), pp. 788–89.

49. Knaus, op. cit.

50. See Franz Kafka, "Zwei Tiergeschichten. 2. Ein Bericht für eine Akademie," *Der Jude* 2, no. 8 (1917): 559–65. This story has been extensively discussed in terms of, among others, Kafka's relationship to Zionism, his Jewish identity, language, and his encounter with Yiddish, as well as his relationship to Brod. See for example Howard M. Sachar, *Dreamland: Europeans and Jews in the Aftermath of the Great War* (New York: Alfred A. Knopf, 2002), pp. 158–59 and Spector, *Prague Territories*, pp. 192–93.

51. Fritz Mauthner, *Wörterbuch der Philosophie*, vol. 2 (Leipzig: Felix Meiner, 1924), pp. 316–17.

52. For the ethical character of Wittgenstein's construct of music, see Martin Alber, ed., *Ludwig Wittgenstein und die Musik: Briefwechsel Ludwig Wittgenstein–Rudolf Koder* (Innsbruck: Hayman, 2000), pp. 154–55.

53. Mauthner, *Prager Jugendjahre*, pp. 545–49.

54. No doubt Brod believed that Janáček's accomplishment was partly the result of his isolation from modern cosmopolitanism and his deep connection to a Czech tradition relatively insulated from modernity. The return to a premodern linkage of music and life was implausible within German culture, particularly after Wagner.

55. Kurt Singer, *Musik und Character* (Vienna: Universal, 1929), p. 111.

56. Ibid., p. 110.

57. Brod, "Leoš Janáček's *Jenůfa*," and "Noch ein Wort zur *Jenůfa*" in *Prager Sternenhimmel*, pp. 17–30, 40. The complete text of Max Brod's review of *Jenůfa*, translation by Susan H. Gillespie, can be found in Appendix A of this chapter.

58. Brod "Leoš Janáček's *Jenůfa*," pp. 17–30. It is significant that Brod underscored the role Janáček's music could play in defining a distinct Czech identity, more important politically than "the world-shattering question of mono- or bilingual street signs." He criticized the Czech "oversight" of Janáček. Here is an analogy for Brod's hopes for a defining cultural renaissance using music, not merely language, within the Zionist movement. Ibid., p. 19.

59. Brod "Noch ein Wort," p. 38.

60. See Max Brod, "Die Reise zu Janáček," in *Prager Sternenhimmel*, pp. 42–49.

61. One can infer this from the suspicious attitude displayed about the Stössels as Jews by Janáček's wife in her 1935 account of her life, a factor absent in Janáček himself. See John Tyrrell, ed. and trans., *Intimate Letters: Leoš Janáček to Kamila Stösslová* (Princeton: Princeton University Press, 1994), pp. 6–9. Curiously, Janáček's wife makes little or no

reference to Brod. See John Tyrrell, ed. and trans., *My Life with Janáček: The Memoirs of Zdenka Janáčková* (London: Faber, 1998).

62. The finest accounts of Janáček's theories of composition are found in Michael Beckerman, *Janáček as Theorist* (Stuyvesant, N.Y.: Pendragon Press, 1994), particularly chapters 3–6; Miloš Štědroň, "Direct Discourse and Speech Melody in Janáček's Operas," in *Janáček Studies*, ed. Paul Wingfield, (Cambridge: Cambridge University Press, 1999), pp. 79–108; and, in terms of each opera, John Tyrrell, *Janáček's Operas: A Documentary Account* (Princeton: Princeton University Press, 1992); see also Richter, *Leoš Janáček*, pp. 31–36. For the background in Czech operatic tradition, see John Tyrrell, *Czech Opera* (Cambridge: Cambridge University Press, 1988), particularly chap. 8.

63. Max Brod, "Jenůfa Übersetzung," in *Prager Sternenhimmel*, pp. 34–35.

64. It should be noted that the example of Berg's *Wozzeck*, for which Janáček had admiration, represents yet another alternative to the relation of text and music. See Leoš Janáček, *Uncollected Essays on Music*, ed. and trans. Mirka Zemanová (London: Marion Boyars, 1989), p. 123.

65. Michele Girardi, *Puccini: His International Art* (Chicago: University of Chicago Press, 2000), pp. 100–103, 191.

66. Janáček, *Uncollected Essays*, pp. 174–75.

67. See, for example, the few passing references in Theodor W. Adorno, *Philosophy of Modern Music* (New York: Seabury Press, 1973).

68. These reviews, in translations by Susan H. Gillespie, are printed in their entirety in Appendix B of this chapter. The originals can be found in Theodor W. Adorno, *Gesammelte Schriften*, vol. 19 (Frankfurt: Suhrkamp 1989): pp. 149–53.

69. Adorno, Appendix B. A brief survey of German language opera handbooks dating from the 1920s into the Nazi era reveal that *Jenůfa* remained regarded, with polite appreciation, as essentially a Czech folk opera and Janáček's only lasting work. Most make reference to Janáček's use of speech melody. Others make comparisons to Charpentier, Strauss's *Salome, Boris,* and verismo and cite Janáček's resistance to reconciling the local color with a "western European tonal language." Scholtze argued that Janáček resisted the use of "musical-thematic transformation and complexity." See Alexander Eisenmann, *Das grosse Opernbuch* (Stuttgart and Berlin: Deutsche Verlags-Anstalt, 1922), pp. 398–401 and 411; Heinz Wichmann, *Der neue Opernführer* (Berlin: Paul Franke, 1930), pp. 355–58; Johannes Scholtze, *Opernführer* (Leipzig: Justus Dörner, 1936), Janáček entry, n.p.; Otto Schumann, *Meyers Opernbuch* (Leipzig: Bibliographisches Institut, 1936), pp. 384–85; and Julius Kapp, *Das Opernbuch* (Leipzig: Hesse and Becker, 1941), pp. 396–402.

70. Janáček, *Uncollected Essays*, p. 226.

How Janáček Composed Operas

JOHN TYRRELL

It was exactly halfway through Janáček's middle opera—number five out of nine—that he hit upon a method of writing operas that sustained him for the remaining eleven years of his life. It meant that in these eleven years he was able to write four and a half operas; the previous four and a half had taken him thirty years. Janáček began composing *The Excursion of Mr. Brouček to the Fifteenth Century* (the second half of *The Excursions of Mr. Brouček*) on May 5, 1917, and completed it by the end of that year. The new speed of composition was helped by the fact that he had a libretto in front of him and that the characters were based on those from the first half of the opera, *Mr. Brouček's Excursion to the Moon*, but even so, the eight-month gestation of this half of the opera makes a striking contrast to the eight-year gestation of the first half.

Essential for Janáček's composing of operas was confidence. He seems to have had plenty of confidence in writing his early operas, *Šárka* and *The Beginning of a Romance*. The first version of *Šárka* took less than seven months, *The Beginning of a Romance*, admittedly in a single act, took only six weeks. It is not surprising that these were relatively quick jobs: in subject matter, and to some extent in idiom, *Šárka* fitted into the existing patterns of Czech nationalist opera. With *The Beginning of a Romance*, an extension of his folk-arrangement phase, Janáček was mostly recycling his earlier arrangements of folk dances. In both cases, too, he began with existing librettos. It would seem also that Act 1 of *Jenůfa* did not present too many problems, although his method was beginning to change. The voice-and-piano versions of his first two operas (orchestration came later) gave way in *Jenůfa* to a two-stave draft containing voice part and accompaniment, which was then worked out in full score. The one surviving draft page is witness to this method, as are Janáček's sketches in 1906–1907 for *The Mintmaster's Wife*. In this way the composition of Act 1 of *Jenůfa* took little over a year.

But in 1896 Janáček stopped writing *Jenůfa*. One reason why he interrupted his work was the impact of Tchaikovsky's opera *The Queen of Spades*, which he saw in Brno early in January 1896, and the far greater possibilities this opera opened up for him. It meant a return to the drawing board and to an extensive rethinking of his operatic style, further enriched with his developing ideas about speech melody. Once he returned to the opera, by late 1901, the rest went quickly. He completed the remaining two acts in about fifteen months.

This rate was not sustained for the next two operas. *Fate* and *The Excursion of Mr. Brouček to the Moon*, unlike any previous or later operas, had problematic librettos that slowed Janáček down; in *Brouček* this led to enforced periods of inactivity. Furthermore, in their genre and idiom these were experimental operas and their difficult genesis is evidenced by the many versions that each underwent. In the end Janáček abandoned *Brouček* in 1913 because he saw little chance of its being produced, at least outside Brno, and took it up again only in 1916.

This is when the picture changes completely. The production of *Jenůfa* in Prague, and the possibility of its performance abroad, produced a demand that had not existed before. *Jenůfa*'s success, the wonderful reviews, the warmth of reception from many leading Prague composers and critics, and even a few polite words from Richard Strauss did wonders for Janáček's confidence. He completed *Brouček* (both its *Moon Excursion* and its *Fifteenth Century* sequel), revised *Šárka* and set out—at the age of sixty-five—to compose a cluster of new operas. His style would continue to evolve and each of the remaining operas would be very different from its predecessor, but from now on we can talk of a unified method of composition.

Texts

With the chosen text before him Janáček would begin work. In *The Excursion of Mr. Brouček to the Fifteenth Century* the chosen text was a commissioned libretto but one that Janáček would hack to pieces in the course of composition. As its stoic librettist F. S. Procházka observed when seeing the result, there had been a fundamental failure of communication. Procházka had intended it for a whole evening; Janáček for just half.[1] It was Janáček's last commissioned libretto and thereafter he was on his own, either adapting stage plays (*Káťa Kabanová*, *The Makropulos Affair*), as he had done in *Jenůfa*, but also taking on novels that he now adapted himself. In *The Cunning Little Vixen* there was some attempt at writing a preliminary libretto extracted from dialogue in the novel, but in *From the House of the Dead* he simply worked from a brief scenario with page references to his copy of the Dostoevsky. All texts, whether plays or novels, bear witness to Janáček's engagement with the material through his copious underlinings, side-linings, and marginal comments. It is clear that choosing the words to set was all part of the creative process and went hand in hand with composition and that Janáček had clear ideas about exactly what sort of words were suitable. In judging a libretto competition in 1900 he explained why he had not liked any of the submitted librettos: he wanted concrete words, not too many of them, and they shouldn't be too "rough": "Some of them, because of the wateriness of the imagery, were not suitable for melodic song; how many words there were before a thought came! With others I remember the unprecedented roughness; elevate it all through singing?"[2] Or, as he put it to Viktor Dyk in 1916, what he wanted was "concise speech, trenchant verse."[3]

Music

Janáček wrote out the opera, in full score, very fast: essentially a type of improvisation involving a large number of musical motifs and not much repetition or development. There was no preliminary sketching, as there had been for *Jenůfa*, no planning of motifs. Janáček simply wrote. The result is a continuous draft but one whose musical logic is precariously thin at times. This was his way of grasping the potential of the material. He would write each act like this, usually with a long pause in between.

One should not be fooled by all of Janáček's ringing declarations that he was "finished" with a particular act or opera. "Finished" often meant that he got to a stage where he had a continuous draft for a particular act and had sorted out its shape and character in his mind. When he put a date to the end of an act or apprised one of his correspondents of the fact, he usually had a long way to go, and what he had written in this draft resembled the final version only fitfully.

Revision followed, usually after a gap (ideally after a holiday), a process often taking almost as long as the drafting. "I'm now calmly cleaning up individual scenes of the last act," Janáček wrote of *The Excursion of Mr. Brouček to the Fifteenth Century* to Gabriela Horvátová on 30 November 1917, having got to the end of his first draft.[4] Three operas later, the method is just the same: "I've finished the 300-year-old," he wrote to

Kamila Stösslová on 23 February 1925, "but now comes the worst bit: copying it out. I would like to teach you how to paste over the crossed-out stuff, to square it up, tear off, replace—then it would go quickly for me."[5]

During revision ("copying," as he had called it to Mrs. Stösslová, is a misnomer) he discarded most of the motifs thrown up in his initial improvisation and stretched out the remaining ones, or even new ones, over longer passages by means of his usual variation techniques. When commenting on Fibich's *Šárka* in a review for the periodical *Hlídka,* he specifically criticized Fibich's large number of themes: "So many themes are a waste and detract from the effect of the whole work" (XV/160).[6] Janáček's thinning down of thematic material and elaborating it is where the real composition took place; the first draft can be regarded more as part of the process of getting ideas.

A clue as to how he set about developing themes is provided in some of his speech melody studies where, having set down what he heard spoken, he demonstrated its musico-dramatic potential by creating a short piece from it. In *The Beginning of a Romance* (1922; XV/237) he simply added harmonies for the overheard speech melodies to make up a four-bar piece (Example 1). In *He had an Excellent Ear* (1924; XV/249) the four-syllable speech melody *"tys nebyl tam"* generated a three-bar piece in which the "tune" is heard twice: once on top against descending lower parts, once in an inner part against full harmonies. The two harmonizations, both pianissimo, are, however, interrupted by a pause and then a dramatic gesture with a crescendo to a sforzando (Example 2). In *The Mouth* (1923; XV/246) Janáček took the three-note *"prosím vás"* and six-note *"nevyhánějte mne"* themes, harmonized and positioned them to create the melodic core, while the four-note *"dyt' je zima,"* with its

Example 1. *Počátek románu* (The Beginning of a Romance).

Example 2. *Měl výtečný sluch* (He Had an Excellent Ear).

up-and-down pitches speeded up, provided a typical four-note ostinato and interruption (Example 3).

Breaks

The breaks between acts or revisions were an important part of Janáček's
creative process. He believed in letting things lie around so the unconscious—though he didn't put it like this—could take over the creative
process. "Then I want to let the work 'lie' until I forget about it. Only
then does a fellow look soberly at his own work—and sends the whole
piece packing if necessary."[7] "It is a habit of mine to let finished work
lie—until another flood of mood has passed over it. After a time one gets
different eyes. A work should not drown the whole man, all his thoughts."[8]

The breaks were also Janáček's way of organizing his work. They were
usually planned in advance with holidays, or trips away, providing tar-
get deadlines. Act 1 of *Kát'a Kabanová* (in first draft) was finished before
Janáček's summer holidays of 1920, the whole opera on 24 December
that year, just before he stopped work for Christmas. In *The Excursion
of Mr. Brouček to the Fifteenth Century* Janáček announced that he hoped
to finish Act 1 before his summer holiday in 1917.[9] He made it with
two days to spare. When Procházka wrote to him in Luhačovice about
the next act, he was fobbed off. It is clear that the opera (for whose libretto
Janáček had been pressing Procházka very hard) would be off Janáček's
desk for a good while, during which period Procházka must please not
bother him.[10] The completion of the work's second act (in its original
three-act version) did not fall quite so comfortably before a long holiday,

Example 3. *Ústa* (The Mouth).

but nevertheless Janáček gave himself a short trip to Prague as a treat: "I badly need diversion after hard mental work. . . . In Prague I want to hear lots of music, to receive and not to give."[11]

The method worked well in *The Excursion of Mr. Brouček to the Fifteenth Century* but there was one important refinement that Janáček adopted in his next opera, *Kát'a Kabanová*, and its successors. Instead of drafting an act and then revising it before a break, he now wrote the whole opera in draft (with pauses between acts). After taking a break Janáček then revised the whole opera, act by act, into its final shape.

Chronologies

A comparison of the composition dates of Janáček's last operas provided by the accompanying charts reveals interesting differences, and highlights fluctuations in Janáček's confidence and state of mind. *The Excursion of Mr. Brouček to the Fifteenth Century* should be treated as a special case. For a start Janáček was evolving his method; for another he was still teaching and administrating at the Organ School. It is not clear whether the two months working on Act 1 before the summer of 1917 also included revision. Probably it did, since there was little time after he got back from holiday before he finished the first draft of Act 2. The revision of this act took exactly a month. The short Act 3 is barely more than a scene (it was later absorbed into the previous act) and Janáček drafted it in a matter of days.

In the following operas an act generally took slightly over a month in first draft—for instance, Acts 2 and 3 of *Kát'a Kabanová*, or all four acts (as then conceived) of *The Cunning Little Vixen*. What particularly stands out in these two operas is the six-month composition span of the first-draft Act 1 of *Kát'a Kabanová*. It is, of course, longer than Act 2: forty minutes of music as against thirty minutes for Act 2. It is also the last act of any opera that he composed against the background of his administrative duties (he retired in the following summer). However, it is clear from Janáček's correspondence at this time that the composition of the work was much interrupted by other matters: frequent trips to Prague to sit in on rehearsals of *The Excursions of Mr. Brouček* and continual ill-health. It was not until the *Brouček* premiere (April 20, 1920) was out of the way that Janáček could at last sit down to sustained and systematic work on his opera.

What is also striking about *Kát'a Kabanová* is the single-minded concentration on the opera, interrupted by almost no other work. If we regard the January 5 date as a false start and if, rather, we date the real work from late April 1920, then the entire opera, including revision, was finished in about a year. Janáček allowed himself almost two months of holiday after composing Act 1, but thereafter the breaks are short—just a few days between drafting Acts 2 and 3. He managed to get Act 3 done just before Christmas and gave him himself only two weeks off before beginning his revision of the whole opera. Curiously, he revised the acts in reverse order, not a practice that he ever repeated. The last two acts took forty days to revise, the revision of Act 1 almost as long. Then there was further tinkering for another three weeks.

During the writing of *The Excursion of Mr. Brouček to the Fifteenth Century* Janáček had declared that he would not write any more operas.[12]

However, while composing *Kát'a Kabanová* he was planning the next one, *The Cunning Little Vixen*, and while composing *The Cunning Little Vixen* he was deciding what should be the one after that. For *The Vixen* there was no secret about what he had in mind: barely a month after finishing *Kát'a Kabanová* he gave an interview in *Lidové noviny* about the new opera that he was looking forward to writing (XV/226) and a month later he published a feuilleton, *The Little Goldfinch* (XV/227), whose protagonist was described as one of the Vixen's "companions." With all this mapped out so clearly one might then have expected Janáček to have begun work perhaps after his summer holiday in 1921 but here caution restrained him. He had had such trouble getting *Jenůfa* and *Brouček* onto the Prague stage (and, when it did eventually arrive, the Prague *Brouček* was a huge disappointment). This time he waited not just for the Brno stage production of *Kát'a Kabanová* to take place (amazingly quickly, by the end of 1921) but also for other signs of interest, such as Otaker Ostrčil's application to perform the work in Prague. With that in hand he began *The Cunning Little Vixen* a few days later.

At this point Janáček seems to have slipped into what seems like a two-year cycle of opera-writing: he began *Kát'a Kabanová* in January 1920; he began *The Cunning Little Vixen* in January 1922. In the second opera, however, there were not all the distractions that had slowed down the writing of Act 1 of *Kát'a Kabanová* and the opera proceeded in an orderly fashion, with the draft of Act 1 complete by the end of March 1922. We lack an exact date for the beginning of work on Act 2 but what with various diversions, including Rosa Newmarch's visit to Janáček in Brno (April 20–24, 1922) and the premiere (April 24) of his violin sonata, it seems unlikely that he could have begun much before these were out of the way. If "Act 2" (i.e. the first half of the present Act 2) took the usual month—it was complete in first draft by June 5—then he would have been at work by late April 1922. The remainder of what is now Act 2 was finished before Janáček went to Luhačovice in early July. In this way Janáček completed two full acts (in its final numbering) before his summer holidays, in contrast to the single act of *Kát'a Kabanová* composed before the summer of 1920. Despite an even longer summer holiday (July–September), he had the whole opera in draft by the end of October.

Changing Horses, Other Distractions

Whereas with *Kát'a Kabanová* Janáček got on with the revision with only a short Christmas–New Year's break, and then continued almost without stopping until he had finished revising the piece, his growing confidence in his opera writing is attested by the longer breaks he now allowed himself between acts and versions and by the fact that he undertook other work in these breaks. He wrote one of his finest choruses, *The Wandering Madman*, before revising *The Vixen*. During the revision of *The Vixen* he began writing a large-scale orchestral work, *The Danube*. There was a very long summer break (during which he revised his *Fairy Tale* for cello and piano) before he began revising the final act.

The transition from *The Vixen* to *Makropulos* was much shorter than the transition from *Kát'a Kabanová* to *The Cunning Little Vixen*. This time he did not feel the need to see the previous opera on stage before beginning the next, and he did not even wait for his winter break. Less than a month after signing off *The Vixen* he began his new opera.

Before he began *The Vixen*, Janáček made elaborate preparatory studies in order to shift himself into the different atmosphere of his new opera. For a start there were the nature feuilletons. Since the summer of 1921 Janáček had been describing and celebrating nature with a series of articles: about the goldfinch (XV/227), about the mountains of Slovakia (XV/230), about trees and wood (XV/234), about the springs and wells in Hukvaldy (XV242), about the Demänová caves in Slovakia (XV/248). And not only did he think and write: in December 1921 Janáček bought a cottage, his piece of earth in his native village of Hukvaldy. He went for his first winter visit "to cut the trees" on his "estate."

Just as a chance visit to a performance of *Madama Butterfly* seems to have set *Kát'a Kabanová* in motion, *The Cunning Little Vixen* may have been sparked by a couple of important encounters with Debussy. In the first three months of 1921 there were three performances in Prague of Debussy's *La Mer*, the first in the Czech lands since 1910. We cannot be sure that Janáček heard any of them; however, he was in Prague at the time of the March performance. Incontestable evidence of his getting to know Debussy's great nature picture comes from a substantial analysis he made of the piece at this time (XV/336)—his manuscript is dated 11 March 1921, shortly before the Prague performance that month. And from then on the sound of Debussy's music left its traces on Janáček's. His interest in *La Mer* may have been prompted by a Brno performance of another major work by Debussy, *Pelléas et Mélisande*, whose first night Janáček attended on February 4, 1921. Within a couple of months Janáček had confronted two major works by Debussy. A year later, these new influences absorbed, he began work on *The Vixen*.

One looks in vain for any pattern in similar preparation preceding or accompanying the creation of *Makropulos*. Equally striking is the way that the process of writing other non-operatic works simultaneously that had begun during *The Cunning Little Vixen* now continued and accelerated during *Makropulos*, with the composition of *Youth*, the Concertino, and *Nursery Rhymes*. All of these changes in his work patterns suggest a far greater confidence and a fecund creative mind with ideas flowing over into other works. As he wrote to Max Brod on 13 February 1925, "I'm now finishing the final scene of *The Makropulos Affair*—nevertheless "children's rhymes" [*Nursery Rhymes*] with their melodic and harmonic somersaults get into my fingers."[13]

Alternatively, one could argue that Janáček found *Makropulos* difficult and let himself be distracted. Within a month of beginning the opera he had drafted two hundred pages of Act 1, if we can believe his estimate in a fragmentary letter to Brod.[14] The remaining sixty-nine pages, however, took him another two months. It is true that work was interrupted by his fury over the court case that Mrs. Kovařovicová had initiated over her late husband's additions to *Jenůfa*. (The Prague National Theatre was playing the opera in Kovařovic's version, but had stopped paying her a royalty.)[15] It is interesting that the point where Janáček got stuck, or at least slowed down, was in the long scene between Marty and Gregor, one of the longest spans in this opera (or in fact in any Janáček opera) and compositionally demanding. Either because of Mrs. Kovařovicová or because of the piece's compositional difficulties, the time for drafting the act stretched out from the usual month (*Kát'a Kabanová* and *The Cunning Little Vixen*) to three.

The same is true of the draft of Act 2, written between 19 March and 16 June 1924. Here again some external factors may explain another three-month span. Janáček began Act 2 of *Makropulos* buoyed by his delight at the wonderful Berlin premiere of *Kát'a Kabanová* but also heavy with flu which he caught during his trip there. In the end the flu got the better of him and prevented effective work on the opera for a month. One gets the feeling, however, that things were not going quite so well with this opera. When, a month after he began, he wrote to Brod reporting that he had been "sick in bed for a month," he added, "How could Smetana compose during that illness! With me while I'm ill hardly a motif comes to the surface, it just hides."[16]

Soon after he completed Act 2 Janáček turned seventy (another "deadline") and fled to Hukvaldy to escape the visitors and the fuss in Brno. If he followed the pattern of previous operas he would then have taken a break of at least two months before resuming work on the opera. By this stage Janáček was punctilious about putting down dates for beginnings and endings of his works. He noted when he ended each act of *Makropulos*; he noted when he began Act 1 and Act 2. But for his beginning work on Act 3, there is no date: perhaps forgetfulness, or a lost sheet could explain this—or maybe even faltering confidence in resuming work on this problematic opera. In a letter to Adolf Veselý on 29 September 1924 Janáček had mentioned that he was working on *Makropulos*.[17] Even if this is true Janáček would hardly have had much time, since his autumn was also thoroughly disrupted by the schedule of seventieth-birthday concerts that took place in Brno and Prague. There is in fact no further mention of the work in his correspondence until, on 5 February 1925, Janáček declared himself to be happily at work on it.[18] By 23 February he was able to tell Kamila Stösslová that he had "finished" his opera. The first draft of *Makropulos* had taken him almost fifteen months in comparison with the nine-month spans for *Kát'a Kabanová* and *The Cunning Little Vixen*. Revisions started soon after. The first two acts were revised in the four months before his summer holidays of 1925, the third act after his summer break.

As significant as the longer composition span of *Makropulos* is the fact that in the year that followed Janáček began no new opera. The year 1926 was full of wonderful compositions: the Sinfonietta, *The Glagolitic Mass*, the Capriccio for piano and chamber ensemble, an expanded *Nursery Rhymes*, a draft violin concerto, but no hint of an opera. It would seem, rather, that just as he needed to see *Kát'a Kabanová* onstage and convince himself of its success Janáček needed to see *Makropulos* in performance and make sure that his new opera, with its grittier musical vocabulary and greater demands on singers and orchestra, was viable. And even if it was a close-run thing, it was in Kundera's words a "joyful première."[19] "They say it is my greatest work," Janáček wrote to Kamila on 21 December, three days later. "But it's still possible to go higher."[20] By February 1927 Janáček, now in his seventy-third year, was hard at work on his final opera, *From the House of the Dead*.

Janáček's concentration in this final work is reminiscent of the composition of *Kát'a Kabanová*: Act 1 drafted in just over six weeks, the whole opera drafted in eight months (less if one discounts Janáček's summer break); revisions begun immediately afterward and concluded in just over six months, though Janáček continued to tinker with the copyists' fair copies until his death in August 1928. Not since *The Beginning of a Romance* had he written an opera so fast. Apart from the second string quartet and some short occasional pieces there were no distractions. His mind was set on his opera and the new stage of his passion for Kamila Stösslová, which had blossomed more or less simultaneously. The urgency with which he was writing his final opera is documented in many of his letters to her at the time. "So I am finishing one work after another—as if I had to settle my accounts with life. . . . With my new opera I hurry like a baker throwing loaves into the oven!"[21] "And I am completing perhaps [my] greatest work—the latest opera— excited almost to the pitch where my blood would want to spurt out."[22]

Once he had finished his autograph version of the opera (i.e., the revised draft), Janáček would hand it over to a copyist. The copyist would make a fair copy, which Janáček would then correct, add to, and "authorize" by adding his signature, producing a so-called authorized score. In time Janáček discovered that his copyists had difficulties deciphering his characterful but often illegible manuscript, and that, moreover, when he saw his musical thoughts in the clear light of day, he had further thoughts, or different ones. So, from *The Vixen* on, copyists began to be used additionally as amanuenses, with Janáček sitting down with them, dictating to them, or writing out individual instrumental parts for them, which would then get reproduced neatly in the final copy. In *From the House of the Dead* this process is well documented and occupied a period between March and 10 June 1928.[23]

The Empty Head

Now I have an empty head. Thoughts fly away from me which I have held several years. What now?
—*Janáček to Gabriela Horvátová, 5 December 1917*

An essential requirement for Janáček in his later operas was the "empty head" that preceded composition. It is striking that with the success of *Jenůfa* in Prague there was no thought of starting out with new operas immediately. Unfinished business had to be dealt with first. The rest of 1916 was taken up with feverishly getting *The Excursion of Mr. Brouček to the Moon* into shape, a process that spilled over into expanding it (in 1917) to create a two-excursion "bilogy," *The Excursions of Mr. Brouček*. Other unfinished business included the radical revision of his first opera *Šárka* (1918–1919); the decision—after much heart-searching—to abandon his fourth opera *Fate* when even the faithful Max Brod could not suggest how to make it more stageworthy; and the completion of his fragment of *The Diary of One Who Disappeared*, begun in a fit of enthusiasm in the summer of 1917 after meeting Kamila Stösslová. Only after all this was out of the way could he begin to think of what next to do operatically. "I've put my first opera in order, written thirty-one years ago," Janáček wrote to Kamila Stösslová on 12 January 1919. "Now I have nothing to do—until something occurs to me again."[24]

"So what now?" Janáček wrote to Max Brod on 10 January 1922, shortly before beginning *The Cunning Little Vixen*.[25] "In my head it's empty as if burnt out. I don't know what to bite into." This is disingenuous in view of the fact that for at least a year Janáček had been assiduously preparing himself for his next opera and just a month before this letter had invited Brod to wish him "luck" with *Liška Bystrouška*.[26] But the clearing of the mind, the empty slate, seemed psychologically important to Janáček despite whatever thinking and reflecting he had done previously. The same images persist to the end of his life. With *Makropulos* successfully staged Janáček could write to Kamila, on 27 December 1926: "For the first time I've got an empty head—I'm not writing anything."[27] The next day he spelled it all out in a letter to Brod: "I've never had such an empty head as now after *Makropulos*, the *Glagolitic Mass*, Capriccio, and *Nursery Rhymes*. Usually at the end of one work there was the beginning of the next—waiting out the time like a goose for an ear of grain."[28] With the head cleared and empty he was able to start work on his final opera just over a month later.

How Ideas Occur

Then into the empty head came ideas. Janáček never wrote any account of how he got started with the composition of an opera but, valuably, did leave a description of his early work in the cantata *Amarus*, one of the compositions that he wrote while "stuck" on *Jenůfa*. It is possible that much of the process described here could be applied to other large-scale works such as operas. In the article *How Ideas Occurred* (XV/313), unpublished during his lifetime, Janáček painted a portrait of himself at work on *Amarus*, reading the text late at night, going to sleep and then waking up with a vision of sound that he needed to notate:

> I fell asleep again. Awoken by the usual family bustle the next morning, I rush to get down the motifs that have "occurred." My memory has kept them safe, that faithful memory of mine. I know by now that every time I will have lots of them to hand. They will grow and more will come. In all circumstances of my profession. Motifs are the shadow that even the sun won't bleach. You can't talk them out of it, shout them down—until they mature.

The article is an extraordinary piece of writing. In later life Janáček would provide introductions to some of his compositions, but this is his only account of the actual process of composition. In a stream of consciousness Janáček describes how he listens to the "music of the soul," sees it "clearly noted down" (Example 4).

Example 4. *"How Ideas Occurred."*

He describes the details:

> The tune in the soprano stands out with its fuller sound: the colors of the melancholy oboe have been darkened by the muted strings con sordini. The metrical rhythm comes across clearly to me above the bass. And around the whole picture lights twinkle, here ever quicker in intertwined circles, or in innumerable little stars. The idea doesn't recede from the mind. The end dies away—and once again in bursts the beginning. An evenly measured Adagio.

Janáček was describing the piece at a very early stage. The music example he supplies has the clear A-flat minor tonality and 12/8 key signature of the third movement. The key is confirmed by the dwelling on the dominant note E flat, with a leap up an octave (related to a motif in the third movement of *Amarus*) and the upward scale on horns and cellos, though beginning on a different note. Thereafter description and finished piece diverge. In its final form this passage has a clear-cut trombone motif in the bass and a different continuation in the top line. Janáček's mention, in virtually the same breath, of the "tune in the soprano" coupled with an oboe can refer, in the finished composition, only to a middle section in the second movement; the mention of the "evenly measured Adagio" can only mean the fifth movement. For his next example he provides the following commentary: "A further melody on the viola is accompanied by the muted harp [Example 5]. I must not forget the last eighth-note quadruplets: they will form a bridge to a reminiscence

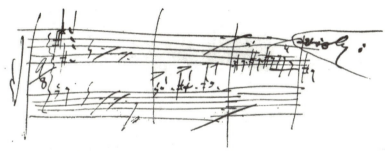

Example 5. *"How Ideas Occurred."*

of the beginning. By means of a ritenuto each eighth note will be prolonged into a dotted quarter note." This tune, at a different pitch and
never on viola or with muted harp accompaniment, became the theme
that holds together the section of the third movement where Amarus
sees and then follows the lovers (Example 6). The "eighth-note

Example 6. *Amarus*, piano-vocal score, 3rd system, mm. 2–3.

quadruplets" do indeed link this movement to the four sixteenths of the
chief theme of the opening movement (Example 7), but the continuation

Example 7. *Amarus*, 2nd system, mm. 3–4, viola and horn part.

that Janáček goes on to describe in *How Ideas Occurred* was abandoned:

> I draw attention also to the speed with which thoughts penetrate
> consciousness. In time they would get lost, like water in sand—dur-
> ing improvisation, for instance. One has to stop the whole flow
> and draw the memory tight over just the main phrases.
>   Later we'll bridge the gaps between these now firm pillars of the
> whole piece.

This description sounds much like Janáček's later practice in his operas in which a piece begins as a continuous improvisation, with many unrelated themes. When revising the draft Janáček would take just a few themes and elaborate them, in a sense, bridging "the gaps between these now firm pillars of the whole piece."

Thickening, Compressions, Insertions

Further insights are, of course, provided by the score itself: much crossing out, scratching out, writing over, and replacing. One curiosity of the revision process is that Janáček maintained the original page numbering, presumably in an attempt to rescue individual pages from the first draft. The page numbering of the final version is thus an eloquent record of omissions and insertions. A page number such as "13–17" indicates the omission either of the original pages 13–16 or of the original pages 14–16; a page number sequence of "19a, 19b, 19c, 19d" indicates an insertion.

This type of pagination reveals not only the physical makeup of Janáček's scores but also the psychology of composition. Janáček regarded the compression of passages revealed in a "13–17" page number as a method of "thickening." "I didn't care for the Epilogue for *Brouček*. I have done it differently, cut it, thickened it, unified it with the motif of the Housekeeper's indignation."[29] This is how Janáček describes the compression he made in Act 3 of *The Excursion of Mr. Brouček to the Moon*, an act subsequently abandoned when he decided to add *The Excursion of Mr. Brouček to the Fifteenth Century*. But this process is evident in all his operas, for instance, in the opening scene of *Fate*: "I have shortened the first scene; it begins immediately on the full spa grounds. It will be more striking. But I will insert little episodes into it. Here and there you will correct the odd word for me."[30]

The "little episodes" inserted was the reverse side of the coin. Janáček created the domestic act (Act 2) for *Fate* by taking Živný's monologue and inserting into it the "little episodes" of the other characters and their interaction with Živný.

The insertions and compressions often led to a form of montage, a typical Janáček compositional procedure, with extra layers added. "Well, in the end it's necessary for it to be thicker, parallel currents are necessary," he wrote to Procházka when trying to diagnose potential problems in the *Brouček* epilogue.[31] And it is this sort of montage that allowed him occasionally, although it would seem to go against the grain of Janáček's word-led composition, to add words to existing music. Procházka, Janáček's most amenable librettist, was sometimes pressed into service to do this ("I need just a few lines in it [for *Šárka*]. Would you do them for me? They are underlined in red, the dots indicate the number of syllables."[32] When soliciting revisions for *Fate* from another librettist, he needed "a few lines of reaction from all concerned." "So, that's what I suggest, it would fit my music excellently."[33]

And Afterward?

Although most of Janáček's operas up to *Brouček* had been heavily revised, once Janáček got his eye in and sorted out his method, the confidence and speed with which he wrote was striking, as was the lack of revision once an opera got to the stage. *The Excursion of Mr. Brouček to the Fifteenth Century* needed adjustments, he felt, and he instructed Ostrčil accordingly,[34] but the following operas went into production and print virtually as he wrote them down, give or take a little tweaking of the orchestration at rehearsals. He resisted attempts to give Boris an aria in *Kát'a Kabanová* and was chary of taking in any of Max Brod's other bright ideas that came out of his translation work.[35] The most substantial pieces of post-compositional changes came about because of the cumbersome scene changes: in both *The Vixen* and *Kát'a Kabanová* Janáček subsequently extended the scenic interludes, the wonderful horn fanfares before the final scene in *The Vixen* and the intra-act interludes in Acts 1 and 2 of *Kát'a Kabanová*.

Apart from the changes forced on Janáček in the sadly cut-down version of *Brouček* for its Brno airing in 1926, the only other substantial changes Janáček made of a work that he had already seen staged were in 1907–1908, when he made a thorough-going revision of *Jenůfa*, which had been given its premiere in 1904. In 1906 its conductor, C. M. Hrazdira, had suggested tightening up some of the ensembles and these had been put into effect at the performances that autumn.[36] Janáček went along with Hrazdira's suggestions, incorporating them all when he made a thorough revision of the opera before the publication of the piano-vocal score in 1908. Bohumír Štědroň made a useful assessment of the changes, but the material that he was able to comment on was limited.[37] It is only recently, with a huge amount of patient detective work, that Mark Audus has been able to reconstruct the 1904 score, lying beneath various layers of later changes. More than the jettisoning of longer ensembles, and the tucks taken into flabby orchestral interludes, what is revealing here is the bread-and-butter stuff of bar-to-bar composition. Generally the more tuneful and memorable passages remained. To take examples from the first scene of Act 2, the opening orchestral prelude, the closing "good night" music or *Jenůfa*'s "baby music" in the middle stayed much as they were. In many other cases the chief change was to tighten up the brief orchestral interludes between sung passages: six bars typically reduced to two, or two-bar interludes excised altogether. In some cases the cuts are more radical. Originally, in the opening scene, Jenůfa reacted to the Kostelnička's objection to the baby's crying (*"Ale bude bečat'"*). In the 1907 revision Janáček discarded her rather aimless music together with its few lines of text. One of the most striking changes in this early scene is to Kostelnička's 26-bar solo *"Už od té doby."* After Janáček's changes in 1907 this became a recitative-like passage, with occasional orchestral gestures interrupting the voice. In 1904, however, it was sung against a continuous four-note ostinato. Here Janáček's changes provide a strong texture contrast and allow the voice (and its crucial words) to come through very clearly. Such examples could be multiplied. Taken together they show evidence of a growing dramatic intelligence brought to bear on the existing musical material. Interestingly, it is the orchestral part that was most changed; Janáček left the voice parts largely intact apart from a few large-scale cuts or small-scale alterations to improve the word setting. This is the precise opposite of Janáček's 1918–1919 changes to *Šárka*, where the orchestra stayed much the same while the voice part became radically altered into a less melodic, more "realistic" guise. A difference between the two, of course, is that Janáček had still not seen *Šárka* on the stage, and that there was a thirty-year gap between composition and revision, during which time his style shifted out of all recognition.

John Tyrrell

Opera Composition Chronologies
(Abbreviations used for sources explained in endnote 1.)

The Excursion of Mr. Brouček to the Fifteenth Century

Date	Action	Source
5 May 1917	Begins Act 1	Date in autograph
1 July 1917	Ends Act 1	BR123

3–30 July 1917: Holiday in Luhačovice, meets Kamila Stösslová
9–22 August 1917: Begins writing *The Diary of One Who Disappeared*

26 August 1917	Resumes work on *Brouček*	BR126
10 September 1917	Ends Act 1 (revision?)	Date in autograph
18 September 1917	Ends Act 2 (draft)	BR134
18 October 1917	Ends Act 2 (revision)	Date in autograph

1–4 November 1917: In Prague for long weekend

8 November 1917	Tries to begin work on Act 3	Janáček to Roman Veselý
18 November 1917	Begins Act 3	Janáčkův Archív, vol. 3, p. 52
27 November 1917	Finishes Act 3 (draft)	Janáčkův Archív, vol. 6, pp. 29–32; date in autograph
2 December 1917	Finishes Act 3 (revision)	BR145
4 December 1917	Adds Kunka's lament	BR146
12 December 1917	Revises *"márně skuháš"* section	BR150; date in autograph

---

Kát'a Kabanová

---

5 January 1920	Begins Act 1 (draft)	Smetana, 1948, p. 113

Composition interrupted by *Brouček* rehearsals in Prague and illness

6 July 1920	Ends Act 1 (draft)	Date in autograph

10 July – late August 1920: Holidays in Luhačovice and Hukvaldy

14 September 1920	Begins Act 2 (draft)	Date in autograph
15 October 1920	Ends Act 2 (draft)	Date in autograph

24 October 1920	Further revisions to Act 2 (draft)	Date in autograph
28 October 1920	Begins Act 3 (draft)	Date in autograph
24 Dec 1920	Ends Act 3 (draft)	Date in autograph

Christmas (1920) and New Year (1921) holidays

8 January 1921	Begins Act 3 (first revision)	Date in autograph
17 February 1921	Ends Act 2 (first revision)	Date in autograph
27 March 1921	Ends Act 1 first revision	Date in autograph
17 April 1921	Ends further revision	Date in autograph

The Cunning Little Vixen

| 22 January 1922 | Begins Act 1 (draft) | Date in autograph |
| 26 March 1922 | Ends Act 1 (draft) | Date in autograph |

Early April 1922: Trip to Prague
20–24 April 1922: Visit of Mrs. Newmarch to Brno

Late April 1922	Begins Act 2, First half (draft)	———
5 June 1922	Ends Act 2, First half (draft)	Date in autograph
7 June 1922	Begins Act 2, Second half (draft)	Date in autograph
End June 1922	Ends Act 2, Second half (draft) ?	LB12

3–24 July 1922: holiday in Luhačovice
18 August (or earlier) to 18 September 1922: holiday in Hukvaldy

| By 30 September | Begins Act 3 (draft) | LB14 |
| 25 October 1922 | Ends Act 3 (draft) | Date in autograph |

Late October 1922: *The Wandering Madman*, trip to Prague
November 1922: Preparations for Prague premiere of *Kát'a Kabanová*
28 December 1922 – 11 January 1923: Holiday in Hukvaldy

| By 26 January 1923 | Begins Act 1 (revision) | LB22 |
| 22 February 1923 | Ends Act 1 (revision) | Date in autograph |

March 1923: Revisions of *Fairy Tale*
24 March 1923: Bratislava premiere of *Kát'a Kabanová*

| By 3 April 1923 | Begins Act 2 (revision) | LB17 |

18, 20 June 1923: Dated work on *The Danube*

29 June 1923	Ends Act 2 (revision)	Date in autograph

4–19 July 1923: Holiday in Štrbské pleso
20 July – 1 August 1923: Holiday in Hukvaldy
Early August 1923: In Salzburg for ISCM festival
16 August – 1 September 1923: Holiday in Luhačovice

Early September ?	Begins Act 3 (revision)	——
10 October 1923	Ends Act 3 (revision)	Date in autograph

The Makropulos Affair

1 November 1923	Begins Act 1 (draft)	Date in autograph
18/19 February 1924	Ends Act 1 (draft)	Date in autograph

26 February 1924: Writes feuilleton (XV/250)
Early March 1924: Trip to Prague; visits and lectures
15–18 March 1924: In Berlin for premiere of *Kát'a Kabanová*

19 March 1924	Begins Act 2 (draft)	Date in autograph

March–April 1924: *Makropulos* slowed down by flu;
several feuilletons (XV/252 and XV/253)

16 June 1924	Ends Act 2 (draft)	Date in Janáček's copy of play

By 24 June 1924: Work on *The Vixen* proofs
25–6 June 1924: Prague Conservatory exams; then trip to Písek
3–16 July 1924: Holiday in Hukvaldy
15–30 August 1924: Holiday in Luhačovice

September 1924 ?	Begins Act 3	Janáček to Adolf Veselý

9 October – 8 December 1924: Seventieth birthday concerts
in Brno and Prague

18 ? February 1925	Ends Act 3 (draft)	Date in autograph
15 March 1925	Begins Act 1 (revision)	Date in autograph

July 1925: Completes movement of *The Danube*

27 July 1925	Ends Act 2 (revision)	Date in autograph

August 1925: Work on *The Danube*
31 August – 10 September 1925: Venice ISCM festival
13 September 1925 onward: Ill with shingles
5–14 October 1925: Holiday in Hukvaldy

Mid-October 1925 ?	Begins Act 3 (revision)	——
12 November 1925	Ends Act 3 (revision)	Date in autograph
3 December 1925	Final revisions	Date in autograph

From the House of the Dead

---

18 March 1927	Begins Act 1 (draft)	Date in autograph
2 April 1927	Ends Act 1 (draft)	Date in autograph

17–23 April 1927: Visit to Stössels in Písek

By May 1927	Begins Act 2 (draft)	ZD8
By late June 1927?	Ends Act 2 (draft)	——

28 June – 3 July 1927: ISCM festival in Frankfurt
13–23 July 1927: Holiday in Hukvaldy
16 August – 2 September 1927: Holiday in Luhačovice
September 1927: Mostly away: In Písek, Radhošt', Hukvaldy,
Berlin, Prague, Písek
4 October 1927: Back in Brno

17 October 1927	Ends Act 3 (draft)	ZD13
By 22 October 1927	Begins Act 1 (revision)	ZD14

By 9 November 1927 Composes *Kát'a Kabanová* interludes

By 18 December 1927	Ends Act 2 (revision)	ZD18

4 January 1928	Ends Act 3 (revision)	ZD21

29 January – 19 February 1928: Composes String Quartet no. 2

10 March 1927	Working with copyists	ZD23

27 March – 2 April 1928: Composes *Chorus for Laying Foundation Stone*

24 April 1928	Ends Act 3 (final version)	Date in autograph
1 May 1928	Further work on Act 2	ZD26
7 May 1928	Ends Act 2 (final version)	ZD21

8 May 1928: Composes *Reminiscence*
31 May – 5 June 1928: Drafts *Schluck und Jau*

| 20 June 1928 | Copyist's work complete | ZD37 |

NOTES

1. F. S. Procházka to Janáček, Prague, 23 December 1917, in John Tyrrell, *Janáček's Opera: A Documentary Account [JODA]* (London: Faber, 1992); BR152, *The Excursions of Mr. Brouček (Výlety páně Broučkovy)*. (Abbreviation refers to the Czech title of Janáček's opera, the number following refers to the document as catalogued in *JODA*; hereafter opera title is identified in first cite.)

2. *Dopisy Leoše Janáčka z archívu Družstva Národního divadla v Brně* (Janáček's letters from the archive of the Družstvo of the National Theatre in Brno), ed. Leoš Firkušný, *Musikologie* 1 (1938): 130.

3. Viktor Dyk, "A Memoir of Leoš Janáček," *JODA*, BR71.

4. *Korespondence Leoše Janáčka s Gabrielou Horvátovou* (Letters to Gabriela Horvátová), ed. Artuš Rektorys, vol. 6, in Janáčkův Archív, first series, general ed. Jan Racek (Prague: Hudební matice, 1950), pp. 33–34.

5. Janáček to Kamila Stösslová, Brno, 23 February 1925; *JODA*, VM19, *The Makropulos Affair (Věc Makropulos)*.

6. The numbers in parentheses refer to catalogue numbers to be found in Nigel Simeone, John Tyrrell, Alena Němcová, *Janáček's Works: A Catalogue of the Music and Writing of Leoš Janáček* (Oxford: Clarendon Press, 1997).

7. *Korespondence Leoše Janáčka s Gabrielou Horvátovou*, ed. Rektorys, pp. 33–34.

8. Janáček to F. S. Procházka, Brno, 19 December 1917; *JODA*, BR151.

9. Janáček to F. S. Procházka, Brno, 2 June 1917; *JODA*, BR115.

10. *Korespondence Leoše Janáčka s F. S. Procházkou* (Letters to F. S. Procházka), ed. Artuš Rektorys, vol. 3, in Janáček Archive, first series, general ed. Jan Racek (Prague: Hudební matice Umělecké besedy, 1948), p. 46.

11. *Hádanka života: dopisy Leoše Janáčka Kamile Stösslové* (The riddle of life: the letters of Leoš Janáček to Kamila Stösslová), ed. Svatava Přibáňová (Brno: Opus musicum, 1990), no. 29.

12. *Korespondence Leoše Janáčka s Gabrielou Horvátovou*, ed. Rektorys, pp. 32–33.

13. Janáček to Max Brod, Brno, 13 February 1925; *JODA*, VM16.

14. Janáček to Max Brod, Brno, n.d., winter 1923–1924; *JODA*, VM13.

15. Anna Kovařovicová to Janáček, Prague, 28 May 1923; *JODA*, JP146ff., *Jenůfa* (*Její pastorkyňa*).

16. *Korespondence Leoše Janáčka s Maxem Brodem* (Letters to Max Brod), ed. Jan Racek and Artuš Rektorys, vol. 9, in Janáček Archive, first series, general ed. Jan Racek (Prague: Státní nakladatelství krásné literatury, hudby a umění, 1953), p. 154.

17. Janáček to Adolf Veselý, 29 September 1924, Janáček Archive of the Music Division of the Moravian Provincial Museum, Brno, shelf B 2205.

18. Janáček to Kamila Stösslová, Brno, 5 February 1925; *JODA*, VM15.

19. Ludvík Kundera, "Janáček's *The Makropulos Affair*"; *JODA*, VM56.

20. Janáček to Kamila Stösslová, Brno, 21 December 1926; *JODA*, VM57.

21. Janáček to Kamila Stösslová, Brno, 30 November 1927; *JODA*, ZD16, *From the House of the Dead* (*Z mrtvého domu*).

22. Janáček to Kamila Stösslová, Brno, 1–2 December 1927; *JODA*, ZD17.

23. Janáček to Kamila Stösslová, Brno, 10 March to 9 June 1928, passim.; *JODA*, ZD23–34.

24. Janáček to Kamila Stösslová, Brno, 12 January 1919; *JODA*, KK1, *Káťa Kabanová*

25. *Korespondence Leoše Janáčka s Maxem Brodem*, ed. Racek and Rektorys, pp. 98–99.

26. Janáček to Max Brod, Brno, n.d., after 10 December 1921; *JODA*, LB9, *The Cunning Little Vixen* (*Příhody Lišky Bystroušky*).

27. Janáček to Max Brod, Brno, 3 December 1926; *JODA*, ZD2.

28. *Korespondence Leoše Janáčka s Maxem Brodem*, ed. Racek and Rektorys, p. 211.

29. Janáček to Roman Veselý, 18 February 1917, Janáček Archive of the Music Division of the Moravian Provincial Museum, Brno, shelf B 1620.

30. Janáček to Fedora Bartošová, Brno, 3 December 1903; *JODA*, OS18, *Fate (Osud)*.

31. *Korespondence Leoše Janáčka s F. S. Procházkou*, ed. Rektorys, p. 19.

32. Janáček to Otakar Ostrčil, Brno, 21 January 1926; *JODA*, SR20, *Šárka*.

33. Janáček to František Skácelík, Brno, 10 October 1907; *JODA*, OS59.

34. Janáček and Otakar Ostrčil, letters 27 April–25 August 1920; *JODA*, BR238–44.

35. For example, Janáček to Max Brod, n.d., after 10 December 1921; *JODA*, KK83.

36. C. M. Hrazdira to Janáček, 11 July 1906, Janáček Archive of the Music Division of the Moravian Provincial Museum, Brno, shelf B 83.

37. Bohumír Štědroň, *Zur Genesis von Leoš Janáčeks Opera Jenůfa* (The Genesis of Leoš Janáček's Opera *Jenůfa*), 2d ed. (Brno: University J. E. Purkyně, 1972).

Janáček and the Captured Muse

DIANE M. PAIGE

Because you're in me, because you've dominated me completely,
I don't long for anything else. I don't have words to express my
longing for you, to be close to you. . . . I know that my compositions will be more passionate, more ravishing; you'll sit on every
little note in them.

—Leoš Janáček to Kamila Stösslová
30 April 1927

Leoš Janáček's relationship to Kamila Stösslová, a woman nearly four
decades his junior, has become an essential part of the composer's biography. Relations between the two are generally treated as a titillating
aspect of the composer's personal life, and there is a general assumption that she played some role in Janáček's creative process. Much of
what is known of their eleven-year relationship stems from the voluminous surviving correspondence. The letters penned to her, while
they abound in courting gestures and evocations of his feelings, por-
tray much more than the impractical obsessive feelings of an old man
to an unlikely woman; rather, they hint at a central entity that guided
Janáček's mature works.

The muse, the enigmatic female figure credited with the creation of
many works throughout Western history, was an integral element in
Janáček's creative process. Despite the pervasiveness of the muse, it is
a topic rarely approached in the musicological literature. Given this, a
short history of the muse and her appearance in the works of Janáček's
contemporaries, such as Franz Kafka, will help to establish parameters
of what she embodies for the creative artist.

Since antiquity the female muse has served as creative helpmate to
artists of all kinds.[1] In early Greek culture, the muses were imagined
as beautiful erotic beings who compelled men to irrationality, a state that

favored the creative impulse. "A poet is a delicate thing, winged and sacred, and unable to create until he becomes inspired and frenzied, his mind no longer in him; as long as he keeps his hold on that, now man can compose or chant prophecy," remarked Socrates in the *Ion* of Plato.[2] In another Platonic dialogue, Socrates classified this process as "possession and madness from the muses, seizing a tender and untrodden soul, arousing it and exciting it to a Bacchic frenzy toward both odes and other poetry."[3] Plato further warned that men should be wary of her powers, since such frenzies could interfere with matters of state. "If you admit the Muse of sweet pleasure, whether in lyrics of epic, pleasure and pain will rule as monarchs in your city, instead of the law and that rational principle which is always and by all thought to be the best."[4]

In the Christian Middle Ages, the Classical muses, active singers who overtook their artists, were reconfigured as passive inspirers. Yet, the imagery of the muse and the link between sexual desire and poetic invention still remained part of her visage well into the Renaissance. Exaltations of the beloved, whether by troubadours or Elizabethan poets, spoke of the muse's beauty and creative potential. A significant alternative view of the muse that held sway in the Middle Ages and Renaissance noted the muse's ability to bring the artist closer to God, a stance which helps to explain Dante's Beatrice, the cult of the Virgin Mary, or Milton's "Heavenly Muse" in *Paradise Lost*. With the advent of Romanticism, English poets epiphanized a third aspect of the muse: her—and, by extension, all women's—inherent connection to nature, her natural creative force, and her ability to help man reconnect with the lost paradise.[5]

The muse appears in several forms: as an erotic/sexual being, as a spiritual channel to God, or as a vital force in the natural world. Whether they are configured as pure virgin or as Mother Earth, all muses share certain characteristics. All are objects captured by the artist. They are, as Mary K. DeShazer contends, "vehicles, catalysts, emblems against and through which the male poet asserts his imaginative power."[6] It is through this assertion that male artistic prowess is complemented and completed by feminine creativity. One such case of a captured muse involves writer Franz Kafka, who channeled this feminine power into his writing largely by means of letter writing. His relationship to this captured muse reveals many standard tropes of the poet-muse relationship.

Under the invisible presence of Felice Bauer, Franz Kafka found his artistic powers renewed, and works such as "The Metamorphosis" were released in a torrent of creative energy. Kafka's muse took on several guises in his mature works and functioned as inspiration, as helpmate, and as an idealized creative force. In a diary entry dated 20 August 1912, Kafka recalled his initial meeting with Felice, Berlin Jewess and distant cousin to his friend Max Brod. He wrote:

> Miss F. B. When I arrived at Brod's on August 13, she was sitting at the table. I was not at all curious who she was, but rather took her for granted all at once. Bony, empty face that wore its emptiness openly. Bare throat. A blouse thrown on. Looked very domestic in her dress although, as it later turned out, she by no means was. . . . Almost broken nose. Blonde, somewhat straight, unattractive hair, strong chin. As I was taking my seat I looked at her closely for the first time, by the time I was seated I already had an unshakable opinion.[7]

One month later, on September 20, Kafka began a daily correspondence with Felice, an act that initiated his most productive period as a writer. The short stories "The Judgment," "The Stoker," and "The Metamorphosis," were written in the span of a few months, and these works define Kafka's coming of age as a writer. Three days after the first letter to Felice, on September 23, Kafka quickly and effortlessly penned "The Judgment," whose painless creation prompted him to note in his diary:

> This story [The Judgment] I wrote at one sitting during the night—23rd, from ten o'clock at night to six o'clock in the morning. . . . The fearful strain and joy, how the story developed before me as if I were advancing over water. . . . Only in this way can writing be done, with such coherence, with such complete opening of the body and the soul.[8]

Doubtless, this was a powerful epiphany for a man who only six weeks earlier had declared in his diary, "I have achieved nothing."[9]

Kafka's use of letter writing to Felice in Berlin from the safe environs of his native Prague was a way to achieve intellectual intimacy through physical distance.[10] Though his letters to Felice abound with conventional courting gestures, they give but only the appearance of intimacy; Kafka never fully intended to pursue her romantically, a fact evidenced by his two broken engagements to her within the next five years. By projecting an intimate relationship upon Felice from a distance, Kafka assigned to Felice the role of his muse and soon found himself able to write with the fervor and direction he had found lacking. Not only did he send her letters daily, but encouraged her to do likewise, for he needed to know every detail of her daily life so that he could indeed fully capture her image from afar. The exchange of letters was central to Kafka's success as a writer; when the correspondence waned, so too did his literary output. He clearly recognized Felice's role in his creative life when he queried Max Brod in a letter "Could it be that one can take a girl captive by writing?"[11]

Elizabeth Boa summarizes the ways in which Felice Bauer served Kafka: as an initiating inspiration, as one who hovers silently during writing, as the receiver of the writing, as one who becomes a figure within the writing, and as a companion who stands by when the writer faces his public. For Boa, "writing is a secret act of possession from a distance" and such an act allowed Kafka to channel the illusory power he held over the image of Felice into his writing.[12]

Not only have literary figures such as Kafka relied on the muse for creative inspiration; several examples exist among composers from the nineteenth and twentieth centuries as well. Tchaikovsky's correspondence with the widow Nadezhda Filaretovna von Meck from 1876 to 1890 offered the composer the safe, distant company of a confidante. Not only did von Meck serve as inspiration for such works as the Fourth Symphony, but she provided strength and comfort as the composer battled self-doubt and anthropophobia.[13] While von Meck offered Tchaikovsky moral and psychological support, Anežka Schulzová (1868–1905), the muse of Zdeněk Fibich (1850–1900), became the musical subject for his most bizarre composition.[14] *Nálady, dojmy, a upomínky* (Moods, impressions, and remembrances) from 1892 to 1899 is a cycle of 376 small works for piano solo. While many offer musical reminiscences of their love affair, others are explicit descriptions of Schulzová's body; Fibich intended to capture his muse musically in all of her guises, both emotional and physical.

Other composers, like Alban Berg, captured the beloved through symbolic musical compositions.[15] His wife, Helene, for example, was represented by the key of D minor, and in his first letter to her some three years before their wedding in the spring of 1907 he called out "I kiss that hand of yours, my most glorious Symphony in D Minor!"[16] For much of their courtship, their contact was limited to letters due to Berg's health and family commitments, and Helene's domineering father who felt the young Berg an unworthy suitor. The composer wrote of the anticipation of her next letter and confessed that "figures of imagination" appear after one appears by post. He reports of "first, the kindly muse-figure, the wise counselor and helpmate, the dispenser and general kindness and love."[17]

Perhaps the most tangible evidence of Helene's influence is found in the famous D-minor interlude at the end of *Wozzeck*, based on the early, unfinished *Klavierstückerl* in the same key from 1914. Berg confessed in a letter dated 27 May 1922 that "the Interlude at the end I owe to you and you alone. You really composed it, I just wrote it down."[18] It is not surprising that references to Helene's role as muse virtually disappear once the couple married. Part of the allure of the muse is her unattainable nature and her illusory power. Marriage affords neither. Although correspondence continued during the couple's frequent separate holidays, travels, and the like, the contents are decidedly mundane. Though Berg still professed love for his wife, her role in his creative life seems to have become either tacitly accepted or no longer acknowledged or needed.

Later in his marriage, Berg found another source of inspiration, and references to this muse, Hanna Fuchs-Robettin, are embedded in the *Lyric Suite*. Because her presence there is encoded, Berg prepared a specially annotated score for her use, detailing where she and the composer appear in the work. Berg's choice of the hidden clues no doubt stemmed from the fact that both he and Fuchs-Robettin were married, but there are more compelling reasons than simply concealing an affair of the heart. By this time, the composer's compositional process was highly emblematic and he sought out hidden codes in numbers and pitches of his compositions.[19] It is not surprising that he should hide his muse among such symbols, for her presence was just as "hidden" and as emblematic in his works. Such examples demonstrate the rich history of the muse in music, and offer a basis to discuss Janáček's muse and how she shaped his most creative period as a composer.

Like Felice Bauer and Helene Nahowski-Berg, Kamila Stösslová, Janáček's muse, was also captured through letter writing. Janáček's admiration, his wooing, and his preoccupations with this dark beauty provided part of the impetus to produce four masterful operas and several other works. These cathartic works inspired by Kamila allowed the composer to vent frustration over the loss of youth and his unhappy romantic situations. By vicariously attaching himself to her personality, Janáček accessed the creative energy necessary to create several masterworks within the short span of a decade.[20]

Janáček's string quartet subtitled "Intimate Letters" is perhaps the most famous reference to his feelings for Kamila, but aspects of the relationship resonate in all of his late major works, including the operas *Kát'a Kabanová*, *The Adventures of Vixen Sharpears*, and *The Makropulos Case*, as well as the chamber work *The Diary of One Who Vanished*. Theirs was a bizarre relationship—highly erotic and yet unconsummated, intimate and painfully honest, yet with few personal contacts.[21]

The two first met at the popular Moravian spa town Luhačovice in the summer of 1917. The sixty-two-year-old composer was immediately attracted to Stösslová, a twenty-five-year-old with dark hair and eyes. Upon returning home from his holiday, he wrote to her:

> You are so lovely in character and appearance, that in your company one's spirits are lifted; you breathe warmheartedness, you look on the world with such kindness that one wants to do only good and pleasant things for you in return. You will not believe how glad I am to have met you. Happy you! All the more painfully I feel my own desolation and bitter fate.[22]

This "bitter fate" was self-inflicted. Janáček's marriage to Zdenka Janáčková had nearly come to an end the previous year because of his flagrant affair with the singer Gabriela Horvátová.[23] As a result of the composer's indiscretions, an out-of-court legal separation was drawn up in January of 1917, dictating that the couple remain wedded on peaceful terms, continue to keep house together, but sleep apart.[24] By contrast, Kamila's marriage to David Stössel seemed a happy one, and Janáček directed his energies toward their seemingly idyllic relationship.

Later that summer, the Stössels visited Janáček's summer home in Hukvaldy. While Zdenka Janáčková initially regarded Kamila as a diversion from Janáček's lingering thoughts of Horvátová, she was understandably wary of her husband's intentions, given his past indiscretions.[25] In her memoirs from 1935, Mrs. Janáček recalled her early impressions of Kamila:

> She gained my husband's favour through her cheerfulness, laughter, temperament, Gypsy-like appearance, and buxom body, perhaps also because she reminded him of Mrs. Horvátová, although she had none of that woman's demonic qualities or artfulness. She was natural, sometimes almost uninhibited. One couldn't exactly say that she won my husband over, for she didn't try to. . . . She herself was completely unimpressed by my husband's fame, and also by his person; sometimes she laid into him quite sharply and at other times he seemed almost ridiculous in her eyes. . . . I felt I'd no option when I saw how desperately Leoš wanted this friendship. I said to myself that she could be a good support for me against Mrs. Horvátová.[26]

Kamila and Janáček shared a one-sided relationship, with the composer relentlessly pursuing Kamila through his many letters, and she responding infrequently and coolly. A typical example of their friendship involved an invitation to Vienna for the German-language premiere

of *Jenůfa* in February 1918. Kamila failed to later thank the composer
for her inclusion in this important event and her silence brought a
sharp response from Janáček. "A mistake! I waited for your first response
after returning from Vienna, and nothing, absolutely nothing from
you."[27] As his muse, Kamila was not allowed to waver in her support
of the composer, especially when he was to face his public.

Such dynamics were to characterize the relationship until Janáček's
death a decade later. In an effort to please his muse, Janáček made myr-
iad offers for visits, concerts, and the like and found such invitations
were refused. Often he simply received no acknowledgment of his gestures or received, at best, sporadic replies. Clearly, Kamila did not
consider the relationship as serious as he did, and though she may
have been humored and flattered by his effusive prose and nonstop letters, it is evident that she never seriously considered the relationship
anything more than that of an acquaintance. Even the anniversary of
their first meeting in Luhačovice, considered highly significant by
Janáček, was marred by an obscure public incident involving the two
that forced the composer to write on 29 July 1918 that "I wanted to
take my leave of you; however you humiliated me in front of the servants. After all I have never so insulted you."[28] Still, for all the discourtesy
and lack of acknowledgment that Kamila displayed, Janáček was quick
to forgive. "And if I am more passionate than other people, that is just
my pain, my suffering. Forgive me if I was in the way. I believed that I
had sincere friends in you and your husband; that's why I sought your
company."[29] Though this unlikely muse seemed nonreceptive and
unsupportive of Janáček's work, the composer persisted and began to
create a visage of her in his mind that would sustain his creative energies. Soon she became the subject of musical works.[30]

Shortly after that first meeting in the summer of 1917, Janáček began
work on the song cycle *The Diary of One Who Vanished* after reading a
lovers' tale in the local newspaper *Lidové noviny* (The people's news).
The work is based on the erotic story of a young man who falls in love
with a beautiful Gypsy girl, fathers a child by her, and then abandons
his family to wander with her.[31] The central themes expressed in the
song cycle of passionate, consummated love, the fathering of a child,
and the abandonment of worldly responsibilities were to become the
basis for Janáček's imagined relationship with Kamila and central elements in works inspired by her.

In a letter dated 10 August 1917 Janáček first noted the link between
Kamila and his sketches for *The Diary of One Who Vanished*. "In the morning I potter around in the garden; regularly in the afternoon a few motifs
occur to me for those beautiful little poems about that Gypsy love.

Perhaps a nice little musical romance will come out of it—and a tiny bit of the Luhačovice mood would be in it."[32] More than a year later, Janáček wrote to Kamila, complaining, "It's too bad my Gypsy girl can't be called something like Kamilka. That's why I also don't want to go on with the piece."[33] Janáček often referred to Kamila as his "Negress" or "Gypsy" (among other pet names) because of her strong, dark features, and in 1924 he fully admitted the central role she played in the genesis and conception of work:

> And that black Gypsy girl in my *Diary of One Who Vanished*, that was especially you. . . . That's why there's such emotional heat in these works. So much heat that if it caught both of us, there'd be just ashes left of us. Luckily it's just I who burn—and you who are saved.[34]

Kamila's connection with the work was so obvious to Janáček that he wanted the first printed edition to feature a likeness of her on the cover with her hair down. The 1921 edition featured a woodcut by Ferdis Dusa depicting a woman with long, dark hair embracing her lover, an apt reference to the woman who was both the initiating inspiration and an important figure with the work. That Janáček compared his muse Kamila to the dark, exotic Gypsy of the *Diary* further enforces Kamila's role in the composer's creative life: the muse not only arouses the artist's creative energies but also his sexual desires.[35]

The *Diary* was the first of several works inspired by Kamila. After completing this work, Janáček was able to attend a production of Nikolay Ostrovsky's play *The Storm* in March 1919. The story of an unfaithful wife and her tragic end compelled him to begin sketches shortly thereafter. A December production of Puccini's *Madame Butterfly* seems to have further inspired the composer. "I've just come from the theatre," he writes to Kamila on December 5. "They gave *Batrflay* [*sic*], one of the most beautiful and saddest of operas. I had you constantly before my eyes. Batrflay [*sic*] is also small, with black hair. You could never be as unhappy as her."[36] Kamila had now become emblematic of the married woman's woes as she became central to his newest work, *Kát'a Kabanová*. One month later, he announced the work's genesis to her. "I've begun writing a new opera. The chief character in it is a woman, gentle by nature. She shrinks at the mere thought [of hurting, of evil]; a breeze would carry her away—let alone the storm that gathers over her."[37] While at work on *Kát'a*, Janáček's fantasies of his imaginary marriage to Kamila surfaced. This was no doubt fueled by the gift of a ring to him from Kamila in August 1919 after he wrote to complain that his own had been damaged and then lost. References to the ring peppered the correspondence thereafter, further suggesting Janáček's idealization of her as a wife of sorts.

Janáček's mode of adaptation of Ostrovsky's play suggests Kamila's central role as well. Rather than set the numerous roles and the symbolic presence of the storm found in the original, Janáček produced a libretto that focused on the character of Kát'a, her lonely life, and cruel treatment at the hands of her husband and mother-in-law. And while Kát'a still suffers the obligatory death of an adultress, Janáček's audiences were left with a more sympathetic reading of her plight than is found in the Russian original. Janáček considered Kamila an omnipresent force during the creation of the opera and stated in a letter dated 25 February 1922, "During the writing of the opera I needed to know a great measureless love. Tears ran down your cheeks when you remembered your husband in those beautiful days in Luhačovice. It touched me. And I always placed your image on Kát'a Kabanová when I was writing the opera."[38]

While Kamila was willing to confide in Janáček about the loneliness that accompanied her marriage to David, she was wary of any attempts Janáček made to spend time alone with her. When he suggested in October 1921 that she attend the Prague premiere of *The Diary of One Who Vanished*, she replied, "It's not possible for me to come to Prague for my husband has not arrived back. . . . If you bring your wife with you then I might come without my husband but in this way it's impossible."[39] Like Kafka, Kamila understood the safe distance created by letter writing, one that would be jeopardized if the two parties met. Her reluctance intensified Janáček's feelings, thus further idealizing her in his mind. Had she capitulated to his advances, she could not have been his muse. As poet Robert Graves writes, "The White Goddess [his term for the original muse figure] is anti-domestic; she is the perpetual 'other woman,' and her part is difficult indeed to play for more than a few years."[40]

A year later, in February of 1922, Janáček began work on the opera *The Adventures of Vixen Sharpears*, an Arcadian tale on the themes of man and nature, the circle of life, and the twilight of one's existence. That fall he had purchased a cottage in Hukvaldy, his retreat and birthplace, and intended that the quiet, secluded home would serve as a place for his retirement. The correspondence continued as usual; his contact and replies from Kamila were few, and despite his entreaties their relationship remained one separated by physical distance.

Because physical proximity to Kamila was impossible, the composer stepped into the opera with his muse. "I have begun writing *The Cunning Little Vixen*. A merry thing with a sad end: and I'm taking up a place at that sad end myself. . . . And I so belong there!"[41] The opera tells the story of the Vixen who is captured by the covetous Forester, escapes to the forest, and marries and bears children. Her eventual recapture and death at the hand of the poacher Harašta is the final link in the circle of life.

Themes of life, death, and regeneration by offspring resonated with the septuagenarian composer, who wrote the following April that "I caught Bystrouška for the forest and for the sadness of the late years."[42] Sentiments of sadness and regret became more evident with the passing of Janáček's seventieth birthday, and yet his ardent fervor for Kamila remained. On 1 July 1924 he sent a newspaper clipping with the following remarks:

> I'm enclosing a cutting. I wanted to escape from every sort of celebration of those damned seventy years but it just can't be done. It wasn't too bad when a German newspaper called me a "*Greis-Jungling* [old man/youth]." If the second epithet were true I'd carry you off even if you were behind seventy-five locks! But I know that you wouldn't let me. For you have not only the power of eloquence, but also the strength to break bones. But nevertheless I'd overpower you![43]

Although the opera addresses the powerlessness of old age and the inevitability of death, these dark themes are tempered by the regeneration following the Vixen's death. Likewise, Kamila represented a regenerative force for Janáček. While countless accounts of the composer's life speak of his passionate obsession with her, few note her important role as a maternal figure. Like the muse, the mother is a creative being through whom man can channel his creative and procreative energies. Janáček's comments about Kamila's increasing girth and roundness were probably references to the imaginary child she carried.[44]

> Oh you know Kamila, I'm so unutterably fond of you. I'd call out Kamila all the time! And sometimes, ah, I fear to say it . . . because it's something not to be uttered. Not for this passion, for something higher. . . . They say of me that I'll live for ever; that's metaphorical. But it's possible to live for ever in other ways. Eternal life springs from you, from that dear Kamila.[45]

So too did the creative impulse to compose.

In November 1923 Janáček announced plans to write an opera that once again addressed themes of life, longevity, and death. It was based on Karel Čapek's play *The Makropolus Affair*: "I've begun a new work and so I'm no longer bored. A 300-year-old beauty—and eternally young—

but only burnt-out feeling! Brrr! Cold as ice! About such as woman I shall write an opera."[46] Emilia Marty, the opera singer who holds the secret to eternal life, must decide if immortality is worth the price of the boredom of living century after century, the pain of outliving every lover, and the sorrows that accumulate in an immortal's lifetime.

At one point in the opera Emilia is visited by old Hauk, a lover from long ago, and their scene captures the essence of the relationship between the young, vibrant Kamila and the aged Janáček. The reunion of two lovers whose lives are now out of sync, is poignant and captures fully the futility of old Hauk's ardor for the eternally youthful Emilia. At first she fails to recognize the decrepit madman as her former lover, but once she remembers his identity she declares, "I was in love, you see, fifty years ago, in 1870." He sings of the *chula negra* (dusky beauty) a woman for whom he "left everything behind, including his mind. . . . I haven't really been alive since then—just dozing." Emilia (or Eugenia, as he knew her) served as a vital force in Hauk's life, one whose absence stripped him of all vitality. As the eternal beauty caresses the aged, witless Hauk, one can only imagine the passionate relationship the two enjoyed fifty years earlier. Janáček himself must have wondered if his relationship with Kamila was as futile, for in the last year of his life he referred to her as his "hoped for wife" and announced that he wanted to dedicate his String Quartet no. 2 to "Mrs. Kamila Janáčková."[47] Like Hauk, Janáček loved a woman whose lifetime was out of sync with his own, and one whose inspiring nature served as a vital life source.

Perhaps the most prevalent characteristic assigned to Kamila was her elusive nature and thus nearly invisible presence in Janáček's life. Unfulfilled longing for the intangible is a central theme in the correspondence and operas, as evidenced by this excerpt from a letter from 1924:

> How can one not want you, when one loves you? But I know, don't I, that I'll never have you. Would I pluck that flower, that family of happiness of yours, would I make free with my respect for you, whom I honour like no other woman on earth? Could I look your children in the eye, your husband and parents? Could I walk into your home? You know, we dream about paradise, about heaven and we never get to it. So I dream about you and I know that you're the unattainable sky. But not to want you, though that's an impossibility—I can't do that. You are entire in my soul; so it's enough for me to want you always.[48]

The most explicit compositional reference to Kamila is the second string quartet, subtitled "Intimate Letters." Written in the last year of

Janáček's life, it reflects, in part, the couple's decision to make their relationship public. Such a decision was prompted by a domestic quarrel between the Janáčeks on New Year's Day 1928 and shortly afterward by Kamila's wish to have the relationship publicly acknowledged.[49] Despite entreaties from family and gossip circulated by those close to the composer, Janáček persisted in openly recognizing Kamila's importance to his personal and professional well-being. A less public but symbolic move toward openly declaring the relationship occurred the previous fall when Kamila purchased a small album for Janáček's use while at her Písek home. It was to contain the thoughts, speech melodies, small compositions, and other reflections that occurred to him during his visits.[50] (For more detail on this, see the next essay in this volume.)

Amid the tumult precipitated by Janáček's public avowal, the composer was compelled to seek advice from Max Brod, the translator of the German versions of several of his libretti, in a letter dated 18 January 1928. He wrote from Hukvaldy:

> Tell me, is it possible to reveal upon which human grew the crystals of my motifs? Has any writer ever told the public? With the painters it is no secret. . . . But a composer? Would it be taken amiss if this spiritual relationship, this artistic relationship were to be openly admitted? . . . I am aware of the psychological side to this tendency of the motifs to incline toward perceptions of the tangible, real. This is the sort of composing which has nurtured me and brought me to maturity.[51]

Brod's reply does not exist, and later letters from Janáček to him do not mention the issue again. Perhaps the composer received no reply, or could no longer wait for one, since he penned an article for the magazine *Venkov* (Outdoors) six days later. When the article, entitled "Dusk Approaches," appeared in print two weeks later, it acknowledged Kamila and her role in his works and allowed the composer to defend his use of Kamila's image as a means to inspiration.

> Composing music is not as easy as an innocent mind would have it. To create an image through music is, in large part, one of the graphic arts. It becomes such an art when, as if by miracle, the vision catches a glimpse of itself in a real being.[52]

January 29 must have been a day of epiphany, for Janáček wrote four separate letters to Kamila. While the second letter testified to his resolve: "I'll never hide anything . . . you're half my soul," the last, written later that night, announced the early stages of work on a quartet to be called "Love Letters" (*Listy milostné*).[53] Janáček wrote the quartet between 29 January and 19 February and later stated that it reflected experiences both real and imagined that he and Kamila had shared. Thus, it is not surprising that there are many references to her throughout. The opening movement, for example, features the so-called Gypsy scale, an apt reference to a woman that Janáček often called his "Gypsy" or "Negress."[54] On 1 February 1928 Janáček reported to Kamila, "I'm now working on the second movement. I think that it will flare up in the Luhačovice heat [one word inked out]. A special instrument will particularly hold the whole thing together. It's called the viola d'amore—the viola of love."[55] This movement refers to the spa town where the couple first met, and may further denote an important event that took place in Luhačovice on 26 August 1927, when Kamila allowed Janáček his first kiss.[56] The viola d'amore held special significance for Janáček, who used it in several works. For example, it appears in the early opera *Osud*, where it represents Mrs. Kamila Urválková, whom Janáček characterized in his autobiography as "the most beautiful woman. Her voice was like a viola d'amore."[57] Not only does the instrument appear in this work, but in others such as *Kát'a Kabanová*, *The Makropolus Case*, and the third movement of the Sinfonietta.[58]

The quartet's third movement depicts what Janáček called the day "when the earth trembled."[59] During a week-long visit to Písek in March 1927, Janáček openly revealed his love for Kamila. He recalled the incident in a letter two months later:

> My Kamila, whom I told that I love infinitely and I think perhaps that she also loves me! For it seemed that the earth burst open when I said it to her and she was silent, she ran and stood still again, I stood and ran after her again—yes, just like the birds do—who don't lie about love."[60]

The main theme of the quartet reappears in the final movement and describes the "great longing—and as if it were fulfilled."[61] It seems that Janáček was struck by his vivid portrayal of his personal life, for soon after completing the work, Janáček changed the title from "Love Letters" to the more ambiguous "Intimate Letters" (*Listy důvěrné*). His reason given to Kamila for the change was "I won't deliver my feelings to the tender mercies of fools."[62]

Upon hearing the work, one that "sprang from directly experienced feeling," Janáček was struck by its profound effect.[63] The first private performance took place in his home and was given by the Moravian

Quartet on 27 June. That evening, he reported the event to Kamila and spoke as if his compositional choices were not conscious decisions, but rather the result of Kamila's image:

> I listened to their playing today. I listen. Did I write that? Those cries of joy, but what a strange thing, also cries of terror after a lullaby. Exaltation, a warm declaration of love, imploring; untamed longing. Resolution, relentlessly to fight with the world over you. Moaning, confiding, fearing. Crushing everything beneath me if it resisted. Standing in wonder before you at our first meeting. Amazement at our appearance; as if it had fallen to the bottom of a well and from that very moment I drank the water of that well. Confusion and high-pitched song of victory: "You've found a woman who was destined for you." Just my speech and your amazed silence. Oh, it's a work as if carved out of living flesh. I think that I won't write a more profound and a truer one.[64]

Janáček's last opera, *From the House of the Dead*, is unique in that it features no central female roles. Set in a men's prison, the work seemingly has little room for Janáček's muse, and yet he found ways in which to project her image onto this work. In reworking Dostoevsky's original, the composer found two characters to attach to his muse: Aljeja, a young Tartar boy, and Akulka, a long-dead victim of one of the prisoners. In a newspaper article, Janáček confessed the connection: "You in whom Ostrovsky sought his Kát'a Kabanová; you who Dostoevsky would call the tortured soul of Akulka, and in whom I find the pure child's soul of Aljeja."[65] Throughout the opera, women are conspicuously absent, and men mourn those they have wronged, long for the sisters and mothers left behind, and see the feminine in the guise of a prostitute who appears briefly and in prisoners in women's costume for a holiday farce. The oppressive atmosphere of the prison is doubly suffocating without a palpable feminine presence, just as Janáček held fast that he could not create without the visage of Kamila with him.

In light of his relationship with Kamila it might be tempting to consider Janáček as a man who saw women in idealized terms. In truth, Janáček's view of women was sharply divided among the real and the ideal. As his maid recalled, "He respected women of talent, especially artistic talent, but his general view was the same of most men in those days: women belong in the kitchen."[66] On one hand, he adhered to patriarchal norms and considered most women aesthetically pleasing objects, and looked forward to his spa holidays because they were filled with, as he said, "an annual congress of beautiful women."[67] His extramarital affairs with women such as Gabriela Horvátová support the view that in many ways his dealings with women were base or obligatory. And yet he was also able to sublimate his desires into other outlets and mythologize some women into ideals. His relationship with Kamila depended on her physical distance and his lack of real experience with her as a lover. As long as she was not his, she could remain an ideal. This persistent dichotomy is eloquently captured in a letter sent by Baudelaire to his beloved Apollonie Sabatier, a woman he had loved for five years. When she finally gave in to his amorous advances, he fled, for now that he knew her as a woman, she could no longer be his "White Venus."

> You see my dear, my beauty, that I have hateful prejudices about women. In fact, I have no faith; you have a fine soul, but, when it's all said, it is the soul of a woman . . . a few days ago you were a deity, which is so convenient, so noble, so inviolable. And now there you are, a woman.[68]

Despite Janáček's more mundane associations with women, he clearly idealized Kamila and all that she represented. She embodied central aspects of the muse, a notion evident in the voluminous correspondence of Janáček and by the recurring elements within his works. And yet she has often been dismissed as a potential inspirational source; she was undereducated, not terribly attractive, rather large, and hardly had the intellect to satisfy someone as astute as Janáček.[69]

While one can criticize her for all of the above, such qualities made her the perfect muse for Janáček. Her full and maternal figure represented a vessel through which compositions took root and could be brought forth. Her reticence, her physical distance, and perhaps her lack of education were crucial factors in determining her suitability, for a muse does not criticize her artist. On the few instances where Janáček felt Kamila to be critical or rude, no matter how trivial the issue, he immediately issued a strong response. She was to be his passive conduit, his perfect helpmate.

Kamila's sensual nature and Janáček's desire for her were important to the creative relationship as well.[70] She was a dark beauty, his Negress, his Gypsy girl, who represented earthly desires, and one who, like the young woman of the *Diary*, could pull a man away from the mundane world into another, more intoxicating, more liberating. But he created an image for her more complex than that, for like all muses, she embodied the erotic woman whose sexual nature provokes creative genius, the spiritual being who allows the composer a glimpse of the face of God, and a being whose necessary and deep connection to nature provides the composer with a window to paradise. Through Kamila, Janáček found a means through which to assert his creativity. After a short visit with her in May 1927, he summarized the illusory, yet necessary connection to his captured muse in a letter to her: "I rushed into work so vigorously that my heart began to pound. However, you were like a peaceful shade for me—when the heat was troublesome[;] and like the sun—when I needed to be warm: in short under your image I work well."[71]

NOTES

This article is a refinement of a chapter from my doctoral dissertation "Women in the Operas of Leoš Janáček," University of California, Santa Barbara, 2000.

1. For an overview of the muse in antiquity, see Pierre Boyancé, *Le Culte des Muse: Chez les Philosophes Grecs, Etudes d'Historie et de Psychologie Religeuses* (Paris: Editions E. de Boccard, 1936).

2. Plato, *Ion. Hippias Minor. Laches. Protagoras*, trans. R. E. Allen (New Haven and London: Yale University Press, 1996), p. 14 (535b).

3. Plato, *Gorgias and Phaedrus*, trans. James H. Nichols, Jr. (Ithaca, N.Y.: Cornell University Press, 1988), p. 174 (245a).

4. Plato, *Plato's Republic*, trans. G. M. A. Grube (Indianapolis: Hackett Publishing, 1974), p. 251 (607a).

5. Mary K. DeShazer, *Inspiring Women: Reimagining the Muse* (New York: Pergamon Press, 1986), pp. 2–9. While DeShazer's study is concerned with the ways in which female artists imagine the muse figure, her introduction outlines the history of the muse and supplies the three categories I have used here.

6. Ibid., p. 26.

7. Franz Kafka, *The Diaries of Franz Kafka, 1910–1913*, ed. and trans. Max Brod (London: Secker & Warburg, 1948), p. 276.

8. Ibid.

9. Ibid., p. 266.

10. Such means are well documented throughout the history of the arts. Consider, for example, the relationship of Michelangelo to Vittoria Colonna, Marchesa di Pescara. The couple's exchange of passionate sonnets occurred only after Colonna withdrew from society and joined a convent.

11. Elias Canetti, *Kafka's Other Trial: The Letters to Felice*, trans. Christopher Middleton (New York: Shocken Books, 1982), p. 7. For a summary of the role of letter writing between Kafka and Felice, see Elias Canetti, "Letters from a Bachelor: Kafka's Letters to Felice Bauer," in *Reading Kafka: Prague, Politics, and the Fin de Siècle*, ed. Mark Anderson (New York: Schocken Books, 1989), pp. 229–240.

12. Elizabeth Boa, *Kafka: Gender, Class, and Race in the Letters and Fictions* (Oxford: Clarendon Press, 1996), p. 65.

13. See the introduction by Edward Garden in Pyotr Ilich Tchaikovsky, *"To My Best Friend:" Correspondence between Tchaikovsky and Nadezhda von Meck 1876–1890*, ed. Edward Garden and Nigel Gotteri, trans. Galina von Meck (Oxford: Clarendon Press, 1993), pp. xix–xxvi; and Alexander Poznansky, "Two Women," in *Tchaikovsky: The Quest for the Inner Man* (New York: Schirmer, 1991), pp. 195–214.

14. See Gerald Abraham, "An Erotic Diary for Piano," in *Slavonic and Romantic Music: Essays and Studies* (New York: St. Martin's Press, 1968), pp. 70–82 and Zdeněk Nejedlý, *Zdeňka Fibicha milostný deník* (Zdeněk Fibich's erotic diary) (Prague: Hudební matice, Umělecké besedy, 1925). Nejedlý offers a lengthy essay entitled "Umělec a žena" (The artist and woman) as well as appraising the women in Fibich's life and how they may have shaped his creative personality.

15. See, for example, Constantin Floros, *Alban Berg: Musik als Autobiographie* (Wiesbaden: Breitkopf & Härtel, 1992) for a summary of the ways in which the composer's life and music were connected.

16. Alban Berg, *Alban Berg: Letters to His Wife*, ed. and trans. Bernard Grun (New York: St. Martin's Press, 1971), p. 19.

17. Ibid., p. 62. Letter dated 16 July 1909.

18. Ibid., p. 299.

19. See, for example, George Perle, *Style and Idea in the Lyric Suite of Alban Berg* (Stuyvesant, N.Y.: Pendragon Press, 1995).

20. From 1917 until his death in 1928, Janáček wrote the operas *Kát'a Kabánová*, *The Makropolus Case*, *The Cunning Little Vixen*, and *The House of the Dead*. He also penned such works as *The Diary of One Who Vanished*, the two string quartets, the Sinfonietta, and *Glagolitic Mass* in this fruitful decade.

21. Attempts to chronicle the couple's relationship include a sanitized version of events by Antonín Hloušek, *O přátelství Leoše Janáčka s Kamilou Stösslovou* (On the friendship of LJ with Kamila Stösslová) (Kladno: Kladenský lis, 1963); a listing of all of the known "loves" of Janáček by Jaroslav Slavický, *Listy důvěrné. Z milostné korespondence Leoše Janáčka* (Intimate letters: From the romantic correspondence of LJ) (Prague: Panton, 1966) and the novelized version of the couple's relationship by František Kožík, *Po zarostlém chodníčku* (On the overgrown path), 3rd ed. (Prague: Československý spisovatel, 1983).

22. Leoš Janáček, *Intimate Letters: Leoš Janáček to Kamila Stösslová*, ed. and trans. John Tyrrell (Princeton, N.J.: Princeton University Press, 1994), p. 3. The complete correspondence in the original Czech is *Hádanka života: dopisy Leoše Janáčka Kamile Stösslové* (The riddle of life: The letters of Leoš Janáček to Kamila Stösslová), ed. Svatava Přibaňová (Brno: Opus musicum, 1990).

23. Horvátová and Janáček become romantically involved when she was cast as the Kostelnička in the 1916 Prague production of *Jenůfa*. The fervent rate of correspondence between the two parties is as impressive as the tawdry content. See *Korespondence Leoše Janáčka s Gabrielou Horvátovou* (Correspondence of Leoš Janáček with Gabriela Horvátová) ed. Artuš Rektorys (Prague: Hudební matice, 1950). For a brief overview of their affair, see Charles Susskind, *Janáček and Brod* (New Haven: Yale University Press, 1985), p. 38.

24. Tyrrell, *Intimate Letters*, p. 354.

25. For a highly personal and often painful account of the couple's life together, see Zdenka Janáčková, *My Life with Janáček: The Memoirs of Zdenka Janáčková*, ed. and trans. John Tyrrell (London: Faber and Faber, 1998). The typed manuscript of her memoirs remain in the Janáček Collection of the Moravian Museum in Brno, Czech Republic, but are "unavailable" for consultation. Parts of the original Czech were published in *Opus musicum* in 1993 and 1994 after John Tyrrell uncovered a photocopy of the manuscript through an antiquarian. See Zdenka Janáčková-Marie Trkanová, "Můj zivot," *Opus musicum* 25, nos. 5–6 (1993): 182–88; no. 8 (249–56); nos. 9–10 (305–14); 26 (1994) no. 1 (25–32); nos. 2–3 (84–96); nos. 5–6 (142–51); nos. 8–9 (277–88, 314–36). These memoirs still do not "officially" exist; archivists contend that Tyrrell's copy is the only one they have in possession in the Janáček Collection.

26. Janáčková, *My Life with Janáček*, p. 162.

27. Tyrrell, *Intimate Letters*, p. 15. Letter dated 16 March 1918.

28. Ibid., p. 20. Letter dated 29 (correctly, 27) July 1918.

29. Ibid. Letter dated 28 July 1918.

30. Kamila Stösslová was not the first woman to inspire or to appear in Janáček's works. His early opera *Osud* (Fate) features the composer Živný whose situation is modeled on Janáček's, is set in the Moravian spa town of Luhačovice, and tells the story of old lovers reunited. The heroine, Míla, is a portrait of Mrs. Kamila Urválková, a guest of Luhačovice who attracted the composer's attentions when she sent three red roses to his table during a stay in August 1903. This was not the first opera that Urválková inspired; she appears in the 1897 opera/melodrama *Kamilla* by Ludvík Vítězlav Čelanský as the irresponsible and faithless sweetheart of the composer. Janáček's opera was to be a rebuttal to Čelanský's acerbic portrayal of Urválková; once Janáček realized that this Kamila was not all he had imagined, he altered the opera so that Živný, not Míla, was the main protaganist. See Theodora Straková, "Janáčkovy opery *Šárka, Počátek románu, Osud* hudebnědramatická torza (Ke genezi děl, stavu pramenů a jejich kritické interpretaci)" (Janáček's operas *Šárka, The Beginning of a Romance, Fate,* and musico-dramatic fragments; On the genesis of the works, the establishment of the sources, and their critical interpretation), *Časopis Moravského muzea* 65 (1980): 149–58; and "K problematice Janáčkovy opery Osud" (On the problematics of Janáček's opera *Fate*) in *Leoš Janáček a soudobá hudba: Mezinárodního hudebené vědecký kongres, Brno 1958,* ed. Jaroslav Jiránek and Bohumil Karásek (Prague: knižnice hudebních rozhledů, 1963), pp. 289–93; Jaroslav Jiránek, "On the Dialects of Personality and Work of Art," *Acta Janáčkiana: Společnost Leoše Janáčka,* ed. Jiří Vysloužil, 2 (1958): 34–35; and John Tyrrell, "Janáček's Stylistic Development as an Operatic Composer as Evidenced in his Revisions of the First Five Operas." Ph.D. diss.; Oxford University, 1968.

31. The poem detailing the lovers' fate originally appeared with the byline "*Z pera samoukova*" (From the pen of a self-taught man) and it was believed for decades after that the poems were the authentic testimony of a young man who had chosen to live with his Gypsy lover and abandon society. Recent research has revealed the identity of the poety to be Josef Kalda (1871–1921), a Moravian writer. See Jan Vičar, "Autor veršů Janáčkova Zápisníku zmizelého objeven," (Author of the verses for Janáček's *Diary of One Who Vanished* discovered) *Hudební věda* 4, no. 97 (1997): 418–22; and the book-length study of Kalda and the *Diary* by Jan Mikeska, *Tajemství P.S. aneb odhalení autora textu Janáčkova Zápisníku zmizelého* (Secret P.S. or the revealed author of the text to Janáček's *Diary of One Who Vanished*) (Vizovice: Nakladatelství Lípa, 1998).

32. Tyrrell, *Intimate Letters*, p. 10.

33. Ibid., p. 23. Letter dated 2 September 1918.

34. Ibid., p. 53. Letter dated 24 July 1924.

35. The exotic female Other has been associated with sexual desire and release in the West for centuries. See, for example, Mario Praz, *The Romantic Agony*, 2d ed., trans. Angus Davidson (London: Oxford University Press, 1970), passim; Ralph P. Lock, "Constructing the Oriental Other: Saint-Saëns' *Samson et Dalila*," *Cambridge Opera Journal* 3, no. 3 (November 1991): 261–302; and Susan McClary, "Structures of Identity and Difference in Bizet's *Carmen*," in *The Work of Opera: Genre, Nationhood, and Sexual Difference*, ed. Richard Dellamora and Daniel Fischlin (New York: Columbia University Press, 1997), pp. 115–30.

36. Tyrrell, *Intimate Letters*, p. 29. Clearly, Janáček transliterated "Butterfly" into his native Czech; here, Tyrrell has chosen to let it stand in its original form.

37. Ibid., p. 30.

38. Ibid., p. 38.

39. Ibid., p. 34. Letter dated 17 October 1921.

40. Robert Graves, *The White Goddess: A Historical Grammar of Poetic Myth*, ed. Grevel Lindop (Manchester: Carcanet Press, 1997), p. 440. This is a recurrent theme in Graves's examination of the muse; if the poet chooses her as a wife, she can no longer be his muse, and thus his art will suffer. The muse must remain distanced from the artist.

41. Tyrrell, *Intimate Letters*, p. 37.

42. Ibid., p. 42.

43. Ibid., p. 47.

44. Ibid., pp. 354–55.

45. Ibid., pp. 49-50.

46. Ibid., p. 43.

47. Ibid., pp. 124 and 289, respectively. Letters dated 1 July 1927 and 29 May 1928, respectively.

48. Ibid., p. 52. Letter dated 15 July 1924.

49. Jaroslav Vogel, *Leoš Janáček: A Biography*, rev. and ed. Karel Janovický (New York: W. W. Norton, 1981), p. 364. Vogel states, "There were no more secrets at home"; that is, Janáček refused to hide his need for Kamila and his lack of sympathy for his wife's position. There is a reference to Kamila's wishes in a letter from the composer to her dated 10 January 1928 as well as Kamila's appellation, "my future wife." Tyrrell, *Intimate Letters*, p. 183.

50. The album dates from 2 October 1927 until 10 August 1928, just two days before the composer's death and includes the fourth codicil to his will that names Kamila as a major heir. Kamila had purchased this album after the couple agreed to burn all letters sent to each other. While Janáček did indeed burn nearly all the correspondence he had received from her, she never followed through. The album is available in facsimile with commentary and translation: Leoš Janáček, *Album for Kamila Stösslová*, ed. Jarmila Procházková, trans. John Tyrrell (Brno: Moravian Museum, 1996). See also Jarmila Procházková, "Památník Leoše Janáčka psaný pro Kamilu Stösslová," (The album Leoš Janáček wrote for Kamila Stösslová) *Opus musicum* 26, nos. 8–9 (1992): 266–77.

51. Vogel, *Janáček: A Biography*, pp. 364–65. The letter, in its original Czech, is in Leoš Janáček, *Korespondence Leoše Janáčka s Maxem Brodem* (Correspondence of Leoš Janáček with Max Brod), ed. Jan Racek and Artuš Rektorys (Prague: Státní nakladatelství krásné literatury, hudby a umění, 1953). There is another, more complete English translation of this letter published in Hans Hollander, *Janáček—His Life and Work*, trans. Paul Hamburger (London: John Calder Publishers, 1962), pp. 83–84. However, Vogel is more faithful to the original, since it has been translated but once, and still retains the flavor of Janáček's language and the syntax of the original Czech.

52. The original article appeared as Leoš Janáček, "Smráká se" (Dusk approaches), *Venkov* 23, no. 31 (5 February 1928). The cited English translation is Leoš Janáček, *Janáček's Uncollected Essays on Music*, ed. and trans. Mirka Zemanová (London and New York: Marion Boyars, 1989), pp. 118–19.

53. Tyrrell, *Intimate Letters*, pp. 191 and 193, respectively. Both letters dated 29 January 1928. Janáček announced the new work a few days later from Brno on February 1, p. 196.

54. Not only was Kamila linked with the Gypsy of the *Diary*, but also in more general terms. His term "Negress" probably alluded to her dark complexion and penchant for sunbathing. Both titles suggest the exotic, the unknown, and the sexually forbidden.

55. Tyrrell, *Intimate Letters*, p. 196.

56. Janáček's long association with the spa town is chronicled in Bohumír Štědroň, *Leoš Janáček a Luhačovice, 1 část: (K 10. výročí mistrova úmrtí)* (Leoš Janáček and Luhačov-

ice, Part 1: On the tenth anniversary of the master's death) (Luhačovice: Zvláštní otisk z výroční městké spořitelny v Luhačovicích, 1938).

57. Leoš Janáček, *Leoš Janáček: Pohled do života a díla* (Leoš Janáček: A look at the life and works), ed. Adolf Veselý (Prague: Fr. Borový, 1924), p. 94. On Urválková, see endnote 32.

58. For an overview of the composer's use of this instrument, see John Tyrrell, "Janáček and the Viola d'Amore," in *Leoš Janáček: Kát'a Kabanová*, ed. John Tyrrell (Cambridge: Cambridge University Press, 1982), pp. 154–61. Tyrrell considers the use of this instrument to be "a secret code" and as an "inspirational device," pp. 158 and 159, respectively. For a history of this instrument, see Werner Eginhard Kohler, "Beiträge zur Geschichte und Literatur der Viola d'Amore," Ph.D. diss., Freidrich Wilhelms Universität zu Berlin, 1938.

59. He announced the content and completion of this movement in a letter dated 18 February 1928. Tyrrell, *Intimate Letters*, pp. 206–07.

60. Ibid., p. 111. Letter dated 7 May 1927.

61. Ibid., p. 208. Letter dated 19 February 1928. In this letter Janáček also reported that he revealed to his wife the importance of his relationship with Kamila. Following the composer's death, Stanislav Tauber reported that Zdenka said, "What could I do, when he says to me that Kamila inspires him and that she is needed for his composing?" See his *Můj hudební svět* (My musical world) (Brno: Vlad. Hapala, 1949), p. 73.

62. Tyrrell, *Intimate Letters*, p. 210. Letter dated 20 February 1928.

63. Ibid., p. 282. Letter dated 18–19 May 1928.

64. Ibid., p. 317. Letter dated 27 June 1928.

65. Leoš Janáček, "Schytali je!" (They caught them!) *Lidové noviny* 35, no. 333 (3 July 1927), pp. 108–09.

66. Trkanová, *U Janáčků* (Brno: Simon Ryšavy, 1998), p. 101. This excerpt does not appear in the first edition of the memoirs published in 1959.

67. Janáček, *Pohled do života*, p. 69.

68. Quoted in Patrick Bade, *Femme Fatale: Images of Evil and Fascinating Women* (New York: Mayflower Books; London: Ash and Grant, 1979), p. 10. On the ideal versus real women, see, for example, Ruth Crego Benson, *Women in Tolstoy: The Ideal and the Erotic* (Urbana, Ill.: University of Illinois Press, 1973) and Melvin Kalfus, "Richard Wagner as a Cult Hero: The Tännhauser Who Would be Siegfried," *The Journal of Psychohistory* 11, no. 3 (winter 1984): 315–82.

69. Examples of Kamila-bashing are abundant. See, for example, Eva Hoffman, "'My Dear Beloved Riddle of Life': The Correspondence Between a Great Composer and His Improbable Muse," *New York Times Book Review,* 31 July 1994 p. 12. Hoffman considers her an "unlikely object" for Janáček's compositions. Kurt Honolka, in his *Leoš Janáček: Sein Leben, Sein Werk, Seine Zeit.* (Stuttgart: Bessler, 1982), p. 182–83, wonders what about Kamila could have fascinated the composer so. Even the composer's wife was dismissive, and, as her maid reported, "regarded the relationship as only a friendship, if a rather incomprehensible one, but those who shared the master's life had to get used to incomprehensible things." Marie Trkanová, *U Janáčků (podle vyprávění Marie Stejskalové)* (At the Janáčeks', according to Marie Stejskalová) (Prague: Panton, 1959), p. 115.

70. Jan Vičar considered Janáček's physical desire for Kamila to be the means through which she motivated his compositions. He states that "Janáček kept a portrait of Kamila on his work table, and this photograph uplifted and augmented his fantasy and desire, which was projected onto his other female characters." See his "Leoš Janáček's 'The Diary of One Who Vanished,'" in *Acta Universitatis Palackianae Olomucensis Facultis Philosophica, Musicologica* II, vol. 14 (Olomouc: Vydavatelství Univerzity Palackého, 1995), p. 53.

71. Tyrrell, *Intimate Letters*, p. 119. Letter dated 31 May 1927.

Reinterpreting Janáček and Kamila: Dangerous Liaisons in Czech Fin-de-Siècle Music and Literature

GEOFFREY CHEW

Kamila Stösslová, Leoš Janáček's Adulterous Muse, the Key for Interpreting His Work?

In July 1917 the Czech composer Leoš Janáček first encountered Kamila Stösslová, the young, relatively uneducated wife of a Jewish antique dealer, David Stössel, when he and the Stössls were on holiday at the spa town of Luhačovice. From then until the composer's death in 1928 there were regular meetings between Janáček and Stösslová, at first formal, and later passionate, at least on his side. These twelve years were the most productive of his entire life as a composer. In the hundreds of letters he wrote to her, he represented her as almost his sole source of inspiration, and made her somehow present in the narratives of most of his major works. In his vision she became the heroines of *Kát'a Kabanová*, *The Cunning Little Vixen*, and *The Makropulos Case*, the maltreated woman of Tolstoy's *Kreutzer Sonata* in the First String Quartet, and the recipient of the composer's "Intimate Letters" of the Second String Quartet; she walked with him in procession in the forest in the *Glagolitic Mass*; she was the dark Gypsy Zefka who seduced the young Czech herdsman Jeník in *The Diary of One Who Vanished*; in the absence of almost any female characters, she was even the vulnerable young Tatar boy Aljeja in *From the House of the Dead*.

It might seem self-evident, then, that scholars and critics should use both the letters and associated documents—including the so-called

Album for Kamila Stösslová, an amorous diary which will be further discussed in a later section of this article[1]—as well as the (rather frank) memoirs of Zdenka Janáčková, Janáček's wife,[2] since their publication (the Stösslová letters in a Czech edition in 1990 and an English edition in 1994,[3] the *Album* in 1996 and the Janáčková memoirs in 1998), as unambiguous, authentic biographical evidence of direct relevance to Janáček's oeuvre. A different situation prevailed during the Communist period, when these documents were swept under the carpet and withheld by archivists even from scholars, because they cast the composer in a scandalous light, even though the affair had been fairly common knowledge, and various codicils to Janáček's will, including one on a page in the *Album*, had come to light after his death in the law courts and had gained a certain notoriety. Instead, Janáček was represented as possessing a lofty vision of humanity informed and elevated by the "sparks of God," as he puts it (following Dostoevsky) with reference to the *Notes from the House of the Dead*.[4]

But this older view of the composer and his work has seemed sanitized and inadequate to more recent writers, who have replaced it with a straightforward romantic picture of an elderly composer trapped in an unhappy marriage, with his creativity at long last released through his defiance of conventional respectability in favor of adulterous love. As John Tyrrell writes, concerning the letters:

> [The corpus of letters between Janáček and Stösslová] is by far the most important source for the understanding of Janáček's emotional and creative life in the last twelve years of his life—the period in which he became famous and in which he composed his greatest works. . . . Biographers have been working on incomplete and misleading information for this period of Janáček's life, and only now is a proper perspective on it possible. . . . These letters are valuable as being the most beautiful and self-revealing ever written by Janáček. He was always a gifted and imaginative letter writer but these letters go to the heart of his inner life. And within them, they contain a great love story.[5]

And so the story of Kamila Stösslová has come to dominate Janáček interpretation in recent years, to a far greater extent than, say, in their different ways, the stories of Harriet Smithson for Berlioz, of Mathilde Wesendonck for Wagner, of George Sand for Chopin, or of Nadezhda von Meck for Tchaikovsky.

Yet this new use of the Stösslová affair and its impact on Janáček's work should open up some new problems, and also reopen some old questions. If this affair had been openly admitted by Czech music critics earlier last century, before or during the Communist period, they would have almost certainly considered it necessary to discuss Janáček in terms of Decadence, since these were the terms in which the composer Fibich was discussed due to his involvement in a comparable episode. And there are independent grounds for considering some of Janáček's music as Decadent, although Czech (and other) writers have generally skirted around this issue. So some discussion of Decadence itself, together with related concepts, will be necessary.

And this will be supplemented with an exploration of some of the ways in which the motif is constructed and criticized, in Czech fin-de-siècle literature and music, of the creative, artistic genius whose vocation is enabled and authenticated by a liaison, often adulterous, with his Muse, in order to provide a framework within which Janáček's life and work may fruitfully be reassessed.

Provisional Definitions of Key Terms (Naturalism, Realism, Decadence)

A variety of stylistic and period terms might be used to describe Czech music of the half-century between 1880 and 1930, including Janáček's; the situation is complicated by the fact that current usage in literary history and criticism does not map very well onto current usage in musical history and criticism, and neither of those corresponds very closely with the terminology used in the Czech criticism of the period. A thorough treatment of the issues would exceed the bounds of this discussion, so I shall confine the discussion to three such terms—Naturalism, Decadence, and Realism—all of which have been used in writings on music as essential concepts for interpreting Janáček and his contemporaries. Since Naturalism and Decadence, at least, arguably remain useful for this purpose even in twenty-first-century criticism, it will be necessary throughout this discussion to hold in tension two different basic definitions of each term (each admittedly allowing for some variation): one, of the term as understandable today, and the other, of the term as understood by Czech writers before the Second World War. Brief definitions of current practice are offered below; some distinctive polemical meanings of the terms in Czech criticism will emerge in later sections of this article.

Currently there is no single generally accepted definition of Naturalism. However, the term will be used in only one modern sense here, referring not to "the poetic evocation of a vital reciprocity between man and his living natural environment," but rather to an opposite, essentially anti-Romantic concept of subjecting art to quasi-scientific ideals, "characterized by meticulous attention to the details of the world used to convey a sense of the given work's distinctive social milieu and psychological peculiarity."[6] These two concepts may best be distinguished from each other, perhaps, by referring to the former as "naturalism" and the latter as "Naturalism," with lower-case and upper-case N respectively. The latter of the two, Naturalism, which concerns us here, was defined in a well-known essay on Balzac by Hippolyte Taine in 1858 and outstandingly exemplified in the novels of Emile Zola.[7] Its characteristic method—the placing of representatives of a particular social, national, regional, or racial group under a laboratory-style microscope, on the assumption that if they are placed under stress, they will reveal their distinctive characteristics—was pioneered in Czech drama by Gabriela Preissová in her *Gazdina roba* (1889, a play that formed the model for J. B. Foerster's opera *Eva*, and was also considered for setting as an opera by Janáček) and her *Její pastorkyňa* (1890, the model for Janáček's opera of the same name, which is often called *Jenůfa* outside its homeland).

Decadence as a literary movement or cultural category, as currently understood, has been given a useful seven-point definition by Robert Pynsent:

> Decadent art is self-centered; gives the artist a special role; adopts particular stylistic poses; expresses an awareness or even a philosophy of decay; expresses also an awareness of existing in a period of transition; does not relay messages or express didactic opinions; but may strive to mock or shock or provoke the bourgeois or the Establishment.[8]

This also may serve as a point of departure here (particularly for present purposes in its second point, though others are relevant also). Even though the term Decadence has never been consistently adopted in musical historiography as a general category for discussing the period, its musical pedigree is impressive. One might mention in passing the use of the term by Stanislaw Przybyszewski to make constructions of sickness and neurosis in the music of Chopin;[9] and Friedrich Nietzsche, further quoted below, who did the same for Wagner, devoting "Der Fall Wagner" to a construction of Wagner as the "artist of Decadence" achieving his selfhood through the gift of pessimism from Schopenhauer as the "philosopher of Decadence."[10] Moreover, from the analytical point of view, we might expand Pynsent's third point with a frequently quoted sentence from Nietzsche which refers to the concentration on detail at the expense of overall unity, which makes Wagner for him a miniaturist (because a Decadent):

> How may every type of literary Decadence be characterized? In that there is no longer life in the whole. The word becomes sovereign and springs out of the sentence; the sentence encroaches upon and obscures the sense of the page, the page achieves life at the expense of the whole—the whole is no longer a whole.[11]

Thus it is in Decadence, in particular, that Classical and Romantic notions of unity and coherence might be expected to be exploded in modernist music.[12]

Although Naturalism has much in common with Realism if the latter is taken to mean the "prosaic" presentation of subject matter, it depends, like Decadence, on the distortion of external reality (Naturalism generally veers towards the unpleasant and Decadence toward the hedonistic, but in neither case is this always so), and there are other correspondences between Naturalism and Decadence also, some of which will emerge in the discussion below. The relationship with Realism is an important point, given that the incorporation of elements of external Nature or Life into literary or musical works of art was, as we shall see, seldom separate in the minds of Czech critics from value judgments. But in any case "realism" is always a chimera in art; and for a variety of reasons it seems advisable to avoid the use of the term "Realism" to denote a cultural movement in the present discussion in any modern sense, though it must inevitably come under discussion later owing to its use by Czech writers. (For the record, it should be added that T. G. Masaryk promoted Realism as a desirable "direction and method" to guide the "literary revolution" to be set in motion by the new generation, in his influential *Česká otázka* (The Czech question).[13] Realism has much in common with *verismo* in Italian opera, Janáček's interest in modern Italian opera, especially Puccini, is well documented, and the composer's work has recently been discussed in terms of "Verismus" by Miloš Štědroň.[14] One of the most impressive discussions available on Realism is that of Roman Jakobson, also from the Czech sphere, which—unusually—frees the concept from its normal moral connotations and relativizes it in aesthetic as well as historical terms, by starting from sharp distinctions between four types of Realism—that of the artist's intention and the recipient's perception, each in a radical and a conservative variant.)[15]

Constructions of Czech Modernist Adulterous Muses in Literature and Music

The creative artist's enabling Muse, in whom Art can be seen to flow from Life, is hardly a new or distinctively Decadent motif in the late nineteenth century; in some ways it is a Romantic commonplace, as is the aesthetic of artistic genius and of the intimate relationship between Life and Art on which it is based. It is already fully developed on the one hand in the relationship between Robert and Clara Schumann and the series of works that he (and she) produced around the time of their marriage. It is also manifest, no doubt, in the stereotyped redemption-through-love theme of many nineteenth-century German operas from *Fidelio* to *Der fliegende Holländer, Götterdämmerung,* and beyond. But there are new aspects to it in the fin de siècle. First, the topos is often presented in a consciously modern setting, and so can construct modernism, sometimes in opposition to Romanticism. Secondly (a related issue), it has a necessary whiff of scandal about it, and its deliberate clouding of distinctions between Life and Art, autobiography and fiction, and private and public spheres of activity, involves a sense of risk. The artistic inspiration that the lover provides is private, but its results are bound to be public; the authentication that she or he provides must be publicly perceptible, but its scandalous nature means that it cannot be universally acknowledged if the lover is not to be brought to ruin. It is the art of revelation through concealment.[16] Thirdly, it expresses a threefold ontological anxiety: that of the fin-de-siècle male required to be adequately masculine when confronted with emancipated womanhood, that of the fin-de-siècle genius required to be adequately original when confronted with modernism in artistic style, and that of the fin-de-siècle Czech artist when confronted with the sophistication of modern international European society; these issues are closely interrelated, but it may be advisable not to conflate them with one another.[17] And finally, too, the conventional relationship between Nature and Art is sometimes paradoxically reversed in the late nineteenth century, as in Vivian's aphorism in Oscar Wilde's *The Decay of Lying* (1889): "Art is our spirited protest, our gallant attempt to teach Nature her proper place."[18]

Czech fin-de-siècle literature and music offer a surprisingly wide variety of treatment of the topos of the artist's Muse, and it was well-known to Janáček, who is misrepresented if thought of as naive or lacking in self-awareness.[19] I shall compare several different literary and musical versions of it below, mostly in chronological order, including Janáček's. In presenting the versions thus, I do not intend to imply that there was any direct line of influence joining them all, nor that Janáček or any other Czech musician was necessarily aware of them all: I hope nevertheless to illustrate the limits within which the topos usually functioned, and some of the social conditions to which it represented a response. Owing to the modern neglect of most of these works, even including Janáček's, it seems advisable to discuss them in some detail.

Julius Zeyer (*Jan Maria Plojhar,* 1887–1888): "Il faut méditerraniser la Muse"

A classic example of the Adulterous Muse in Czech literature occurs in Julius Zeyer's novel *Jan Maria Plojhar* (written between November 1887 and February or March 1888).[20] In a number of respects, the hero, Jan Maria Plojhar, is a precursor of Czech Decadent heroes.[21] Plojhar is a modern Czech poet of genius (even though he apparently publishes only one volume of verse). For health reasons, he lives chiefly in Greece and Italy rather than in the northern Czech fogs: he is pale and tubercular, having sustained a lung wound in a duel fought to defend the honor of Bohemia. He is abnormally sensitive to external stimuli; he is set apart from his fellows by virtue of his calling as an artist, and he achieves this calling (if at all, for he is passive apart from his duel) through the quasi-mystical mutual love between him and his ideal Muse, with whom finally he shares a love-death, freely chosen on her part.

Plojhar has successive sexual encounters with three women whom he hopes will fulfill the role of his Muse—and the account is partly autobiographical, for they have parallels in the Englishwomen with whom Zeyer himself was involved, even though he was homosexual. His first, paní Dragopulos, is a married woman, a Romanian femme fatale with Gypsy blood: Zeyer goes so far as to put the phrase "smrtonosná siréna" (death-dealing siren) into the mouth of one of his characters, referring to her.[22] She brings him close to ruin "mortally wounded and robbed of his most beautiful illusions."[23] Some of the imagery associated with her is musical, and there are unexpected nuances. For instance, one might have expected her to be an enthusiast for Wagner and for *Tristan.* Yet it is Bizet and his recently composed *Carmen* that symbolize her, for Carmen too is a Gypsy: paní Dragopulos introduces Plojhar to it and plays it for him at first from a piano reduction, and they meet later at the Teatro Argentina in Rome, at a fateful performance of *Carmen* that is replete with Decadent imagery:

Meanwhile the music began to play; its Spanish coloring, dreamy and at the same time fiery, produced a sweet, sensuous pleasure in him, blended with a certain melancholy. It was an enchantment like that of fumes of hashish.[24]

Carmen is, however, richly allusive for the purpose: it was used around this time by Nietzsche as a model of the "Mediterraneanization" (or Africanization or Indianization) of music, and the passivity, which he argues in *Der Fall Wagner*, using his famous phrase, *"Il faut méditerraniser la musique,"* is needed as an antidote to the Decadence of Wagner's *unendliche Melodie*. Nevertheless, he too sounds under the influence of hashish, and happy to wallow in Decadence of a sort, when he writes:

And indeed, each time I heard *Carmen,* I thought myself more of a philosopher, a better philosopher than I ever think myself otherwise: I became so patient, so happy, so Indian, so *sedentary.* . . . Sitting for five hours—the first step towards holiness![25]

Moreover, Nietzsche's pose should be understood within the context of contemporary Bizet reception, in which the composer was at times seen as too Wagnerian for comfort.[26]

Even though paní Dragopulos is Mediterranean (or at least southern European, and Mediterranean by adoption), and quite as enthusiastic as Nietzsche about *Carmen*, she is not stimulated to holiness by it. Her Decadence is thoroughgoing, and she is perversely, "monstrously," attracted to Plojhar precisely because of his illness: she muses, with a hint of necrophilia:

To love one who is ill is also a kind of perversity. I understand that great lady of the Middle Ages whom I have heard yielded herself to a leper. How enchanting, to wrestle with death over him! A danse macabre! . . . Oh, that will be something new, never hitherto experienced![27]

And her affair never threatens her marriage, for she is able to keep it semi-secret: unlike her husband, she is multilingual, and so she speaks of forbidden matters with Plojhar openly, even in front of her husband—in Russian. No doubt the husband is aware of what is going on, but is prevented by the rules of polite social intercourse from confronting either of them with his suspicions.

Plojhar's second affair is with the prostitute Gemma, who is by contrast attractive, sisterly, and kind, but the relationship is not spiritual;

in retrospect he reflects dispassionately that "good Gemma was an object rather than a person, perhaps a blossom."[28] But in the third woman, Caterina, an impoverished Italian contessa, we find the true counter-balance to paní Dragopulos. Unlike Dragopulos, she has a generosity in love that enables her to comprehend and meet Plojhar's needs. She understands the pain he feels on behalf of Bohemia, and sympathizes with his literary tastes, reading Shelley with him in private tutorials in the garden of her country house. In turn she becomes Jan Maria's Mediterranean Muse, his salvation rather than his ruin: in the south-ern sun his Czechness is constructed, for implicitly his genius would not be recognized except abroad. He comes (ostensibly in order to conva-lesce) to live in her house; this arrangement seems scandalous to her conventionally minded acquaintances, since the couple is not married, and even the final death-bed marriage between the two seems more like a mystic operatic apotheosis (say, the final union between Senta and the Dutchman in *Der fliegende Holländer*) than a straightforward rectifica-tion of domestic irregularities. Even more operatic is her final suicide, for which she and the reader are prepared by the stories of death and self-immolation she encounters from exotic, archaic traditions. She has read of Nachiketas in the Upanishads, who—believing in reincarnation, perhaps unlike her—willingly went to meet Yama, the god of death, and she applies this to Jan Maria.[29] And she takes very seriously the gift she has received of the wedding jewels of a girl in an Etruscan tomb who, she thinks, "followed him [her lover] into the shadow and the darkness willingly, sacrificed herself and died with him."[30]

There is, admittedly, a lack of consistency in Zeyer's projection of Jan Maria's search for his Muse in terms of three women. In this novel, people, events, and concepts are repeatedly grouped in threes, the number serving primarily to generate a sense of comprehensiveness, comple-tion, and inevitability, and this is important especially for the effectiveness of the book's ending. But Gemma has little weight in the narrative: only two of these women count, paní Dragopulos and Caterina, and, even more important, the relationships of these two women with Plojhar have much more in common than appears through Plojhar's, and per-haps even Zeyer's, own eyes. The life-giving love (*láska*) offered by Caterina and the death-dealing passion (*vášeň*) offered by Dragopulos are both foreign and Mediterranean, both arise equally irrationally, both fill his entire horizon, both exclude questions of conventional bourgeois respectability, and both depend on the scent of death the two women detect in him. To Plojhar it seems self-evident that his artistic creativity and integrity must depend on the lifelong devotion of a sin-gle woman; yet Caterina's love is no more than the obverse of that of paní Dragopulos and is not adequately comprehensible except as such. In passing it may be noted that this fin-de-siècle scenario of two equal, opposing, and yet interdependent worlds of Sensuality and Art, linked through death, is developed in German-language literature in Austria in a different way in the innovative short novel of Leopold Andrian, *Der Garten der Erkenntnis* (1895).[31] In the discussion below, it should become clear that there is almost always a narrow dividing line between the inspiring Muse and the femme fatale.

Otakar Auředníček (*Malířské novelly,* 1892): Salon Versions of the Muse

The topos recurs in the short stories in Otakar Auředníček's *Malířské novelly* (Short stories about painters) of 1892:[32] several take as their subject the modern bohemian life (in the other sense) of (usually male) Czech artists and their sexual liaisons.[33] Jan Maria Plojhar had already been an artist in financial difficulties, but Zeyer's novel is built on the pleasant fiction that a Muse with money and a glamorous lifestyle (paní Dragopulos) is less authentic than one who can share the poverty of the artist and live in decaying splendor with him (Caterina). Auředníček permits no such nonsense, and money regularly changes hands in this book, usually in favor of the male artist and usually at the expense of Zeyer's high tone. But there is none of the social or psychological criticism that this might have implied, which would have raised these tales beyond the level of salon literature: Auředníček, by constructing them as the anecdotes that an insider in the bohemian world of artists might hear, and also in his frequent embedding of anecdotes within other anecdotes, attempts to flatter the reader into uncritical complicity with the attitudes of the narrator. The detached tone that this generates is compounded by the occasional, and usually misconceived, attempts at comic writing.

The narrator in "Malířovo romanetto" (A painter's romance), the first of these stories, is Machek, a handsome, talented, and idle twenty-five-year-old painter: a feckless Czech, on whom we are evidently not expected to stand in judgment. In the pub he tells his artist friends how he received an unexpected proposition from Marie Pokorná, a bored married Czech woman of means living in Italy, and spent several ecstatic and cliché-ridden weeks living in a hotel in a decaying, decadent Venice with her, at her expense. She became his Mediterranean Muse while, "kissed by the sun," they were bathing in the sea at the Lido: "Then I felt artistic inspiration so immense that I was incapable of expressing it."[34] Later he met her husband, Pokorný, who, unaware of the situation, invited Machek to spend the winter with them. Paní Pokorná was appalled at Machek's sudden appearance at the family house: "'Whatever made you do it?' she groaned. 'You will ruin me!' And she began to weep."[35] When their adultery was, inevitably, uncovered, he was forced to make a quick escape to Bohemia. The story depends on a combination of excited titillation and slapstick and seems a parody, though probably unintentional, of Plojhar's situation.

In the third tale, "Plesové šaty" (The ball gown), the role of the sexes is reversed in some, though not the most important, respects. The heroine is Karolina, another talented Czech painter in search of her Muse: she is sincere and conventionally deserving of sympathy, for she is orphaned (though evidently from a well-to-do bourgeois family) and thus forced to work for her living. But unlike most of Auředníček's artists she lives in moderate comfort, since she is constructed as a woman, spending her time selling her pictures instead of drinking in the Prague pubs like the men, and fulfilling the woman's role in these stories of providing her man with financial handouts.

The recipient of Karolina's generosity and her unsuitably chosen Muse, Břetislav Hampl, is a curious, imperfectly Decadent hero. As a dependent man he is, from Auředníček's point of view, inadequate; perhaps for this reason, the author attempts to make him comic as well as *fatal*, and so the story again inadvertently but strongly constructs fin-de-siècle male anxiety (that of the author as well as that of the hero) in the face of the self-sufficient woman. No ill-starred aristocrat, Hampl is merely a good-looking bank clerk: his classical features and blue eyes are a mask half concealing a self-contained, dandyish (and by that token Decadent) indifference to the world around him, which he manages to maintain, although the only genius he possesses is that of his haircut:

> Hampl was a man whose face could be reckoned handsome by a superficial observer, for his features were classically regular, his sensual lips were finely formed, and his gleaming brown hair flowed in ringlets of genius over his temples. But this face lacked soul: it was a decorative mask, whose large, beautiful blue eyes were also lifeless, staring indifferently out at the world. . . . In his impeccable attire there could be observed an almost comic pettiness and conceit.[36]

(As Robert Pynsent points out, his dandyism is not thoroughgoing enough to prevent him from being embarrassed by Karolina and blushing, for he is a "Czech depressed by his milieu beneath the mask.")[37]

Perhaps more comic than Hampl's triviality is the way in which Karolina literally derives death-dealing inspiration from him by passive smoking, cigarettes being a regular symbol of modernity in Czech literature of this period—though the author did not intend this image to be funny:

> She laid her head gently on his shoulder, and her delicate, quivering nostrils rapturously breathed in the bluish drifts of fragrant smoke which he exhaled from his lips.[38]

Karolina is melodramatically cut down to size by her Muse, for her chef d'oeuvre is the result of a trivial commercial commission to paint flowers on a ball gown for the (much richer) woman who turns out, unfortunately all too predictably, to be Hampl's secret betrothed. Nevertheless, even Hampl's mercenary infidelity does not ultimately detract from Karolina's art. At the end, Life is represented as intersecting with and authenticating it: as she realizes what a cad he has been, a single desperate tear of hers rolls onto the gown and ruins the painting while inestimably raising its value as a human, and therefore aesthetic, document. Superficially this seems the same point as is made in the misogynistic and xenophobic tale-within-a-tale of the fourth story, "Lionardo da Vinci," where a young male painter (Polish this time, not Czech) forces his German model against her wishes to pose nude for him by holding her out of a fifth-floor window and threatening to drop her into the street. She gives in, and the resulting painting, of the death of Jezebel thrown from the window to the dogs, is an artistic sensation. But the contrast is telling. Easy, "fashionable" (*módní*) art, or kitsch, is all a female artistic genius in Auředníček's world can be expected to produce when Art crosses Life, heart-rending though it may prove; serious, full-blooded, "modern" (*moderní*) art is evidently expected of the male artist when the same happens to him (further on the opposition between fashionable and modern in the culture of this period, see the discussion of *Bludička* below).[39]

Jaroslav Kvapil (*Bludička,* 1896): The Muse as Social Critic of the Artist

The social and ethical problems associated with the theme of the Czech artist and his Muse—and indeed the attitudes exemplified by Auředníček and Czech salon literature—are criticized fully in Jaroslav Kvapil's four-act drama *Bludička* (Will-o'-the-wisp, 1896); the seriousness of this play ought not to be obscured for a modern reader by the melodramatic denouement, in which the hero shoots himself after an unfortunate purple-passage farewell to Prague.[40] Unlike Kvapil's libretto for Dvořák's *Rusalka* of a few years later, this play has a modern setting. The hero, Kamil Dušek, a thirty-two-year-old painter, has been living in the Lesser Town since returning to Prague from his student days in Paris, when his ambition was to paint scenes from Murger's *Vie de Bohème* and enhance his genius by finding a *petite femme* for himself.[41] For the past six years this role has been fulfilled by Stáza Faltysova, a milliner's assistant.[42] But now he feels that she, and his bohemian way of life, are cramping his potential as an artist, and so he makes a break with Stáza, forcing her to avoid ruin by leaving Prague for anonymous poverty in Vienna (brutally, he asks her why she feels she has to go, and adds insult to injury by reacting impatiently when she bursts into tears).[43] Almost immediately, Dušek tries to enter the world of the *haute bourgeoisie*, getting the rich young Helena Lindnerova to sit for him, taking her on as his pupil in painting, and finally declaring his love for her.

It is not entirely easy to classify this play, combining as it does Decadent and Naturalist features; Naturalist elements include the quasi-realistic treatment of the material, the microscopic attention that is paid to this particular class of people as representatives of a particular time and milieu, and to their mentality, as well as the placing of the principal characters, both Dušek and Lindnerova, in situations of extreme stress to examine their responses to them.[44] And there are clear messages, concerning the politics of art as well as the politics of sex, in contemporary Austria-Hungary.

Some aspects of the play, however, are distinctly Decadent, such as the pessimistic (though perhaps accurate) view of fashionable Czech society as a mere illusion, a "will-o'-the-wisp," for a genuine artist, even one like Dušek who essentially shares its bourgeois values, which will inevitably destroy him. In Act 2 we meet the upper ranks of rich Prague bourgeois society, who have come to the salons of paní Hellerová, Helena's aunt, to hear a mixture of indifferent music-making by amateurs and (marginal) professionals. Their commitment to art is slender and does not extend except grudgingly and meanly to financial support. And none of them is prepared to accept Dušek socially, apart from the stupid and romantically inclined paní Fabiánová, who has brought her small daughters along to play Dvořák's Slavonic Dances as a piano duet. (Even she is reminded that she would never allow either daughter to marry Dušek after they are grown up.)[45] Of the gathering, only paní Hellerová has some serious interest in culture, though even she finds modernism hard to stomach: "Forgive me, gentlemen—but your modern art is too difficult and mysterious for us ordinary mortals."[46]

And Helena herself admits she finds salons more attractive, less demanding, than galleries when she is in Paris.[47] As the cynical Dr. Nedoma points out, Dušek will never be more than a *parvenu* in this society, and, worse, a penniless *parvenu*;[48] it is, indeed, the financial dependence of the artist on his Muse that makes the relationship unsustainable in the end.[49] Moreover, in entering the world of the salon, Dušek has lost more than his independence: he has had his judgment perverted, and has given up his serious painting in favor of designing Helena's ball gowns; it is the beginning of Decadence (*začátek úpadku*).[50] In Nedoma's words to him, "So you are in no way becoming a modern artist, but a fashionable one!"[51] And in Act 2 Nedoma goes on at some length to voice what may well be Kvapil's own hostile criticisms of "fashionable" salon music and salon literature, the latter here personified and satirized in the figure of Bohuš Vladimír Novák, "básník pražských salonů?" (poet of the Prague salons), whose kitsch is, one might say, a *culture fatale*, and with whom Dušek has been trying to curry favor.[52]

Helena, too, displays Decadent features, in some respects embodying the powerful, threatening femme fatale. As Dušek eventually discovers at their final showdown, she is far from playing the role of a submissive adjunct to him (he complains that she has made it impossible for him to believe any longer in the young lady's devotion,) nor is she willing to cooperate in his hypocritical sentimentality in sexual matters.[53] Indeed she is a remarkable creation, a thoroughly self-possessed, modern woman, without sentimental illusions. She knows very well that Dušek has had his recent liaison with Stáza, but is happy to accept the fact,[54] even though she has a clear idea of the double standards in sexual morality governing male and female behavior at the time, with women expected to remain virgins until marriage but men allowed to sow their wild oats;[55] and, while preferring for herself freedom from domesticity and indeed freedom from sexual fidelity,[56] she is able to reflect coolly on the status and interrelationship of the financial and sexual transactions that are carried on clandestinely in her society: "Our whole society is a kind of market in several different currencies."[57] She has moral standards, but they are absolutely at variance with the public morality of her class: she refuses to sell herself or compromise in any way, and she astonishes Dušek, who does not begin to comprehend the sexual politics of his situation or hers, with the notion that he might be more to blame than she in the shortcomings of their relationship.

Even at the end, when Dušek is devastated by the discovery that Helena has all along been the lover of Dr. Vlasák (who is engaged to Helena's friend Klára), he fails to grasp the essential point that she has clearly anticipated: her independence is much less absolute than his, whatever he may think. *His* broken heart, even though he is an artist, ought to be mendable by new conquests, because he is a man; *her* affair, now that he has uncovered it, however, consigns her immediately, and without any alternative, to an unwelcome marriage because she is a woman. The avoidance of her ruin is bought at the price of a lifelong sentence to the hypocritical domesticity she has been dreading, with a man she does not love though she has shared illicit, sexual passion with him and would have liked to have had the freedom to continue to do so. Although the point is obscured somewhat by the concentration on Dušek and his suicide in the final act, it emerges very strongly in Act 3: Helena, too, like Stáza before her, has been deceived and brought down by Dušek's will-o'-the-wisp. (Stáza, it turns out, has also avoided ruin in Vienna, through a quick marriage: Dušek's reaction to the news is typically uncomprehending: "You know—typical woman!")[58] So their final fate is worse than his death.

Even the possible corollary, that Dušek's art could have remained intact if he had stayed with Stáza, is denied by the depiction throughout the play of Dušek's comrades. These bohemian Bohemians divide their time between the well-known Lesser Town pubs U Glaubiců and U svatého Tomáše, in which they make spectacles of themselves. And when Dušek jokes that the "modernism" of their paintings might be a consequence of their unfinished state rather than any aesthetic choice, one might suspect that there is something in what he says.[59] So these constructions of Czech modernism are at the same time reflections of the author's own anxieties about the ability of Czech society to support artists, and of those artists to measure up to international standards.

Emanuel z Lešehradu (*Shroucení*, 1904): The Decadent Anti-Muse

The topos is exemplified very differently in the one-act "lyrical scene" in octosyllabic rhyming couplets, *Shroucení* (Collapse, 1904), by Emanuel z Lešehradu, an occultist and a writer who remained very close to Decadence until just before the First World War, even though Lešehrad is here dramatizing a similar ironic point, that the mystic union between an artist and his Muse is eventually unsustainable if prolonged beyond marriage.[60] It is not for nothing that these fictional artists and their Muses usually die at the moment they achieve their union, and no doubt it is best for them to do so. Nietzsche's earlier formulation of this idea brings out its essential Decadent fear and hatred of women, though his beautifully ironic tone also captures the paradox that redemptive Muse and femme fatale are virtually one and the same construction:

> What happens to the "eternal Jew" idolized and *anchored down* by a woman? He simply ceases to be eternal; he gets married; he no longer interests us. —Translated into reality: the danger for artists, for geniuses—and it is they who are really the "eternal Jews"— lies in Woman: women who idolize them are their downfall.[61]

Lešehrad's piece is a brief melodrama (in the theatrical, not the musical, sense). Jan, a painter, is married to Hilda, and the marriage is approaching breakdown, with Jan unproductive and the couple both unhappy. They are visited by Jan's friend Walter, to whom Hilda makes sexual advances, complaining of being a prisoner and deprived of love. Walter expects her to be satisfied with being the wife of a famous artist; she replies that this is nothing but an illusion. The conversation has been secretly overheard by Jan, who realizes the same thing: Art and Life are reinforcing each other in a downward spiral, and perhaps the banality of Lešehrad's verse is intended to underline the point:[62]

> What is the worth to me of the whole of Art
> when the whole of Life is transformed
> into a tragic, infernal abyss?
> O, be it forever accursed!

And there is a further paradox: it is she, as his Muse, who teaches him this. This is the more thoroughly Decadent converse of the commonplace we have met in Auředníček, of Art being authenticated by Life: here Art is being invalidated, rather than validated, when Life crosses its path. So Jan renounces both Art and Life, and shoots himself. His villa seems to be collapsing as well, as words yield to *son et lumière* (first the windows emit a pink light and then "from the villa are heard some sad piano chords"), while Jan is finally apostrophizing his fatal Muse as an angel.[63]

Lothar Suchý (*Sláva*, 1905): The Anxiety of Impotence

Lothar Suchý's three-act drama *Sláva* (Glory, 1905) focuses especially on the predicament of the impotent Czech artist unable to come to terms with modernism.[64] Miloš Krása, a young dramatist, has been able to pass off as his own a successful drama by his impoverished, tubercular friend Karel Bárta, owing to the latter's death on the night of the Prague premiere. Krása marries his Muse, Lída Žákova, and the riches (as well as honor, the *"sláva"* of the title) he earns from Bárta's play impress his bourgeois merchant father-in-law, pan Žák, who exclaims, pleased with his own joke, "Who would have imagined that dramas like these could earn almost as much as my ham!"[65] But Krása is unable to match Bárta's genius in his next play: as his friend Samek (another writer) says, "It is not as immediate . . . as naively powerful and original . . . there is evidence of work in it!"[66] With Samek, we come to suspect him of stealing his "hypermodern" imagery, all Wiener Sezession, from someone else; the half-drunk Samek suggests that Krása might find an obscure French or Belgian writer useful for plagiarism.[67] Eventually Krása feels he needs a psychiatrist,[68] we find out with Lída that he has been taking a poisonous drug, antipyrine,[69] and a scene toward the end, in which he is confronted by an apparition of Karel Bárta and nearly strangles Bárta's surviving brother, symbolizes the complete disintegration of his personality,[70] before the final scene in which he takes stronger poison and dies.

Throughout all this, Lída plays an ambiguous role as Krása's Muse. She has apparently been worshiped previously from afar by Karel Bárta: he has taught her an idealistic belief in the immortality of the soul and the eternity of love, and she knows by heart his poetry (published, we find, like *Jan Maria Plojhar*, in the journal *Lumír*).[71] Whether or not she is to be believed that she was unaware of Bárta's love and that there was nothing between them, he has provided her with the "capital" necessary to set up as a Muse, just as he has provided Krása with the "capital" necessary to set up as a genius. But expressing their relationship in this way, along lines familiar from Helena Lindnerova's view of society as fueled by transactions in several different currencies, is immediately to cast doubt on the authenticity of such transactions; and in Suchý's world we are not encouraged to trust the good faith or idealism of any of the characters. Moreover, our suspicions are sown early on. Krása is modern and Nietzschean enough to reject his dead friend's idealistic or religious belief: "Unbelief is more profound than faith,"[72] but his is a Decadent unbelief that sees itself in religious terms as sin, which, as he tells Lída, is the currency he will use if necessary to pay for possessing her. She is enchanted by this rhetoric, even though she adopts the pose of pure, maidenly devotion: "How beautifully you speak! How I love you! But I want our love to be pure, undisturbed, far from sin . . . from any sin!"[73]

Once she discovers she is pregnant, and financial considerations are suddenly more important to her, she shows herself just as willing as he is to sacrifice principles to maintain her position, despite her frequent protestations that she would be happy to endure poverty with him. In fact, their roles are, at least in some respects, reversed: once she is aware of his fraud, she prevents him from admitting it publicly, and she becomes increasingly self-sufficient and independent as Krása himself adopts the submissive pose of the conscientious author desperately and obsessively trying to overcome writer's block and redeem himself. In this process, the motif of the drugs increasingly poisoning him becomes symbolic of the change in Lída from inspiring Muse to femme fatale. As she discovers his drug taking and immediately takes over control of the supply of the tablets to him, he praises her for "poisoning" him with his antipyrine: "Are you yourself willing to give me the poison? Oh, how good you are.")[74] Then he switches the drugs for genuine poison, and (in another echo from *Jan Maria Plojhar*) she is again the one to give it to him; when she realizes what has happened, she answers his question: "A já ti sama jed ten podala" ("And it was I myself who administered this poison to you.")[75] The conclusion is profoundly Decadent, allowing no escape. Krása dies in vain without having come to terms with his fraud, and leaves Lída and his unborn child on their own to inherit Bárta's usurped fortune and Bárta's usurped good name; her final act is to become his Muse fully at last, as she burns his signed confession, makes herself responsible for perpetuating his "sin," and witnesses him dying ecstatically and foolishly with her name on his lips.

Leoš Janáček (*Osud,* 1905): The Muse Drawn from Life

To move from literature to opera is awkward, given the passionate, irrational lyricism of the operatic genre, even though the theme of the adulterous Muse might seem obviously "operatic" in the conventional sense—offering as it does an excuse for placing lyrical, essentially Romantic, episodes with a central pair of (probably) soprano and tenor characters at the heart of a musical piece, pleasantly contrasting them with scenes of conflict, perhaps together with comic interludes, in a genre that is fairly tolerant of absurd plots. This is the basis, for example, of the four-act opera *Nepřemožení* (The invincible ones) by Josef Bohuslav Foerster, to his own libretto, as late as 1917, and this work may be quoted in order to point up the unusual qualities of Janáček's version of the topos.[76] Foerster's piece is partly autobiographical: his brother, Viktor, was an artist who had had an unhappy love affair with an aristocrat. Accordingly, the hero, Viktor, a modernist—Straussian—composer and violinist (son of a castle gardener), loves Alba, a countess. When this is discovered, he is banned from the castle, and for mercenary reasons she is married off to a count. But she finally achieves her vocation as Viktor's Muse when he is dying of tuberculosis in Italy, abandoning her unhappy marriage and joining him there in another idealistic, Mediterranean deathbed apotheosis. This opera is unfairly ignored or dismissed as incompetent (or as too "philosophical") in the secondary literature; the key lyrical moments when Viktor expounds the nature of love are well conceived in theatrical terms as well as being musically expansive. But in 1917 it came a generation late; and mystic, snobbish unions in fictional art like this one, between prewar countesses and musicians who are too well bred to have financial or sexual transactions with each other, were already receiving mordantly mocking treatment in K. M. Čapek-Chod's novel of the same year, *Antonín Vondrejc*; his character Skalický summarizes the fictional novel *Tantalus* thus:

> Could anything be more astounding and sensible than this novel of the voracious, insatiable love felt by this pianist from the fifth district employed by a young countess to do the pedaling for her in her piano playing? Consider this invention of the tender, sublime, golden-haired beauty, with completely paralyzed legs [. . .], for whom the conservatoire student must do the pedaling! I tell you, gentlemen, that refinement of those long half-days of love which allow the two young people to enjoy complete certainty that nothing can go wrong! Gentlemen, I know no madder sensation in any literature—and I am conversant with more than one literature— than that evoked in the pages of Falada's *Tantalus* when Stryjski produces his own compositions, when the two of them see no means of escape from their crisis other than a shared death, and when the sublime Stryjski is driven out, even before the catastrophe, because it is found out that he is actually a Polish Jew by origin! And how he concludes his Tantalian torment, when he takes pity on the scorned daughter of a Jewish washer of corpses who has long idolized him, and embraces her, persuading himself most beautifully that he is actually holding his countess in his arms![77]

There are no countesses, however, in Janáček's earlier treatment of this theme, in his three-act opera *Osud* (Fate, 1905), for which his own designation was "tři románové obrazy" (three novelistic scenes); in this work he dared to jettison much of the "operatic" potential of the material in order to depict another psychological breakdown of the sort we have already met.[78] The circumstances of its composition are well-known.[79] In 1903 at Luhačovice, shortly after the death of his daughter Olga, and years before he met Stösslová, he had met another Kamila—Urválková—who told him she had been calumnied in the one-act opera *Kamilla* (1897), by Ludvík Vítězslav Čelanský, whose lover she had been. The eponymous heroine of Čelanský's opera is represented as a flirt who trifles with the heart of a salon poet, and Urválková urged Janáček to put the matter right by writing another opera. Janáček obliged—though possibly principally because he saw an opportunity to dramatize himself in the figure of the composer, and because he was attracted to setting a modern subject. *Osud* was the result, a setting of a text that ultimately stemmed from the composer himself.[80] In a letter to Urválková in October 1903, he sets out his conception for this work, drawing on the adulterous Muse construction already outlined, with its up-to-date combination of modernist "realism," ladies' salons, Mediterranean scenery (some of Act 2 having been envisaged on the Dalmatian coastline, with a crisis provoked by the heroine's jealous husband, before its final location in the composer's flat) and hallucinatory breakdowns:

I want to have Act I completely realistic, drawn from life at a spa. There is a wealth of motifs there! Act II is to be actually a *hallucination*. No more reality, instead the mind, provoked almost to a nervous breakdown, propels the action further to the point where it is hard to say whether it is real or a hallucination, a delusion. While the setting of Act I is magnificent spa scenery, Act II ought to reveal the extravagant interior of ladies' boudoirs, the scenery of southern landscapes. Act III will be strange. . . . The students argue about the opera. Whether real or imaginary, the second act was downright psychopathic. It is drawn from the life of the artist.[81]

In Janáček's final version, the hero, Živný, a composer, meets the heroine, Míla Válková, at Luhačovice around 1880 in the first act.[82] They have previously been lovers and she has borne him a son, Doubek, but she is now married to a rich, elegant bourgeois; they decide, however, to the consternation of Míla's mother, to reestablish their liaison. In Act 2, a little later, they are married, and Živný has been composing an opera about their lives. The doubling of all the characters in the opera with those in the opera-within-the-opera is disturbed in that the first-level composer is "Živný," in which "life-giving" role Janáček is evidently casting himself, and the second-level composer is "Lenský"—in other words, Čelanský, conceived by Janáček as a mediocre composer; and Lenský has echoes of the mediocre poet of the same name in Pushkin's *Yevgeny Onegin*—a work envisaged by Janáček as a model in some respects for *Osud* (see below). From the intertextual complexities and autobiographical enthusiasm of this mismatch spring some fundamental dramaturgical problems, which need not occupy us here. Míla and Živný have not come to terms with the social or emotional consequences of their original affair, which haunts Míla and has driven her mother to insanity. Indeed they have realized that it fundamentally calls into question their personal identity: "Our soul is a forest with an echo," and this is a fearful echo.[83] Živný himself has harbored doubts concerning Míla's fidelity and the authenticity of her relationship with him—indeed her psychological integrity—as he apostrophizes her through his score, in language whose tone is fairly typical of the whole libretto:

> You poisoned flower of revenge! I desired to tear your heart from your body, to parade its wounds and to toll its knell with heartless laughter; to pour out your tears even unto the palms of my hands; to pierce your breast with a sharp dagger and inflict a mortal wound on you; to hold you up to human judgment as a living lie: "A couple of salacious moments behind a shield of pretense behind a mendacious smile."

An epiphany is provoked by the four-year-old Doubek, reinforcing these doubts by telling Míla that she does not know what love is: he has seen it, and it is what the servants Žán and Nána do below stairs when they are fond of each other.[84] His words, "Mami, víš, co je láska?" (Mummy, do you know what love is?), are so central to the conception that they were considered as the title for the piece. Perhaps, then, idealistic artistic inspiration is nothing but adult self-deception, and love nothing but raw sex, a stinking can of worms. Yet the logical connections are undercut throughout the opera; there is no direct connection, for example, between this central turning point and the melodramatic mad scene at the end of the act, where Míla's mother sings an incoherent monologue about the seduction of Míla by Živný and his music, about a mysterious songbird with a hidden meaning, and about Fate, and then hurls herself down the stairwell of the building, dragging Míla down with her.

In Act 3, now in the present day, Živný's opera is finally reaching its premiere at the conservatory; the students realize that its hero, Lenský, is in fact Živný himself, as they rehearse its ending, which they find "so strange and ridiculous" (*divné tak i směšné*)—a storm instead of a proper denouement. They humiliate Doubek (now a student himself) with the Žán and Nána episode, which has been incorporated into the opera—and we realize (in a strange Nietzschean pre-echo of the "eternal return of Nature" motif in *Liška Bystrouška*) that the sexual couplings at the heart of the opera, dictated by Fate and very possibly destructive, are repeating themselves over and over—in the real life of Čelanský and Urválková, in the opera-within-the-opera between the servants and between Lenský and Míla, and in the first-level opera not only between Živný and Míla, but also between Verva and Součková, two of the students at the rehearsal. When Živný enters and starts to explain Lenský to the students, a real storm blows up; the students are terrified both by the thunder and lightning and by Živný's increasing madness, and Živný finally falls unconscious. Yet he is still alive, insisting that they are wrong to think that this could be the missing last act, which remains and must remain in the hand of God. Like the turning points of the plot, this missing ending can only be awaited as a bolt from the blue, and, like the others, must be followed and obeyed if life is not to be cut off at its source and wither. But even this idea is not developed or allowed to become a peroration. The operatic rhetoric is undercut, with the last brief word given to Dr. Suda, a minor character: *Co jest vám, příteli?* ("Is anything the matter, my friend?") With its dreamlike illogicality this may be insignificant, or may be mysterious and alarming: Suda is a lawyer (Verva had gone in search of a doctor) and has not played an important part in the action, though the first sung words of the opera were also his, where he announced himself as a songbird; but it repudiates normal operatic logic either way. It is not surprising, therefore, that Václav Nosek's radical "flashback" revision of the opera (with Acts 1 and 2 inserted within Act 3) reorganizes the ending, with Živný looking at the last page of his score, musing on the ever-present vision of his dead Muse, and, accompanied by the chorus, invoking the bolt from the blue that will indeed end the action.[85] But this undercuts the radical approach essential to Janáček's conception, and is a miscalculation comparable to that of the "optimistic" ending produced for *Z mrtvého domu* after Janáček's death by his pupils Břetislav Bakala and Osvald Chlubna.

Even though *Osud* is arguably a masterpiece, its relationship to belles lettres is problematic in more than the usual ways. The Janáček documents show that this work was a focus of his ambitions; in December 1903 he was hoping that a work "so new, new!" might be successful "for a wider, even a Prague, public."[86] But it was not based on a recognized literary model (as *Její pastorkyňa* had been), and the composer was not at ease with the idea of competing with professional writers on their own ground; the previous October he had written to Urválková:

> What I'd like now is a libretto that is fresh, modern, bubbling over with life and elegance—the "story of a child" of our time. Oh, but who will write it for me? I have many details for it myself; I'm told that I know how to handle words—but I am frightened among literary people.[87]

And it would appear that he was oversensitive to criticism as a result, embarking on numerous revisions, having second thoughts about his librettist's competence, and approaching some writers—including Kvapil—who sensibly declined to help in matters that were faits accomplis.

The curious qualities of the work may be illustrated here from three extracts—two from the libretto and one from the music. First, the quotation above from Act 2 illustrates the lexis of the libretto in general terms. Its highly contrived and anti-natural language (no doubt together with the composer's avoidance of normal operatic structure) has been one of the principal reasons why Czech producers have so seldom mounted this opera. Janáček had invented Czech *Literaturoper* by setting *Její pastorkyňa* in the prose of Preissová's play, bypassing the usual versification for a libretto, and adhering rather faithfully to the actual words of the original; by setting these words with a "realistic" approximation of speech rhythms, he produced a very radically realistic Naturalism, though this does not rule out highly lyrical moments. He must have felt that this Naturalism would not suffice for *Osud*, and that the new opera should be more poetic; yet his lack of confidence in dealing with librettists persuaded him to make use of a young (and inexperienced) teacher of his acquaintance, Fedora Bartošová, who had been a friend of his late daughter. Bartošová versified a prose model which he provided, encouraging her to use the form of verse employed by Pushkin in *Yevgeny Onegin*.[88] The result might be termed a modernized version of Pushkin. However, in writing the music he then revised and exploded the verse almost beyond recognition, so that it ended virtually as a series of "prose poems"—lyrical and highly stylized, but nonmetrical and apparently formless.

This process may be exemplified in detail through a second extract, a comparison of Bartošová's versified libretto and its revision by Janáček, on the basis of the extract from the beginning of Act 2 that is shown in Figure 1:

Bartošová's Version	Janáček's Version
1 Spí tóny moje . . . moje tóny – divné! tóny spí.	Echo našeho života dříme, bledé
2 Teď všechny dřímou. *(jde ku klavíru)* Probudit vás ze sna?	*(Rozžehne svíčky u klavíru)*
3 Ne! nezbudím vás! Tíhu mojí duše	Tíhu našich duší
4 na křídlech máte. Odpočiňte! Zítra,	na křídlech máte. Kdy
5 již zítra slavně, zářivě a v lesku	as, kdy zářivě a v lesku
6 se rozleťte! A bodnete-li pravdou,	se rozletíte?!
7 jen hluboko, až do krve! A láskou	Až láskou
8 když zašeptáte, měkkounce a teple	si zašeptáte, měkkounce, teple
9 se přitiskněte ku mladému srdci.	si přisednete k mladému srdci.
10 Svých křídel vzmachem utajujte každý	Svých křídel stínem utajujte každý
11 hluboký vzdech. A závistníkům bledým	hluboký vzdech!
12 uleťte v dáli, jak bzučící komár.	
13 Ale vás, řady umlčených tónů,	Ale vás, řady umlčených tónů,
14 zapřené lidem, zakřiknuté v duši,	zapřených lidem, a vás, zakřiknuté
15 jež do řady jste navlečeny dlouhé	
16 jak řada perel bělostných, Vás vzbudím!	vlastním svědomím, mám vzbudit naposled?

1 My notes sleep . . . my notes . . . strange!	The echo of our life is slumbering, pale notes sleep.
2 Now they all slumber. *(Goes to piano)* Awaken you from dreams?	*(Lights the candles at the piano)*
3 No, I shall not! The weight of my soul	The weight of our soul
4 bears on your wings. Rest on! Tomorrow,	bears on your wings. When,
5 soon, solemnly, gloriously and in splendor	O when, gloriously and in splendor
6 take flight! And if you stab with the truth,	will you take flight?
7 do so deeply, drawing blood! And with love	When in love
8 when you whisper, softly and warmly,	you whisper to yourselves, softly, warmly,
9 press yourselves to a young breast!	take your seat by a young heart!
10 In the spreading of your wings	In the shadow of your wings

hide every	conceal every
11 deep sigh. And from pale, envious people	deep sigh!
12 fly far away, like a buzzing gnat.	
13 But you, sequences of silenced notes,	But you, sequences of silenced notes,
14 hidden from the people, cowering in the soul,	hidden from the people, and you, cowed
15 which are strung into a long series	
16 like a string of gleaming pearls, I shall	by your own conscience, must I at last
awaken you!	waken you?

The librettist cast the whole of the beginning of this act (extending further than the extract in Figure 1) as a long monologue by Živný, which is broken up by Janáček into a dialogue between Živný and Míla, with offstage interjections from Míla's mother. The sixteen lines illustrated are nearly all regular hendecasyllables, long eleven-syllable lines that give the verse a reflective weight (Bartošová moves to shorter lines as soon as Živný begins to quote from the opera-within-the-opera). The diction is undoubtedly "literary" and noncolloquial; indeed, the poet may have over-reached herself, since the metaphors are contrived and unpleasant even for verse (Janáček was undoubtedly right in omitting the metaphor of the buzzing gnat), and they are impossible for a libretto.

Nevertheless, the sense is plain. Živný is about to bring his "sleeping" notes to life and is considering the consequences of doing so. His physical move to the piano coincides with a change from third person to second person in referring to the music, a change that itself implies increased resolution. But Janáček changes the first line so that it makes a deliberately puzzling, self-reflective statement. Moreover, for the purpose he transfers into this line attributes with Decadent (or at least neo-Romantic) resonance, used by Bartošová simply in passing elsewhere in the act— "echo," *"bledý"* ("pale," from line 11 in this extract)—thus investing them with obscure, mysterious, but not necessarily satisfactorily poetic, significance. And every other alteration he makes serves a comparable purpose, confusing and obscuring the sense of Bartošová's text, presumably with the aim of increasing the poetic power of the original: the reassurance Živný gives, that the notes will not wait longer than "tomorrow" to take flight, becomes a doubt that they will ever do so; the word "zakřiknuté" (cowed), which for Bartošová is merely a conventional word to signify the inactivity of the music, becomes for Janáček a word to signify the self-awareness of the music as culpable and as dangerous. So the artificiality in style of Bartošová's original libretto is compounded in Janáček's setting into an artificiality and obscurity of subject matter comparable to that found in the poetic output of some of the minor Czech poets of the fin de siècle.

Besides his alteration of the content, Janáček undermines the coherence of Bartošová's libretto by destroying the original metrical scheme. There was some encouragement to do so in that so many of Bartošová's lines run on in enjambment, with punctuation dividing many of the lines by contrast in the middle; and Janáček's frequent practice is to omit either the first or the second half of such lines (for example, lines 3, 6, 7, 11 in the extract), often inserting brief orchestral phrases in their place; when he retains the full hendecasyllable, the density of the words sometimes encourages the use of a parlando, as in the artificially lengthened first line of the text of the act (see Example 1), and so the manner of revising the text has some bearing on the music that resulted from setting it.

Yet the artificial qualities of the libretto and its setting coexist with a Naturalistic "realism" throughout the opera, which, as in *Její pastorkyňa*, is the result of using material drawn from life. In this, Janáček's assumptions about the relationship between Art and Life are only too reminiscent of the naive ideas of Auředníček's artists—such as the Polish painter in "Lionardo da Vinci," cited above—who assume that the most powerful effects in Art come from the direct observation of extreme situations in Life. Indeed, Janáček wished to model all the effects in this opera if possible on speech melodies, as if he were an artist painting his model from life. These included the incidental local color from Luhačovice—he wrote to Urválková in a letter, perhaps from October 1903, that he had been noting "snatches of melodies from speech and overheard talks" at Luhačovice, and referring also to a phrase uttered by her five-year-old son, "with the classic answer to the question: 'What is love?'"—the phrase that found its way into Act 2, with minimal revision.[89] But it also included even the mad scene at the end of Act 2: he approached insane asylums in Brno and Prague to find suitable speech melodies for it, and wrote a letter to a doctor at the Prague Institute for the Insane (though this was probably never sent), including the following request:

> May I request you to permit me to listen to the patients in the women's section of the Prague Institute. I have a twofold aim. First, I am interested in the speech melody of the insane in general; secondly, I am looking for a particular case where miserliness was the cause of the illness. A wealthy widow did not want to marry her

Geoffrey Chew

Example 1. Leoš Janáček, *Osud,* Act II, scene 1, mm. 1–5 (opening of Živný's monologue).

daughter to a "beggarly" artist. When a marriage nevertheless took place, she went mad. She feared that she might be robbed even of her jewel box. One day, when running away, she jumped from a staircase and killed herself. This, briefly, is the type—possibly rare; I have failed to find one, even in the Brno Institute for the Insane.[90]

So the extreme situations in *Osud* drive the music to an exaggerat-edly deformed "realism," more extreme than that shown above in Example 1, and whatever the methods adopted to arrive at this music, its Decadent aspect is very clear. Generally, the (typically Naturalist) pessimistic exploration of social conditions in *Její pastorkyňa*—infanticide, poverty, extended families of half-brothers and foster-daughters and reli-gious bigotry—has been replaced here by a (typically Decadent) pessimistic exploration of mysterious psychological conditions and insanity. Nevertheless, numerous equivalent moments in *Její pastorkyňa* and *Osud* will illustrate the closeness of Naturalism to this Decadence. For exam-ple, the central aria "Co chvíla" in *Její pastorkyňa,* of the Kostelnička, is a point at which she is subjected to maximum stress, as a respected, reli-gious person and a caring foster mother, who must nevertheless jeopardize her own eternal salvation and kill Jenůfa's infant if she is to rescue Jenůfa from ruin; she stands on the brink of the madness of the abyss, as Naturalist characters may do. But, even though Míla's mother (Janáček's idea, an addition to the cast during composition) is a far more negative character than the Kostelnička, her scene at the end of Act 2 of *Osud* is comparable to "Co chvíla," though more extreme: she is already in the psychological abyss of madness and, in suicide, also consigns herself to the physical abyss.

Example 2 gives a further flavor of the musical method in an extract from this aria, if it can be called that; the piece dramatizes breakdown in an operatic parallel (as Janáček's letter, quoted above, suggests was his intention) to the hallucination scene in Suchý's *Sláva*, but more radical, owing to the fact that it is not constructed as a final unraveling of the plot's problems. It is equally more radical than traditional operatic mad scenes, whether or not it is drawn from life, for though it is certainly constructed as an exaggerated, feminized, hysterical response, it is not made to correspond with erotic passion. In the example, Míla's mother has not yet disintegrated into total incoherence (though she has been mad for the whole act): the music moves from a lyrical reminiscence, in regular four-measure phrases, of the words between Živný and Míla—"Myšlenku cítím bloudit kol nás" (I sense a thought drifting around us)—through fragmented utterances that turn the scene into a recognition scene, an anagnoresis—"Znám tě! Tys svůdce mojí dcery!" (I know you! You are the seducer of my daughter!)—accompanied in the orchestra by increasingly deformed versions of the four-measure phrases, before the first great outburst, accompanied by fortissimo percussion—"Ó, těžká ti zavolá má duše" (O, my heavy soul invokes you)—and leading to the great invocation (not shown here) of "Fatum."

Nejedlý contra Helfert: Theorizing Janáček and Theorizing the Adulterous Muse in Czech Music

Both Decadence and Naturalism were, and remained, essentially pejorative terms for Czech critics throughout, and beyond, the first half of the twentieth century. It is almost exclusively the latter term that was used as a weapon against Janáček, however, and this is largely the consequence of the fact that it was overwhelmingly *Její pastorkyňa* (*Jenůfa*) with which Janáček made his national and international reputation. The understanding of Naturalism in this context was fixed even before the First World War by Zdeněk Nejedlý (a critic and musicologist long before

Example 2. Leoš Janáček, *Osud,* Act II, scene 6, mm. 1–47 (monologue of Míla's mother).

he became the well-known Stalinist ideologue and government minister under the Communists in the late 1940s and in the 1950s), in a sense
rather different from that used above in this article, even though it was
also seen to apply particularly to *Její pastorkyňa*. For example, in his criticism of the Prague premiere of the opera in 1916, Nejedlý finds the
composer an upholder of primitivism against culture—and he terms this
Naturalism:[91]

> Today we term this view *Naturalist*, because it proceeds from the
> presumption that one can simply introduce real, natural forms, as
> life presents them, into art, and that the work of art itself becomes,
> by this means, natural and veracious—the old error of all Naturalism,
> which does not fully take into account the importance of active
> artistic creation, which alone brings to life all the dead material that
> is natural.[92]

In this review, he writes that Janáček's "speech melodies" represent
the "real, natural elements" that are the stock in trade of the Naturalist;
and Janáček's decision to set his opera largely in Preissová's prose (rather
than to recast the text in verse in the manner of Foerster's *Eva*, a
Preissová adaptation that Nejedlý thinks far superior to *Její pastorkyňa*)
is, once again, evidence of the composer's fatal Naturalism, which, indeed,
he links with the *verismo* of the 1890s.[93] This view of Janáček as fatally
tainted with Naturalism was one with which the composer had to contend for the rest of his life and posthumously. In a well-known monograph
(based on a series of lectures held in České Budějovice in 1923), the composer Josef Bartoš repeats Nejedlý's verdict on Janáček's Naturalism,
linking it with the fragmentation and incoherence one might rather
associate with Decadence, and suggesting that foreigners might find it
more acceptable than Czechs as a manifestation of Czech nationality in
music.[94] In 1924 or 1925, Janáček himself drafted a fascinating document
on Naturalism in music (unpublished until recently, and included in
this volume in translation), understanding by it the use of elements from
the natural (and human) world, processed artistically to a greater or lesser
extent, and quoting the practice of a variety of Czech and foreign composers: he concludes, "nebát se naturalismu," "one should not fear
Naturalism."[95] Still, after 1948, at the time of the reconstruction of
Czechoslovak culture along Soviet lines, the charge of Naturalism remained
an obstacle to be overcome before he could be admitted to the canon of
music acceptable under the new watchword of Socialist Realism.[96]

Also due to Nejedlý, however, is another and quite different theoretical construction of direct relevance to our subject, and as we shall

see, well known to Janáček himself, which is Nejedlý's edition in 1925 of the amorous diary ascribed to the composer Zdenĕk Fibich. In the decade preceding his death in 1900, Fibich had published several sets of small piano pieces, entitled *Nálady, dojmy a upomínky* (Moods, impressions and reminiscences). It was always obvious that these had some sort of narrative content; for example, the second series contains a sequence of pieces entitled *Novella*, with pieces entitled "Preface," "Chapter 1," "Chapter 2," "Epilogue," and so on. But the content of the narrative, even in the *Novella*, is unspecified, and might have remained so but for the intervention of Nejedlý, who had been a composition pupil of Fibich's in the last decade of the nineteenth century. In that decade, Fibich had an extramarital affair with a sophisticated and educated writer, Anežka Schulzová. He and Schulzová kept a diary that provided a secret key to the piano pieces, all of which apparently referred to day-to-day events in the life of the lovers, reflections on the physical attributes and beauty of Schulzová, the parts of her body, her attire, and so forth, and it had come into the hands of Nejedlý after Schulzová's suicide in 1905.[97] (It should be added that, despite the appearance of disinterested scholarship on Nejedlý's part, questions remain, not only about the motivation for the publication, but also about the extent to which the published diary reflects interventions both by Schulzová during her lifetime and Nejedlý thereafter. These questions cannot be addressed here.)

In a substantial introductory essay, Nejedlý first presents a theoretical rationale for the importance to the creative artist of amorous liaisons that contravene conventional morality; and then he applies his general conclusions to an interpretation of Fibich and his music. First, he distances himself from what he terms Romantic notions of Woman, according to which an egoistic artist places her on a pedestal at an unattainable distance and turns her into his slave. The same is true, he thinks, of the conceptions of Woman of the Naturalists and Realists, whom he regards as the heirs of the Romantics in this respect. None of these attitudes allow Woman, nor indeed Man, to be a human being, but merely the instrument of artistic inspiration. A true man (he gives Wagner as an example) or a true woman (here the example is the author Božena Němcová, equally canonic for the Czechs) will always be grateful enough to his or her lovers to allow them to be themselves, and will also embrace suffering as well as joy. And the most important aspect is the nature of the love between them. It is no bolt from the blue, appearing instantaneously and fatefully as the Romantics irresponsibly think, but is generated by the needs of the soul of the artist, and this "higher, better" love may be directed at friends, home, humanity, nature, or culture as well as at a woman, if it is the love of a true artist who is aware of his or her vocation. This means that it is no business of the bourgeois public to stand in judgment on the amorous liaisons of a true artist.

Nejedlý then proceeds to interpret Fibich's output. Each of the three decades between 1870 and 1900 corresponds to the involvement of Fibich with one of his women, and each generates a distinct period in his work. (There is a strange parallel with the fictional construction of Jan Maria Plojhar's three women by Zeyer.) First, Fibich married Růžena Hanušová in 1873; Nejedlý says she was a "dreamy, Schumannesque" type, and that she corresponds to the "lyrical" works of the 1870s, marked as they are by the (from his point of view canonic) personality of Smetana. After Růžena's early death in 1874, Fibich married her sister, the singer Betty Hanušová; Nejedlý regards this marriage as one entered into for the sake of art rather than love, and interprets the "heroic" works of the 1880s as corresponding to her personality. And finally there emerges in the 1890s the true love of Fibich for Schulzová, which inaugurates the third, "passionate, erotic" period in Fibich's work. According to Nejedlý, this represents a key moment in the development of Czech music, when literary modernism is wedded to it: as a woman up to date with modern French and Russian literature, Schulzová is a typical modern, fin-de-siècle figure, the necessary complement to Fibich's art.

In this extraordinary argument, Nejedlý thus interprets the adulterous liaison of Fibich as a guarantee of immunity against all three crises of the time: with Schulzová, Fibich's ideal manhood is constructed, as are his status as a thoroughly modern artist (safe from the possible ravages of Naturalism and Realism) and his status within the acceptably national Czech tradition inherited from Smetana. It is classic special pleading, for Schulzová herself had written:

> Fibich maintained an insurmountable aversion toward all extremes in modern trends, in music just as in literature and in the fine arts. This aversion extended to a contempt for the significance of modern art.[98]

And, significantly enough, Nejedlý in this text almost completely avoids any mention of the possibility of interpreting Fibich's life and works in terms of Decadence, except to assert baldly at one point, without qualification, that Fibich was a *"člověk nedekadentní"* (a non-decadent person).[99]

When the book was published, it was greeted with mixed reviews in the Czech journals, with a hostile review from the distinguished Brno academic and champion of Janáček, Vladimír Helfert.[100] Helfert directly contradicts Nejedlý on several points and interprets Fibich as Decadent, as he does also later in his monograph on twentieth-century Czech music:

> Is it possible to believe in such artistic and aesthetic naivety on Fibich's part? . . . For in that there would be such Decadence, such a cruel rupture in creative individuality, that it would far surpass my convictions hitherto that Fibich's period with Anežka Schulzová represents the period of the turning point in Fibich's artistic career![101]

He argues that Nejedlý cannot see this because he himself fundamentally adheres to a "výrazový naturalismus" a (naturalism of expression), since his aesthetic, as displayed in the book, permits the possibility of the direct "expression" in music of phenomena in external Nature—such as Anežka wearing a light blue dress rather than one of another color.

Corresponding to Helfert's negative interpretation of Fibich and his music is a positive interpretation of Janáček—which prevailed over Nejedlý's view after 1948, even though Helfert had died during the Second World War and Nejedlý had become a leading architect of Stalinist cultural policy after the accession to power of the Communists. In his writings Helfert had developed the idea of *"hudební myšlení"* (the equivalent of "musikalisches Denken," a concept possibly new within the Czech tradition though with parallels elsewhere), which was measurable through the technical analysis of specific compositions and capable of demonstrating specific national traits both in the compositions and in their composer.[102] This idea supplied him with an effective argument against Nejedlý's conception of Naturalism as the unmediated incorporation of raw natural elements into art works—though there is irony in the fact that the idea is itself a Naturalist tool, if Naturalism is understood as more than a simple insult.

In these terms Helfert expounds Janáček's "musical thought": the composer's impatience and impetuosity make him an opponent of Classicism, yet he is no pure Romantic either, for he subjects his Romantic inspiration to a process of artistic transmutation:

> His expressiveness and his subjective eroticism in particular have many Romantic elements. But all this concerns a source of inspiration. As soon as some musical thought wells up from this source, it immediately loses its Romantic character. For Janáček neither stylizes nor idealizes his musical inspiration in the Romantic manner. . . . He develops motifs in their raw state, and takes sudden possession of them as his most personal musical reality. By this quality

of his musical thoughts alone, Janáček is a new phenomenon in Czech music: a representative of musical Realism.[103]

Helfert goes on to expound this central idea of Janáček as Realist in relation to specific technical aspects of the music, drawing on his comprehensive familiarity with the composer's oeuvre, and in particular emphasizing his achievement in forging a "new Czech dramatic style, the Realist style," at a time when modernism was taken to mean Wagnerianism in music.[104] And at the end of this classic account of Janáček's music, the argument with Nejedlý reemerges and is explained in terms of an incompatibility between the aesthetic of Prague and that of Brno. Not only did Janáček's career suffer because the Czech culture of Brno was inhibited by the proximity of Vienna, but

> in addition even the novelty of his compositional style, which was not readily accepted in Prague, appeared as mere whimsical idiosyncrasy; this is understandable, for a style as new and untraditional as that of Janáček could not be comprehended all at once in Prague, brought up as it was in the Classical and Romantic styles.[105]

This enables Helfert to construct a line of succession in the canon of Czech music that stretches from Classicism though Romanticism to the true modernism of Realism, in which the main names are Smetana, Dvořák, Fibich (in other words, with a nod of concession to Nejedlý), and Janáček. And though this is a line of succession rather distinctly different from the Prague-oriented view favored by Nejedlý, it provides the narrative that has generally found favor in histories of Czech music since the Second World War, both at home and abroad.

But it is a view that would have been fatally compromised on its own terms if Helfert had attempted to interpret Janáček's "musical thought" within the framework of the Stösslová affair as writers do nowadays; and Helfert, well aware of that affair and of at least some of the important documentary evidence bearing on it, was clearly not prepared to bring it out directly into the open. (He comments on the impropriety of doing such a thing in front of the vulgar public even with Fibich, in his Nejedlý review.) So he is one of those who thought it best to suppress the Stösslová documents, not indeed to pretend that the affair had not existed, but rather to maintain the typically fin-de-siècle dynamic of risky semi-concealment through which this whole construction functioned most effectively as a guarantee of manhood, of genius, and of Czech identity.

Leoš Janáček (*Památník pro Kamilu Stösslovou,* 1927–1928): The Muse Drawn from Art

When Janáček encountered Stösslová in 1917, he had already moved beyond Decadence; it is perhaps significant that in looking back to *Osud,* his principal Decadent work, he wrote of it in his autobiography of 1924 in gendered terms, thus distancing himself from it, as "sighing in tone, feminine in its diction."[106] And after the First World War, as we have seen, the Adulterous Muse topos had itself already begun to change in Czech literature, as had the Czech reception of Nietzsche that influenced it.[107] It could hardly remain in the Zeyer mold—indeed it could hardly survive—after the creation of figures like Helena Lindnerova, and subsequent constructions of Woman by fin-de-siècle Czech feminists, who were able to use Nietzsche's misogyny for their own purposes:

> Women have learned all too well from Nietzsche to believe in the omnipotence and justification of their demands and drives and are thus not in the least willing to sacrifice these demands and drives to any moral commandment.[108]

Yet Janáček's beliefs about Art and Life and the connections between them remained essentially unchanged for the rest of his life, so that any romantic liaison that he might enter upon subsequently was subject to substantial constraints. He could probably not have fallen in love with a thoroughly modern woman (although in this story the improbable constantly occurs); essentially, he continued to construct his ideal Muses, including Stösslová, as devoted women, in ways that were determined by the traditional literary topos—in other words, to construct Life according to models from Art, the converse of the "Naturalism" with which he constructed Art according to models from Life. It is not surprising, then, that his communications to Stösslová tend constantly to emphasize her status as an outsider combining unacceptability with enchantment, constructing her, whatever his (undoubtedly genuine) feeling for her, as an enchanting Jewess, an enchanting Gypsy, an enchanting negress—indeed an enchanting southern Muse; and she was—apparently fairly willingly—manipulated into adopting these constructed roles.[109] But his ability to see his Muse, conceived in this way, in a wide variety of literary models, from Tolstoy and Dostoevsky through to modern ones, Karel Čapek, Rudolf Těsnohlídek, and others, enabled him to maintain a fundamentally old-fashioned, fin-de-siècle aesthetic while making use of an unprecedentedly modernist musical style.

Once again, this extraordinary story does not end there, and a new combination of Art with Life emerged in 1927. During that year, the relationship between Janáček and Stösslová became more intimate, after a visit of his in April to Písek, where she lived. On 26 August, they first kissed, according to Janáček's recollection, and that month they made a pact to burn their letters. Janáček burned Stösslová's letters with many regretful tears. (A large number survive; Stösslová, in particular, did not quite keep her side of the bargain.) Perhaps as a result of this episode, the *Album* was started, a document that finally contained entries between 2 October 1927 and 10 August 1928.[110] Stösslová had persuaded her husband to buy the leather-bound volume preferred by Janáček, and he made entries in it each time he visited Písek. During Janáček's final illness in Hukvaldy, Stösslová brought it there, and one of the last entries is a codicil to his will made at Hukvaldy in her favor. Unlike the letters, the *Album* contains brief compositions (most left fragmentary) for a keyboard instrument, as well as speech melodies and fragments of song, and even the will concludes with an incomplete piece, "Čekám Tě!" (I am waiting for you!) None of the pieces lasts longer than a minute, and they are scarcely performable independently: in other words, they can hardly be accorded an aesthetic interpretation outside the context of the *Album*. Thus several performances of the whole *Album* have so far been undertaken in order to recover the pieces for a concert public. When this is done it has the effect of conferring on the *Album* the curious status of a (public) musical work rather than the (private) archival source it might seem on the surface, although it is clear that the relationship between public and private in a document of this sort is problematic.

The *Album* may also have been influenced by the long shadow of Nejedlý's writings. In 1927, Janáček himself acquired a copy of Nejedlý's edition of the Fibich diary and gave it to Kamila Stösslová to read. His letter of 13 December 1927 to Stösslová shows him, in the most delicate way, using it to manipulate her into her role as his Muse, and at the same time betraying his own anxieties by casting the self-sufficient Schulzová as a dowdy bluestocking (yet one of strange sexual power over a thoroughly masculine man), so as to forestall any possibility that Stösslová might attempt to emulate her and make the fatally easy transition from Muse to femme fatale:

It greatly cheered me that you're interested in Fibich and his Anežka. Whatever's very learned in the book, skip it. What's there that applies to us, remember it well and then tell me. Anežka must have had something strange in herself for a strong man like him, a big fine fellow, to fall for her. And you have strange charms within you with which you bind me to you. You haven't thrown a net around me; Anežka surely threw such an enormous net that he could not break out of it. I found the charm of a body and a natural soul, he found a frump and the grammar of words. He threw notes at a hump and sensuality, I would cover your beautiful waves of the Otava with melodies, your legs as swift as pikes, your mouth like a little window into the sanctuary where things are burning. Into your womb I'd put the most beautiful things that would ever occur to me.

I'd even make a joke of your flexible toes and your big toe.

But I'd not leave to the clutches of the common crowd the thing that would bind us irreversibly for ever. This is the way I'd do it—and will do it.[111]

The letter also shows him concerned that they should keep their affair safe from the eyes of the vulgar herd; this further links Nejedlý's publication of Fibich's intimate diary with Janáček's own amorous diary, since it will have reminded him of the possibility that scandal might "ruin" Kamila. Nejedlý in the book says this is what irresponsible Romantics are prepared to do to their women; and Janáček's *Album* contains a speech melody attributed to Kamila, with the phrase "Vy byste mě byl zničil!" (You would have ruined me!) In any case, that this possibility was in their minds is suggested by the episode with the burning of the letters.

The *Album*, then, became a quasi-artwork, the final manifestation of the Adulterous Muse in Czech music, with Life returning into Art for the last time. From the lovers' point of view, it would have seemed a more securely private codification of the shared moments that had hitherto been written down only in letters. And, very largely, this is the impression it projects. The successive dates are symbols of times spent together; the construction is that of a diary, so that they not only provide the structural outline but also apparently negate the possibility of the author's imposing any kind of nonchronological form on the material. The content appears to represent Janáček's actual words to Kamila; even the elements that go beyond the letters, the speech melodies, the inconsequential interpolations and the brief, fragmentary piano pieces, further build up this image of random, heartfelt immediacy.

But the narrative of the *Album* is in reality far from unmediated as a record of shared moments. Where Kamila speaks, it is effectively only via Janáček—as if through the medium of his notebook of speech melodies; yet several of these fragments of speech are not responses to previous remarks, and so they have a grotesque disconnectedness, reminiscent of some of the dialogue in *Osud* or, for that matter, *From the House of the Dead.*

Further, there is a shape to the narrative: at the beginning it is constructed as a public fiction; there is an implied third-party reader, who is not a voyeur so much as a potentially skeptical critic, and the narrative appears to question its own status as reality, as if it were preempting the accusations of a hostile public. The title page (signed by both Janáček and Kamila) apostrophizes this implied reader, whose sympathy cannot be taken for granted: "Tak čtěte, jak jsme si svůj život jen domýšleli, z celého srdce přáli!" (So read here how we have only worked out our life in our minds, wishing it from the bottom of our hearts!) In the first part of the diary, similar appeals to the reader occur when delicate matters are raised: "A zase si slibujeme, slibujeme ty děti—ale jen ty domyslené, ale tak živě domyslené—ach! rozuměj kdo čteš" (And again let us promise ourselves, promise ourselves those children—but only those imagined ones, but so vividly imagined—oh! understand, you who are reading.)

This narrational voice changes during the course of the *Album*, constructing a different, more neutral reader. In its central section the *Album* becomes the document of a private covenant, with the appeals to external witnesses effaced in favor of passionate, private (and be it said, distinctly manipulative) appeals to Kamila for her fidelity in this private covenant. Nevertheless, here too the music effaces the distinction between private and public, and thereby serves to seal the authenticity of the narration. That this is possible is, throughout, the result of the disagreement between words and music: considered on their merits as music, the pieces are obviously the work of a professional composer; considered on their merits as literature, the words often veer into kitsch, the work of a rank amateur; here again, the awkward disjunction of music and literature we noted above in *Osud* comes to the fore.

The *Album* concludes as a publicly attested covenant, in his will, which brings the public aspect of the beginning and the private aspect of the central narrative together in a highly public manner. So even in the codicil to the will, at the end of the *Album*, it is the piano piece "Čekám Tě" that authenticates it (effectively if not legally), rather than the composer's signature.

So the *Album*, with its semi-abolition of the listener, and its tiny, fragmented pieces, is the most radical realization imaginable in Art of the semipublic nature of the Adulterous Muse complex as it was inherited from the Decadents; it illustrates, in the clearest possible way, the radical overlapping of public and private spheres that this topos invites. So it is an extreme example of a characteristic method in which distinctive Czech modernism was created in music, and in which the national traditions in literature and music were seen to intersect in the first half of the twentieth century through the Decadent "explosion" of the relative coherence of the Romantics. But it is characteristic of the whole of Janáček's mature output, and of relevance to other composers as well; and in some ways, it indeed justifies the claim of Nejedlý in his Fibich monograph: that it is in works like these, reflecting the Adulterous Muse, capital *A*, capital *M,* that Czech modernism in music most fully encompasses the modernism of Czech literature and constructs itself as Czech.

NOTES

1. Jarmila Procházková, ed., *Památník pro Kamilu Stösslovou: Album for Kamila Stösslová* (Brno: Moravské muzeum, 1996); the translation is by John Tyrrell.

2. Marie Trkanová, *Paměti: Zdenka Janáčková—můj život* (Brno: Šimon Ryšavý, 1998); English translation in John Tyrrell, ed., *My Life with Janáček: The Memoirs of Zdenka Janáčková* (London: Faber and Faber, 1998).

3. Svatava Přibáňová, ed., *Hádanka života: dopisy Leoše Janáčka Kamile Stösslové* (Brno: Opus musicum, 1990); John Tyrrell, ed., *Intimate Letters: Leoš Janáček to Kamila Stösslová* (London: Faber and Faber, 1994).

4. The frequently quoted phrase occurs in the interview with Janáček published in *Literární svět* on 8 March 1928, of which an English translation is printed for example in Mirka Zemanová, ed., *Janáček's Uncollected Essays on Music* (London and New York: Marion Boyars, 1989), pp. 120–24.

5. Tyrrell, *Intimate Letters*, p. xi.

6. Michael Winkler, "Naturalism," in *The New Princeton Encyclopedia of Poetry and Poetics*, Alex Preminger, T. V. F. Brogan et al. (Princeton, N.J.: Princeton University Press, 1993), pp. 818–19.

7. Hippolyte Taine, *Essais de critique et d'histoire* (Paris: 1858). Taine famously outlines three principles for Naturalist writing: race or heredity, environment (milieu), and "moment"—the force of immediate circumstance.

8. Robert B. Pynsent, "Conclusory Essay: Decadence, Decay and Innovation," in *Decadence and Innovation: Austro-Hungarian Life and Art at the Turn of the Century*, ed. R. B. Pynsent (London: Weidenfeld and Nicolson, 1989), pp. 111–248, this quotation, p. 142. Compare Robert Vilain, "Temporary Aesthetes: Decadence and Symbolism in Germany and Austria," in *Symbolism, Decadence and the Fin de Siècle: French and European Perspectives*, ed. Patrick McGuinness (Exeter, Eng.: University of Exeter Press, 2000), pp. 209–24.

9. Przybyszewski, himself a Decadent writer, wrote first in German but also published some pieces in the Czech journal *Moderní revue*, corresponded with Czech Decadent writers such as Karásek and Hlaváček, and generally exerted a major influence on Czech Decadence. On the musical aspects of his writings, see especially Lukas Richter, "Zur Musikanschauung von Stanislaw Przybyszewski," *Deutsches Jahrbuch der Musikwissenschaft*, year 18 (= *Jahrbuch der Musikbibliothek Peters*, year 65) (1973–1977), pp. 59–79.

10. "Die Wohltat, die Wagner Schopenhauer verdankt, ist unermeßlich. Erst der *Philosoph der décadence* gab dem Künstler der *décadence sich selbst.* . . ." Friedrich Nietzsche, "Der Fall Wagner: Ein Musikanten-Problem," in *Friedrich Nietzsche: Werke in drei Bänden*, ed. Karl Schlechta (Munich: Carl Hanser, n.d.), vol. 2, pp. 901–38; this passage, p. 911.

11. Ibid., p. 917.

12. One should add that the converse might also be Decadent, the concentration on formal perfection at the expense of content; so modern "formalism" is from at least one point of view closely related to modern "formlessness."

13. See T. G. Masaryk, *Česká otázka*, in *T. G. Masaryk: Česká otázka, O naší nynější krizi, Jan Hus*, Knihy pro každého, year 3, vols. 1–2, ed. Zdeněk Franta, (Prague: Státní nakladatelství, 1924), p. 176ff. But I take my cue from Winkler ("Naturalism," p. 818): "There are advantages to retaining an essential distinction between realism and n[aturalism] and to accepting the Ger[man] trad[ition] of using the former to denote a way of looking at things artistically, and the latter a literary movement."

14. Miloš Štědroň, *Leoš Janáček a hudba 20. století: (Leoš Janáček and twentieth-century music)* (Brno: Nadace Universitas Masarykiana, Nakladatelství Georgetown, Nakladatelství Nauma and Masarykova univerzita, 1998).

15. Roman Jakobson, "O realismu v umění," *Červen* 4, (1924): 300–304, quoted in *Roman Jakobson: Poetická funkce*, ed. Miroslav Červenka, (Jinočany: H&H, 1995), pp. 138–44. I owe this reference to the kind suggestion of Štěpán Kaňa.

16. Compare the secret program of Berg's Lyric Suite, comprehensively discussed in George Perle, *Style and Idea in the Lyric Suite of Alban Berg* (Stuyvesant, N.Y.: Pendragon Press, 1995).

17. For a useful introduction to this topic, see Robert B. Pynsent, "Conclusory Essay: Decadence, Decay and Innovation" (cited in n. 8); on the construction of Czechness in music, see in particular Michael Beckerman, "In Search of Czechness in Music," *Nineteenth-Century Music* X, no. 1 (1986–1987): 61–73.

18. Oscar Wilde, "The Decay of Lying: a Dialogue," *The Nineteenth Century: A Monthly Review* 25 (January–June 1889): 35–56, later published in *Intentions* (1891).

19. I should like to acknowledge the help of Robert Pynsent in suggesting key texts from Czech fin-de-siècle literature that exemplify the topos; the opinions expressed about these texts are, of course, my own.

20. *Jan Maria Plojhar* was first published in installments throughout vol. 16 of *Lumír* (1888) and was published by Otto in their series Salónní bibliotéka as a book in 1891; for the 1891 edition, Zeyer restored some phrases that had been altered in deference to censorship. The second edition (Prague: Šimáček, 1900–1901), with some further alterations, was published as part of the collected edition of Zeyer's works while the author was still alive, but so ill as not to have played a part in correcting proofs. Rudolf Skřeček re-edited the book as Julius Zeyer, *Jan Maria Plojhar* (Prague: Státní nakladatelství krásné literatury a umění, 1964). Although this is not a critical edition in the full sense, the editor claims to be restoring the 1891 text (see his editorial note, pp. 311–12), and page numbers quoted in footnotes here refer to this 1964 edition.

21. Though Zeyer is often regarded (as a German-speaking author writing in Czech) as outside the Czech tradition proper, he became an influential figure in Czech literature; on him, and on Czech Decadence, see especially Robert B. Pynsent, *Julius Zeyer: The Path to Decadence*, Slavistic Printings and Reprintings, ed. C. H. van Schooneveld, vol. 290 (The Hague and Paris: Mouton, 1973), and on Central European Decadence more broadly, the same author's "Conclusory Essay: Decadence, Decay and Innovation" (cited in n. 8).

22. Zeyer, *Jan Maria Plojhar*, p. 61: "smrtonosná siréna."

23. Ibid; p. 66: "až k smrti raněn, oloupen o nejkrásnější iluze."

24. Ibid; p. 135: "Mezitím začala hudba hráti, španělský, snivý a ohnivý zároveň její kolorit působil mu sladkou, smyslnou rozkoš, smíšenou s jakousi melancholií. Bylo to kouzlo jako páry hašiše."

25. Nietzsche, "Der Fall Wagner," p. 905: Und wirklich schien ich mir jedesmal, daß ich *Carmen* hörte, mehr Philosoph, ein besserer Philosoph, als ich sonst mir scheine: so

langmutig geworden, so glücklich, so indisch, so *seßhaft*. . . . Fünf Stunden Sitzen: erste Etappe der Heiligkeit!

I am not suggesting, however, that Nietzsche was not concerned to overcome Decadence in art. For Nietzsche's phrase "il faut méditerraniser la musique" and his use of *Carmen* to exemplify it, see ibid., pp. 906ff. See also Nelly Furman, "The Languages of Love in *Carmen*," in *Reading Opera*, ed. Arthur Groos and Roger Parker, (Princeton, N.J.: Princeton University Press, 1988), pp. 168–83, which takes Nietzsche rather one-dimensionally: "The sentimental relationship represented in Wagner's *Flying Dutchman* is, according to Nietzsche, essentially a product of culture, while the passionate feelings expressed by Carmen and José are truer to nature" (p. 170).

26. On the contemporary reception of Bizet see Susan McClary, *Georges Bizet: Carmen*, (Cambridge, Eng.: Cambridge Opera Handbooks, 1992), chap. 6, pp. 111–29. McClary shows that the French were more aware of the Wagnerian undertones of the work than the Viennese were.

27. Zeyer, *Jan Maria Plojhar*, p. 146: Milovat nemocného je také jakousi monstruozitou. Chápu tu velkou dámu v středověku, o které jsem slyšela, že se poddala malomocnému. Jaké kouzlo, rvát se o něj se smrtí! Une danse macabre! . . . Ó to bude něco nového, posud nepocítěného!

28. Ibid., p. 100: "Dobrá Gemma byla spíše předmětem než osobou, třeba květem."

29. The story is found in the Katha Upanishad; Zeyer's version in *Jan Maria Plojhar* is at pp. 113–16 and pp. 127–29.

30. Zeyer, *Jan Maria Plojhar*, p. 106: "Šla za ním do stínu a tmy dobrovolně, obětovala se, zemřela s ním."

31. Leopold Andrian, *Der Garten der Erkenntnis* (Frankfurt a. M.: S. Fischer, 1970): The young, tubercular aristocrat, who is the hero and is just as passive as Plojhar, dies young, "ohne erkannt zu haben" (final sentence of the novel, p. 58), but not before "es schien ihm die königliche Verschwendung des Daseins und die unsagbare Erhabenheit der Seele in … [einsamen] Begegnungen zu liegen; es war wunderschön, daß der einsame Tod, welcher das Leben ist, uns nicht verhindern kann, eine fremde Schönheit, die wir nicht verstehn, die sich uns nicht enthüllen und uns nichts geben wird, nur weil sie schön ist, zu bewundern; es war wunderschön, daß wir, obwohl Menschen, dennoch Künstler sind, Künstler wieder darin, daß wir nicht einmal klagen, wenn uns diese Schönheit entgleitet, sondern sie grüßen und über sie jubeln, weil uns ein Schauspiel mehr wie unser Schicksal ist" (p. 38). The novel, and its new narrative style, were admired by Hugo von Hofmannsthal and Stefan George among others.

32. Otakar Auředníček, *Malířské novelly* (Prague: Fr. A. Urbánek, 1892).

33. In part these go back, no doubt, to the tradition exemplified in Henry Murger's short stories published between 1845 and 1849 and reworked in the five-act play *La vie de Bohème* (Paris, 1849), the source also for Puccini's *La Bohème* of 1896; see also the reference to Murger below in the discussion of Jaroslav Kvapil's *Bludička*.

34. Auředníček, *Malířské novelly*, p. 13: "Cítil jsem v té době umělecké inspirace, tak nesmírné, že jsem byl neschopen je vyjádřiti. . . ."

35. Ibid., p. 19: "Cos to vyvedl? zastenala. Ty mě zničíš! A počala plakat."

36. Ibid., p. 48: Břetislav Hampl byl mužem, jehož obličej by mohl povrchní pozorovatel nazvati krásným, neboť jeho tahy byly klasicky pravidelné, smyslná ústa měla ušlechtilý, něžný tvar a hnědý, lesklý vlas splýval v geniálních prsténcích kolem jeho skrání. Ale obličeji tomu scházela duše; byla to ozdobná maska, jejíž velké, krásné modré oči byly též bez života a zíraly lhostejně do světa. . . . V jeho bezvadném oděvu bylo lze pozorovati až komickou titěrnost a samolibost.

37. Pynsent, *Julius Zeyer* (cited in n. 21), p. 172.

38. Auředníček, *Malířské novelly*, p. 49: Ona položila jemně svou hlavu jemu na ramena a její jemné, chvějící se nozdry vdechovaly s rozkoší modravé obláčky vonného kouře, které vypouštěl z úst.

39. Compare the use of the same motif in the Austrian composer Franz Schreker's opera *Die Gezeichneten* (Frankfurt, 1918, to his own libretto, which had been requested by Zemlinsky before Schreker decided to set it himself). The hero, Alviano, a crippled aristocrat, poses for Carlotta, a talented painter, and it is her declaration of love that evokes from him the ecstatic expression that will make the painting a masterpiece. Though she is no chocolate-box painter, she turns out not to be serious about him as her Muse, even when about to die; and the Italian Renaissance setting also indicates that this is another branch of contemporary Decadence, though not without its parallels in the Czech sphere.

40. Jaroslav Kvapil, *Bludička: Drama o čtyřech dějstvích* (Prague: F. Topič, 1896).

41. *Bludička*, p. 22. See n. 33 on Murger.

42. The traditional practice, though already being questioned by some academics at the time, is followed in the quotations here, with feminine surnames distinguishing between -*ova* (treated and declined as a possessive adjective) for unmarried women, and -*ová* (treated and declined as a normal adjective) for married women.

43. Kvapil, *Bludička*, p. 16.

44. See Robert Pynsent, "Conclusory Essay: Decadence, Decay and Innovation" (cited in n. 8), pp. 152–53, for illuminating remarks on the differences between Decadence and Naturalism; he asserts, "Naturalists and Decadents are concerned both with decay and with the part man has played in causing decay. As long as one is speaking about serious literature. . . . I believe one will barely be able to distinguish between Naturalism and Decadence in Austria-Hungary. Except in one point: a Naturalist work will usually have a conscious message. Perhaps Naturalism is frequently little more than Decadence with a message" (p. 153). Perhaps, then, *Bludička* is really Naturalist.

45. Kvapil, *Bludička*, pp. 66–67.

46. Ibid., p. 23: Odpust'te, pánové—ale vaše moderní umění je pro nás, obyčejné smrtelníky, příliš těžké a záhadné."

47. Ibid., p. 24.

48. And his name is significant—"*ne doma,*" (not at home.)

49. Kvapil, *Bludička*, pp. 48–49.

50. Ibid., p. 50.

51. Ibid., p. 40: "Z vás se tedy stává nikoli moderní, ale módní umělec?!"

52. Ibid., p. 48.

53. Ibid., p. 99.

54. Ibid., p. 54.

55. Ibid., p. 91.

56. Ibid., p. 72–74.

57. Ibid., p. 90: "Celá naše společnost je takovou tržnicí o několika měnách".

58. Ibid., p. 112: "To víš—ženská!"

59. Ibid., p. 28.

60. Emanuel šl. z Lešehradu, *Shroucení: Lyrická scéna o jednom dějství* (Prague: [The Author], 1904).

61. Nietzsche, "Der Fall Wagner," p. 909: "Was wird aus dem 'ewigen Juden,' den ein Weib anbetet und *festmacht?* Er hört bloß auf, ewig zu sein; er verheiratet sich, er geht uns nichts mehr an.—Ins Wirkliche übersetzt: die Gefahr der Künstler, der Genies—und das sind ja die 'ewigen Juden'—liegt im Weibe: die *anbetenden* Weiber sind ihr Verderb."

62. Lešehradu, *Shroucení*, p. 14: "Co platno mi vše umění, / když celý život přemění / v pekelný jícen tragický? . . . / Ó, prokleto buď' na vždycky!"

63. Ibid.

64. Lothar Suchý, *Sláva: Drama o třech dějstvích*, in Repertoir českých divadel, vol. 130 (Prague: F. Šimáček, 1905).

65. Ibid., pp. 31–32: "Kdo by si byl pomyslil, že taková dramata mohou vynášet téměř tolik, jako moje šunky."

66. Ibid., p. 39: "Není to tak bezprostřední ... tak naivně silné a neurvalé. . . . je na tom vidět práci!"

67. Ibid., p. 42.

68. Ibid., p. 59.

69. Originally a trade name for "a toxic white powder, $C_{11}H_{12}N_2O$, formerly used to reduce fever and relieve pain." *American Heritage Dictionary of the English Language*, 4th ed. (2000).

70. In this scene, a classic solo melodrama, Suchý might be said to prefigure the psychologizing interest in depicting unstable heroes of later Czech authors such as Egon Hostovský or Václav Řezáč.

71. Suchý, *Sláva*, p. 19.

72. Ibid., pp. 16–18: "Nevěra jest hlubší nežli víra."

73. Ibid., p. 21: "Jak krásně mluvíš! Jak tě miluji! Ale já chci, by naše láska byla čistá . . . klidná . . . vzdálena hříchu . . . hříchu každého . . . !"

74. Ibid., p. 73: "Ty sama mi chceš dáti jed? Ó, jak jsi dobrá."

75. Ibid., p. 76: "A já ti sama jed ten podala."

76. J. B. Foerster, *Nepřemožení: Zpěvohra o čtyřech dějstvích, op. 100* (Vienna and Leipzig: Universal Edition, 1918); for summary of the plot and commentary, see Josef Hutter and Zdeněk Chalabala, eds., *České umění dramatické: Zpěvohra* (Prague: Šolc a Šimáček, 1941), pp. 245–48.

77. Karel Matěj Čapek-Chod, *Antonín Vondrejc: Příběhové básníka*, 8th ed., Česká klasická próza, ed. Marie Liehmová (Prague: Odeon, 1971), p. 194: "Může být něco úžasnějšího, senzitivnějšího nad tento román žíznivé a neukojitelné lásky, kterou pociťuje jeho pianista angažovaný z páté čtvrti k mladičké komtese, aby jí ve hře na klavír šlapal pedál? Už tato invence o něžné nádherné zlatoplavé krasavici [. . .], vážnivé mistryně Lisztova nástroje, které musí pedál šlapat konzervatorista! Pánové, ta rafinovanost těch dlouhých půldnů lásky, jež dovolují oběma mladým lidem prožívati v úplném bezpečí, že se nemůže nic stát! Pánové, neznám šílenějších senzací v žádné literatuře—a v literaturách jsem obeznámen—nad stránky Faladova 'Tantala,' když Stryjski přinese své vlastní skladby, když oba nevidí jiného východiště ze své krize než společnou smrt a když spanilého Stryjského ještě před katastrofou vyženou proto, že se na něho prozradilo, že je vlastně původem polský žid! A jak svá tantalovská muka ukončí, slitovav se nad opovrženou dcerou židovského umývače mrtvol, která jej dávno zbožňuje a kterou objímá v překrásné autosugesci, že v náručí chová vlastně svou komtesu!"

78. The opera remains so far unpublished, except for rental scores. For details of sources, the circumstances leading to its composition and revisions, earlier versions of the title, further bibliography, etc., see Nigel Simeone, John Tyrrell, and Alena Němcová, *Janáček's Works: A Catalogue of the Music and Writings of Leoš Janáček* (Oxford: Clarendon Press, 1997), no. I/5, pp. 18–25. For recent comment, see John Tyrrell, "Czech Opera," in *National Traditions of Opera,* ed. John Warrack (Cambridge: Cambridge University Press, 1988), pp. 123–24; Štědroň, *Leoš Janáček a hudba 20. století* (cited in n. 14), passim.

79. They are best followed in John Tyrrell, *Janáček's Operas: A Documentary Account* (London: Faber and Faber, 1992), pp. 108–60.

80. It is somehow typical of the whole Adulterous Muse complex that Čelanský himself was envisaged as the conductor of the performance of *Osud* planned (but not realized) at the Vinohrady Theatre in Prague in 1907.

81. See Bohumír Štědroň, "K Janáčkově opeře Osud," *Živá hudba*, vol. 1 (1959), pp. 169, 174; John Tyrrell, *Janáček's Operas: A Documentary Account* (quoted in n. 79), p. 113:

"Chci míti tedy I. jednání zcela realistické, odkresleno ze života lázeňského. Tam jest motivů bohatost!

"II. jednání má býti vlastně *přelud*. Není tu skutečnosti více, ale do prasknutí nervů podrážděná mysl vede děj dále tak, že nastává rozpor, jest to skutečnost neb halucinace, přelud?

"Jest-li byla I. jednání scenerie lázně nádherné, tož v II. jednání má ukazovati přepych interieru dámských pokojů, scenerii jižních krajin.

"III. jednání bude divné. [. . .] Elévi hádají se o opeře. Bylo-li druhé jednání skutečností neb vybájené, pak tu byla přímo choroba duševní. Jest to z uměleckého života."

82. The name Míla Válková is of course an abbreviation of Kamila Urválková, as the name Lenský for the composer in the opera-within-the-opera is an abbreviation of Čelanský.

83. "Les s echem je duše naše." The allusions to echoes, incidental in the original libretto, were built up by Janáček as an important thread in Act 2. Several of them are suppressed in the bouncy English translation used for the Welsh National Opera recording: this translation may streamline the admittedly problematic dramaturgy, but it loses a good deal of the dreamlike allusiveness of the original conception, turning 1880s Luhačovice at times into a hearty 1940s British seaside resort.

84. Zan is, in other words, "Jean": French servants represent success among bourgeois Czechs of this period. The original speech melody on which this line was based had "Johan" for this name. The name Nána may represent an echo of *nyanya*, the Russian word used for Tatyana's nurse in *Yevgeny Onegin*.

85. This version is reflected in the 1964 rental vocal score: Leoš Janáček, *Osud: Opera o předehře, dvou dějstvích a dohře v úpravě Kurta Honolky* (Prague: Dilia, 1964); a copy is available in the British Library.

86. "Tak nové!"; "Pro velké, i pražské publikum." See Theodora Straková, "Janáčková opera Osud," *Časopis Moravského muzea, Social Sciences* 41 (1956): 216; John Tyrrell, *Janáček's Operas: A Documentary Account* (cited in n. 79), p. 123.

87. See Štědroň, "K Janáčkově opeře Osud" (cited in n. 81), pp. 167–68; Tyrrell, *Janáček's Operas: A Documentary Account* (cited in n. 79), p. 112: "Teď bych si přál libreto svěží, moderní, překypující životem a elegancí—tak "román dítěte" času našeho. Ach, kdo mi ho napíše. Tak bych měl plno detailů: povídají, že umím i perem vládnout—ale bojím se mezi literáty."

88. See his letter of 12 November 1903 to Bartošová: Tyrrell, *Janáček's Operas: A Documentary Account* (cited in n. 79), p. 116.

89. "Samá nota, samé kousky nápěvné z mluvy a řečí zaslechnutých." See Štědroň, "K Janáčkově opeře Osud" (cited in n. 81), p. 169ff; Tyrrell, *Janáček's Operas: A Documentary Account* (cited in n. 79), pp. 109–110.

90. "Osměluji se Vás žádat, abyste mi umožnil poslechnouti si choromyslné ženského ústavu pražského.

"Účel mám dvojí: jednak jde mi o melodii mluvy choromyslných vůbec, jednak hledám zvláštní případ, kde byla příčinou lakota onemocnční.

"Bohatá vdova nechtěla vydat dceru svoji za "žebráka" umělce. Když k sňatku přece došlo, zešílela. Bála se, aby nebyla okradena i o schránku se skvosty.

"Jednou při útěku seskočila se schodiště a zabila se.

"Ťoť v krátkosti typ, který jest řídký snad; nenalezl jsem jej ani v brněnském ústavu choromyslných."

Janáček Archive, MS A 3319, Brno, Moravian Museum, previously unpublished. I owe the transcription to the kindness of Štěpán Kaňa; translation published in Tyrrell, *Janáček's Operas: A Documentary Account* (cited in n. 79), p. 129. The rationale for the mad scene and, for example, the use in the action of the jewel box, may be fairly clear in this letter, but it is hardly realized in the opera, where Janáček as usual juxtaposes disparate images in surreal and powerful fashion.

91. Nejedlý's views on this subject had appeared earlier in his *Česká moderní zpěvohra po Smetanovi* (Prague: J. Otto, 1911), but may be conveniently taken from this review: Zdeněk Nejedlý, "Leoše Janáčka Její pastorkyňa," *Hudební knihovna časopisu "Smetana,"* 22 (Prague: Melantrich, 1916).

92. Nejedlý, *Leoše Janáčka Její pastorkyňa* (cited in n. 90), p. 6: "My dnes nazveme si tento názor *naturalistickým*, poněvadž vychází z předpokladu, že do umění lze vnášeti prostě skutečné, přirozené tvary, jak je život podává, a tím že pak i umělecké dílo stává se přirozeným, pravdivým—starý omyl všeho naturalismu, nedoceňující význam aktivního tvoření uměleckého, jež teprve oživuje všechen mrtvý materiál přirozený."

93. Ibid., p. 11.

94. Josef Bartoš, "O proudech v soudobé hudbě," *Knihovna Okresního sboru osvětového ve Kdyni* 3 (Kdyně: Okresní sbor osvětový ve Kdyni, 1924).

95. Brno, Janáček Archives, MS S.72–73, published in Štědroň, *Leoš Janáček a hudba 20. století* (cited in n. 14), pp. 241–47. This document, which is included in English translation in Part II of this volume, is fundamental to an understanding of Janáček's conception of program music.

96. See Ludvík Kundera, "Janáček ve světle nové hudby," *Hudební rozhledy* I, nos. 2–3 (1948), pp. 35–36 (the journal had been recently revised as the organ of the Union of Czechoslovak Composers and Musicologists, which functioned along the lines of its Soviet equivalent).

97. Zdeněk Nejedlý, *Zdenka Fibicha milostný deník: Nálady dojmy a upomínky* (Prague: Hudební Matice Umělecké Besedy, 1925), reprinted as "*Zdeněk Nejedlý: Zdeňka Fibicha milostný deník*," ed. Václav Pekárek, *Sebrané spisy Zdeňka Nejedlého* 20 (Prague: Melantrich, 1949).

98. Ludvík Boháček, ed., "Anežka Schulzová: Zdenko Fibich, hrstka upomínek a intimních rysů," *Knihovna Společnosti Zdeňka Fibicha*, vol. 3 (Prague: Orbis, 1950), p. 19: "Fibich choval nepřekonatelný odpor ke všem krajnostem moderních směrů, jak v hudbě, tak v literatuře a v uměních výtvarných. Odpor ten stupňoval se až k despektu vůči významu moderního umění."

99. Nejedlý, *Zdenka Fibicha milostný deník*, p. 255.

100. Kundera, *Hudební rozhledy* 2 (1925–1926), pp. 99–101, 117–18, reprinted in ed. František Hrabal, *Vladimír Helfert: Vybrané studie I., O hudební tvořivosti* (Prague: Supraphon, 1970), pp. 73–83.

101. "Lze věřit v takovou uměleckou a estetickou naivnost Fibichovu?. . . Vždyť v tom by byla taková dekadence, tak krutý zlom tvůrčí individuality, že by to daleko překonalo dosavadní mé přesvědčení o tom, že Fibichovo období s Anežkou Schulzovou je dobou přelomu Fibichova vývoje uměleckého!" This passage is quoted from Ibid., *Vladimír Helfert: Vybrané studie I.*, p. 76; for his verdict on Fibich in the monograph, see Vladimír Helfert, "Česká moderní hudba: Studia o české hudební tvořivosti, *Knihovna Tempa* 1 (Prague:

Tempo, 1937): 38: "[Fibich] nakonec se zcela oddal čistě romantickému subjektivismu, jsa v tom věrným členem své romantické a dekadentně nalomené generace (Fibich finally yielded totally to pure Romantic subjectivism, being in this a faithful member of his Romantic and Decadently impaired generation)."

102. Compare the essays collected in Rudolf Stephan, *Vom musikalischen Denken: Gesammelte Vorträge*, ed. Rainer Damm and Andreas Traub (Mainz: Schott, 1985); for the eighteenth-century prehistory of the concept, see Adolf Nowak, "Der Begriff 'Musikalisches Denken' in der Musiktheorie der Aufklärung," in *Neue Musik und Tradition: Festschrift Rudolf Stephan zum 65. Geburtstag*, ed. Josef Kuckertz, Helga de la Motte-Haber et al. (Laaber: Laaber-Verlag, 1990), pp. 113–22.

103. Helfert, *Česká moderní hudba* (cited above, n. 100), p. 45: "Zvláště jeho výrazovost a jeho subjektivní erotismus má mnoho romantických prvků. Ale to vše se týče spíše inspiračního zdroje. Jakmile však z tohoto zdroje vyvře nějaká hudební myšlenka, ihned ztrácí charakter romantický. Neboť Janáček své hudební inspirace nestylisuje a neidealisuje po způsobu romantickém. . . . Exponuje motivy v jejich syrovém stavu, zmocní se jich prudce jako své nejvlastnější hudební reality. Již tímto charakterem svých hudebních myšlenek je Janáček novým zjevem v naší hudbě—představitelem hudebního realismu."

104. Ibid., p. 47.

105. Ibid., p. 50: "K tomu pak přistupovala i novost jeho komposičního směru, jenž byl přijímán v Praze s nedůvěrou, jako pouhá svéhlavá zvláštnost; je to pochopitelné, neboť v Praze, odchované stylem klasickým a romantickým, nemohl být naráz pochopen styl tak nový a netradiční, jako byl Janáčkův."

106. Tyrrell, *Janáček's Operas: A Documentary Account* (cited in n. 79), p. 109.

107. The process is followed through in Urs Heftrich, "The Early Czech Nietzsche Reception: T. G. Masaryk, O. Březina, F. X. Šalda," in *East Europe Reads Nietzsche*, ed. Alice Freifeld, Peter Bergmann, and Bernice Glatzer Rosenthal (Boulder, Colo.: East European Monographs, and New York: Columbia University Press, 1998), pp. 107–44.

108. Juliana Lancová, "Nietzsche a ženy: volná úvaha," *Ženský obzor* 7 (1907–1908): 36, quoted from Heftrich, (cited in n. 107), p. 114. I have not been able to secure access to the original text.

109. However, his recollection in 1925 of their first meeting in 1917 was that he had seen her sitting on the grass and that his opening gambit had been, "You must be a Jewess!"; her recollection in the same year was that she would have preferred not to reply. Moreover, Stösslová's son in old age recalled to John Tyrrell (private communication) that the almost daily arrival of missives from the maestro was generally greeted with impatience by his mother—though he may have been influenced in his recollection by the fact that presents for himself were seldom forthcoming from Janáček.

110. Procházková, ed., *Památník pro Kamilu Stösslovou* (cited in n. 1).

111. Přibáňová, *Hádanka života* (cited in n. 3), letter 534, p. 264; Tyrrell, *Intimate Letters* (cited in n. 3), pp. 161–62: "Těšilo mne nesmírně, že se zajímáš o Fibicha a jeho Anežku. Co bude v knize moc učené, přeskoč. Co tam bude, co se na nás hodí, to si dobře zapamatuj a mi potom pověz. Musela mít Anežka něco v sobě divného, že on silák, velký pěkný člověk, jí podlehnul. A Ty máš v sobě kouzla divná, kterými mne k sobě vážeš. Ty, sítě jsi nevyhodila na mne, Anežka jistě tak obrovskou vyhodila, že ji roztrhat nemohl. Já půvab těla našel a přirozenou duši, on šeredu a gramatiku slova. On házel noty na hrb a smyslnost, já melodií bych přikryl ty Tvoje krásné vlnky Otavy, Tvou nožku hbitou tak ty štiky, Tvá ústa jako okýnka do svatyně, v kterých to hoří. V Tvůj život vložil bych, co mi nejkrásnějšího kdy mohlo napadnout.

"I žert bych udělal s Tvými ohebnými prstíčky i s tím paleček na Tvé nožce.

"Ale všednímu davu nedal bych napospas, co by nás nezvratně navždy spojilo. Tak bych já to udělal—a udělám."

A Turk and a Moravian in Prague:

Janáček's *Brouček* and the

Perils of Musical Patriotism

Derek Katz

Leoš Janáček's *The Excursions of Mr. Brouček* is a decidedly odd work. The excursions in question take the title character through both space and time. Mr. Brouček is first sent to the moon, where he shocks the ethereal local Lunarians with his crass eating habits, and then back to the fifteenth century, where he proves himself a coward in battle. Even in the context of Janáček's better-known operas, whose protagonists include singing animals, immortal sopranos, and infanticides, this stands out as peculiar. *Brouček* has also been the subject of some unfortunately memorable invective. The baritone Václav Novák, for instance, who created the part of the innkeeper Würfl, claimed that the part would ruin his voice, and fumed that he was not going to "throw all that [he] had learned with such difficulty . . . for the sake of someone who has only to sit down and write notes easily with his pen, who is probably mad and does not care in the least whether his notes are singable or not."[1] Even Max Brod, Janáček's translator and biographer, described the opera as "a grotesque that chokes on its own excesses."[2]

Despite all this, when Janáček took his seat in the Prague National Theatre for the April 23, 1920, opening of *The Excursions of Mr. Brouček*, he had every reason to believe that he was about to complete his elevation from a provincial Moravian chorus master to an opera composer of international stature. Although the 1916 Prague premiere of *Jenůfa* had been much delayed and fraught with controversy, *Jenůfa*'s eventual success had created a demand for Janáček's work. Even before *Brouček* opened, three publishers had fought for the rights to the new opera, with Universal Edition winning out over Prague's Hudební matice and Berlin's Drei Masken-Verlag.[3]

The *Brouček* premiere came not only at a propitious point in Janáček's career but also at a critical juncture in the history of the Czech lands. With the collapse of the Habsburg Empire at the end of the First World War, an independent Czechoslovak Republic had existed for a year and a half. Janáček was now not only a Czech composer but also a Czech citizen. For the second of Mr. Brouček's excursions, Janáček chose a suitably patriotic subject, the Battle of Vítkov Hill, in the hopes of celebrating a new Czech state by evoking the one great military triumph in Czech history. Despite Janáček's well-founded optimism, *Brouček* was not a success. Janáček left Prague after the premiere, returning to Brno without seeing the second performance, or even waiting for the (indifferent) reviews. He might not have been so hasty had he realized how scarce opportunities would be to see the opera. *Brouček* only lasted a year in the National Theater repertoire, and was not given a new production until 1948. The only other production during Janáček's lifetime was in Brno in 1926, but even in his hometown he did not hear the second excursion, which was omitted.[4]

Brouček's failure to thrive is easy to explain. Janáček had hoped that the fifteenth century setting of Brouček's second excursion would stir audiences on the brink of political independence. In a letter written during the composition of the second excursion, Janáček referred to the fifteenth century as "the most sacred period for every Czech."[5] While soliciting a libretto from F. S. Procházka, he wrote "A new time is coming, it's just around the corner, and [it would be wonderful] to place it before a pure mirror at Vítkov."[6]

Brouček, though, would not see a flattering reflection of himself. In the same letter to Procházka, Janáček declared that "our small-mindedness is embodied in Brouček,"[7] and later wrote in a *Lidové noviny* feuilleton, "We see many Broučeks in our nation...I would like such a person to be disgusting to us."[8] Janáček also compared Brouček to the indolent protagonist of Ivan Goncharov's *Oblomov*, suggesting that "we see as many Broučeks amongst our people as there are Oblomovs amongst the Russians."[9] The simplest explanation for Brouček's woes is that a satire was not a timely gesture. In addition, Janáček may have held up a mirror to his time more effectively than he realized. The Brouček affair betrays conflicts between Janáček's national and regional identities, between Czech national rhetoric and demographic realities, and between nationalist musical symbols and operatic tradition.

Hussites

The Battle of Vítkov Hill took place on July 14, 1420. The hill, which provided access to Prague from the east, was invaded by a crusader army of mixed nationality (including Germans, Austrians, Hungarians, and royalist Czechs) led by King Sigismund, the same Sigismund responsible for Jan Hus's execution five years earlier.[10] Sigismund's army was repelled by a Hussite army, under the command of the one-eyed Taborite general Jan Žižka. After this victory, Žižka's forces continued on to capture the Prague strongholds at the Vyšehrad garrison and the Hradčany castle. These Hussite victories eventually led to the installation of a Czech king, Jiří z Poděbrad in 1458, and a period of Czech autonomy that lasted until Bohemia became part of the Habsburg empire in 1526. The nineteenth-century national rebirth movement would look back on the Hussite era as a source of national pride, and glorified everything connected with the triumph at Vítkov Hill.

One of the reasons the battle was such a powerful and enduring symbol was that it could be easily reinterpreted in different ideological contexts. Before the nineteenth century, it was seen as a religious conflict, between Catholics and Protestant Hussites. For nineteenth-century nationalists, attempting to construct a politically viable community of Czech speakers, the battle was a revolt by Czechs for the right to worship and, by extension, participate in civic life, in the vernacular. Toward the end of the Habsburg era, patriots framed it as a national struggle, with loyal Czechs defending their native Prague against German and Austrian interlopers. The fact that Žižka defended Vítkov with a peasant army was useful to Marxist historiographers, who saw a proletarian rebellion against the aristocracy and urban elites.[11] A 1904 drawing of Žižka's army by Mikoláš Aleš contains a typical profusion of symbols. The religious dimension is represented in the drawing by bread and wine. The Hussites, although not Hus himself, insisted on communion of both kinds for all. Žižka is led by a priest carrying bread in a monstrance and followed by a man with a banner depicting a chalice. For good measure, Aleš throws in another chalice, on a shield in the lower right-hand corner. Despite these references to Hussite dogma, it is the military man Žižka, mounted on a white charger and presented as completely blind, with a bandage over his eyes, who occupies the middle of the composition. The peasants that follow him carry as weapons farm implements, including flails, emphasizing the rural origins of the army. Many of these elements are encountered by Janáček's Brouček on his trip to Vítkov.

Aleš also included a musical allusion in his drawing. Both the words and music for the Hussite battle hymn "Ye who are God's warriors" ("Kdož jste boží bojovníci") are inscribed in the lower half of the picture. This hymn was easily the most potent aural symbol for Hussite glory. When the Prague National Theater opened in 1883, the first music to be heard was Bedřich Smetana's opera *Libuše*. The opera concludes with a series of tableaux, each depicting a great moment in Czech history, as foretold by the prophetess *Libuše*. The fourth of these visions is of the noble Hussites, led by Žižka. Significantly, Smetana's librettist, Josef Wenzig, chose Žižka rather than Hus himself to represent the Hussite era, thereby emphasizing military prowess over religious affiliation. As Libuše exclaims that the peasant armies will mow down enemies of the people as easily as they harvest wheat, the same Hussite war song depicted in Aleš's drawing rings out from the orchestra pit.

This hymn is also the main thematic material for the last two tone poems from Smetana's *Má vlast*, "Tábor" and "Blaník." The potency of this musical symbol was lost neither upon the Nazis, who banned performances of those tone poems in occupied Czechoslovakia, nor upon the makers of the Oscar-winning film *Kolya*, who used this same music to accompany a montage of footage from the 1989 Velvet Revolution. Following Smetana's lead, Antonín Dvořák used the battle chant in his *Hussite* Overture, also written for the inaugural season of the National Theater. When Dvořák died, Janáček was in Warsaw, considering the directorship of the Warsaw Conservatory. He attended the Warsaw Philharmonic concert that evening, to which the Hussite Overture had been added to commemorate Dvořák's death.[12] Dvořák's son-in-law and favorite pupil, Josef Suk, also used the song, albeit in a slightly less recognizable version, as the main theme of his symphonic poem, *Praga* (1904).

Even after the establishment of the Czechoslovak Republic, "Ye who are God's warriors" remained an emblem of resistance both in the Czech lands and near it. Karl Amadeus Hartmann's 1939 *Concerto funèbre* paraphrases the hymn in its introductory movement, and the song was also deployed by two composers who were interred in the Terezín concentration camp and died at Auschwitz. Janáček's student Pavel Haas used it in his 1939 Suite for Oboe and Piano, and Viktor Ullmann quotes its beginning near the conclusion of his Seventh Piano Sonata, written in Terezín in 1944. A more recent example of a politically motivated use of the hymn comes from Karel Husa's *Music from Prague*, written to commemorate the "Prague Spring" of 1968.

Inevitably, Janáček also used "Ye who are God's warriors" in *Brouček*. In the second act, Brouček hears the hymn from a distance, sung offstage by the armed men marching to Vítkov. The fact that Brouček fails either to add his voice to their song or his body to their numbers is just one of the many ways in which he fails to measure up to the standards of his Hussite hosts. Janáček's evocation of the Hussite era in *Brouček* was not his only patriotic gesture of this time. The first published edition of *Brouček*[13] carried a dedication "to the liberator of the Czech nation, Dr. T. G. Masaryk,"[14] an inscription which was suppressed in the later CSSR editions of the score. Immediately after Czechoslovak independence was declared on October 28, 1918, Janáček composed a substantial choral setting of a poem lauding the military prowess of the Czech Legion at the Battle of Amiens, a piece which was a huge hit in the early years of the First Czechoslovak Republic. A year later, he began another obviously nationalistic work, the orchestral tone poem, the *Ballad of Blaník*. According to legend, Blaník Hill is the burial place of the knights of St. Vaclav, who will emerge from their tomb to rescue the Czech nation in times of trouble. The knights of Blaník had already inspired a Smetana tone poem and an opera from Zdeněk Fibich. The *Ballad of Blaník* was also dedicated to Masaryk.

That Janáček should have indulged in these patriotic gestures is unsurprising, given the political circumstances. It may be worth noting, though, that none of these overtly patriotic pieces have been popular beyond their immediate historical circumstances. These pieces also represented a significant departure for Janáček, whose career had largely been based on establishing himself as a specifically Moravian composer, rather than as a more broadly Czech figure. Perhaps poor Brouček's reception has something to do with Janáček's failure to move from a musical language based on exotic regional music to one that deployed national musical symbols, or, to put it another way, his failure to move from defining Czechness from a periphery to defining it from the center.

Moravians

Conflicts and intersections between his various regional and national identities shaped Janáček's early life and career. Although a resident of Brno since the age of eleven, he was marked as a country boy by his Lachian dialect.[15] When he entered the German secondary school in Brno, he was registered as *böhmisch* (Czech).[16] Pavel Křížkovský, Janáček's childhood teacher at the Brno Augustinian monastery, exposed him to the Cyrilo-Methodius movement, which encouraged him to identify with a larger Slavonic community, and probably led to his lifelong obsession with Russian culture.[17] Janáček, although fluent in German, was

fiercely and famously devoted to the Czech-speaking minority in Brno.
As an adolescent, Janáček affected a Sokol hat,[18] the emblem of a Czech
gymnastics society.[19] Later in life, he insisted that his wife, Zdenka, a
native German speaker, speak only Czech at home, forbade her to read
German books, and refused to speak German with her family or to visit
her German-speaking relatives. The Janáčeks were forced to move
closer to the Brno Organ School in 1910, because Janáček was boycotting
Brno's German-owned trams.[20] Janáček's patriotism was particularly
galling to his in-laws. He insisted on having his wedding banns read in
Czech and wore a traditional Moravian coat, the *čamara,* to the cere-
mony.[21] Zdenka's father, Emilian Schulz, was also Janáček's supervisor
at the Brno Teachers' Training Institute. At a point when Leoš and Zdenka
had separated, Schulz attempted to start disciplinary proceedings against
Janáček, citing his son-in-law's "nationalist fanaticism giving an impression of madness."[22] From Schulz's point of view, this fanaticism could
be expressed either through broadly Czech gestures, like Janáček's
insistence on the Czech language, or through specifically Moravian
ones, like Janáček's affectation of the *čamara.*

For all his patriotism, though, Janáček was painfully aware that in
Prague he was a Moravian. In 1903, while *Jenůfa* was being rehearsed
in Brno, he complained in a letter, "And Prague papers? You can wait
a long time before you read anything there! They ignore everything
that concerns Moravia."[23] Janáček may have felt confined to the margins of Czech culture, but his career to that point had largely been built
on exploiting his various regional identities. His Moravian origins
allowed him to present himself as part of a more exotic, Slavonic, and
less Western European Czech culture. Moravia had long been a symbol for a region that was distant and somewhat foreign, yet still Czech.

One musical illustration of Moravia's status in Czech culture comes
from Smetana's *The Bartered Bride,* the archetypal Czech national opera.
Jeník, the barterer of *The Bartered Bride,* is a native of the unnamed
Bohemian village in which the opera is set, but he has recently returned
from exile. In the first act, he explains that he had gone out into the
world and taken up "with foreign people." In the next act, Jeník reveals
that he comes from "far, far away; on the Moravian border." The distance that Jeník has traveled to return to Bohemia is emphasized by a
sudden move from G major to A-flat major for the mention of the
Moravian border. Another example comes for the career of Dvořák, whose
Moravian duets, based on Moravian folk poetry, were his first works published in Germany, and were instrumental in establishing him as a
distinctively Czech figure outside of the Czech lands.[24] In Milan
Kundera's *The Joke,* the protagonist explains that "Prague musicologists

have long claimed that European folk song originated in the Baroque. . . . Now, that may be the case in Bohemia, but the songs that we sing in Moravia can't be explained in this way. . . . Our songs are sung in modes that court orchestras never dreamed of!"[25]

Janáček's first stage successes drew on the folk life of his native northern Moravia and of Moravian Slovakia. Despite the fact that he was already active as an ethnographer, receiving a state grant to collect and transcribe folk songs, he seems to have been perfectly comfortable in his role as a purveyor of provincial exotica for urban audiences. Janáček's first surviving works for full orchestra are a set of dances, eventually published as the Valachian Dances, op. 2. Augustin Berger, ballet master at the Prague National Theatre, heard a Brno performance of four of these dances, and opened negotiations that eventually led to the ballet *Rákoš Rákoczy*.[26] This ballet was performed during the 1891 Prague Provincial Jubilee Exhibition, as part of the Moravian exhibit. The exhibition drew visitors from throughout the Czech lands, and became a major site of nationalist expression when Prague's German-speaking community boycotted the festival. Typically, this display of national culture in urban citadels of high art, like the National Theatre, focused on the folk culture of peripheral areas. Janáček's melange of folk dances and choruses fitted this political agenda perfectly, coming not just from Moravia, but from the hinterlands that bordered on Slovakia. That these songs and dances were from distant and exotic locales was sufficient, but that they represent a particular local culture was not necessary. The ballet was advertised as "a scene from Moravian Slovakia" on the poster for the premiere.[27] The work contains choruses and dances from a variety of Moravian districts, including Janáček's native Lašsko and the Moravian Highlands, but none are actually from Moravian Slovakia. Despite this, *Rákoš Rákoczy* was hailed as a "Slavonic national ballet" by Josef Merhaut of the *Moravská orlice*,[28] and it was highly successful, receiving eight performances during the Jubilee summer.

The success of *Rákoš Rákoczy* prompted Janáček to produce another distinctive regional work, the folk opera *The Beginning of a Romance*. The opera is set in Moravian Slovakia, but characters express themselves mostly in literary Czech, breaking into Slovakian dialect occasionally for songs. Again, Janáček produced a Moravian spectacle by combining regional elements. The folk arrangements that Janáček recycled for the opera are mostly of music, not from Moravian Slovakia, but from farther north and east. Gabriela Preissová, the opera's librettist, was convinced that the result would be "our *first* Moravian opera."[29] The same process that Janáček followed for *Rákoš Rákoczy*, using folk material from the border areas of Moravia to serve as markers of regional identity in Brno and of national allegiance in Prague would also serve him well for *Jenůfa*. Again, a story set in Moravian Slovakia provided the scenario, and again folk music from various regions is alluded to, albeit in only a handful of numbers. When *Jenůfa* was finally produced in Prague, it was perceived as a national event, despite its regional character. Much of the audience wore national costumes, rather than traditional evening dress.[30]

Janáček longed to establish himself in Prague. In 1918, after *Jenůfa's* appearance in Prague, but before *Brouček's* premiere, he wrote: "I simply must go to 'golden' Prague. I feel like part of the clock's mechanism. . . . If I had to stay in Brno I should become as useless as the part which has been taken out."[31] Janáček's desire to have his works heard outside of Brno is understandable for reasons of professional advancement. In the context of his success with distinctively Moravian works like *Rákoš Rákoczy*, *The Beginning of a Romance*, and *Jenůfa*, his insistence on a Prague premiere for his next opera, *Fate*, despite the Brno National Theatre's pleas to be permitted to produce it, and his choice of urban Prague settings for the two halves of *Brouček*, may also be read as an attempt to establish himself as a Czech composer operating from the center, rather than one providing bulletins from the margins. Janáček never succeeded in making this transition. After the *Brouček* premiere, he felt that Prague was "like a foreign city,"[32] and, in 1921, at a time when an artist of his stature might have been expected to finally relocate to the capital city, he instead purchased an estate in his birthplace of Hukvaldy. In his glorious last decade, Janáček returned repeatedly to exotic settings, be it the Moravia of *The Cunning Little Vixen*, or the Russia of *Káťa Kabanová* and *From the House of the Dead*. Nonetheless, he continued to insist on his stature as a national figure, complaining in 1926 that "I am a Czech composer and not only a *Moravian* one as they nowadays like to pretend in Prague."[33]

Brouček's Reflection

If Janáček hoped to establish himself in Prague as a Czech national composer by choosing stories set in Prague and parading icons of the Hussite era onstage, he could hardly have chosen a less worthy protagonist than Matěj Brouček. Brouček's trip to the fifteenth century is based on Svatopluk Čech's novel *The New Epoch-Making Excursion of Mr. Brouček, This Time to the Fifteenth Century*, published in 1889. Čech's story is a satire, whose comedy is propelled by Brouček's cowardly shirking of his duties as a Hussite warrior. Janáček's librettist, F. S. Procházka, was well aware that the work was a burlesque, describing the libretto as a *karikaruta* in a letter to the composer.[34] Procházka's use of the word *caricature* probably was suggested by a lengthy paean to the sun from Čech's novel, which concludes with the thought that the sun has set on the glorious Hussite era, but that it might rise again, and be welcomed by a future poet with ringing words, instead of Čech's "petty caricatures."[35] Procházka included a condensed version of Čech's ode at the beginning of the excursion, sung in the opera by an apparition of Čech bathed in a green light, even adding a question to the sun: "Why do you light my words with irony, rather than with ardent odes?" Beyond the mere unsuitability of such an ironic text for a patriotic screed, Janáček's intentions were further undermined by both the highly specific ways in which Brouček failed to embody Hussite ideals and by Czech society's failure to become less Brouček-ridden in the time since Čech's novel.

Matěj Brouček is a negative image of the Hussite warriors that defended Vítkov. Brouček is a coward among heroes, a Catholic among Protestants, and an urban landowner in a peasant army. In addition to failing tests of courage, religion, and class, Janáček's Brouček rather carefully rejects the specific emblems of the Hussite era. Not only does Brouček resist conscription, asking what Sigismund has done to him that Brouček should fight against him, but he refuses to wield a flail, that very implement that stood for the rural origins of Žižka's army in Aleš's drawing. This reminder that Brouček is no peasant farmer follows closely on a theological discussion in which Brouček not only reveals his Catholicism, but also insults his hosts by suggesting that only sheep would celebrate mass without vestments. This comment by the tipsy Brouček shows him to be ignorant of Taborite practice, and it is particularly galling given that one of the humiliations inflicted upon Jan Hus before being burned at the stake was being dressed in vestments, which were then removed while Hus was ceremonially cursed.[36]

Brouček also fails the test of linguistic nationalism. Brouček's modern, German-inflected Czech is barely comprehensible in fifteenth-century Prague, and he is mistaken for an imperial spy. Brouček talks himself out of this dilemma by replacing chronological displacement with geographical dislocation. Instead of trying to convince his interlocutors that he comes from the future, he claims to have been traveling in the land of the Turks and to have forgotten his mother tongue.[37] The explanation is accepted, but when Brouček becomes embroiled in religious controversy, he is accused of being a "foul Mohammedan."[38] Here Brouček is read, not as a traveler in foreign lands, but as a foreigner. In both cases, he is viewed as being even more exotic than first suspected: not merely German, but Turkish, not just Catholic, but Muslim. At the end of the opera, after the victorious forces of Žižka have returned, it is revealed that Brouček had attempted to go over to the other side, kneeling in front of a German knight and crying out (in a mixture of broken German and Czech) "My Lord, my Lord! It's me! Not a Praguer! Not a Hussite! Mercy!" Here Brouček renounces both his language and the Hussites' religion by attempting to speak German and denying Hus. This time, he even denies Prague, explicitly tying together language, religion, and nationality.

Brouček's linguistic and religious failings were all too typical, not just of his time in 1888 but of Janáček's in 1917. The Czech lands had not become a Czech-speaking area in the fifteenth century, despite the Hussite victories. Although there was substantial consolidation of urban Czech society, by and large, most German communities stayed German after 1420, and most ethnically mixed communities stayed ethnically mixed.[39] Half a millennium later, Janáček's Czechoslovakia remained a linguistically and ethnically mixed nation. In 1921, Czechoslovakia was still nearly a quarter German (23 percent), and, even counting the Slovaks as Czechs, just over 65 percent Czech.[40] The percentage of Germans was even higher in Bohemia, where they constituted 33 percent of the population.[41] Similarly, a definition of the Czech nation in linguistic terms would implicitly disenfranchise a huge portion of Janáček's nation.

A view of the Czech nation as being made up largely of Czech speakers could reasonably be entertained in Prague, where the proportion of Germans had plummeted from 64 percent in 1847 to 15 percent in 1880 and to 7 percent in 1910,[42] but while Brouček may have departed for his excursion from "Golden Slavic Prague," as the city had been known since the 1880s,[43] this pretense of linguistic purity was harder to sustain in outlying areas. These census figures should be approached with some caution. Citizens were allowed to choose their own ethnic and linguistic identity, and in a city where "thousands of people spoke both languages badly,"[44] the declining German population reflects a change in the social status of the two languages, as well as a movement of ethnic populations. In the middle of the nineteenth century, German was the respectable linguistic identification for a bilingual Praguer; by the end of the century Czech would be the politically prudent response from the same citizen. The liberal sprinkling of German elements in Brouček's speech may have been an uncomfortable reminder that the Czech nation was a multiethnic state. This would continue to be the case throughout Janáček's lifetime. Even by 1930, the Czechoslovak population had risen only slightly to 67 percent.[45] A linguistically homogenous state could only be approximated by the forced expulsion of Germans after the Second World War.

A definition of a Czech nation bounded by language, though unrealistic, was at least a plausible goal. Brouček's theological failings, however, reveal an even deeper inconsistency in nationalist discourse. As one might expect from Čech's novel, Catholicism fared poorly in nineteenth-century Czech political discourse. The Counter-Reformation was seen as a foreign imposition and the contemporary church as an agent of the Habsburgs. Despite repeated attempts, no Catholic political party was established in Bohemia.[46] Nonetheless, the Czech lands were solidly, if only nominally, Catholic. Brouček's Catholicism is just as typical of 1888 Prague as is his slightly Teutonic Czech. In 1910, 96 percent of Bohemia and 95 percent of Moravia were Roman Catholic,[47] and even when a Czech national Hussite church was established in 1919, fewer than half a million of the newly minted Czecho-Slovaks joined.[48] This figure did not rise significantly in the next two years. In 1921, more than 75 percent of Czechoslovakia was still Roman Catholic (adding Uniates and Old Catholics pushes the figure over 80 percent), with the number of Czech nationals (3.86 percent) roughly equal to that of Lutherans (3.93 percent), and significantly less than that of the atheists (5.32 percent).[49]

Reverence for the Hussite period has also obscured the significant role played by Catholic clergy in the nineteenth-century national rebirth. Although clerical support for patriotic institutions declined toward the middle of the century, it remained substantial.[50] Janáček, although by the end of his life a nonbeliever (famously responding to review of the Glagolitic Mass, "Not an old man! Not a believer"),[51] was educated as a Catholic choirboy and never broke from the church, remarking, "Why should I leave the [Catholic] Church? The Church hasn't done anything to me."[52] Janáček hoped that *Brouček* would disgust operagoers, but those very people would have shared many characteristics with the Czech Oblomov.

Beer, Bagpipes, and Turks

If Brouček's reflection in "Vítkov's pure mirror" was uncomfortably familiar to Janáček's potential audiences, the music that he brought with it might well have added confusion to disgust. At various times, music and musical associations undermine the intentions of the libretto; at others they fatally reinforce its devastating portrayal of the protagonist.

One of the running jokes of Čech's novel is that Brouček's home base is his local pub, and that he drinks rather more that he ought, a gag that is carried over into both operatic excursions. The first excursion opens on the steps of the Vikarka Inn; Brouček first appears calling for the innkeeper Würfl, too drunk to stand upright, and assumes that his presence on the moon is but a beery hallucination. When he falls asleep on the moon, Brouček automatically orders more beer. In both excursions, Brouček's eating and drinking habits separate him from his hosts. The Lunarians neither eat nor drink and are appalled by the carnivorous Brouček. In the second excursion, Brouček boasts of his beer-drinking exploits, but chokes on Hussite mead and is mocked as a "hero of the hops," and as a man "whose only god has been your stomach and altar a full barrel!" Beer is also implicated in Brouček's forceful expulsion from the past and return to the present, when, after his failure in battle, he is immolated in a keg (in fact, sixteen prisoners were burned in barrels by the victorious Hussites after the battle of Vítkov Hill).[53] Instead of being roasted in the fifteenth century, Brouček wakes to find himself merely damp in the nineteenth, emerging from a keg in Würfl's courtyard.

The contrast between the two journeys poses an obvious problem. On the moon, however comic Brouček may be, we are clearly intended to sympathize with him, rather than with the ludicrous moon dwellers (who are caricatures of a group of Czech poets). Brouček, while crude and tipsy, is a Prague Joe Six-Pack, a regular guy who is justified in snoozing during a pretentious lunar poetry slam. The very same man, though, is intended to be an object of scorn in the second excursion. This problem is exacerbated by earlier Czech operas that use drinking as a marker of national identity.

One of the most famous choruses in the Czech repertoire is the hymn in praise of beer ("Beer is certainly a heavenly gift!") that opens Act 2 of *The Bartered Bride*. Drinking is here an activity that joins the community, as well as one that imparts specific benefits. The villagers sing that beer chases away worry and trouble, and grants strength and courage. There is also a chorus that praises beer at the beginning of Brouček's first excursion,[54] but, unlike Smetana's Jeník, Brouček is excluded from a community (Hussites, and by extension, Czechs) while drinking, and lacks exactly those qualities (strength and courage) that Smetana's beer should have bestowed upon him. Another example comes from Dvořák's *The Devil and Kate*, which opens with shepherds and farmhands drinking at a country inn. Jirka, the hero, takes a swig of beer before singing his first lines. When the devil appears, he insinuates himself into village life by drinking with the villagers at a dance. In this opera, drinking and dancing are rural activities that separate the "us" of the (Czech) villagers from the "them" of their (foreign) rulers. Once again, the situation is reversed in *Brouček*. In the first excursion, he drinks and dances like one of Jirka's fellow shepherds, but by the second he is an urban outsider, unworthy to join a peasant army.

When Brouček first encounters the Hussite army, he hears them singing a battle hymn from offstage, led by a bagpiper toward the Týn cathedral. Janáček, probably under the influence of either Čeněk Zíbrt or Zdeněk Nejedlý, associated bagpipes with the Hussite period.[55] He wrote to Zíbrt in 1918 that he "needed [bagpipes] as a musical, orchestral indication of that period" and that he valued them "for their softness and for their melancholy tone; they bring with them the refined tone of the organ to the modern orchestra but are nevertheless more spiritual."[56] Bagpipes do not appear, however, in any of the well-known musical tributes to the Hussite period listed above. Instead, they are associated with same kinds of bucolic dramas in which the drinking songs are found. Orchestral bagpipe imitations shortly occur after the curtain opens in both *The Bartered Bride* and *The Devil and Kate*, and Karel Kovařovic's *The Dogheads* even has a bagpiper as a singing character. Janáček's inclusion of pipes to accompany the march to the Týn cathedral, while musically effective, sends a mixed message. Janáček is still working within the nationalist framework established by Smetana, but has transposed one of its symbols. In terms of Smetana's cycle of tone poems, *Má vlast*, the bagpipes belong at the rural wedding celebration heard beside the Moldau, but Janáček has moved them to Tábor. Two types of Czech national identity, the pastoral and the legendary, are conflated as bagpipes lead the Hussites, as if Jan Žižka were marching hand-in-hand with Mařenka, Jeník's bartered bride.

As the Hussites (and their bagpiper) appear from the distance, Brouček is interrogated about his suspiciously unintelligible Czech and accused of being a spy for Emperor Sigismund. This is the point at which he concocts his story about returning from Turkey, a detail not found in Čech. Janáček specifically requested such a reference, writing to Procházka after receiving the Act 1 libretto, "I would still need another sort of line which would perhaps refer to Brouček's *Mahometanism*."[57] Apparently, Janáček was inspired by the reference to Muhammedanism in the vestments argument to introduce a Muslim country earlier in the story. Having been given a literary excuse for musical exoticism, Janáček seized it with authority.

Immediately after Brouček is accused of espionage, the bagpipes are heard from the distance. The chorus of armed men is then heard from offstage, singing a chorale whose second phrase is derived from the bagpipe music. This little tune, then, could hardly be more steeped in Czechness, having been linked to both the iconic bagpipe and used for a Hussite chorale.

Example 1. *Brouček*, bagpipes to chorale, VS 193.

When Brouček tries to explain himself, the bagpipe music moves into the orchestra, and the underlying harmony shifts from B major to a diminished triad on B. The melody itself is enharmonically renotated to use flats instead of sharps, and the fifth note is raised a half step, shrinking the descent of a perfect fifth into a tritone. With these changes, the tune is both stripped of its symbolic associations when wrested from the bagpipes and deprived of its harmonic and melodic integrity. Instead of a familiar diatonic fragment, already heard seven times without alteration, using perfect intervals and pure triads, it is now a mere motif, subject to various instrumental and harmonic perversions.

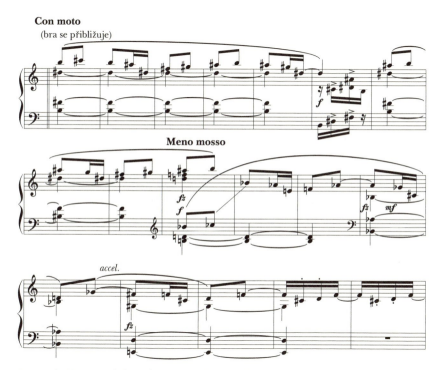

Example 2. *Brouček*, bagpipes to orchestra, VS 194.

The suspicious tritone continues to figure in Brouček's alibi. When Brouček explains away his modern Czech by claiming to have been far away, in Turkish lands, the words "far away" are accompanied by the bagpipe music (from the violins), this time not literally in the distance, but removed from B major to E-flat major, the most distant key possible. Although the melody is heard in its original form, the bass pedal is the fifth, rather than the root, and is further destabilized by a persistent trill. The melody breaks off after the third bar of the motif, no more capable of completing itself than Brouček is of finishing his thought. When the melody halts on a C, the accompanying G is dropped to G♭, creating an exposed tritone, which is reiterated twice (Example 4).

Brouček finally lights upon an explanation and, at the mention of Turkish lands, a familiar motif enters. The music now played by the bassoons was first heard in the overture to the first excursion (also in the bassoon) and has been associated with Brouček throughout the two operas (Example 3).[58] But now, the second note has been raised a half

Example 3. *Brouček*, motif from opening, VS 1.

step, changing the mode from the expected gapped natural minor to Lydian. The Lydian tritone is exposed and repeated, in a textbook demonstration of musical exoticism worthy of Mozart's Turks or of Verdi's Egyptian priestesses (Example 4). As the explanation is accepted, the music returns to simple tonic-dominant alternations in E-flat major, interrupted by forte tritone cackles from flutes surrounding the words "from Muhammedan lands." When Brouček's name is cleared, both chorale and bagpipe return, and the act builds to its noble conclusion.

Here Janáček only too effectively deploys musical devices to deny Brouček his national identity. Like Jeník in *The Bartered Bride*, Brouček has come from far away, and, once more, that physical distance is represented by a tonal metaphor. Unlike Jeník, Brouček will not be welcomed back home in Bohemia (at least not in the fifteenth century). Any hope of presenting Brouček as either sympathetic or distinctively Czech is dashed by musically coding him not just as an exotic figure, but as a Turk, the most stereotypically sinister of operatic villains.[59]

The final irony of this situation is that Janáček's *Brouček* was done in by exactly the same relation between periphery and center that had buoyed Janáček's career to that point. Brno audiences were happy to read the exotic dances and mores of Moravian Slovakia as manifestations of Moravian identity. Prague audiences saw those same songs and rituals as part of a broader Czech culture, with the distance to the Slovakian border merely indicating the scope of the nascent state. This reverence for the rural, however, prevents the landlord Brouček from being a proper Czech hero. Mr. Brouček, unlike the farmers and shepherds of uncertain provenance found in the timeless pastoral spaces of

Example 4. Turkish Stuff, VS 196.

Dvořák's and Smetana's operas, is a city slicker with an address, an occupation, and a historical location. Even were he not a coward, these attributes would disqualify him from wielding a flail with Žižka.[60] The music, though, is magnificent. The end of the first act, in which bagpipes and warriors approach, leading to a glorious, organ-soaked final chorale, is an exemplary operatic finale. In fact, the combination of hymn, marching soldiers, and a church is strongly reminiscent of Act 3 of Giacomo Meyerbeer's *Les Huguenots*,[61] in which a soldiers' chorus is combined with an *Ave Maria*. Perhaps now it is time to hear Janáček's *Brouček* as a music-drama that does not depend on a coherent political message. Meyerbeer's Huguenots are accepted as excuses for characteristic music and scenic spectacle. Janáček's Hussites should stand by them on the world stage.

NOTES

1. Ian Horsbrugh, *Leoš Janáček: The Field that Prospered* (Newton Abbot: David & Charles, 1981), p. 131.

2. Max Brod, *Leoš Janáček: Leben und Werk*, rev. ed. (Vienna: Universal, 1956), p. 44.

3. John Tyrrell, *Janáček's Operas: A Documentary Account* (London: Faber and Faber, 1992), pp. 227–28.

4. Svatava Přibáňová, "Přehled inscenací jevištního díla Leoše Janáčka z let 1894–1998," in *Svět Janáčkových oper* (Brno: Moravské Zemské Muzeum, 1998), pp. 111–12.

5. Letter to Kamila Stösslová, 17 October 1917. Bohumír Štědroň, *Leoš Janáček: Letters and Reminiscences,* trans. Geraldine Thomsen, (Prague: Artia, 1955), p. 148.

6. Tyrrell, *Janáček's Operas*, p. 204.

7. Ibid.

8. 23 December 1917. Jan Racek and Leoš Firkušný, *Janáčkovy Feuilletony z L. N.* (Brno, 1938), p. 60.

9. Ibid.

10. Peter Demetz, *Prague in Black and Gold: Scenes from the Life of a European City* (New York: Hill and Wang, 1997), p. 160.

11. František Šmahel, "The Hussite Movement: An Anomaly of European History?" in *Bohemia in History,* ed. Mikuláš Teich (Cambridge: Cambridge University Press, 1998), p. 81.

12. Mirka Zemanová, *Janáček* (Boston: Northeastern University Press, 2002), p. 94.

13. The 1919 Universal vocal score

14. Nigel Simeone, John Tyrrell, and Alena Němcová, *Janáček's Works: A Catalogue of the Music and Writings of Leoš Janáček* (Oxford: Clarendon Press, 1997), p. 38.

15. The terms "Lachian" and "Valachian" were used inconsistently in late-nineteenth-century Moravia. Janáček, a native of Hukvaldy in what is now called Lašsko, would have called himself a Valachian, at least until 1891. Simeone et al., *Janáček's Works*, pp. 187–88.

16. Zemanová, *Janáček*, p. 19.

17. Jaroslav Vogel, *Leoš Janáček: A Biography*, trans. Geraldine Thomsen-Muchova, rev. Karel Janovický, (Prague: Artia, 1981), pp. 44–45.

18. Zemanová, *Janáček*, p. 20.

19. The Sokol societies were based on the German *Turnverein*. Janáček joined a Brno section in 1876 and wrote a piece to accompany Sokol Indian club swinging in 1893. The first Prague performance of the Sinfonietta took place at a Sokol rally, and the opening

fanfares may have been written for a Sokol society. Simeone, et al., *Janáček's Works*, pp. 254–55, 208–11.

20. John Tyrrell, ed. and trans., *My Life with Janáček: The Memoirs of Zdenka Janáčková* (London: Faber and Faber, 1998), pp. 16–17, 28, 104.

21. Tyrrell, *My Life*, p. 23. The *čamara* was a braided black coat. The Janáčeks' wedding picture, showing Janáček in the *čamara*, is reproduced on the cover of the cited work, in Vogel, *Leoš Janáček*, pp. 112 and 113, and in Zemanová, *Janáček*, pages 176 and 177.

22. Zemanová, *Janáček*, pp. 46–47.

23. Zemanová, *Janáček*, p. 92.

24. The title page of Simrock's 1878 edition of the Moravian duets (with, incidentally, only German texts) is reproduced in Klaus Döge, *Dvořák: Leben, Werk, Dokumente*, 2d ed. (Zürich: Atlantis Musikbuch, 1997), p. 164.

25. Milan Kundera, *The Joke* (New York: HarperCollins, 1992), p. 130. For these last two examples, and more on the place of Moravia in Czech national consciousness, see Michael Beckerman, "Kundera's Musical Joke and 'Folk' Music in Czechoslovakia, 1948–?" in *Retuning Culture: Musical Changes in Central and Eastern Europe*, ed. Mark Slobin, (Durham, N.C.: Duke University Press, 1996), pp. 39–41.

26. Simeone, et al., *Janáček's Works*, p. 7.

27. Ibid., p. 5.

28. Vogel, *Leoš Janáček*, p. 97.

29. Tyrrell, *Janáček's Operas*, p. 26.

30. Zemanová, *Janáček,* p. 127.

31. Štědroň, *Leoš Janáček: Letters and Reminiscences*, p. 128.

32. Zemanová, *Janáček*, 161.

33. Štědroň, *Leoš Janáček: Letters and Reminiscences*, p. 183.

34. 30 April 1917. Tyrrell, *Janáček's Operas*, pp. 205–6.

35. Svatopluk Čech, *Výlety Pana Broučka I–III* (Prague: Slunovrat, 1985), p. 256.

36. Demetz, *Prague in Black and Gold*, pp. 144–45.

37. In Čech's novel, Brouček has been far away, but he does not specify where. Čech, *Výlety Pana Broučka*, pp. 158–59.

38. "Muhammedan" was an epithet used by the Hussites, albeit for Orthodox Christians. Demetz, *Prague in Black and Gold*, pp. 146.

39. Šmahel, "The Hussite Movement," p. 84.

40. Richard and Ben Crampton, *Atlas of Eastern Europe in the Twentieth Century* (London: Routledge, 1996), p. 61.

41. Carol Skalnik Leff, *National Conflict in Czechoslovakia: The Making and Remaking of a State, 1918–1987* (Princeton, N.J.: Princeton University Press, 1988), p. 16.

42. Gary B. Cohen, "Ethnicity and Urban Population Growth: The Decline of the Prague Germans, 1880–1920," in *Studies in East European Social History*, ed. Keith Hitchins, vol. 2 (Leiden: E. J. Brill, 1981), p. 3.

43. Gary B. Cohen, *The Politics of Ethnic Survival: Germans in Prague, 1861–1914* (Princeton, N.J.: Princeton University Press, 1981), p. 13.

44. Ibid., p. 5.

45. Crampton, *Atlas*, p. 61.

46. Leff, *National Conflict in Czechoslovakia*, pp. 20–21, 21 n. 19.

47. Ibid., p. 21.

48. Derek Sayer, *The Coasts of Bohemia: A Czech History* (Princeton, N.J.: Princeton University Press, 1998), p. 140.

49. These figures are somewhat misleading, since there were major regional differences. Most of the Uniates and Orthodox were in Ruthenia, and the non-Czech National

Protestants were most numerous in Slovakia. The greatest concentration of Czech Nationals was in Eastern Bohemia. R. and B. Crampton, *Atlas*, pp. 62–63.

50. See Miroslav Hroch, *Social Preconditions of National Revival in Europe: A Comparative Analysis of the Social Composition of Patriotic Groups Among the Smaller European Nations*, trans. Ben Fowkes (New York: Columbia University, 2000 [first published 1985]), p. 45ff.

51. Janáček's postcard to Ludvík Kundera is reproduced in Mirka Zemanová, *Janáček's Uncollected Essays on Music* (London: Marion Boyars, 1989), p. 124.

52. From the memoirs of Janáček's servant, Marie Stejskalová, in Marie Trkanová, *U Janáčků* (Brno: Šimon Ryšavý, 1998), p. 117.

53. Demetz, *Prague in Black and Gold*, p. 162.

54. The text of the Brouček chorus is vaguely reminiscent of the Smetana Act 2 beer chorus, while its music, in particular the middle section in the parallel minor, resembles that of the opening chorus in *The Bartered Bride*.

55. Nejedlý, citing Zíbrt, traces bagpipes back to the fifteenth century. Zdeněk Nejedlý, *Dějiny Husitského zpěvu*, Book I (Prague: Československá Akademie Věd, 1954), p. 172. First published as *Dějiny předhusitského zpěvu v Čechách* in 1904.

56. Tyrrell, *Janáček's Operas*, p. 216.

57. Tyrrell, *Janáček's Operas*, p. 212.

58. Mirka Zemanová hears this moon theme and suggests that its return is connected to Turkey as the land of the half-moon. Zemanová, *Janáček*, p. 144.

59. "Turkish" music is also used to characterize the Devil in *The Devil and Kate*, another unfortunate association for poor Brouček.

60. Although, as Tibor Kneif has wryly pointed out, why should Brouček risk his neck in a battle that he knows has long since been won? Tibor Kneif, *Die Bühnenwerke von Leoš Janáček* (Vienna: Universal Edition, 1974), p. 43.

61. An opera that Janáček reviewed in 1880.

Zdenka Janáčková's Memoirs and the

Fallacy of Music as Autobiography

Paul Wingfield

For Rachel

I

Oscar Wilde once remarked that "everybody has disciples," but it is "Judas who writes the biography." I share Wilde's antipathy to biography. A brief elaboration of my objections will provide a convenient frame for my principal topic: the memoirs of Zdenka Janáčková.[1] My worries can be grouped under three broad headings: evidence, ethics, and explanatory force. Regarding evidence, a crucial factor is that the survival of documentary detritus about any individual's life is random. In fact, a biographer rarely has access to all the extant material. Moreover, the accuracy of biographical matter is dubious: letters are tailored to individual recipients; memoirs and diaries are forms of self-invention. Interviews with surviving family, friends, and acquaintances are no more reliable, not least because memory is fallible. And, of course, a vast proportion of an individual's life and thought goes entirely unrecorded. In short, biographers are deeply ill-informed about their subjects' lives. Yet they are inclined to design narratives attempting to conceal this ignorance, imposing seamless patterns of cause and effect where none exist. Worse still, few biographers possess the skills of a good novelist and so tend to fall back on clichéd narrative strategies such as the concept of the inevitable. To put it bluntly, most biographies fail to convince as either history or fiction.

My reservations about the ethics of biography are just as strong. Donald Reimann makes a valuable distinction between three types of document: *public* documents are "accessible to a multiplicity of readers"; *confidential* ones are "shared by members of a limited community"; and *private* ones are "addressed to specific people."[2] Reimann asserts that "discretion and tact" should be the fundamental basis of responsible scholarship. If researchers gain access to *confidential* and *private* documents and are thereby able to avoid error, they can draw attention to these sources in footnotes. Scholars ought to make every effort to distinguish themselves from "sensationalist journalists." However, "discretion and tact" are in short supply among biographers, who are apt to winkle out every last morsel of scandal. In the words of Geoffrey Braithwaite, the narrator in Julian Barnes's novel *Flaubert's Parrot*: "If you are reckless enough to write a book, this puts your bank account, your medical records, and the state of your marriage irrevocably into the public domain."[3] James Joyce memorably characterizes the biographer as a pursuing hound called the "biografiend." The biografiend's motivation is elegantly encapsulated by Richard Holmes as a "suppressed desire to devalue greatness, to find the feet of clay and the rattling skeleton in the cupboard."[4] It is no compensation that a few biographers acknowledge their own bad faith: Humphrey Carpenter—author of books about Ezra Pound and Benjamin Britten, among others—openly declares his aim "to tarnish great artists."[5]

In this climate of denigration, the biographers' holy grail becomes sexual transgression. As Geoffrey Braithwaite puts it: "All biographers secretly want to annex and channel the sex lives of their subjects."[6] Even highly regarded biographical authors seem unable to resist the lure of tabloid journalism. For example, the 1975 "popular" selection of James Joyce's letters by the widely acclaimed Richard Ellman is heavily weighted toward the sexual and has a dust jacket that actually directs readers to the most salacious passages.[7] If one also considers that biographers can expect larger publishing advances, more royalties, and far less rigorous critical scrutiny than academic authors, then one is entitled to be suspicious. Indeed, Peter Ackroyd's quip to a journalist that biographies reveal more about their authors than their subjects provides a basis for an indictment of the whole discipline.

One area of broad agreement among biography's proponents and critics is the importance of explanatory force. On a simple level, biographical research is useful for establishing matters of chronology and the authenticity of sources. Nevertheless, clerical documentary work attracts neither public nor academic renown, so biographers are principally concerned with what Wittgenstein calls the "inner life." So-called critical biographies are invariably founded on the assumption that "a writer's life illuminates the works,"[8] an assumption that is never accorded sustained theoretical examination. In a review of David Rigg's *Life of Jonson*, Ian Donaldson questions this assumption on two counts.[9] First, if an author's writings do indeed reveal something about his life, "how exactly (and how dependably) do they do their revealing?" And second, what kind of relationship can we assume to exist between an author's texts and his life, and through what "distorting lenses do we read the latter in the former?" Anne Thwaite raises another important stumbling block. As the author of a biography of A. A. Milne, she expresses incredulity at the idea that her book might be thought to "illuminate" *Winnie-the-Pooh*.[10] This leads one to ask what sorts of work might be deemed to be susceptible to biographical elucidation and why? No one ever attempts to answer such questions.

Musical biographers face a yet more daunting task, because of the essential differences between music and language. This may explain why, as Maynard Solomon argues, serious musicology "withdrew from interpretive biography" once the naive nineteenth-century view of music as "autobiography in tones" was abandoned.[11]

II

Autobiography is a particularly troubling sub-branch of biography. It is a discourse of anxiety, compromised by its lack of self-awareness and the impossibility of reconciling fact with the urge to shape public image. Zdenka Janáčková's memoirs are a particular minefield. Zdenka apparently dictated these between 1928 and 1935 to a confidante, the journalist Marie Trkanová, who then revised them and supplied an introduction and afterword.[12] Disquietingly, Trkanová admits in her preface that she found Zdenka's account "flat, cold, uninvolved," so she "hit on the method of trying to put herself in [Zdenka]'s place and then narrating her story in her own words" (pp. xiv–xv). John Tyrrell's 1998 English translation introduces changes to the "sentence and paragraph construction" and insertions of material from two further sources: a populist biography by one of the composer's pupils, Robert Smetana,[13] and the memoirs of the Janáčeks' maid, Marie Stejskalová.[14] The "I" of the 1998 English translation is thus a composite of no fewer than five people. Thus every time hereafter that the author of these memoirs is referred to as "Zdenka," this comes with an official warning.

To make matters worse, the very fact of publishing this material is problematic. The project was Marie Trkanová's brainchild. She seems to have viewed Zdenka as an unjustly disparaged yet loyal wife whose story needed to be told. Zdenka was a reluctant contributor. Moreover,

Trkanová's introduction states that "from the beginning both of us were aware that because of their intimate character the memoirs . . . would remain simply as study material for those dealing in detail with Janáček" (p. xi); i. e., the document is *confidential*. As a result, the early Janáček biographers Vladimír Helfert and Jaroslav Vogel merely cited the memoirs in footnotes, where necessary.[15] At some point, Trkanová's original and revised typescripts were given to the Janáček archive in Brno specifically on condition that neither should be published.[16]

In his introduction to the English translation Tyrrell asserts that "one might have imagined that such a frank memoir . . . would be a key source, familiar to all those interested in Janáček" (p. ix), although he does not explain why. His focus on Janáček rather than Zdenka is evidenced by his omission of her account of her life after her husband's death and his changing Marie Trkanová's title from *Zdenka Janáčková: My Life* to the more cumbersome *The Memoirs of Zdenka Janáčková: My Life with Leoš Janáček*. The result of this alteration is a generic confusion compounded by the additional claim that "Zdenka's story" *is* in fact a valuable piece of social history in its own right (p. xvii). Nor does Tyrrell's description of the memoir's content ameliorate my concerns. He writes that "one of the remarkable features of Janáčková's account is her frankness in sexual matters," then dwells on Janáček's "torrid affair" with the "predatory" singer Gabriela Horvátová (p. xiv). The dust jacket throws in a suicide attempt for good measure. Tyrrell adds to the list of charges against Janáček in a 1999 newspaper article.[17] After dwelling on Janáček's alleged marital misdemeanors, he directly relates Janáček's "cruelty" to his music:

> What emerges on almost every page is the composer's appalling cruelty. . . . At first it seems hard to imagine that Janáček's operas . . . could have been the product of someone who behaved so vilely to his wife. But then one forgets how much cruelty there is in the operas, most strikingly in . . . *From the House of the Dead*.

Since no one has hitherto presented the case for the defense, I should like to do so now. My arguments will be divided in three parts: first, I will contend that the memoirs have been misrepresented; second, I will question their reliability from the viewpoint of modern psychotherapy; and third, I will argue that they cannot be convincingly related to Janáček's music, and in particular to his final opera, *Z mrtvého domu* (*From the House of the Dead*) (1927–1928).

III

A brief outline of the lives of the Janáčeks is given in Table 1. There are two columns, the first containing births, deaths, and marriages, and the second detailing other notable events.

Tyrrell's 1999 article makes six specific accusations of cruelty against Leoš:

1. Leoš forbade Zdenka to see her parents more than once a week.
2. He made her trudge off on her own to her parents when in labor.
3. He refused to pay for treatment when their children became ill.
4. He attacked Zdenka when she was holding Olga, causing the 1882 separation.
5. There were other women almost from the start, one even while Olga was dying.
6. His affair with Gabriela Horvátová, resulting in a pregnancy and a miscarriage (or abortion), led Zdenka to attempt suicide.

A cursory reading of the memoirs reveals some of these accusations to be contentious. Leoš did not *make* Zdenka trudge home when in labor.

Table 1
Life Chronology of Janáček

Date	Births, Deaths, Marriages	Other Events
3 July 1854	Leo Eugen ("Leoš") Janáček born in Hukvaldy	
30 July 1865	Zdenka Schulzová born in Olomouc	
October 1865		Leoš becomes a choirboy in Brno
8 April 1866	Jiří Janáček dies in Hukvaldy	
1871		The Schulz family moves to Kroměříž
1872		The Schulz family moves to Brno
July 1872		Leoš begins work at the Czech Teachers' Institute in Brno

Table 1 continued

Date	Births, Deaths, Marriages	Other Events
1877		Leoš employed to teach Zdenka the piano
August 1879		Leoš and Zdenka become informally engaged
18 May 1880	Leo Schulz born in Brno	
12 July 1881	Leoš and Zdenka marry in Olomouc	
15 August 1882	Olga Janáčková born in Brno	
September 1882		Leoš begins work as director of the Organ School in Brno;
		Leoš and Zdenka separate
April 1884		The separation is annulled
August 1884		Zdenka and Olga return to live with Leoš
16 November 1884	Amálie Janáčková dies of cancer in Hukvaldy	
February 1888		Olga ill with rheumatic fever
16 May 1888	Vladimír Janáček born in Brno	
October 1890		Olga contracts scarlet fever
7 November 1890		Vladimír catches scarlet fever
9 November 1890	Vladimír dies of streptococcal meningitis in Brno	
February 1894		Olga again contracts rheumatic fever
August 1894		Marie Stejskalová becomes the Janáčeks' servant
1899		Emilian Schulz retires; the Schulzes move to Vienna
April 1902		Olga contracts typhoid fever in St. Petersburg
August 1902		Olga again ill with rheumatic fever

Table 1 continued

Date	Births, Deaths, Marriages	Other Events
September 1902		Leoš and Zdenka buy Olga a poodle, "Čert"
26 February 1903	Olga dies of rheumatic heart disease in Brno	
November 1903		Leoš retires from his job at the Teachers' Institute
2 July 1910		Leoš and Zdenka move to a villa on the grounds of the Organ School
Summer 1915	Čert dies	
May 1916		Leoš begins an affair with Gabriela Horvátová
10 July 1916		Zdenka "attempts suicide"
19 January 1917		Leoš and Zdenka sign a "voluntary legal divorce" contract
July 1917		Leoš meets Kamila Stösslová
June 1918		Leoš's affair with Gabriela Horvátová ends
18 December 1918	Anna Schulzová dies of pneumonia in Vienna	
12 February 1919	Eleonora Janáčková dies in Švábenice	
July 1919		Emilian Schulz returns to Brno
28 July 1923	Emilian Schulz dies of pneumonia in Brno	
August 1923		Zdenka acquires a new puppy, "Čipera"
April 1927		Marital crisis for Leoš and Zdenka over his friendship with Kamila
12 August 1928	Leoš dies of pneumonia in Ostrava	
17 February 1938	Zdenka dies of liver cancer in Brno	

The couple had a disagreement about where Zdenka should have the baby, Leoš favoring the hospital and Zdenka her parents' home. Zdenka's avowedly prejudiced opinion was that "no decent lady would have gone into a maternity hospital" (p. 37), so she went home on her own. Moreover, the alleged attack was not in fact the catalyst for the 1882 separation: Zdenka states that the final straw was Leoš's intention to bring his ailing mother, whom she feared, to live with them (p. 38). This is Zdenka's only accusation of physical violence on the part of Leoš. That scarcely marks him as a wife beater, and it should be measured against Zdenka's confession that in 1902 she herself attacked Leoš's sister, Josefka (p. 77).

Nor does the "other women from the start" claim bear much scrutiny. Zdenka does express some anxiety about her husband's female friends. But she declares that Leoš was, before 1915, the year of his sixty-first birthday no less, "innocent" in "erotic matters" (p. 128). And she describes confronting the "other woman" when Olga was dying, only to be told: "I assure you that . . . we didn't do bad things together" (p. 214). On this evidence, Leoš hardly qualifies as a Don Juan. The Gabriela Horvátová pregnancy and miscarriage scenario is equally murky. What Zdenka actually alleges (pp. 153 and 158) is that Horvátová duped Leoš into believing that she had conceived, then lost his baby.

Tyrrell's other accusations are called into question by only modest probing. Leoš's hostility to Zdenka's family has to be viewed in the light of Zdenka's maternal grandmother's behavior: she strongly objected to Zdenka's speaking Czech with the staunchly nationalistic Leoš; to her, "anyone who didn't speak German wasn't an educated person" (p. 17). Similarly problematic is Leoš's alleged refusal to pay for medical treatment for the sickly Vladimír. Leoš did call a doctor, who recommended a wet nurse. Zdenka acknowledges that they could not really afford a wet nurse, but her middle-class opinion was that "it is was our duty to . . . find the money at any cost" (p. 49). Leoš was from a poorer family and four of his siblings died in infancy. Inevitably, he viewed matters differently. In the event, Zdenka's parents paid for the wet nurse, although this did not prevent Vladimír from dying when he was two. By today's standards, child mortality rates in the late nineteenth century were simply very high.

The truth regarding Zdenka's supposed suicide attempt is yet more elusive. Her account is as follows (pp. 136–37): On the evening of 10 July 1916, after a bitter argument, she took about twenty barbiturate tablets and an unspecified quantity of morphine. She was found the next morning by the maid, who shouted for Leoš. He summoned a doctor, who in turn called an ambulance. At the hospital Zdenka's stomach was then pumped out. Zdenka disingenuously maintains that she "did it out of love for my husband so that he could be free." As Tyrrell points out, "By the morning the stomach pump . . . would not have been much use." He suggests that Zdenka may have taken an underdose as a "cry for help." But one might see the whole episode as a calculated attempt to induce guilt.

There is another important consideration. If autobiography is a discourse of anxiety, it is also a discourse of crisis. Descriptions of domestic harmony are insufferably boring. In Table 2 I have summarized the structure of the English translation of the memoirs. The narrative lurches from disaster to disaster. More than half the book is devoted to the death of Olga, Leoš's affair with Horvátová, and the 1927–1928 marital problems. Vast stretches of time go all but unrecorded: in chapter 6, Tyrrell inserts ten pages of his own to plug the gaps. Intriguingly, Zdenka's few comments about the periods 1903 to 1915 and 1918 to 1927—which amount basically to half of the Janáčeks' life together—

Table 2
Chapter Structure of *Memoirs: Zdenka Janáčková—My Life*

Chapter	Title	No. of Pages	Years	Principal Events
1	Childhood	6	1865–1877	Move to Brno
2	Betrothal	14	1877–1881	Engagement and marriage
3	Marriage. A Child. Separation	15	1881–1882	Olga's birth Separation and return to parents
4	Return	14	1882–1889	Reconciliation with Leoš Birth of Vladimír
5	Our Children	40	1890–1903	Death of Vladimír Olga's early illnesses Čert's arrival Olga's final illness and death (20 pages)
6	New Home. The World War	23	1903–1915	Leoš's retirement from the Teachers' Institute Rapprochement with Leoš Move to a new house Outbreak of the First World War Death of Čert

Table 2 continued

Chapter	Title	No. of Pages	Years	Principal Events
7	*Jenůfa* in Prague	42	1915–1918	Leoš's affair with Gabriela Horvátová
				Zdenka's "suicide attempt"
				Horvátová's alleged miscarriage
				"Voluntary legal divorce" from Leoš
				Leoš meets Kamila Stösslová
8	Coup d'État The Death of My Parents	16	1918–1924	Death of her mother
				Leoš's retirement as director of the Organ School
				Death of her father
				Čipera's arrival
9	Seventieth Birthday. Reconciliation	17	1924–1926	Leoš's seventieth birthday celebrations
				Resumption of marital relations
10	Leoš's Death	41		Leoš's intimate friendship with Kamila
				Leoš's death, funeral, and aftermath

form a striking counternarrative to the predominant tale of woe by detailing twenty-odd years of domestic concord:

> Leoš and I were now living at peace with one another. . . . It seemed as if our relationship was constantly rejuvenated (1903; p. 97). . . . And now there was a time of peace and contentment for me (1904-8; p. 101). . . . Leoš behaved very tenderly toward me (1909; p. 102). . . . I was happy. . . . We didn't have much money, we had to count our pennies all the time. But our happiness wasn't bought by money, it was within us (1909–1910; p. 106). . . . A peaceful time full of contentment came (1910; p. 109). . . . A beautiful, beautiful time (1910–1915; p. 111). . . . The relationship between

me and Leoš improved (1917; p. 163). . . . Leoš showed a new kindness to me (1918; p. 166). . . . Leoš was very good to me, he looked after me and showed great sympathy toward me (1918; p. 174). . . . This was a joyous time—full of things which invigorated us and reconciled us to everything bad that had gone before (1925; p. 190). . . . He was charming as before, he captivated me (1925; p. 193). . . . Everything had become rejuvenated, joyful (1925; p. 194). . . . We were both overjoyed when we were together again. At home he caught me impetuously in his arms and went on kissing me so that I found it all too much (1926; p. 200).

All this suggests that any representation of the Janáčeks' marriage as unremittingly unhappy is grossly oversimplified. Furthermore, Zdenka emerges from the memoirs as highly unstable, prone to manic mood swings and enmeshed in past pain. In fact, anyone disposed to view these memoirs as reliable testimony would, it seems, be presented with an insoluble conundrum: their author seems to have been suffering from a psychopathological condition, a major characteristic of which is an inability to construct a coherent narrative.

IV

Let's imagine then that, for all the reservations I have so far voiced about biography, we were to turn the spotlight on "Zdenka" as autobiographer in order to probe the veracity of her "memoirs." What might be the most valid type of biographical approach, and what might we find? Psychoanalysis might at first seem the natural avenue of exploration. Certainly, since the advent of the 1950s "psychobiography," even traditionally oriented biographers have unthinkingly employed Freudian terminology. However, as the psychiatrist Anthony Storr contends, psychoanalytical causal interpretation has not so far yielded convincing results.[18] Indeed, Freud's own forays into biography were disastrous.[19] Storr thus advocates instead a more scientific approach based on clinical psychiatry. His diagnosis of Kafka as schizoid is certainly persuasive. So let's follow Storr and toe a clinical line.

A close relative of psychiatry is of course psychotherapy, perhaps the most powerful tool of which is modern attachment theory, as formulated by John Bowlby and developed by many similarly minded researchers.[20] A brief technical digression at this point is unavoidable. At the heart of attachment theory is the notion of what Jeremy Holmes calls "the psychological immune system."[21] Just as "defense and the integrity of the individual organism are central to physical health," so a sense of security is the basis for psychological well-being. For Bowlby, psychological security is founded on the attachment bond.[22] The newborn infant has a biological need to stay close to caregivers in order to guard against predators; separation from protectors results in anxiety. Attachment is a "primary motivational system" that works independently of other systems such as feeding. A healthy attachment bond creates a stress-free environment—known as the "secure base"—in which the infant can explore. Attachment is hierarchical: at the top of the ladder is a single figure, usually but not necessarily the mother. Since attachment theory, unlike classic psychoanalytic theory, does not correlate caregiving roles with sexual identity, the convenient term "mother" from now on refers to a primary attachment figure of either sex.

Attachment proper begins to form after the age of six months. Up to the age of three an infant seeks to keep close enough to its mother to use her as a secure base for exploration, also exhibiting separation protest when threatened. An infant's exploratory behavior may be inhibited in one of two main ways: an overprotective or intrusive mother stifles her infant; an inattentive mother triggers fear of abandonment. With the advent of language, children begin to acquire a sense of individual identity and the capacity to interact. The growing child builds up a set of models of the self and other people. A securely attached child stores a model of a responsive and reliable caregiver, has a sense of self-worth, and develops the ability to forge strong, healthy relationships. Conversely, an insecurely attached child stores a model of a neglectful or inconsistently attentive caregiver, lacks self-esteem, and tends to approach relationships with undue caution.

There are four basic types of attachment, which are, in order of frequency of occurrence: *secure*; *insecure-avoidant*; *insecure-ambivalent*; and *insecure-disorganized*. About two-thirds of children form *secure* attachments. *Avoidant* infants try to minimize their needs in order to forestall rebuff; *ambivalent* children cling submissively to their caregivers; and *disorganized* infants develop a variety of more serious pathological conditions. As children become adolescents they are able to tolerate longer separations from caregivers, retreating to the parental home principally when threatened. Nevertheless, the progression from parental attachment via peer-group attachment to adult pair-bonding is a fraught process. A long-term partnership is the adult version of attachment. Just as the mother–infant relationship is not primarily based on feeding, so adult pair-bonding cannot adequately be explained through sexuality alone. The attachment cycle repeats itself as parents form bonds with their own offspring.

Attachment theory has undergone considerable empirical testing. A major contribution was made by Mary Ainsworth, who devised what is known as the "Strange Situation": a set pattern of interactions between a mother, a child, and an experimenter, culminating in the mother and the experimenter leaving and then returning to the child.[23] An infant's reactions when reunited with the mother can be categorized in terms of the four types of attachment. On the basis of Ainsworth's work, Daniel Stern developed the notion of *maternal attunement*.[24] What matters is not the quantity of mother-child interaction but the quality. Mothers of ambivalently attached children, for instance, intrude on their offspring when they are playing contentedly and rebuff them when they are distressed.

Mary Main conducted a study in which ten-year-olds, who had previously been classified in the Strange Situation at the age of one, were asked for an oral autobiography.[25] Three-quarters of the children had the same attachment classification at one and at ten. The stories told by secure children were consistently more coherent, exhibited greater powers of recall, and showed superior self-awareness. Main is also principally responsible for the so-called Adult Attachment Interview.[26] This is a semi-structured interview of a mother, which aims to "surprise the unconscious" into self-revelation.[27] The most significant aspect of Main's approach to the interviews is her concentration on style and structure as well as content. Secure individuals tend to be forthcoming and coherent; avoidant people incline towards the brief and idealized; ambivalent ones tend to be rambling and entangled in past difficulties. Remarkably, a number of studies have suggested that there is about an 80 percent correspondence between assessments of infants in the Strange Situation and their mothers' performances in the Adult Attachment Interview.[28] Peter Fonagy has pinpointed the defining aspect of secure adult narratives: *reflexive function*—the capacity to reason cogently about past trauma.[29]

The upshot of all this is that relationship patterns established in the first year or so of life are strikingly enduring. Avoidant infants tend to become bullies, while ambivalent ones are predisposed to turn into victims. Also, transmission of attachment patterns between generations is common: "The neglected psychopathic child grows up to become the neglectful psychopathic parent," and so on.[30] Naturally, other factors are involved; for example, social environment, temperament, and family structures. Nor are childhood attachment patterns irreversible: sometimes a person pulls through despite an appalling start to life; for instance, because of a supportive partner or even therapy. Nor are avoidant and ambivalent attachment patterns mutually exclusive: a person may display different behavioral patterns depending on circumstances. The notion of "developmental pathways" is probably the best way of conceptualizing differences in how children turn out. A specific attachment pattern will tend strongly to indicate a particular pathway, although a person may forge out in a new direction as the result of relationship changes or other nodal experiences. Ultimately, there is often hope even for the seriously disturbed.

V

How does all this impinge on "Zdenka" as autobiographer? Well, for a start the very first sentence of the memoirs would have any self-respecting psychotherapist reaching for a notebook. It reads: "Painfully, I have to admit to myself that only my childhood was a time of brightness and well-being in my life" (p. 1). Unrealistic idealization of childhood is a surefire indicator of insecurity, and engulfment by past pain points to ambivalent attachment. The initial childhood chapter of Zdenka's memoirs as a whole rates very poorly in terms of quality of recall and coherence. She mentions nothing before she was six, a prime indicator of insecure attachment. More worryingly, her account actually comprises two contradictory narratives jumbled together, a tendency among ambivalently attached individuals.[31] Zdenka's two stories can readily be unraveled. Her first narrative is a short tale of complete harmony, in which her father is especially idealized:

> I was the only child of young parents. As a family we had a happy life together at home. Papa was uncommonly good-natured and cheerful. From the early morning he'd sing or whistle Czech folk songs to himself. He was very popular with his students. Mama loved me very much. [She was] beautiful, slim, elegant, with strict moral principles. At our house there was an atmosphere of love and peace. Yes, my childhood was joyful.

In contrast, her second narrative is a more substantial story of what in the U.K. today is classified as child abuse:

> Mama didn't allow me to get away with anything. She lived only for her household, which she ran frugally. I remember clearly what it was like in our first Brno flat. I was intrigued by the activity in the street below. But I was allowed to see this only through closed windows. It was almost my only contact with the outside world. I didn't have friends with whom I could have played. I was almost always alone. Mama strictly forbade me to take books from the

[book]shelf. I didn't go to school, I had lessons at home. Papa taught me and got angry with me many times. We didn't go anywhere and visitors very seldom came to us. I almost ached for the company of other children, for someone who would like me. I had one friend: our little dog Žoli. He was a wise, long-suffering brown terrier. But then he grew old. My parents had him put down so I wouldn't know about it.

Clearly, Zdenka's first chapter entirely lacks *reflexive function*. She desperately asserts joy while at the same time undermining this protestation.

The cultural context makes matters worse. Zdenka's upbringing is a notable early example of what Frank Furedi terms "paranoid parenting."[32] Significantly, Zdenka's education was viewed as abnormal by at least one acquaintance. Robert Smetana—author of the largely sycophantic, informal biography that I mentioned earlier—attributes it to "*affected* maternal love." Smetana cites Zdenka's parents' reason for not sending her to school as ill health, yet there is no evidence of this.[33] Thus the opening chapter of Zdenka's memoirs clearly indicates ambivalent attachment: she inadvertently details the telltale cocktail of unfounded maternal anxiety and stifling of personal development. The problem seems to have been compounded by her unassertive father, who left the child rearing to his control-freak of a wife. Like the caged canaries she fed daily, Zdenka was shut off from the learning process of independent existence.

Robert Smetana gives us a further clue about the character of Anna Schulzová, describing her as someone "who always cared about the social position of her husband."[34] Zdenka's memoirs endorse the impression that her mother's primary concern was to enhance the family's standing by grooming a compliant wife for an upper-middle-class man. She comments that it was her mother "who had cultivated within me the feeling for duty, economy, and modest personal requirements." At some points in her narrative Zdenka herself actually teeters on the brink of recognizing this—for example, her reflections on her mother's death describe her as "obstinate and domineering" (p. 173)—but she ultimately shies away from painful revelation.

Anna Schulzová's social ambitions for her daughter were seemingly dashed when Zdenka announced her intention to marry the then impecunious Leoš Janáček. At first, Anna and her husband objected strongly, but Zdenka's obstinacy carried the day. Anna seems then to have transferred her ambitions to her son Leo. From this point onward, a family tree is probably necessary—see Figure 1, which has been compiled from details supplied by Zdenka. Since maternal attachment relationships seem

Figure 1
Zdenka's Maternal Family Tree

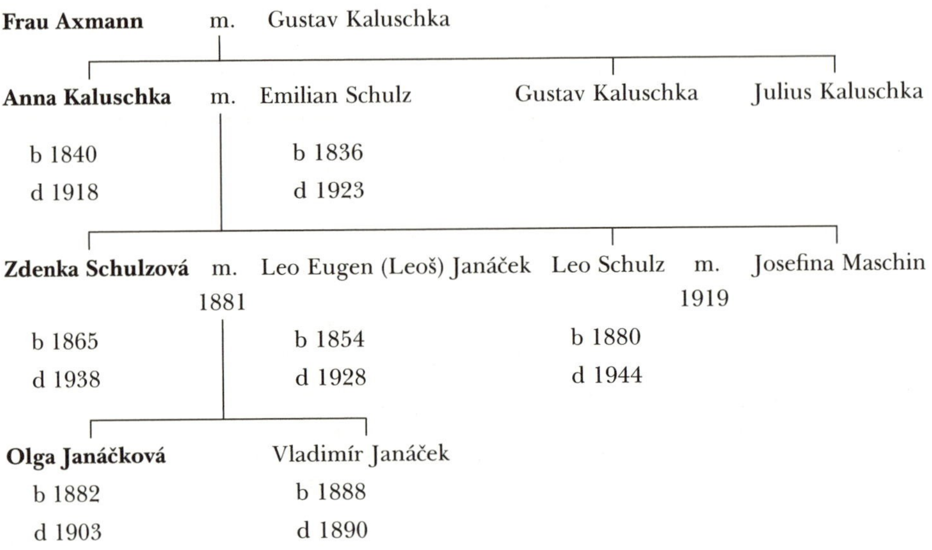

Frau Axmann   m.   Gustav Kaluschka

Anna Kaluschka   m.   Emilian Schulz   Gustav Kaluschka   Julius Kaluschka

   b 1840   b 1836

   d 1918   d 1923

Zdenka Schulzová   m.   Leo Eugen (Leoš) Janáček   Leo Schulz   m.   Josefina Maschin
          1881   1919

   b 1865   b 1854   b 1880

   d 1938   d 1928   d 1944

Olga Janáčková   Vladimír Janáček
   b 1882   b 1888
   d 1903   d 1890

to have been most important to Zdenka's development, this family tree privileges the female line. Leo Schulz incurred his mother's wrath when as a student he fell for the working-class Josefina Maschin. Leo was more compliant than Zdenka: for seventeen years he bowed to Anna's opposition to the match, finally marrying Josefina only after his mother's death. In the Schulz family, concern about social status ultimately took precedence. For instance, the principal concern of Zdenka's parents about the 1917 informal divorce from Leoš was that her "social position was unshaken" (p. 154). Equally damagingly, the Schulzes apparently found it excruciatingly difficult to discuss important matters openly. Zdenka writes of her mother's pregnancy with Leo: "Something was being concealed in our family. Mama used to be sad, often upset; she and Papa had sharp exchanges which suddenly subsided when I came in sight" (p.14). When Anna Schulzová eventually did admit the truth to her daughter, Zdenka felt from the tone that "she was ashamed, and that she was asking my pardon" (p. 14).

Of course, the tendency toward transmission from generation to generation would suggest that Anna Schulzová's relationship with her own mother was likely to have been ambivalent, and that Zdenka would probably repeat the pattern with her own children. All the information offered in the memoirs implies as much. Zdenka's maternal grandmother seems to have been inconsistent and intrusive in her parenting, too. Zdenka describes how at dusk one day her grandmother scared her out of looking at herself in the mirror; apparently, Zdenka was so affected by this childhood experience that forever after she felt ill if she looked into a mirror at twilight (p. 5). Furthermore, Zdenka was overprotective with her own children. For example, she banned Olga from what she calls "childish pursuits" such as running, skating, swimming, and dancing, even at times when Olga was well (p. 57), and she would have stopped Olga from going to school had Leoš not objected (p. 62). Fittingly, when Olga was dying Zdenka gave her a caged canary (p. 78).

VI

If my diagnosis of the attachment bond between Anna and Zdenka as *insecure-ambivalent* is accurate, one might expect confirmation through Zdenka's adult character and development. The insecurely attached are trapped in a vicious circle of anger, fear of abandonment, suppression of feelings, and low self-esteem. Unsurprisingly, this can have a devastating impact on adult relationships. There is copious evidence of such tendencies in Zdenka's makeup. Furthermore, the defining events in her life correspond precisely to the classic developmental pathway of an ambivalently attached individual.

As John Bowlby observes, an insecurely attached person is likely to marry precipitously to an unsuitable mate.[35] Zdenka, of course, married Leoš before her sixteenth birthday. As Jeremy Holmes argues, a common pattern of unsuitable marriage is the phobic-counterphobic alliance in which an ambivalent person marries an avoidant one.[36] There is abundant evidence that Leoš had avoidant leanings. As the ninth child of thirteen he received little attention from his mother; he effectively left home when he was eleven; his father died when he was twelve;

he seems to have been emotionally detached, and so forth. Indeed, *his* "autobiography," far from being enmeshed in past pain, erects a barbed wire fence around personal matters.[37]

Zdenka's low self-esteem dominates her account of her early married life. She remarks about her charitable activities: "Nothing on earth would have induced me to speak publicly or give my opinion aloud; I'd rather have crawled into a mouse hole" (p. 32). As a result, when her marriage ran into trouble she was incapable of confronting her husband with her grievances and simply fled back to her parents, on whom by her own admission she depended "completely" (p. 40). What Zdenka writes about money is also revealing, since, as Jeremy Holmes notes, the "way in which people relate to money is powerfully indicative of attachment styles."[38] Money means relatively little to avoidant people, whereas ambivalent individuals are overpreoccupied with money matters. Zdenka persistently accuses Leoš of fiscal fecklessness. Yet there is evidence to the contrary: early on, despite severe lack of funds, he supported his mother and one of his brothers (p. 33), and he later made regular payments into an insurance policy for Olga (p. 84).

Probably the most self-destructive aspect of Zdenka's adult character as revealed in the memoirs is what Martin Seligman would term her "learned helplessness."[39] This is the belief that one cannot influence the outcome of events. It is a crucial factor in the development of depression, and its major cause appears to be parents' paranoid fears about their children's health. Zdenka's learned helplessness is apparent in virtually everything she writes. She describes being overcome by doubts shortly before her wedding but claims that "it wasn't in my power to stop the course of events which were already in motion" (p. 22). Her approach to conflict in marriage was similarly passive: "I learnt to suffer without hope, without retreating, without a way out" (p. 39). As her life progressed, Zdenka appears to have become increasingly superstitious, perceiving herself as the hapless victim of Fate. In her memoirs she often reorders events to delude herself about the validity of alleged portents and premonitions. An obvious example of this is her description of a 1902 trip that she and Leoš made to a church outside Brno. She writes: "When we arrived . . . a funeral procession was . . . taking a young girl to her grave. . . . The next day we got the news that Olga had fallen ill with typhus" (p. 73). As Tyrrell notes (p. 74), according to correspondence held in the Janáček Archive in Brno, this trip actually took place a month after news of Olga's illness arrived. The narrative strategy of the memoirs, such as it is, reinforces the portrait of Zdenka as victim through its clichéd reliance on the notion of the inevitable and cliff-hanger conclusions to chapters.

VII

The most telling signs that Zdenka suffered from a psychopathological disorder occupy the domain of grief. Grief constitutes an extreme case of separation anxiety, because loss is permanent. Broadly speaking, there are four phases.[40] The first is an apparent calmness resulting from *numbing* or emotional shutdown. The next stage, *the search for the lost object* through *yearning* and *protest*, is the center of the mourning process. Visual images of the dead person haunt the bereaved, and the expression of anger is an important preliminary to recovery. Stage three, *disorganization and despair*, is a quasi-depressive state in which the bereaved person is constantly questioning, but in which the reality of loss is absorbed. The final phase, *reorganization*, sees the relinquishing of the old attachment bond and the gradual return of a capacity to form new attachments. A lot can go wrong with the grieving process. There is copious evidence of a strong relationship between loss and increased vulnerability to psychiatric disorder, particularly among the insecurely attached, even if supportive current relationships sometimes act as a buffer.[41] Similarly, people who attempt suicide are more likely to have experienced loss than those who do not.[42] More controversially, a 1989 U.K. study suggests that women are more liable than men to develop disorders after bereavement.[43]

Pathological grief follows a number of pathways, the most relevant of which for present purposes is what is known as *chronic grief syndrome*: the bereaved "becomes locked into a state of despair from which there seems to be no escape."[44] Such sufferers are often ambivalently attached and have usually shown lifelong dependency on parents and partners. *Chronic grief* is especially common in cases of multiple bereavement.[45] Four common indicators are: (1) prolonged depression; (2) persistent anger and resentment; (3) ideas of suicide, conceived especially as a means of rejoining the dead person; and (4) "mummification": the preservation of objects, rooms, or even entire houses exactly as they were when the deceased was alive.[46] Pertinent to our inquiries is a 1987 study that suggests the loss of a child regularly gives rise in a parent to a remarkably persistent state of *chronic grief*.[47] Mothers of dead children are particularly prone. You will probably be unsurprised to learn, then, that divorce rates are extremely high after the death of a child; all too often, both parents are "so grief-stricken that neither can provide a secure base for the other."[48]

Zdenka Janáčková's accounts of her reactions to the deaths of her two children might almost have been lifted from a psychotherapy manual.

The two-year-old Vladimír's death was unexpected. Strained marital relations seem to have meant an absence of mutual comfort between Zdenka and Leoš. Young parents commonly conceive soon after the death of a child,[49] and Zdenka indeed claims to have begged Leoš for another child, a plea which Leoš allegedly refused (p. 56). Zdenka entered a prolonged state of pathological mourning, in which her overprotectiveness of Olga reached obsessive proportions. She describes what must have been a hellish ten-year period in which "Hour after hour in the darkness of the night I listened to Olga's breathing, or jumped up from my sleep with the terrifying thought that Olga's heart had stopped beating" (p. 58).

When Olga did later die of typhoid fever, Zdenka was even less able to cope. Having given vent to outbursts of despair and irrational "wild hate" for her husband while Olga was dying (p. 90), she now became unnaturally calm, immersing herself in housework. Her description of the night of the funeral contains a worrying pointer to *chronic grief syndrome*. This quasi-necrophylic passage is perhaps the most disturbing part of the whole book (p. 95):

> I . . . spent the night in the child's room, where everything was just as it was from the funeral. . . . I caught something here which was uncommonly precious to me and which was vanishing irrevocably: the odour of Olga's corpse . . . the last thing that emanated from her body—I couldn't give up that. When later we rearranged the child's room as it had been during her lifetime, I slept on her bed. . . . I wished with all my being that she'd materialize, coming to me in the night as a spirit. She promised me this before she died. But she did not come.

Zdenka's rather gruesome attempt to be reunited with Olga is obviously part of the *yearning* stage of mourning, but her "mummification" of her lost child's bedroom suggests susceptibility to *chronic grief*. Unable to conjure up a vision of her lost Olga, Zdenka continued to oscillate between *numbing* and *yearning*.

After a while, Zdenka agreed with Leoš that she would go to stay with her parents in Vienna. She claims that

> what I'd longed for so much in vain at home came to me at my mother's house. I saw Olga in a dream. Radiant and beautiful, she came and said to me: "Mamuška, I'm fine." It relieved me in a trice. . . . Olga came and is with me (p. 96).

Zdenka was thereafter able to go through the motions of living, but she achieved this reduced functional capacity at a price: she never accepted that her daughter was gone, and so *chronic grief* and its attendant depressive state were to afflict her permanently. She confides "It was then that I got out of the habit of laughing; I lost it for the rest of my life" (p. 58). Even thirty or so years later when she was dictating her memoirs she was continuing to contest the loss: Olga "could be living if she hadn't got that typhoid fever," she protests (p. 90). Olga herself apparently predicted this situation shortly before she died: "Mamička, I know that you're the one in greatest need. Daddy will recover from this, but you'll remain abandoned" (p. 83). Zdenka's inability to recover from the deaths of Vladimír and Olga is bound up with acute dependency; she writes: "They were my surest support, they were . . . my everything" (p. 53).

VIII

After Olga's death, Zdenka had such low expectations that happiness to her meant merely the avoidance of permanent separation from her husband. She was now acutely vulnerable to further trauma. Ambivalent individuals are prone to compulsive caregiving, and she became neurotic about Leoš's personal well-being, worrying incessantly about his health, safety, diet, and clothes. Nevertheless, she survived without additional serious psychological injury until Leoš began his affair with Horvátová in 1915. Her fragility guaranteed an extreme reaction to renewed danger. Insecurely attached people exhibit an "angry determination to punish their attachment figure for the minutest sign of abandonment,"[50] and it is in this context that her 1916 suicide attempt is best understood. Zdenka makes much of the fact that after this incident a doctor told Leoš that she was "mentally unstable" and so was the rest of her family (pp. 150–51). The doctor was silenced by her lawyer brother's threat to sue. Zdenka fiercely asserts that she needed neither the doctor "nor any of his psychiatric colleagues" (p. 151). Her protestations of mental health are open to doubt.

Zdenka's self-esteem plumbed new depths with the informal 1917 divorce, to which she "gladly agreed" because it gave her the "chance to go on being with Leoš" (p. 156). The deaths of her parents and sister-in-law after the war left her almost entirely isolated. In such extremity, insecure individuals often become overattached to animals or even inanimate objects.[51] All of us have what is called "an internal secure base," and in times of crisis we derive comfort from creature comforts.[52] But excessive reliance of this type points to psychopathology. Throughout her memoirs, Zdenka appears obsessed with clothes, china, and, above all, furniture, which she describes in excruciating detail.[53] Zdenka also seems to have made a considerable emotional investment in Olga's poodle, Čert, between 1903 and 1915 (p. 84). After her father died in 1923, she acquired a second dog, Čipera, who became the object of particularly desperate attachment behavior. Zdenka actually attributes to Čipera the ability to assess human character unerringly by growling at untrustworthy individuals (p. 185).

In spring 1927 Leoš's moderate intimacy with Kamila Stösslová triggered in Zdenka another violent burst of separation protest. This time she undertook what she perceived to be an extremely risky thyroid operation, allegedly thinking that she would die under the knife (p. 208). In the event, Zdenka survived the operation and gave vent to her anger about Leoš's friendship with Kamila in her correspondence with the widow of one of Leoš's cousins.[54] These letters make unsupported allegations of financial impropriety against Kamila and her husband. They also contain a virulent vein of anti-Semitism, which cannot really be excused by the historical context—as Christopher Ricks observes, "not everybody in the 1920s was anti-Semitic."[55] The rhetoric is toned down in the memoirs, but anti-Semitism is unquestionably a powerful undercurrent that surfaces in passages such as Zdenka's charge that "even if you disregarded the difference in race, Mrs. Stösslová didn't exactly have the best reputation" (pp. 224–25).

Zdenka's final attachment crisis before she herself died was of course the death of Leoš. Her remarks about this alone provide compelling evidence of *chronic grief syndrome*. Particularly notable is her anger at Leoš for dying before she could make preparations to join him (p. 244). In January 1928 Zdenka was profoundly affected by the suicide of Rudolf Těsnohlídek, on whose comic strip Leoš based his opera *Příhody lišky Bystroušky (The Adventures of the Vixen Bystrouška)* (1922–1923). Těsnohlídek's wife—whose first name by a bizarre coincidence was Olga—gassed herself when she heard about her husband's death. From then on, Zdenka felt vindicated in her fantasy of dying at the same time as Leoš. The final few pages of the English translation of the memoirs are a testament to an irreparably damaged psyche. Having convinced herself that if she had been with Leoš on his last holiday her attentions to his wardrobe would have ensured his survival, Zdenka ends by agonizing over why Leoš refused to send for her when pneumonia was diagnosed. Her conclusion is (p. 244):

I will never know the real truth. One thing I know for certain: that it thwarted my idea of departing together with him as I'd always imagined and as I'd furthermore written to him after the death of the Těsnohlídeks. Could I come near him for eternity when he didn't want to see me here on earth? It was cruel, very cruel of him to leave me in this way.

To sum up, a close, clinically oriented investigation of Zdenka Janáčková's memoirs indicates the following scenario: the author had an *insecure-ambivalent* attachment relationship with her overprotective mother. This distorted her future development. Having made a problematic phobic-counterphobic marriage, her mental well-being was further assailed by the trauma of losing both her children. Her last thirty-five years or so witnessed a steady decline in the face of *chronic grief syndrome*. Her psychological immune system collapsed altogether when her husband died. Earlier, I talked about insecure attachment in terms of a vicious circle, but Zdenka's life is probably best visualized as a downward spiral. She dictated her memoirs at the nadir of this spiral. This is a desperately sad story. Nevertheless, one must acknowledge that life's victims collude in determining their fate. To put it another way, Zdenka Schulzová was every bit as bad for Leoš Janáček as he was for her. Today, had the Janáčeks' marriage survived as far as the death of Vladimír, the loss would almost certainly have led to divorce. Perversely, that Zdenka and Leoš survived more than two decades of armed neutrality is a considerable achievement in the context of the social pressures of their day. Leoš evidently suffered, too. In several of his letters to Kamila he describes Zdenka as "gloomy," "affected," and "hard."[56] Zdenka herself admits that she was unable to "laugh" (p. 58). Living with someone afflicted by chronic depression is extraordinarily debilitating. Zdenka's memoirs are clearly a spectacularly unsound basis on which to assess the life and character of Leoš Janáček.

IX

I began by disputing the notion that biographical study illuminates a creative artist's "inner life." I then argued that memoirs are particularly unreliable as source material for anyone seeking to propose connections between man and work, because the corrupting desire to mold reception confounds even the most honest autobiographers' attempts to assess their own lives and relationships dispassionately. I further suggested that Zdenka Janáčková's "memoirs" are uniquely problematic

Kamila Stösslová.

Zdenka and Leoš Janáček's wedding picture.

because of the many layers of narrative distortion that they contain. In support of this hypothesis, I have just employed attachment theory—an offshoot of clinical psychiatry and potentially a very promising analytical tool for the biographer—to lay bare the many internal contradictions within "Zdenka's" text. In other words, I have momentarily donned the guise of a biographer in order to undermine the discipline from within. I have chosen this route because the consequences of applying modern biographical modes of inquiry to the memoirs are so utterly intractable: the authorial "I" of this text appears to have been rendered incapable of narrative coherence by a serious psychopathological condition. Of course, I am not proposing that this "I" is identical with the historical Zdenka Janáčková, who is obscured by the clamor of fictionalizing voices (including her own) within the discourse that bears her name. What I am proposing is that the ultimate destination of any genuinely thorough biographical investigation of Zdenka's "autobiography" is a brick wall, and hence that even the most ardent proponent of biography ought to be wary of this source.

So, where does all this leave the claim that there is a strong relationship between the memoirs and Janáček's music? The short answer is dead in the water. Indeed, unlike Janáček's voluminous correspondence with Kamila,[57] the memoirs have remarkably little documentary value, since there are so few concrete details. Interestingly, "Zdenka" is very dismissive of the notion of relating her husband's life and music. She is particularly forthright in pooh-poohing the idea that Kamila inspired many of Janáček's late works: "The powerful genius of his art didn't need a woman for it to work," she writes (p. 221). I shall conclude by briefly problematizing the notion that it ought to be possible to map a pathway between the composer's allegedly "cruel" character and his music.

Tyrrell singles out the libretto of Janáček's final opera *From the House of the Dead* as a representation of extreme cruelty (see p. 168 above). Even if one ignores the fact that concentrating on only the libretto of an opera offers a severely limited perspective, there are still major difficulties with this line of argument. As Robert Vilain and Geoffrey Chew argue, the opera is based on a text by Dostoevsky that powerfully probes the fragile conventional demarcation line between autobiography and fiction. On the basis of an apparent collage of his experiences in a Siberian prison camp, Dostoevsky constructs a narrative that progresses slowly from "death" to "resurrection," revealing "humanity" to be present even in this brutal setting. It was Dostoevksy's "serious commitment to morality, humanity and truth" that seems to have appealed to Janáček.[58] Certainly, his libretto adheres to his model's humanistic narrative thread. On the title page of his score he actually inserted the epigraph: "In every creature a spark of God."[59]

Obviously, in a prison camp violence and punishment are commonplace. In *From the House of the Dead* there is even the added element of cruelty to animals, in the form of the prisoners taunting a wounded eagle that they have captured. Nevertheless, the violence in Janáček's version is essentially less arbitrary than in Dostoevsky's. The character that comes closest to a traditional central protagonist in the original text is Goryanchikov, who is flogged on arrival. Janáček conflated Goryanchikov with another character, a Polish nobleman, thereby converting Goryanchikov from a murderer to a political prisoner. Hence Goryanchikov has affirmed his status as a political prisoner before he is beaten, making his punishment more strongly motivated in the opera than in the book. The flogging is in fact primarily a vehicle for the vein of social criticism so prevalent in many of Janáček's works.[60]

Another act of violence at the end of Act 2 is at the heart of what Janáček's opera appears to be about: one of the prisoners hurls a samovar at Goryanchikov but instead hits Alyeya, a young Tartar boy. The most clearly delineated human relationship in the opera is that between Goryanchikov and Alyeya. Almost all of Dostoevsky's references to Alyeya are contained in a single section of his book. Janáček distributes these across his opera and develops Alyeya's part further, with the result that the burgeoning rapport between Alyeya and Goryanchikov frames the entire work.[61] In Act 1 Alyeya follows Goryanchikov anxiously when he is taken off to be beaten and also stares fixedly at the gate as the guards bring him back. At the start of Act 2, Goryanchikov asks Alyeya about his family and offers to teach him to read. Later in the same act the prisoners put on some amateur theatricals, which Goryanchikov and Alyeya watch side by side. They are drinking tea together when Alyeya is hit by the samovar. Alyeya's injury here is Janáček's own invention, and it provides a reason for Alyeya to be present in the prison hospital at the start of Act 3, where he is watched over by Goryanchikov. In the final scene, the news comes through that Goryanchikov is to be released. He bids farewell to Alyeya. As his fetters are removed, Alyeya throws himself around his neck, declaring "You are my father!" Goryanchikov replies: "Will I ever see you again, I wonder. A new life is beginning! Golden freedom!" At this precise moment, the prisoners symbolically release the eagle, who soars away. What thus occurs over the course of the opera is the formation and eventual relinquishing of a surrogate parent–child attachment bond. Ultimately, Janáček's libretto appears to be predicated on the intensely humanistic notion that strong and secure attachments may be created even under the direst of conditions. The composer's insight is striking, given his apparent difficulty with relationships in real life.

Which brings me finally to the actual music of the opera. Janáček aims for unparalleled immediacy of expression. The orchestral passage that accompanies Goryanchikov's offstage flogging is pulverizing—see the vocal score (hereafter VS), p. 24, mm. 23–30.[62] The main motif here (VS, p. 24, mm. 23–4) first occurs at the start of Act 1 (VS, p. 12, mm. 1–3). Its core trichord of minor second plus major third derives by inversion from the opening sonority of the overture. The trichord's constricted spacing clearly allegorizes physical pain. The "flogging" motif recurs in a yet more vicious variant near the end of Act 1 as Goryanchikov returns from punishment just as a fellow prisoner, Luka, is relating how he was almost beaten to death (VS, p. 53, mm. 3–12). The core trichord also underpins the shattering A-flat minor conclusion to Act 1 (VS, p. 55, mm. 18–39). These musical evocations of pain do stand out in the operatic repertory. Other composers' settings of offstage flogging and torture tend to deem cries of agony as sufficient. Cavaradossi's torture in Act 2 of *Tosca*, for example, does not penetrate Puccini's musical discourse, which concerns itself with the onstage dialogue between Tosca and Scarpio. In Britten's *Billy Budd*, the Act 1 flogging of the Novice occurs out of sight and sound, and when the half-dead victim is brought back the musical response is muted.

But the tender moments in Janáček's *From the House of the Dead* are also astonishingly effective. During the final parting between Goryanchikov and Alyeya the "flogging" motif is transformed into a radiant diatonic affirmation of humanity (VS, p. 204, m. 8 to VS, p. 205, m. 5). This is one of the most arresting passages in the entire opera. To complicate matters further, Janáček recycled much of the introduction to *From the House of the Dead* including the "pain" trichord from an unfinished violin concerto (1927–1928) benignly entitled *Putování dušičky* (The pilgrimage of a little soul). The crucial point is that Janáček's entire musical aesthetic is, as Robin Holloway observes, founded on the concept of music as the intense utterance of feeling of every sort.[63] Hanns Eisler went as far as to describe Janáček as the ultimate creator of musical expression. In the final analysis, what is most remarkable about Janáček's music is its engagement with the whole of human experience. No amount of rummaging about in memoirs and correspondence could ever adequately account for the extraordinary vision and humanity of *From the House of the Dead*. As Flaubert wrote, "The artist must . . . make posterity believe that he never existed,"[64] and this is exactly what Janáček achieves in his last opera.

NOTES

1. Marie Trkanová, *Paměti: Zdenka Janáčková – můj život* (Memoirs: Zdenka Janáčková— my life), (Brno: Šimon Ryšavý, 1998); English version: John Tyrrell, ed. and trans., *My Life with Janáček: The Memoirs of Zdenka Janáčková* (London: Faber and Faber, 1998). Page references throughout the text refer to the English translation of this book.

2. Donald Reiman, *The Study of Modern Manuscripts: Public, Confidential, and Private* (Baltimore and London: Johns Hopkins University Press, 1993), p. 38.

3. Julian Barnes, *Flaubert's Parrot* (London: Picador, 1985), p. 95.

4. Richard Holmes, "Biography: Inventing the Truth," in *The Art of Literary Biography*, ed. John Batchelor (Oxford: Clarendon Press, 1995), pp. 15–25 (p. 18).

5. Humphrey Carpenter, in conversation with Lyndall Gordon, "Learning about Ourselves: Biography as Autobiography," in *The Art of Literary Biography*, pp. 267–79 (p. 275).

6. Barnes, *Flaubert's Parrot*, p. 39.

7. Richard Ellman, *Selected Letters of James Joyce* (London: Faber and Faber, 1975).

8. Paula Bakscheider, *Reflections on Biography* (Oxford: Oxford University Press, 1999), p. xviii.

9. Ian Donaldson, "Life into Text," *Essays in Criticism*, vol. 41 (1991), pp. 253–61 (pp. 260–61).

10. Ann Thwaite, "Starting Again: One of the Problems of the Biographer," in *The Art of Literary Biography*, pp. 201–11 (p. 210).

11. Maynard Solomon, "Biography," in *The New Grove Dictionary of Music and Musicians*, rev. 2d ed., vol. 3, ed. Stanley Sadie (London: Macmillan, 2001), pp. 598–601 (p. 600).

12. See John Tyrrell's introduction to the English translation (note 1), on pp. ix–xviii (pp. ix–xi).

13. Robert Smetana, *Vyprávění o Leoši Janáčkovi* (Stories about Leoš Janáček) (Olomouc: Velehrad, 1948).

14. Marie Stejskalová, *U Janáčků: podle vyprávění Marie Stejskalové* (At the Janáčeks: As told by Marie Stejskalová) 2d ed., (Prague: Panton, 1959; 1964).

15. Vladimír Helfert, *Leoš Janáček*, vol. 1 (Brno: Oldřich Pazdírek, 1939); Jaroslav Vogel, *Leoš Janáček: život a dílo* (Leoš Janáček: life and work) (Prague: Státní hudební vydavatelství, 1963).

16. For further details about Trkanová's typescripts and their history see John Tyrrell, "He Was One of the Great Composers—and Also One of the Cruellest," *The Guardian*, 5 February 1999.

17. See Ibid.

18. Anthony Storr, "Psychiatry and Literary Biography," in *Art of Literary Biography*, pp. 73–86 (p. 73).

19. For critiques of Freud's writings about Dostoevsky and the paranoid psychotic Judge Schreber, see Anthony Storr, "Psychiatry and Literary Biography," pp. 74–75.

20. John Bowlby's main work is his imposing *Attachment and Loss*, 3 vols. (London; Hogarth Press, 1969, 1973 and 1980); for an excellent and readable introduction to Bowlby's ideas and their subsequent development by other researchers, see Jeremy Holmes, *John Bowlby and Attachment Theory* (London: Routledge, 1993); the clinical value of modern attachment theory is powerfully advocated in Jeremy Holmes, *The Search for the Secure Base: Attachment Theory and Psychotherapy* (Hove: Brunner Routledge, 2001). My brief account of attachment theory draws on all three of these texts.

21. Holmes, *Search for the Secure Base*, p. 1.

22. John Bowlby, *A Secure Base: Clinical Applications of Attachment Theory* (London: Routledge, 1988), pp. 11–12.

23. See Mary Ainsworth et al., *Patterns of Attachment: Assessed in the Strange Situation and at Home* (Hillsdale, N.J.: Erlbaum, 1978).

24. Daniel Stern, *The Interpersonal World of the Infant* (New York: Basic Books, 1985).

25. Mary Main, "Metacognitive Knowledge, Metacognitive Monitoring, and Singular (Coherent) vs. Multiple (Incoherent) Models of Attachment: Findings and Directions for Future Research," in *Attachment Across the Life Cycle*, ed. Colin Murray Parkes, Joan Stevenson-Hinde, and Peter Marris (London: Routledge, 1991), pp. 127–59.

26. Mary Main et al., "Security in Infancy, Childhood, and Adulthood: A Move to the Level of Representation," in "Growing Points of Attachment Theory and Research," in *Monographs of the Society for Research in Child Development*, ed. Inge Bretherton and Everett Waters, vol. 50 (1985), pp. 66–104.

27. Main, "Metacognitive Knowledge," p. 141.

28. See, for example, Klaus Grossman and Karin Grossman, "Attachment Quality as an Organizer of Emotional and Behavioral Responses in a Longitudinal Perspective," in *Attachment Across the Life Cycle*, pp. 93–114; see also Mary Ainsworth, "Attachments Beyond Infancy," *American Psychologist* 44 (1989): 706–16.

29. Peter Fonagy, "Thinking about Thinking: Some Clinical and Theoretical Considerations in the Treatment of a Borderline Patient," *International Journal of Psychoanalysis* 72 (1991): 639–56.

30. John Bowlby, *Child Care and the Growth of Love*, rev. 2d ed. (Harmondsworth, Eng.: Penguin, 1965).

31. Main, "Metacognitive Knowledge," pp. 148–51.

32. Frank Furedi, *Paranoid Parenting* (Harmondsworth, Eng.: Penguin, 2001).

33. Smetana, *Vyprávění o Leoši Janáčkovi*, p. 23.

34. Ibid., p. 22.

35. John Bowlby, "Developmental Psychiatry Comes of Age," *American Journal of Psychiatry* 145 (1988): 1–10.

36. Holmes, *John Bowlby and Attachment Theory*, pp. 82–84.

37. A. Veselý, ed., *Leoš Janáček: pohled do života i díla* (Leoš Janáček: A View of Life and Works) (Prague: František Borový, 1924).

38. Holmes, *Search for the Secure Base*, p. 121.

39. Martin Seligman, *Helplessness: On Depression, Development and Death* (San Francisco: Freeman, 1975).

40. A full account is given in John Bowlby, in *Loss: Sadness and Depression*, vol. 3 of *Attachment and Loss* (London: Hogarth Press, 1980; Harmondsworth: Penguin Books, 1981), pp. 85–103. A useful summary can be found in Holmes, *John Bowlby and Attachment Theory* (note 20), pp. 89–94.

41. For a detailed examination of these issues, see George Brown and Tirril Harris, *The Social Origins of Depression* (London: Tavistock, 1978); Colin Murray Parkes, "Attachment, Bonding, and Psychiatric Problems after Bereavement in Adult Life," in *Attachment Across the Life Cycle*, pp. 268–92.

42. Holmes, *John Bowlby and Attachment Theory*, p. 179.

43. Pat Sable, "Attachment, Anxiety and Loss of a Husband," *American Journal of Orthopsychiatry* 59 (1989): 550–56.

44. Holmes, *John Bowlby and Attachment Theory*, pp. 183–84 (p. 183).

45. Parkes, "Attachment, Bonding, and Psychiatric Problems," p. 281.

46. Bowlby, *Attachment and Loss*, vol. 3, pp. 141–51.

47. Darrin Lehman et al., "Long-term Effects of Losing a Spouse or a Child in a Motor Vehicle Crash," *Journal of Personality and Social Psychology* 52 (1987): 218–31.

48. Holmes, *Search for the Secure Base,* p. 14.

49. Bowlby, *Attachment and Loss*, vol. 3, p. 122.

50. Holmes, *John Bowlby and Attachment Theory,* p. 67.

51. Bowlby, *Attachment and Loss*, vol. 3, pp. 165–69.

52. Holmes, *Search for the Secure Base,* p. 9.

53. Tyrrell comments on p. xvii of his introduction to the English translation of the memoirs that he has "cut overdetailed comments about (Zdenka's) furniture and so on," yet it still reads like a catalogue.

54. This unpublished correspondence is briefly described on p. xv of Tyrrell's introduction to the English translation.

55. Christopher Ricks, *T. S. Eliot and Prejudice* (London: Faber and Faber, 1988), p. 64.

56. John Tyrrell, trans. and ed., *Intimate Letters: Leoš Janáček to Kamila Stösslová* (London: Faber and Faber, 1994), pp. 55, 71, and 114.

57. Ibid.

58. Geoffrey Chew and Robert Vilain, "Evasive Realism: Narrative Construction in Dostoevsky's and Janáček's *From the House of the Dead*," in *Janáček Studies,* ed. Paul Wingfield (Cambridge: Cambridge University Press, 1999), pp. 56–78 (p. 60).

59. This manuscript is held under the class mark A 7448 by the Janáček Archive, which forms part of the Music History Division of the Moravian Regional Museum in Brno.

60. Chew and Vilain, "Evasive Realism," pp. 75–76.

61. Further details of the differences between Janáček's libretto are given in ibid.; Marina Melnikova, "Interpretace Dostojevského textu v libretu poslední Janáčkovy opery' (The interpretation of Dostoevsky's text in the libretto of Janáček's last opera), *Hudební věda* 23 (1986): 43–55; and John Tyrrell, disc note to the Charles Mackerras recording (Decca 430 375–82, 1980, reissued 1991).

62. UE 8221 (Vienna, 1930; rev. 2d ed., 1964).

63. Robin Holloway, "Expressive Sources and Resources in Janáček's Musical Language," in *Janáček Studies* (note 58), pp. 1–17.

64. Quoted from Barnes, *Flaubert's Parrot,* p. 95.

Janáček's Vizitka

MICHAEL BECKERMAN

I have Janáček's vizitka.

At some point last year I purchased it from a dealer in paper goods in Olomouc, Czech Republic. The man from whom I bought it, one Josef Dočkal, had previously sold me a photograph by Josef Sudek in one of his eBay auctions. We struck up a virtual conversation in Czech, and when he heard I was interested in Janáček, he offered me the vizitka and a photograph of Janáček, which I declined. When I purchased the vizitka he also sent me various composer stamps. Perhaps he was excited that he'd made a large sale, perhaps he was simply generous, or maybe I overpaid him. Suddenly I am coy about revealing how much I paid for the vizitka. I think it was $50. Maybe it was more. I forget.

"I Forget" as an Approach to History

I forget. This is something you will read several times in this essay. I forget. As Kundera notes in *Testaments Betrayed*, the concrete past is lost to us forever. Not only can we not remember our conversations even minutes later, but the accompanying textures: smells, the sense of the air's weight, a chirping bird outside. All these are gone. I forget what happened a few months ago, as I forget what happened yesterday or this morning. In the fractal world of forgetting, each moment expands into an infinitude of loss. That is why recapturing the past is so exhausting, frustrating. That is why the manipulation of the past is often the province of tyrants. What amount of any past do we have access to? Even the most recent past? What percentage of any past remains to us? One-billionth? One-trillionth? The ungraspable vastness of such tiny swimmers in the vastest ocean.

And as we weave our narrative tapestries we proceed as if this were not so, and do not *feel* as if this is true. Just as we may feel that we have a sizable chance of winning the lottery, when indeed we are more likely to be struck by lightning. Our sense, our aura of closeness to the lottery jackpot is an illusion created by the fact that for most of us there is no practical difference between one chance in fifty thousand, and one chance in ten million. They are both unimaginable, and so we imagine ourselves to be nearer victory than we could possibly be. For all this, we are a million times closer to capturing the lottery than we are recapturing the past, even without a ticket.

This is not deconstruction; not yet another story about the delicate, self-serving, politicized narratives we impose on the past. That comes later. This is about data, or rather, the lack of it. This is why we must impose narratives. Otherwise we might realize just how lost we are.

Just after writing this I found the following passage in Kundera's new book, *Ignorance:* "Without much risk of error I could assume that the memory retains no more than a millionth, a hundred-millionth, in short an utterly infinitesimal bit of the lived life." And there I was suggesting that we have no more than a billionth and a trillionth! Luckily for both of us there is no proof either way. Kundera writes brilliantly about all these same issues and Janáček seems to be part of the process. Could it be a Brno-Janáček-Czech thing that gives rise to such thoughts?

An Example: Moving to New York

I have recently moved with my family from a six-bedroom house in San Francisco—one with a large basement—to a three-bedroom apartment in Manhattan. Here was a concrete problem, and one I should have been able to solve. I stood looking at my empty new digs and asked: Will my possessions fit in the new apartment? They were all packed, but I had made detailed lists, estimates, room plans and drawings. *My* stuff, three months ago. The fairly immediate past. Yes, I thought, it will easily fit. I was drastically wrong. I had at least 50 percent more stuff than I remembered. What had happened? Simply this: in the absence of my *actual* things, I'd made up a kind of story about my things based on what my mind was able to grasp and retain. When we unpack the historical past the infinitesimally few documents we have allow us or even force us—with no opposing evidence extant—to weave a story that makes sense to us, just as in my own narrative my "things" made sense to me—until the "real" stuff arrived. The difference, of course, is that in our study of history it is rare for *real* stuff to arrive, and never does all of it arrive to show us the error of our ways, the amazing falsity of our conceptions.

A short-term example of this chronic forgetting. This morning the man next to me on the train cannot find his ticket anywhere. He had it just a few moments ago. Anxiety and dread. He hunts, his confidence eroded. "Ah, here it is. In my shirt pocket." I tell him I would like to use him in my study, could I have his name? He tells me his first name, Mitchell, but not his last.

Into the Holocaust and Then Out Again

Imagine how uncomfortable were the critical theorists who realized that their methods were being employed by Holocaust deniers! And do the arguments presented here also bolster the gleefully bloody-minded obfuscators who deny? No. For large-scale events involving millions of people we must accept the principle of *convergence of evidence*. Of course, what "really" happened is still lost, the numbers may be off by 50 percent, and debates still rage unpleasantly about whether the Nazi attack on the Roma (Gypsies) was somehow equal to what happened to the Jews, or the Catholics, or the Poles, or . . .

3:02 P.M. and 20 Seconds

Our reconstructions of history are bound to be false because too much detail has been lost, a thousand times more than what we have in any found fossil. We end up trying to imagine, in the case of Janáček, the impossibly vast category of "Brno in the 1890s." Fine, for what it's worth. But what about the color of the light, the feel of the wind, and the odor of burning leaves on October 9, 1894, at 3:02 P.M. and 20 seconds?

We have a sense that the feel and texture of the past moment has vanished forever.

Is there any way the vizitka can help us visit the past? How shall we get information from it?

Vizitky in General

First a brief word about vizitky in general. First appearing in Germany at the end of the eighteenth century, they had become common by the mid-nineteenth century throughout Europe and the United States, sometimes with elaborate rules of use:

To the unrefined and underbred, the visiting card is but a trifling bit of paper; but to the cultured disciple of social law, it conveys a subtle and unmistakable intelligence. Its texture, style of engraving, and even the hour of its leaving combine to place the stranger, whose name it bears, in a pleasant or a disagreeable attitude.

—*Our Deportment*, 1881

The cards of unmarried and married men should be small (about 1.25 by 3 inches). For married persons a medium size is in better taste than a large card. The engraving in simple writing is preferred, and without flourishes. Printed letters, large or small, are very commonplace, no matter what the type may be. The "Mr." before the name should be dispensed with by young men.

—"Rules of Etiquette & Home Culture," 1882

A man never carries or leaves the cards of any other man, nor can he assume any of the responsibilities or etiquette relating to the cards of any of his feminine relatives or friends. Men never presumed to crease or bend their cards, when such habits were in fashion, and they do not do so today.

—*Correct Social Usage*, 1903

In the Czech-Viennese orbit every respectable person had a vizitka. Janáček had several, as we shall see.

Measuring the Vizitka

But this is all too vague. Isn't it the province of historical investigation to measure and quantify? The vizitka is 2¹/2 by 4 inches, or perhaps since it was made in Europe it should be measured in centimeters: 6.5 by 10. Its most notable quality, aside from the composer's name, is the slightly jagged edge. There must be a name for it in the paper profession. So far, my attempts to locate the name of the typeface and card stock have failed. Would knowing that name make the description more accurate and give me greater authority? Let us imagine that I am able to say: "It is a Windsor font visiting card made in 1924 at the Heinzigen paper factory in Březiny in Central Moravia." Even though there is no such factory, the name Windsor is a possibility, but it cannot be confirmed. The typeface seems to match that of several letters marked "Windsor" preserved in the Janáček Archive. (Note how scientific the previous sentence sounds, with its easy command of the facts and the tag "preserved in the Janáček Archive," the word *archive* evoking the world of painstaking scientific investigation. Really, though, pretending to have any authority of the past is a pose.)

The card seems faded, and I suppose particular tests might reveal precisely what color it was. Or perhaps not. Perhaps the real color is lost forever. Of course, what we fear most is that, whatever color it may have been, the way *it appeared to the citizens of the past* is different than anything we know or can know.

The name Leoš Janáček is just above the middle of the card in this "almost Windsor" typeface. More about the provenance later.

On the back is written "*Všeho štěstí přeje.*" Something like "Best wishes"; literally, "I wish you all happiness." Underneath there is a slanted line with two dots on either side. What does this signify?

How do we divine the "meaning" of this document, and is it typical of the documents we find, or is it in any way exceptional? Are there secrets this document possesses, or is it telling us all we need to know?

Contemplating the Status of the Vizitka as Real

But before doing this, we must ask questions about the vizitka's provenance. Is the vizitka real or a forgery? As mentioned above I received it from a man "dealing in paper goods" from Olomouc, a stunning town in the Czech Republic where Mozart fled during the smallpox epidemic of 1765. He told me several things during our transaction, many of which are preserved as "e-mail documents." Now, if part of the contemplation of history may be described as "I forget," another might be called, in continuing, ". . . but I'll check." But what should we check?

E-mail documents may be forged a hundred ways, so there is no way that they should be used as proof of anything, and in fact there is no particular reason you should believe any of this, since I suppose there are many ways I could have made up the e-mails, or figured out a way to send them to myself through a Czech server. Perhaps I do not even have Janáček's vizitka, real or fake. How do you as a reader know? But why would I bother to write this little essay? Why would one do anything? Why not?

But whether it is fake or real, invented by me (certainly possible) or "authentic," whatever that could mean, let us reproduce the vizitka front and back as is:

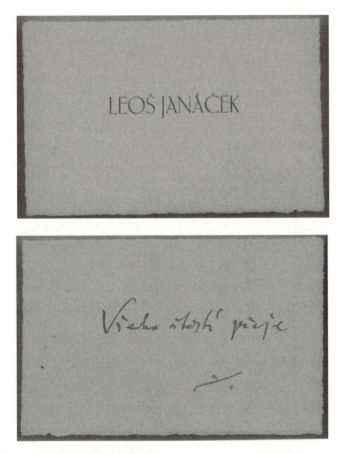

Figure 1. My vizitka front and back

Surely having various e-mail documents gives the illusion that one has control, but there are, I'm sure, various things about my transactions I have erased. I forget. Perhaps I kept them all. Perhaps I am hiding some of them from you because I do not like the way I appear in them. You do not know. You have to trust me, and trust is a sucker's move in the intricate game of history. I don't trust me either. I have a nagging doubt that I might have deleted something unrecoverable. And this causes me, metaphorically, to turn around, the way we do when we think we've left the stove on at home.

Should I consider the possibility that my vizitka is a fake? Surely eBay, as the vanguard of millennial capitalism, is riddled with potential deceits.

Thus, while a fake vizitka might give some insight into the psychology of the forgery of collectibles in 2002, it is absurd to imagine we can learn anything about Janáček from it. Or have we already learned something about Janáček whether or not the card is real? Or whether or not we might have learned something about Janáček even if I have made the whole thing up—even if there is no visiting card at all. I think my vizitka is real, but I cannot prove it. There is only convergence of evidence.

How I Keep My Vizitka

I keep my vizitka in a polyurethane plastic case made for storing sports cards. Simultaneously immanent and reachable, tangible, yet completely safe. This is in keeping with the grand collectible strategies of our time, most astonishingly noted in the Beanie Baby craze, where the cuddly little penguins, clowns, walruses, and ducklings derive their value from the paradox that they had never, would never, be cuddled. Vizitka-like, they are prisoners in plastic with the difference that, "mint condition," they have never been touched after their departure from the factory.

When I moved, I placed the card in a large purple J. C. Penney box (I forget. In this case I had forgotten that there was a second *e* in Penney, although I did not think it was spelled "Penny."). In this box I have for many years kept collected treasures including:

a. A program of a production of *Julius Caesar* directed by my father and in which I played a young boy.
b. A picture of myself taken at about the age of sixteen by my friend Steve Cohen. I am climbing a tree in, I believe, Central Park. I forget.
c. A baseball card called "Dodger Sluggers" featuring Carl Furillo, Gil Hodges, Roy Campanella, and Duke Snider given to me by my best childhood friend, Ed Ellison, who may well have been there when I invented the peanut game (see below).
d. Several oversized "3-dimensional" cards, including, I would have said, Reggie Jackson and Thurman Munson. (Upon examination it turns out that it's really Dave Winfield, and Don Mattingly, and Dave Stieb, and John Tudor. How could I, who have looked so many times in the box over the years, have forgotten Dave Stieb?)
e. A faded letter from a musicologist named Howard Brown, offering me a visiting appointment at the University of Chicago.

While I am listing all these things I gradually become aware that the vizitka is missing. Where is it? I continue listing, but my mind is really on the vizitka. Could I have lost it? I have been unpacking books and boxes in my study. Is it possible that I've actually lost the vizitka, dropped it among the crumpled-up paper? Thrown it in the trash? It occurs to me that this is a danger of unpacking the past. Things get lost, confused. An original order becomes muddled. The deeper one looks, the more the sludge is disturbed.

The Peanut Game

I don't know why, but when I was a small child, I dreamed up a game. Perhaps it started at Herbie Auleta's birthday party. Eddie Ellison might have been there. Peanuts were handed out. For reasons unclear, I decided to see how many times I would remember establishing the "game." And of course, all the game consisted of was remembering the word *peanut* in the context of the game. I cannot say how many times I have "won" the game, but I can say that months, and sometimes even years have gone by without my remembering the game. I am sure that during those lean months or years I eat peanuts, or at least peanut butter, see Mr. Peanut, use the term peanut gallery, and read Charles Schultz's cartoon *Peanuts*. Somehow these do not take me back to the original memory. But suddenly I will remember and "win!" Mine is an individual and even idiosyncratic game, but it may tell us something about the way in which we come to be in our state of constantly-both-remembering-and-forgetting the past, for strange lengths of time, and probably unfathomable reasons.

Am I Repeating Myself?

The lost vizitka appears under the lid of the removed purple box. Did you remember that I had lost it?

In my preface to *Dvořák and His World* ten years ago I wrote about lifting a lid on a table at Dvořák's summer house and finding Josef Suk's initials carved in the wood underneath the false tabletop. Does the fact that I am again speaking of lifting lids connect me with my own past in a profound way or simply reveal that I have traveled nowhere over the period of a decade? In my new book on Dvořák, I include an illustration of a vizitka, the critic Henry Krehbiel's card inscribed to Dvořák. This is something I just remembered. How could I have forgotten this over the last weeks and months as I write about Janáček's vizitka?

Why did I place my vizitka in this box, with other collectibles, bits of nostalgic memorabilia? Was it a coincidence, a simple desire to preserve it? (During the early stages of unpacking I had forgotten completely that the vizitka was in the box and was sure I had lost it.) Is Janáček's vizitka just another collectible to me? Is Janáček? Do the objects of our research become our heroes and is our desire to own bits and pieces, sketches or letters, a bit of primitive totemism? If it turns out that Janáček was or is my hero the way the baseball player Sandy Koufax was forty years ago, does that make me *unfit* to do research on him? Or must I simply be on the lookout for lurking hero worship? But if he were not my hero, why would I waste so much time on him? And what if he was my hero, but is not now? Will my work improve or decline as a result?

My Mysterious Vizitka

Aura. My vizitka is not a mass-produced collectible, but a real thing handled once by the Master. He touched it with his hand, wrote on it. Who cares? And how does someone come to care whether or not such and such a thing was touched by Janáček, or Beethoven, Ty Cobb, Gertrude Stein, Tyrone Power, Philip Roth, or Virginia Woolf? Are these keepsakes—locks of hair, sketches, driver's licenses—like snow globes that we shake to animate the lands of the past?

A Scene from *Kát'a*

When a magician does a trick, say, making an elephant disappear, or sawing a woman in half, the entire audience is expected, more or less, to experience the same thing. In the first case, everyone would say, "It seemed to me as if the elephant vanished." Is a composer like a magician? When Beethoven puts together a symphony in "just such and such a way," does the elephant vanish? Are we all, more or less, expected to have a shared response? Certainly Beethoven has gone to at least as much trouble as the magician in creating his effect.

There is no real answer to this question available to us at this time. While we can teach our students the hierarchical structures of, let us say, sonata form, we cannot prove that in any one piece that "primary" themes are indeed primary. Nor can we ever argue incontrovertibly that something has an unequivocal meaning. We don't know whether slow movements are meant to disappear in our imaginations as the soft center of a work, or whether they may be the artistic core, or whether it differs from piece to piece or listener to listener.

As a more concrete example of this I would like to offer a scene from *Kát'a Kabanová*. It takes place at the end of Act 2 and involves the consummation of the love affair between Boris and Kát'a. Janáček has, however, staged the moment as a contrast between two pairs of lovers, or perhaps even a tug of war. Varvara and Kudryáš are onstage and seem to communicate solely by singing Janáčkian folk songs to each other. When they are not actually serenading each other, they're prattling on about whether or not Kabanicha, the negative authority figure, will find out what they're up to. They are accompanied throughout by a lilting folk song rhythm which first appeared earlier in the second act. Boris and Kát'a, on the other hand, are classical doomed nineteenth century lovers. Their love is endless, hopeless, liberating, and killing: Romeo and Juliet, Tristan and Isolde. Their offstage cries are delivered in the high style, their music soggy with passion, marked by staggering rhythms and melodic leaps.

Janáček, our composer/magician, has juxtaposed these pairs. How are we to understand them? The most obvious reading is that Boris and Kát'a are the *real* lovers—the scene and, by easy extension, the opera, is about them. Varvara and Kudryáš are foils. Whether we are meant to think of them as "charming unassuming lovers" or "insipid lovers" is less important than their function of both musically and dramatically setting up the ideal conditions for observing Boris and Kát'a, or at least imagining them since they are offstage. One could argue for this reading using everything from the title of the opera to the structure of the scene. Certainly the exalted return of Kát'a and Boris from their tryst and the way their music takes over the scene's conclusion would support this view.

But there are other things that do not fit so easily with this scenario. Janáček gives Varvara and Kudryáš a hauntingly charming last song to sing, accompanied by their familiar rocking pulse. They are also accompanied by a drone, and the whole comprises one of the most magnificent idylls in his work. Clearly these two lovers represent another, more stable form of ideal love symbolized by the elevation of the folk song.

Is there any way our vizitka could help us to decide which pair should prevail in our imaginations and our memories?

What Can My Vizitka Tell Me About Janáček?

When I began dreaming of this essay, the idea of a vizitka revealing anything about Janáček was far-fetched. Perhaps the point was supposed
to be that it could reveal nothing. I forget. Yet I've recently received
six photos over the Internet from Eva Drlíková, editor of *Opus Musicum*
and a prime mover in the Janáček Foundation. The six vizitky, with the
exception of one of unknown provenance, date from about 1890 to 1925.
They are reproduced below. They trouble me.

LEOŠ JANÁČEK	LEOŠ JANÁČEK. ČLEN DOPISUJÍCÍ ČESKÉ AKADEMIE CÍSAŘE FRANTIŠKA JOSEFA.
1890	1890–1899
LEOŠ JANÁČEK	*Leoš Janáček:*
About 1910	World War I and after
Dᴿ PH. LEOŠ JANÁČEK	Leoš Janáček
1925	?

As a Man, Janáček Was Always a Stranger to Me*

Through the efforts of journalists, publicists, and some biographers Janáček is usually portrayed as a classic "core personality." Indeed, one of the key images of Janáček is a caricature. Those wishing to carve out a niche for Janáček in the ecosystem of the late twentieth- and early twenty-first-century opera house found his bona fides as a slightly wild Slav, Searcher for Truth extremely useful, and we are led to endorse the composer's maxim "There's only one Janáček and that's me!" Yet some of the people closest to him had other ideas. Here is Maria Calma-Veselá, the woman who, arguably, did more than anyone to get *Jenůfa* produced in Prague: "If Janáček is sometimes portrayed as a sensitive, emotional man, it is either a deliberate, hypocritical attempt to disguise his true colors, or a failure to fathom the depths of so complex a personality. One could write an interesting, [even] enthralling novel about him. But would that help his cause? His contribution to the arts is so great that it outweighs any flaws in his character."

One of his lovers, Gabriela Horvátová, the Kostelnička in the Prague premiere of *Jenůfa,* put the matter more bluntly: "He was very individual, not one person but five or six people rolled into one, and you did not always know which one you were talking to."

Does the representation of Janáček's self through vizitky support Horvátová's picture of a dissociated personality? This is not so flippant a question as I first thought.

Back to *Kát'a*

Janáček has been marketed as if he were an integrated personality, and as if the power of his works derives from this. We should consider the opposite, and count it a necessary condition for an operatic composer. The only person who could inhabit the skin of both the brilliant amoral Vixen and the dried-out old forester, the glamorous yet jaded Marty and the sadistic Prus is someone without the kind of core personality promised by journalists and served up by his biographers. I believe that this is borne out by his behavior. Is it borne out by the vastly different

---

* In an essay like this one it is hard to know if footnotes are in any way desirable. In any case, there are several places they could go. Perhaps, though, they are necessary in this case. Calma-Veselá's remark may be found in Mirka Zemanová's *Janáček: A Composer's Life* (Boston: Northeastern University Press, 2002), p. 133. Horvátová's remark may be found on p. 150 of the same book.

vizitky, each one seemingly unrelated to the other? And is it borne out
by our scene from *Kát'a*, a scene that derives its power, as far as I am
concerned, from the fact that Janáček effectively made *no* choices about
what is primary, because he could make no such choices? The doomed
lovers, Boris and Kát'a represent one scenario, one he craved in his own
life, as his letters to Kamila Stösslová sometimes suggest with their references to self-immolation. Yet the clever folk lovers, in their eternal
balance, are far more than foils and receive far more musical attention.
Was this idyllic stasis also Janáček's goal? Self-immolation and stasis
together?

For all the talk of well-made works, formal perfection, compositional
craft, Janáček's operas—like Beethoven string quartets, Bach's *Art of the
Fugue*, and Stravinsky's *Sacre*—retain their power not because they are
made "just so," according to quantifiable laws, but because they are wildly,
fantastically, overpacked with irreconcilable images.

The Psychoanalytic Review

Just as I am mulling these questions my wife hands me a copy of the
The Psychoanalytic Review belonging to her stepfather, an analyst, and asks
me to read the introduction, which contains a lethal anecdote about Anna
Freud. But I see an article titled "The Search for the Authentic Self,"
just what I happen to be looking for. What coincidence in the writing
of history! The second paragraph includes the following discussion of
Winnicott's 1960 consideration of the role of early parenting in child
development:

> He refers to the idea of the "true self" as the core of personality.
> He also suggests that this core needs to be able to be isolated in
> order to maintain its integrity. This isolation, an aspect of "good
> enough mothering" protects the infant from the anxiety of anni-
> hilation. However, "if maternal care is not good enough then the
> infant does not really come into existence, since there is no conti-
> nuity of being; instead the personality becomes built on the basis
> of reactions to environmental impingement" (p.54.) These con-
> cepts imply a split between what is considered to be true and false
> selves which are organized with what is felt to be an invasive exter-
> nal environment." (Seymour E. Coopersmith, "The Search for the
> Authentic Self," 397–416)

Virtual Vizitky and the Core Personality

Let us consult once again our gallery of "virtual vizitky," whose real existence in the space-time continuum is marginal. They are all very different, and none of them look like my vizitka. Since a vizitka has to do with self-presentation, could one seriously argue for a connection between styles of vizitky and the composer's changing self-image? Perhaps.

We may note the enormous range of typefaces and styles. If we ignore the fact that Janáček simply added information to the earliest one we have, the sense of self implied by the varied cards is dissimilar. Was Janáček's famous "late blooming" more than simply a compositional quest, but rather a search for a full-blown identity?

This seems to contrast with a figure like Schoenberg. According to Schoenberg scholar Joseph Auner, who generously shared information with me, Schoenberg seemed to know who he was, or at least how he wanted to present himself, while still a teenager.

Of course, this is hardly scientific. One could find what one wants to find. But now the search and consideration of vizitky has implications that I did not foresee. My bad.

My Vizitka

What do we know about the historical role played by my actual vizitka? Not much. The typeface is almost certainly associated with Janáček's late period. Drlíková writes to me from Brno, in the mixture of Czech and English and sometimes German that has become a joke over a few decades "*Tvoje vizitka bude asi nejmladší,* [your vizitka is perhaps the youngest] *její* [its] typography is the same as the typography of the title page of the full score of Sinfonietta, published by UE Wien and Hudební Matice Praha in 1927."

If we can date the card, do we have any idea about who the recipient was? I mentioned at the beginning of this study that the man who sold me the vizitka also tried to sell me a photograph: in fact, he insists that it is the last photograph of Janáček ever taken. I cannot remember why I didn't buy it, perhaps it was something about not having any money, or perhaps it was my view that photographs are infinitely reproducible in a way that hand-inscribed vizitky are not. I forget. But now, coming full circle, and finding that the typeface matches that of some of his late works, I must revisit the terms of my original purchase. Fortunately I saved the original picture Mr. Dočkal sent me. It contains both the vizitka and a snapshot of Janáček and his friend Antonín Petzold, director of the cathedral choir in Olomouc.

It is my lucky day. With the picture is an article published in the Olomouc newspaper just after Janáček's death reporting the very recent memory of Petzold describing his time with the composer. Here is a sample:

> "You know what, Leoš," suggested Petzold on July 20, "we should get our picture taken together." "But Tony," laughed Janáček, "do you want to die already? I am not thinking about that yet. Okay, let's go get 'flashed'" [i.e., let's get our picture taken].

Perhaps at that moment, or shortly after, Janáček gave his friend the inscribed vizitka.

How to find out whether the vizitka also belonged to Petzold? Perhaps it had merely been purchased in a lot of Janáčekiana. It has been a year since I sent my last e-mail to Olomouc. I send one with my questions. After a few hours my old correspondent writes back: "It is 115% sure that the man in the photograph was the man to whom Janáček gave the vizitka." Now it seems exciting; since just three weeks after the snapshot, taken on Sunday, August 12, Janáček died, could my vizitka be the last one the composer ever gave out?

The Past

The vizitka, by connecting us to a specific moment when it might have lived fragmentarily as a main player on the stage of Janáček's life, reminds us that his life was filled with such moments. Indeed, Janáček lived well over two billion seconds. Even if we subtract half of them for things like early childhood and sleep (and I'm not sure I've ever seen a description of how long Janáček slept), we are still dealing with more than a billion seconds, or at the very, very least, tens of millions of "moments" when a visiting card could have been handed out, left at someone's residence, or included in a letter. Tens of millions! And we have records of, at most, a few thousand, and those lack all texture.

We live by the implication that the moments we do have allow us to make fairly broad generalizations about the past. But this is a chimera. Lacking records of the past we overrate the documents we do possess, and do this in two ways. First, we assume that they provide more information that they ever could. We naturally fail to "remember" the millions of lost documents for every found one. Second, we forget all the possible information about the document's subject which have gone missing—all the texture and thickness of history.

What Can We Say?

In *Testimony* Shostakovich asks whether it is possible to help one person without harming another. In this spirit we might ask if there is anything we can say about the past or things of the past which is simultaneously:

a. true
b. verifiable
c. interesting
d. significant

An analogy with music: the things upon which we can agree (that we therefore can say we "know" because we all do agree) are mostly insignificant: The *Eroica* Symphony is in the key of E-flat; Picasso's *Guernica* is 349.3 x 776.6 cm (11.5 x 25.5 ft.); leading to the rarely delivered punch line: Grant was buried in Grant's tomb!

Measuring the vizitka, as we did earlier, gives us results that are undoubtedly true, and yet they are not terribly significant. We may be able to verify that the handwriting on the back of the card is Janáček's. But is that interesting? Only in the hermetic world of a scary putative field of "Janáček Vizitka-ology."

Gödel proved that not all true things are verifiable. More bluntly, we know that Janáček moved his bowels. That is incontrovertibly a true statement. We cannot, however, verify it. At the other pole, if we try to argue that a vizitka is an "offering of the self as a proxy body," and therefore "a study of Janáček's visiting cards is in effect a study of Janáček's immanent physicality," it may be interesting, and possibly significant. On the other hand, it is probably utter nonsense, and in any case could never be verified. It could never be a true statement.

What of my suggestion that the varied vizitky can be used to support an argument about Janáček's lack of a core personality? Where is it located on our scale between "true" and "significant"? Here we reach into the ambiguities of history. While the differences between cards seem true and verifiable, different constituencies will evaluate the information in various ways, viewing the whole question as anything from a joke to a profundity. Others might accept the premise completely, but still fail to find it either interesting or significant, saying, so what?

Actually Shostakovich's *Testimony* is perfect for our purposes since no one knows for sure which parts are entirely Shostakovich and which reflect the editorial liberties of Solomon Volkov. So we are told that one must read it quite carefully, and wonder if it is authentic or not. In fact, though, one must read *Testimony* with precisely the same skepticism that one should apply to everything one reads, and certainly to any reading of history. Assuming that everything is a fake is not the worst way to go.

In the End You Will Know Only What You Can Know, and Then You Must Take a Leap

So suggested the scholar Moses Maimonides in his *Guide to the Perplexed*, a lengthy twelfth-century tome that attempts to prove the existence of God in light of modern science. Like knowing the existence of God, the reconstruction of the real past is impossible, more theology than laboratory science. It is always an imaginary past. However, there is something exciting about trying to create an imaginary past that does somehow come closer to some aspect of the real past, rather than further from it.

At first it might appear that this process is akin to muscle memory in the playing of an instrument. One practices and practices, learns scales, arpeggios, plays etude after etude and then, at some point, a great deal of the process becomes more natural, more intuitive, and less conscious. So we might imagine that we fill ourselves up with documents, commentary, news and views, and leap off into the void, into the past.

But I think it is not like that. That past would then become our present, and we know how elusive is our memory of the present. We have to be constantly vigilant that our view of the past does not spiral too wildly out of control; that we are not writing pure fiction. The only way to do this is to assume that any construction is the wrong one. This protects us, to some extent, but perhaps puts us in the position of Janáček's Wandering Madman, who, decade after decade, searches for the stone that turns all objects to gold. He wanders hopelessly until a young boy points out to him that his necklace has turned to gold. But when, or where? He can no longer remember. Even if we stumbled over the real past, would we recognize it?

And even if we caught ahold of the real past somehow, how much of it would our intellects contain? For example, since we are interested in Janáček as a composer, one of the things we might wish to know involves the nature of his thought processes. Do we know what it felt like to be Janáček? Was his mind filled with music? Did he hear it all the time or could he turn it on and off like a faucet? Would the ultimate Janáček research project be a kind of virtual reality helmet, which could momentarily make the wearer feel as if he were Janáček? And would this experience enlighten us, drive us mad, or simply be another amusement?

We haven't a clue.

All the Best

So is the vizitka inscribed. I take it once more from its purple box and hold it under a bright halogen lamp. Underneath the word *štěstí* I think I see the impression of staff lines, perhaps even a fleeting note or two. Could the composer have sketched something on the card? I look at it again, this time with a better angle. It's probably nothing.

Postscript: Plus Ça Change

After bothering Drlíková for weeks and driving her crazy with questions (no, Mike, no one has ever looked at vizitky before, I repeat NO ONE), I write gleefully that I have a line on the last picture of Janáček ever taken, and I float the idea that my humble vizitka may turn out to be Janáček's last—as if the historical role of this little piece of paper should matter. Her response is laconic: "The last snapshot of Janáček was taken by Mrs. Svitáková in Hukvaldy in late July 1928. You can check it out in the book *The Lachian Roots of Janáček's Life and Works*." I have the book at home. More than twenty years ago the author, Jaroslav Procházka, an old-fashioned type if there ever was one, forbade my wife and me to sleep in the same hotel room unless we showed him our marriage license. He may have relented in the end. I forget.

At any rate, I look through his book and somewhat sadly find the photo and the following description: "The last known snapshot of Leos Janáček taken on July 31, 1928 in front of his Hukvaldy home. Amateur photo by Marie J. Svitáková, Prague. (The photo was found in the possession of its owner together with a vizitka with Janáček's signature and with a date attesting to the day the picture was taken)."

In less than twenty-four hours my vizitka has been displaced. At "best" it is *the next to last*. So, I write to Drlíková—research at the speed of e-transfer: Do you know whatever became of the vizitka supposedly included with Svitáková's snapshot? She looks in the file where they are supposed to be. Both the snapshot and the vizitka have vanished. More research is needed. A week passes. Another note from the archive: Procházka, it turns out, was the (unmarried!) lover of one Růžičková. After his death she sold the snapshot and the vizitka to the archive. Drlíková has finally located the envelope which holds them. However, when it is opened, "What a surprise in the archive!" The promised snapshot is there indeed, but instead of the vizitka she finds "a bianco [blank] piece of empty cardboard."

Then perhaps my vizitka was Janáček's last, after all! The end of the same e-mail puts that thought to rest: according to Drlíková, Janáček gave a vizitka to his doctor, Dr. Franta from Hukvaldy, on August 9, three days before his death.

But is mine the next-to-last vizitka or third from last? Did the other one ever exist?

A micro-mystery set in the magnum mysterium that is the past. Shall we try to solve it? Let us begin again.

I have Janáček's vizitka.

I would like to thank the following people for contributing in various ways to this essay. To Joseph Auner for his ideas on Schoenberg, to Maiko Kawabata for discussion about core personality, to Karen Beckerman for giving me a range of insight into the process. To Thomas Langner for ideas concerning the fear of death. To Josef Dočkal for selling me the vizitka and giving me additional information about it. To Paul De Angelis for his helpful suggestions. To Jiří Fukač for being a model thinker. To Milan Kundera and Italo Calvino whose styles and ideas I find profound. And most of all, to Eva Drlíková for making the archival part of the project possible, and for her wonderful ideas on the subject. In the end it turns out that there was never a vizitka in Růžičková's envelope, just a letter. Probably.

PART II

JANÁČEK'S WRITINGS

TRANSLATED BY VÉRONIQUE FIRKUŠNÝ-CALLEGARI AND TATIANA FIRKUŠNÝ
INTRODUCED, AND WITH COMMENTARY, BY MICHAEL BECKERMAN

Introduction: Janáček—Writer

Michael Beckerman

In addition to his activity as a musician, Leoš Janáček was also a prolific composer of prose. Active as an ethnographer, theoretician, pedagogue, and feuilletonist, his literary output sheds light on his goals, his changing ideas on aesthetics, and gives some potent hints about his creative process.

We can find examples of Janáček's writing as early as the mid-1870s with the establishment of the journal *Hudební listy* (Musical pages) and an early *omaggio* to his first great teacher, Pavel Křižkovský (he would later write such homages to Dvořák and finally Smetana). In these youthful efforts he dealt with issues in music theory and pedagogy, and gradually expanded to cover everything from the masses of Orlando Lasso to triadic connections, and from Gounod's *Faust* to medieval manuscripts in the Augustinian Monastery. By the early 1890s he added ethnography to his interests. He published dozens of articles on various aspects of folklore, and especially on his theory of *nápěvky mluvy*—literally "little tunes of speech," usually called "speech melodies." This notion, that the intonational patterns of human speech are an indication of the inner life, is explored in almost all the articles we have included in this book.

In addition to his preoccupation with speech melodies, he continued his theoretical activity, culminating in *A Complete Theory of Harmony*, published in 1912. Although his final decade was a time of prolific compositional activity—four operas, two quartets, and several notable orchestral works—he still found time to revise his theory book and continue writing short articles.

Janáček was influenced by the latest approaches in scientific thought, and in many studies he tried to quantify the world around him. He used Hipp's chronoscope to measure the length of individual notes in some of his folk transcriptions, and based his theory of chord connection on Helmholtz's work concerning the damping mechanism of the inner ear's basilar membrane. Scientific proof, however, was not his ultimate aim; rather, he sought to understand the whole universe, the "whole enchilada" on every possible level. So whenever he encountered a sphere of endeavor that could not be illuminated through the avenue of modern scientific experimentation, he complemented those efforts by turning to the realm of the epigrammatic rhapsody known as the *feuilleton*.

Often these studies lie on the very edge of coherence; they are aphoristic, poetic, with fleeting metaphors scattered throughout. The language is descriptive, idiosyncratic, and often paradoxical. While it might be possible to attribute some of these characteristics to self-indulgence, taken as a whole they represent Janáček's attempts to penetrate in some way the realm we all seek to understand: that uneasy, unmappable intersection between the phenomena of abstract sound and the rest of the world. In these writings, then, we find the composer's most genuine attempts to comprehend the relationship between musical phenomena and human thought in a language simultaneously crystal clear and elusive.

Before he found his astonishing Prague success with *Jenůfa* in 1916, it was easy to dismiss Janáček as a kind of provincial crackpot, whose weird theories of speech and music were precisely what one might expect from a Moravian dilettante. And even recently, Janáček's writings have been treated as little more than a bit of wild Slavic exotica. Historians read documents, and if they are good historians, they read those documents again. And again. And they notice changes with each reading. Janáček's growing success on the world stage should occasion yet another rereading of these documents. After all, whatever unusual approach he might have taken, it seems to have worked, and worked brilliantly. As his operas compete robustly on an international level, scoring new successes each year in London, Paris, San Francisco, and New York, throughout Germany, Japan, and Australia, perhaps we will look differently on his writings, and regard them with some belated wonder, as among the most fascinating prose penned by any composer. And yet we cannot let down our guard: when they seem most transparent they may also be opaque. In the words of the poet James Merrill, their treasure lies in a kind of "revealing by obscuring."

The selections presented here range over four decades and deal with a wide range of subject matter. They begin with *Tristan*, include studies on speech melodies and personal notes on stage direction, and conclude with a lengthy unpublished article on naturalism.

"*Tristan and Isolde* by Richard Wagner"

(1884–1885)

When he wrote this article in 1884–1885 Janáček was still very much in the grip of aesthetic formalism as presented by his Czech contemporaries Josef Durdík and Robert Zimmermann (the dedicatee of Hanslick's famous *On the Beautiful in Music*). This philosophical system stressed the need for pure forms, and argued that the "conditions for musical beauty could only be forms." This article makes it clear that Janáček's champion was Antonín Dvořák, and that he viewed his older colleague and friend as the true representative of Czech music. The name unspoken, and perhaps the one under attack, was Bedřich Smetana, widely perceived as a Wagnerian. This study, and one a year later titled "Bedřich Smetana on Musical Form," marked Janáček thoroughly as a formalist. And we will see echoes of this stance in several of the articles presented here. In the first decades of the twentieth century this alignment came to haunt Janáček, as another round of Dvořák contra Smetana battles arose anew as an open sore on the Czech musical landscape. Only the 1924 publication of "The Creative Mind," on the hundredth anniversary of Smetana's death, revealed Janáček's total abandonment of abstract formalism and his final written reconciliation with that composer.

In this article, he tries to caution Czech musicians and audiences not to give in to Wagner's charisma without thinking about the consequences. It appeared in the journal *Hudební listy* (Musical pages), which Janáček had established several years earlier.

Tristan and Isolde by **Richard Wagner**

Certain Prague music circles are pushing for Wagner's operas to be presented to the Czech public. The purpose behind this happening does not need to concern us. We are of the conviction *that every Czech musician should be familiar with Wagner's works:* these are in their deepest essence the opposite of Dvořák's compositions. It is recommended, however, that *Tristan and Isolde* be given rather than *Lohengrin*, because in *Tristan* Wagner's direction is clear, can be defined; something similar cannot be said about *Lohengrin*.

In the following lines we present a little contribution as proof.

With all its harmonic richness, *Tristan* contains a lot of harmonic roughness, coarseness, and even incorrectness. Examples:

p. 86
l. 4
m. 4

p.103
l. 3
m. 3

p. 125
l. 3
mm. 3–4

By what are these evil sounds justified?
Never by musical beauty; and by the distinction of poetic thought?

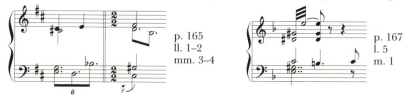

p. 165
ll. 1–2
mm. 3–4

p. 167
l. 5
m. 1

For this distinction, for this agreement with the expressed mood, should modern music adopt such downright ugly musical impressions?

The following harmonic combination is totally incorrect:

p. 209
ll. 4–5
mm. 4–5

I think that the harmonic aspect of Richard Wagner's works needs to be studied with great vigilance: his overflowing buoyancy in this respect is at the same time full of lapses. It is advantageous to spend time with such details: it enables what is really beautiful to emerge more clearly from the whole, and our final judgment will be sober and appropriate.

The closing patterns V:I and IV:I carry great, purely musical importance in the resolution of musical movements. This is why Richard Wagner avoids them in every possible way in *Tristan and Isolde*. *Chromatic progressions constitute Wagner's genuine element. In all* Tristan *there are no other forms with the exception of only two examples.*

A few words about the first of the two. The main movement (MM) begins in A-flat this way:

p. 137
l. 6

and closes in A-flat as well. It is followed by a chromatic progression (P) in the keys of F-flat, C-flat, E-flat, D-flat, and lingers in a nonic harmony in the fifth degree into A-flat; it ends again with the main movement, now, of course, already incomplete. It is difficult to find words to assure the kind reader about the exquisite beauty of this spot! Even the musical form, according to the pattern: MM, P, MM, which is *the first rondo form,* is flawless and perfect. I assert this with the conviction that Richard Wagner used musical forms: to the detriment of others, however, he cultivated only some. In this respect he was one-sided.

The second instance of the use of periodic formations concerns *three* short *movements.*

Especially delightful is the third movement: modern chromatic harmony stands out distinctly even in these small dimensions.

We present this movement:

Every *chromatic progression*, since it does not have a resolution, is more difficult to grasp; continuous modulating, the genuine element of chromatic progressions, tires the listener: thus the composition cultivating solely chromatic progressions overexerts our spirit. *Out of the more than 3,000 bars* which *Tristan and Isolde* consists of *only a little more than 80 bars are allotted to the formation of resolved movements and periods!* So, should this "modern" eccentricity also be imitated? Should "modern" dramatic character reside in this exclusive creation of chromatic progressions? Is there anything *Czech even in this* "Wagnerianism"?

With this we conclude our *small* contribution toward the clarification of the essence of Wagner's compositions.

1. We have pointed out some instances of incorrectness and roughness of harmonic combinations.
2. Since even chromatic progressions are formations (forms), we deny that Wagner supposedly did away with all traditional forms.
3. We have indicated that the exclusive use of chromatic progressions is the cause making total appropriation impossible.
4. Since Antonín Dvořák's compositions contain *all* musical forms, and to speak about one-sidedness in this respect is out of the question, the statement that this genius of ours is the opposite of Richard Wagner is true. We shall certainly be given the opportunity to prove this even from a different standpoint. The music magazine *Dalibor* honored us by calling it "hypocritical bombast."[1]

To prove the incorrectness and roughness of harmonic combinations, *two* harmonic examples suffice: if the esteemed *Dalibor* magazine needs the tempos for this, and what precedes and what follows, we pity it. We were not judging *the whole*. Hans von Bulow vouches *for the complete correctness* of the used examples. That what Richard Wagner created in the field of dramatic music belongs to the best is something we have not denied anywhere, either.

1. Right after the publication of the first part of Janáček's study, the editors of Dalibor 8, no. 2 (1885): 20, in the section "Hlídka časopisu," published the following criticism: "*Musical Pages* no. 4 presents excerpts from Wagner's musical drama *Tristan and Isolde*. These are single bars ripped out of context (without tempo markings and not quite accurate) from which a musician, unfamiliar with either what preceded or followed, cannot judge the whole. The assertion that Wagner's works are the opposite of Dvořák's compositions, and that therefore every Czech musician should get to know Wagner, is hypocritical bombast, which neither we nor the other fans of our Dvořák will be taken by. *Each and every* musician *must* get to know Wagner's works because that, which Wagner created, belongs to the best that has ever been achieved in the field of dramatic music."

"My Luhačovice" (1903)

This and the following four articles were all published in the journal *Hlídka* (Patrol) between 1903 and 1910. All of them deal in one way or another with Janáček's notion of *nápěvky mluvy* or speech melodies, although each of them goes into other realms as well.

Luhačovice spa was Janáček's favorite summer haunt, his home away from home, his shelter from the stresses of the city, with spa waters, flowers, and an endless supply of beautiful young women. Depending on how we view it, the essay "My Luhačovice" is either another example of Janáček's speech melody theory in action or a unique portrait of a specific space-time continuum—Luhačovice, 1903—using speech melodies to anchor the action in concrete reality. Seen in that sense, it is an amazing literary essay, illustrated by sound, a kind of early twentieth-century short story with CD included. In it we find such things as a coachman and a shepherd, a little gypsy child, a "hideous old Jewish woman," a folk tune played on clarinet and bass, a bookkeeper, a bird of prey, and even a cow, all taken down in musical notation. In this essay Janáček states his speech melody credo with rhapsody and astonishing clarity: "There is no artist greater than a human being with the music of his speech."

In several of these feuilletons Janáček uses his own coinage, "*sčasovka*," to refer to a short rhythmic unit, something like a "timelet." We have left the word in its original Czech. Finally, in this and other essays, musical notation is given for the speech melodies as the composer presented them. It is worth considering how we are to hear these. Janáček did not make it clear whether he imagined these notated melodies as sung or spoken. For example, number 5 ("To Ludkovice, to Ludkovice") is represented by three sixteenth notes on A descending to one on D. Played at the piano, one gets a sense of the pitch contour, but spoken language, though it may touch on those pitches, is something different, and it is most likely that Janáček wished us to reimagine the example as speech, not turn it into song.

My Luhačovice

WRITTEN BY LEOŠ JANÁČEK

One doesn't even need to turn around to recognize a familiar person by their voice. So many particular characteristics of every individual are collected along the circuit (ambit) of the melody of their speech, its peculiar coloring, its typical folds or its direction rigidly engraved on a single plane.

Here the ear catches in the speech a frolicking, sparkling play of tone, which has either playfully settled on a consonant and sings out like a nightingale or has run quickly through a whole string of words in a ringing cascade. These personal characteristics of speech are discernable even beside the general characteristics, which dialect imprints on the melody of speech.

Let us listen, for example, to the melodies of two Lachian children. The first lazily drew out every sound:

It was such a sloppy child.

The other asked spiritedly at noontime:

It is the same simple Lachian "*sčasovka*," but the first time so buttery and the next downright crumbly.

For personal musical characteristics, in particular in opera, the melodic fragments are of great importance, even taken from ordinary, what I would call, carefree daily life. It is through their quality that we are able to guess at the truth, to what heights love would move them to jubilate in that person, to what dense froth they would be stirred by hatred, how contorted by envy, to what degree the goodness of this woman's heart would softly round them.

It is first necessary for the composer to establish in detail the basic melody of the personal musical characteristic, before he starts to develop it dramatically: before he tautens it with the horror of a shriek, or sweetens it into amorous waves.

The personal musical characteristic should cling to the singing; the glossiest identifying motif in the orchestra cannot replace it.

Let's follow the trail of these ordinary melodies of speech! They are like water lily blossoms quivering on the calm surface of happy, worriless life.

Accompanied by the song of the village musicians that floated over to us from afar by clarinet and double-bass,

we are arriving in our beautiful spa of Luhačovice. The coachman stopped the horses with his usual:

P - r - r - r, stoj!
Prrrr — whoa!

Before long we are negotiating the price of our lodgings at the Pospíšil's little villa. The lady of the house is still not sure what to charge per week. "At least give us a rough estimate!"

"Ne - bu - de chcet' s mě-chem!"
"He won't want it by the bagful!" *   was her curt reply.

Before it gets dark, to at least refresh oneself with a glimpse of picturesque Slanice. From the broad back of Malá Kamenná hill, a herdsman, anxious to get home, calls out to me familiarly:

Pan - ta - to, ko - lik je ho - dín?
What's the time, sir?

His robust voice moved in broad waves through the pure air.
I meet a woman. "Where will this take me?" I ask. She answers:

Do Lud - ko - vic, do Lud - ko - vic!
To Ludkovice, to Ludkovice!

After a moment she adds:

To se tu na - le - ze!
All this climbing!

* That is, so much money that you would need a bag to carry it.

For some it is much harder to walk down the hill than up it. At least a tiny little boy, dressed neatly and tastefully, about three years old, is enjoying it:

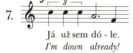

7.
Já už sem dó - le.
I'm down already!

I came closer to him, and he repeated it, but now shyly:

8.
Já už sem do - le!
I'm down already!

I ran across to Velká Kamenná hill. At that moment it seemed to be enchanted. It was resounding with the full fortissimo of a chord:

played by the distant spa orchestra.

When a cow, in the tones of a mocking bassoon, suddenly cut in, the effect was one of indescribable humor:

muá!
Mooaa!

Heading back down a beautiful road coming from the direction of Lhota, I met a sweaty farmer from Dolní [Lower] Lhota. He said to me:

9.
Už cho - dím ko-lik-náct ča - sů.
I've been walking for many clocks.

He was heading home from the market, without having managed to buy a "foal." "Clocks" was in the sense of many hours: a coincidental agreement of Czech and Russian.

They are finishing the bridge leading to where the new villas are, what in the future will be the "Prague quarter." Dark-eyed gypsies were pounding stones into gravel. The children and women were begging. A little gypsy child:

10.
Dej - te mně krej - cár —
Give me a coin —

No sooner did he get the coin than he went running off. But an old gypsy woman thundered after him:

11.
Ar - cha - jel!
Archajel!

The child stopped and thanked me: "God bless!" Could "*archajel*" mean say thank you!?

But if you give to one, a flock of others swarms around pursuing you.

12.
Dyt' ja su vdo - va, pan - tá -to!
Please sir, I'm a   widow!

pleads a tanned-skinned woman with a roguish expression.

We are walking along the stream, and the murkiness of its water is noticed even by a two-year-old child.

13.
Ta je špi - na - vá!
It's so   dirty!   the child said.

14.
Vo - da je be!
The water's blah!   the younger daughter of Mrs. Zahájská, the major's wife, revealed her artistic temperament.

Several ladies along the way egged on the delightful echo from the direction of Jestřabí, calling out to it:

15.
la   la   a a a!
la   la   a a a!

16.
la   la   a a a!
la   la   a a a!

The echo languidly answered them:

It now blended together more intimately with their impish laughter.

The triplets of the evening bells

rang out in three verses and have now long since borne away all the life buzzing along the promenade.

The girls serving the water at the Vincent and Amantka wells in their proud national costumes greeted the earliest spa guest with astonishment the next morning:

17.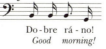

Do - bre rá - no!
Good   morning!

18.

Do bre rá - no pře - ji!
We wish you good morning!

The earliest guest still got to experience the strange night watchman with a fez on his head. He would have avoided him had the latter not greeted him:

Do - bre rá - no!
Good   morning!

The bakers arrive with their hampers and tease the hotel maid: "At the Zápařka's?"

19.

"No   u   Zá - pař - ku!"
"Right, at   Zápařka's!"

she replies. "Till the morning, till morning?"

20.

To   bych ne-by-la tak vy - spa - lá,   kdy - bych by - la do rá - na,
I   wouldn't be   so   rested,   if I stayed   till the   morning,

the maid sasses back. I meet a limping old woman. She's carrying a hamper of herbs. "What do you have there?"

21.

"Pod - bí - lí — Pod - bíl,
"Colt's   foot   — colt's foot,

for my foot. It helps me walk better. My foot hurts."

It was a large leaf, silvery on the bottom and fuzzy.

Are you familiar with the strange buzz in a beehive, when the sun first rests just on the very tip of a mountaintop, gradually moving farther and farther down its slope, until it settles in a low meadow? The basic tone of the buzzing rises; you see a thousand bees, darting about like black dots against the clear sky, suddenly aim straight for the sun as though offering a morning greeting. This is how the sun lured the spa guests out onto the narrow promenade, bringing them brilliantly alive. It was as though one was hearing the hushed hum of a giant orchestra, in which only the solo instruments revealed the now witty, now lamenting, pain-torn melody of life. It's just a pity that it is only in passing that one hears fragments of melodies from which one can draw conclusions about the course of episodes of lives.

A young Slovak woman, from the Hungarian part, with a pale, pleasant face, is suffering "from a tumor." She stops to rest frequently. She is here for the treatment thanks to the kindness of the guests and the spa administration.

22.

od ná - do - ru
from a tumor

The blast of the trumpeting voice of a voluminous, robust woman often comes unbidden and impertinently into one's way; everyone who can tries to avoid it.

She sighs and laments with great fanfare about her loneliness:

23.

Já ta - dy sa - ma ne - o - sta - nu!
I will not stay here all alone!

Just then, the voice of another Slovak woman is heard nearby, melodious and full of motifs:

24.

Tri -nact ro - ku už ma - jú –
He's thirteen already –

25.

Jest mu-o - žem
He's a man

she adds in a moment, self-contented.

26.

E-nom se na ten rýn - sky po - di - vám — už je po něm!
I just take one look at that coin and I've spent it!

complains a lanky female to her neighbor in the voice of a hollow flute.

A hideous old Jewish woman has planted herself in front of a "fellow countryman" from Hungarian Slovakia and in a bubbling voice she is revealing, shamelessly, the effects of the water:

27.

nen - dem nyešt na stra-nu — le - bo
All I do is go to the bathroom because

"Daddy—bye!" the piercing little voice of a very small girl thinks of her father.

28.

Ta - tuš pá!
Daddy, bye!

The drawn-out sounds of the St. Wenceslas chorale have summoned the past and a serious mood all the way to us and the sounds have colored the mood and with it all of the promenade's buzz.

You are losing yourself in thoughts as you wander through the tangle of wooded paths. You have walked deep into the forest, when suddenly in the wistful silence you are frightened by the screech of a startled bird of prey: "Takvititi!"

29.

Tak - vi - ti - ti!
Takvititi!

The magic of the human voice! It quivers just beneath the beating of a heart and ceases under the pressure of will. It unfurls into sweet melodies when flattering, proudly braces its motifs when resisting. It falls to a hushed whisper in wonder when two souls are getting to know each other; is extinguished by tears and laughter. There is no artist greater than a human being with the music of his speech, for no other instrument makes it possible to express one's soul as truthfully as do human beings in the music of their speech. The magic of a pleasant voice inspires trust, secures sincerity, and attunes harmony.

Violetta's love melodies of speech ruled with this strange magic. They were filled with feeling to the point of theatrical affectation.

Like evening shadows they fell suddenly into sad memories and then immediately laughed again with the gilded lightness of heartfelt gaiety. Let us look at several of the melodies of this type; in a way that strikes one as almost too simple they have attached themselves both to rhythm and key.

30.

Pro Bo - ha ži - vé - ho, ne!
For God's sake, no!

31.

O - ni by mne by - li za - bi - li—
They would kill me —

32. Mám ci - tli - vou du - ši –
I have a sensitive soul –

33. Ó ne! Já jí ne - po - tře - bu - ji!
Oh no! I don't need her/it!

34. To jste rá - da, že a - no?
You are pleased, aren't you?

35. Co? Je to pra - vda!
What? It's true!

36. (in astonishment)
A - le tys pro - ti so - bě!
But are you against yourself?

The lovely childish face grew even more solemn. The head dropped lower and lower, until its white forehead fell onto the arms that were crossed over the back of the chair. The soft tones of memories rose like the scent of a broken lily. The musicality of the speech melodies calls for intimate harmonies.

37. Má - te mě rád?
Do you love me?

A sarcastic reply to the sporadic smiles of fate, such was the effect of the sudden transition to reeling gaiety.

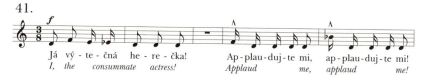

And this directly followed by heartbreaking, tearful laughter, which breaks up into new melodies before you even have a chance to notice the first one.

O - o - o - o - o - o - o - o - o!
O - o - o - o - o - o - o - o - o!

"What is love?" they ask her five-year-old boy. I hear a well-imitated answer:

Když se má Na - na a Jo - han rá - di!
When Nana and Johan love each other!

"He assigned me three Our Fathers as penance," confesses the future husband.

"Mi ta - ké; my má - me stej - ny hří - chy!?"
"Me too; do we sin the same way!?"

probes the cheerful bride like a child.

The hotel restaurant is frothing and smoking and roaring with merriment. Supposedly the cranky gamekeeper saw a woman "who was pretty in the snout!!" The praising motif capriciously skips about:

Po hu - bě! Po hu - bě, po hu - bě! Na - pi - šte si to: po hu - bě!
In the snout! In the snout, in the snout! Write it down: in the snout!

Mne by - ste ta - ké na - psal?
Would you write me down too?

Before he knew it, he was written down too, the nosy student.

Even the affected young damsel from under the shade of the "broken parasol" was written down:

— to už ne - ní?
that doesn't exist anymore?

48.

ingratiatingly in her
singsong voice.

Not even the bookkeeper, that resolute woman, can be left out:

49.

What? I couldn't hear the rest.

50.

Anybody will guess that only an old
Jewish woman could be so insinuating.

Mrs. Místecká was complaining, in the company of a Czech professor,
about Czech education, calling it:

51.

The German one must then be "two-sided" with the other side attaching itself to Prussia.

All the speech melodies "from the hotel tables" fit here reflecting in
the same way the playfulness of carefree life.

It is as if they had just flown out of the splendid hen coop of Jan's
house and nestled closely on the stones, those grand birds in the music
pavilion. Their wings tightly pulled in, their eyes bulging out: that's how
they listen to music that is vanishing high above their heads.

On your last walk you take the turn to the Zápražkas. You are stopped
in your tracks by the trembling, gloomy, screaming variations from the
Jewish house of prayer:

52.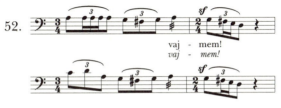

You take a lovely walk from the magnificent Villa Vlasta to the even more magnificent Augustinian house and you become convinced that the dark green of the Luhačovice woods requires buildings of bright, fairy-tale colors.

Everyone wants to add glitter, splendor, coziness and civility to our Czech spa.

A wickerwork carriage is rattling along ahead of me. A tall figure on it is staring fixedly and calling inside:

53.

Sta - ro - sto!   bu - dem   v Lu - ha - čo
Your honor!   *We*   *are arriving in Lu*

Immediately followed in an urgent tone with:

Sta - ro - sto!   bu - dem   v Lu - ha - čo - vi - cích!
Your honor!   *We*   *are arriving in Luhačovice!*

In a moment the carriage with the "extravagant" mayor in it is galloping through Slanice.

"Last Year and This Year" (1905)

"Last Year and This Year" from 1905 is even more encyclopedic in its speech melodies, offering more than one hundred different examples. Here we find what is perhaps Janáček's most famous description of speech melodies:

> The melody of speech is a truthful transient musical characterization of a person; it is his soul and encompasses his entire being in a photographic instant. The melodies of speech are an expression of the comprehensive state of a being and of all the phases of mental activity that arise from that state. They show us a person who is stupid or intelligent, sleepy or still half-asleep, tired or spry. They show us a child and an old man; morning and evening, light and darkness; scorching heat and deep frost; solitude and company.

In this article he makes, by implication, a clear connection between speech melodies and opera: "The art of dramatic composition is to compose a melody which instantly reveals, as if by magic, the human being in a specific phase of life." And further, he explores the implied counterpoint in a single-line melody and argues that contrapuntal forms are not powerful enough to make great drama. For that, something he calls "naturism" is needed. And by this he does not mean onomatopoetic imitation, but something more primal: "It is not only the sound of the spinning wheels that makes spinning parties whir. The atmosphere in a pub has its own tonal din as does a group of drunken recruits." It is these more inchoate examples of nature that attract his attention.

Last Year and This Year

MUSICAL STUDY, WRITTEN BY LEOŠ JANÁČEK

I met with old Kuběna over Christmas in 1903 at a pig feast. Jokingly he said:

1.
"Vči - le   je   kr - maš by - tem."
"Now we can move   into   the   pig sty."

In the snow-covered hamlets of the Wallachian Mountains there is a pig being raised in at least every other cottage. Every week some kind of "hamper" arrives at the homes. For the impoverished and the poor, at least a cup of greasy soup is left over. I ask the landlords' little Lidka (three years old) if the Vlčeks have a pig too? Lidka answers:

2.
"Ni,   už ho pro - da - li."
"No,   they sold it   already."

A strange racket has kicked up in the yard. People are running in and out of the hall. Through the thick wooden walls of the cottage one can hear the pitiful pig's squeals. Lidka, frightened, says:

3.

"Be - či tam pra - sa   na - še."
"It's   crying, that pig   of ours."

We fall inadvertently silent.

There is a strange blending of the piercing scent of pine from the Christmas tree, which still stands by the window with all of its baked ornaments, and the greasy smell of the pig's "jowl," which sits trembling and steaming on a large platter. Old Kuběna reminisces about the hungry years 1847–1848!

4.
"ty   zle ro - ky"
"those bad   years"

He spoke at length about   5.
"Ne - ta - li - i" (Italy).
"N-I-t-a-l-i-a" (Italy).

I was rather more interested in the peculiar modulations of his speech, a compressed and slightly raised melodic wave, that was often repeated in the course of his conversation. He was agitated when speak-

ing about his headaches. He was sitting behind the loom, working the
shuttle, and suddenly:

6.

"Co to je?   Dyt' ja mam dva čun - ky!"
"What's this?   I've   got   two   shuttles!"

Instead of one shuttle he saw two
darting between the taut threads of the woof.

Dusk sets in. The guests have dispersed and only the voices of Lidka
and Vinc (her school-age brother) can be heard twittering in the parlor.
Mrs. Sládečková is lighting up the
tree for them one last time.

7.

"Hen   su, hen,   za   ok - nem!"
"They're there, there, outside   the   window!"

Lidka calls out with glee, spying the reflection of the candles in the window glass. On the tree hang:

8.

"pes,   ka - lik (králík),   ve - ver - ka."
"dog,   wabbit (rabbit),   squirrel"

9.

"To je   mo - ja po - me - ran - ča" —
"that's   my   orange!"

10.

"a   to   su mo - je   dvě"
"and there are my   two apples!"

exclaims Lidka, defending what's hers.

11.

"Ten o - si - lek je ku - pe - ny,"
"That donkey   was   bought,"

12.

"Ne - che   spat!'"
"He doesn't want to sleep!"

His eyes are painted open.

13.

"Ten ko - ni - ček ne - ma po - va - zka" (provázka).
"That   horsey   doesn't have a   stwing"   (string).

Its ear is wooden,   14.

"to   se   ne - u - lo - mi,"
"it   won't break off,"   states Lidka.

She gives a piece of cake to the donkey:

15.

"Bu - de žžat!" (žráti).
"He'll   eat!"

She crumbles the cake and,

16.

"už že - re!"
"he's eating!"

The gifts baked from dough supposedly aren't good.

17.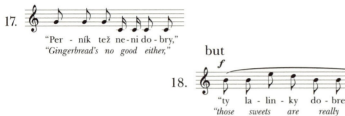

"Per - ník tež ne - ni do - bry,"
"Gingerbread's no good either,"

but

18.

"ty la - lin - ky do - bre su tež."
"those   sweets   are   really   yummy."

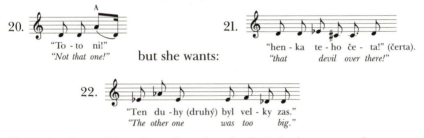

They were made of sugar. More than any gifts, the fish and the devil
captured Lidka's imagination.

19.

"To ni!"
"Not that!"

She doesn't want that candy; she points to another:

20.

"To - to ni!"
"Not that one!"

but she wants:

21.

"hen - ka te - ho če - ta!" (čerta).
"that   devil over there!"

22.

"Ten du - hy (druhý) byl vel - ky zas."
"The other one   was too   big."

She is clearly speaking about the other devil. Only the temporal concept
of was and is, yesterday and today, still confuses her.

23.

Vče - ra spa - dnul do vo - dy   a   zi - tra tež
Yesterday he   fell into the water and tomorrow too

24.

Vče - ra sem se te - ho vel - ke - ho ba - la
Yesterday   the big   one scared   me

and it was a few days ago. Lidka tells Vinc: the devil

and she bites off his leg.

that one's big (the fish)," and she points.

The fish has a golden ring in its mouth. Lidka says:

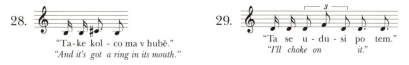

She can only see it from the side, but she knows that it has an eye on either side. She expresses it thus:

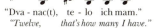

says Lidka.

The counting isn't going so well for Lidka yet either. She counts the chicks in the yard:

And altogether there were three chicks. She counts by pointing.

Lidka counted apples thus:

and she pointed them out. As far as colors go, she comprehends red and gold. Lidka:

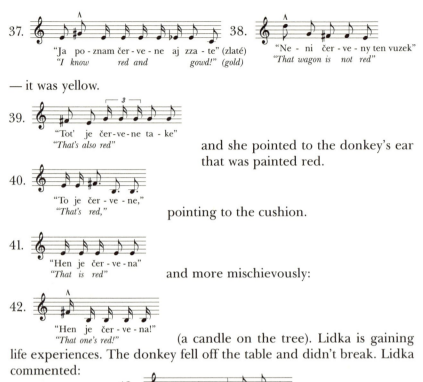

37. "Ja po-znam čer-ve-ne aj zza-te" (zlaté)
"I know red and gowd!" (gold)

38. "Ne - ni čer-ve-ny ten vuzek"
"That wagon is not red"

— it was yellow.

39. "Tot' je čer-ve-ne ta-ke"
"That's also red"

and she pointed to the donkey's ear that was painted red.

40. "To je čer-ve-ne,"
"That's red,"

pointing to the cushion.

41. "Hen je čer-ve-na"
"That is red"

and more mischievously:

42. "Hen je čer-ve-na!"
"That one's red!"

(a candle on the tree). Lidka is gaining life experiences. The donkey fell off the table and didn't break. Lidka commented:

43. "Dyt' je to dře-vo-ve, dře-vo-ve."
"Because it's woodeden, woodeden."

44. "To ja-bko spa-dlo a je už na-hni-le."
"That apple fell, and it's already rotten."

She didn't want to sing by herself.

45. "Sa-ma ne-u-mim,"
"I don't know how alone,"

she said.

All Vinc can think of is sliding and sledding. The ice,

46. "ten zdr-ži"
"it's holding now."

He knows how to slide:

47.

"po ča-pja-ku"
"while crouching"   as well as

48.

"na klu-zi-skách"
"skating on ponds."   He showed me two beech trees that had grown together:

49.

"Ta-ky hu-gač!"
"Such a giant!"   The greens under the candles now started to sputter. One candle went out. Each time, Vinc

50.

"Ko - nec!"
"Finished!"   called out: and Lidka would repeat:

51.

"Ko - nec!"
"Finished!"

Vinc carried the stripped, tattered tree out to the yard. Lidka, as though she wanted to say: The fun is over! Softly she said to herself:

52.

"Už je ven stro-mek!"
"The tree is out!"

Lidka is trying to scare Vinc in the dark, calling out at the same time:

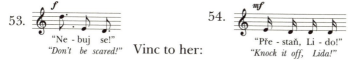

53.

"Ne - buj se!"
"Don't be scared!"   Vinc to her:

54.

"Pře - staň, Li - do!"
"Knock it off, Lida!"

Suddenly, from the darkness, Lidka can be heard crying.

55.

"Co ja - číš?"
"Why are you hollering?"   asks her mother.

56.

"A to cu-kro - ve kaj da - me?"
"And all the sweets, where will we put them?"   comes Lidka's reply.

Those of course weren't supposed to get lost.

The last little melody is delightfully childlike. Let's preserve the harmonic freedom of the first tone E^1 up to the tones of *F sharp^1–F^1*. The raised characteristic tonal modulation E^1–*F sharp^1–F^1* mirrors those childish selfish worries of Lidka's.

Such a motif is not to be found in any single Czech or Moravian folk song and yet it is Czech to the utmost! It is not songlike, but has a lot in common with it, i.e. with a certain expression.

We are at a universal well, full of living, melodic expressiveness.

The speech melody has in it, in its color and force, fear and concern as well as a shade of that hidden childish miserliness and greed, and even the darkness, into which all those sweet morsels have disappeared out of sight.

Let's omit or change one of these circumstances, and the melody will fall out of the soul in different forms, in a different *sčasovka*, a different tonal modulation. In the melody of a song and dance, a certain mood of mind also emerges, although a steadier one. To spell out what it encompasses would require writing out the full literature of song and dance. The initial motifs of songs and dances are still warm with the heat of life, but they cool into the typical mold into which they are poured and to which they adapt with ease. Yet, the changeability of expressiveness in the melody of speech and the steadiness of expressiveness in the melodies of songs and dances are of equal priority.

The melody of speech is a truthful transient musical characterization of a person; it is his soul and encompasses his entire being in a photographic instant.

Everyone who knows her, including myself, would recognize Lidka underneath the Christmas tree by the melody of her speech.

Only such melodies are suitable for the character of a little girl—all would agree.

The melodies of speech are an expression of the comprehensive state of a being and of all the phases of mental activity that arise from that state. They show us a person who is stupid or intelligent, sleepy or still half-asleep, tired or spry. They show us a child and an old man;

morning and evening, light and darkness; scorching heat and deep frost; solitude and company.

To add songlike melodies to Lidka's childish prattling would mean giving Lidka or Olguška or Věrka, etc., a stranger's mask. Imposing such a melody would have the same effect as placing a living eye into a sad, beautiful dead face.

The art of dramatic composition is to compose a melody that instantly reveals, as if by magic, the human being in a specific phase of life.

The motifs in songs, or in general the song motifs of familiar types of compositions, are also the expression of a particular mental state. To want their typical rhythms, their harmonic focus, to adequately provide a complete musical, dramatic description of a being—and here we are not even talking about an entire opera—would be like putting a human being into the uniform of a song. I believe that the current demand for musical declamation is that uniform.

This year, 1904, I again visited my friends at Christmas. Lidka greeted me nicely:

Last year Sládečková couldn't get a peep out of her. The decorated tree stood once again by the window. Again, Lidka had plenty of remarks.

Sládečková appeared with a question:

And Lidka shyly, now louder, now softer, as though she still wasn't sure how to make her lungs work in a song, sang:

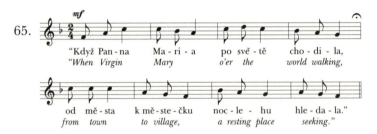

65.

"Když Pan - na   Ma - ri - a   po svě - tě   cho - di - la,
"When Virgin   Mary   o'er the   world walking,

od mě - sta   k mě - ste - čku   noc - le - hu   hle - da - la."
from town   to village,   a resting place   seeking."

Vinc taught her the song.

A song! Who wouldn't discern in it the stagnation of rhythmic prim-
ness in its rhythmic combinations? I recognize it as justified. Who
wouldn't recognize the tonal rigidity, into which every musical motif is
forced?

It is no wonder that in order to proudly build up all those familiar,
purely musical forms, there had to be a certain stability of mental
expression and corresponding to it a rhythmical evenness and harmonic rigidity.

It's not surprising that in dramatic music today, centuries-old contrapuntal forms are shattering and breaking. It goes without saying
that composing modern operas from their bits and fragments is not working and is impossible. Counterpoint usually implies a relationship
between at least two melodies. It is not, however, to be excluded that
one of them cannot, purely through memory, be maintained and fleshed
out in the mind, provided it has adequate support in the second voice.

The structure of many tunes attests to counterpoint. In many a tune,
traces of tunes or of rhythmical combinations of even several tunes are
discernible. The rigidity of the tune is then equal to the rigidity of the
counterpoint.

A different tune presents yet other forms of counterpoint.

It is necessary here to consider even contrapuntal forms as expressions of certain phases of mental activity, but they are not adequate in
musically describing a variety of mental expressions.

The expressiveness of the contrapuntal forms of all of our musical
literature is not sufficient for dramatic music. It is necessary to draw
more deeply from musical "naturism." Musical "naturism" is not to be
found only in nature, provided it expresses itself through sound.

It is now time to move on from imitating a nightingale with a flute.
The grain harvest when done has its own jubilant musical "naturism."
It is not only the sound of the spinning wheels that makes spinning parties

whir. The atmosphere in a pub has its own tonal din as does a group of drunken recruits.

Chopin's noble new contrapuntal forms arise only from the piano.

Lidka finished the eight verses of her Christmas carol. This year she got a play kitchen for Christmas. She placed it on a chair.

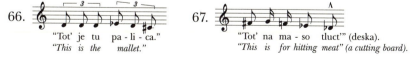

66. "Tot' je tu pa-li-ca."
"This is the mallet."

67. "Tot' na ma-so tluct'" (deska).
"This is for hitting meat" (a cutting board).

She is cooking a "porridge" made of apples.

68. "Pr-sklo do o-ka."
"Squirted in my eye."

69. "Prsk! do o-ka!"
"Spat! into the eye!"

She cuts the apples up and distributes them into all the pots.

70. "A e-šče zas do te-ho."
"And in here too."

And yet again the need to divide:

71. "To bu-de mo-je, to Vin-co-ve."
"This is for me, this is for Vinc."

72. "To su ly-žky" (lžice).
"These are thpoons" (spoons).

Lidka points to the colander:

73. "Na co to tež je?"
"What's this for?"

Vinc has come in and Lidka calls out to him:

74. "To-to ja sem ti ne-cha-la!"
"I saved this for you!"

Now Lidka wants to play hide-and-seek. She cries:

75. "Sko-va-vat'!"
"Hide yourself!"

76. "Sko-vaj!"
"Hide!"

Now almost whining:

77. "Sko-va vat'!"
"Hide yourself!"

Vinc is finally hiding himself. Lidka, her eyes half closed, asks with an impatient, tenuous voice:

78.

p

"Už?   Už?"
"Ready? Ready?"

In a minute Vinc answers from somewhere underneath the bed:

79.

sf

"U!"
"Rea--"

Lidka heads straight for the voice, finds Vinc, and laughs heartily:

80.

f

"Cha-cha-cha-cha-cha-a!"
"Ha - ha - ha - ha - ha - a!"

Vinc with her:

81.

f

"Eche - eche - eche - eche - eche!"
"He - he - he - he - he!"

A blizzard descended from the mountains and with it a fairy tale atmosphere.

82.

mf

"Fu - ja,"
"Fuja,"

pronounced Sládeček. It grew dark in the parlor as though it were nighttime. Lidka sat down in a chair, folded her hands on her lap in the manner of her granny and started to tell a story. I don't know how and why she got the idea. Surely Granny, over in Podoboří, when the shadows grew long in her little room, used to tell Lidka the story about the gingerbread house. I regret that I could not manage to capture all of her talking in notes. I was just able to jot down several motifs in a hurry.

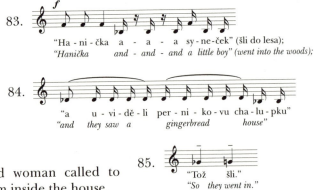

83.

f

"Ha - ni - čka a - a - a sy - ne - ček" (šli do lesa);
"Hanička   and - and - and a little boy" (went into the woods);

84.

"a   u - vi - dě - li per - ni - ko - vu cha - lu - pku"
"and   they saw a   gingerbread   house"

An old woman called to them from inside the house.

85.

"Tož   šli."
"So   they went in."

86. "Kr - mi - la ich —"
"She fed them —"

87. "Ó, ty Han - ko, ty si tlu - sta!"
"My, Hanka, how fat you are!"

88. "Se - dně - te si, sta - řen - ko, na tu lo - pa - tku!"
"Sit down on this shovel, Granny!"

89. "O - na si se - dla a fuk! s ňu do pe - ca."
"She sat down and poof! Into the oven she went."

90. "Po - tem šli na hu - ru," sebrali peníze
"Then they went upstairs," and gathered the money

91. "a u - ti - ka - li - do - mu."
"and ran, ran all the way home."

92. "A věc ža - dnu,"
"And no more,"

Lidka didn't know any more stories.

93. "Byl sklan - ny za - mek,"
"There was a glass castle,"

Nevertheless she began:

94. "A tož, to ne - vim."
"But I don't know the rest."

but quickly added:

This is how the end of the story would go based on the motifs in Lidka's speech in 90 and 91:

95.

I scribbled these few bars to point out for one the beauty of the melodies of speech, as well as something about compositional method. Which nuance in a motif should be set beside another motif, or other motifs? For how long? When? For what reasons? No typical compositional form can answer this for us. The manufactured fabric of tones should have, in dramatic music, color and shape, softness, changeability, a breath of life.

Lidka pointed to the burning candles:

96.
"Žu-lte, čer-ve-ne, mo-dre"
"Yellow,   red,   blue"   and they were. When it came to the colored baked dove she even corrected herself:

97.
"Mo-dre le-bo ze-le-ne? Mo-dre!"
"Blue   or   green?   Blue!"   With counting it was a little trickier.

She repeated the question:

98.
"Ko-lik ich je?"
"How many are there?"   and she answered herself:

99.
"Dva-cet ich je."
"There   are   twenty."

In fact there were thirteen. She counted them over:

100.
"Je-den dva tři pět,"
"One,   two, three, five,"   and on from there without making a mis-take. After thirteen, however, came directly fifteen.

101.
"Tři-nact pat-nact."
"Thirteen,   fifteen."

Old Kuběna wasn't at the pig feast this year. He is resting now along the path from the sacristy to the rectory. From the time that his wife died and the groundwaters destroyed his field in Sklenov, which he spent his lifetime straightening and improving, he deteriorated and deteriorated.

"An Example from Podskalí" (1909)

Four years later Janáček wrote a brief feuilleton featuring a speech melody he heard in the Podskalí district of Prague. In this case, though, the speech melody is used as a wedge to demonstrate the dramatic weaknesses Janáček finds in Smetana's *Libuše*. Janáček considers the opera "unnatural" in terms of his own views, and his criticism is powerfully voiced. In the last part he writes beautifully about "the dead silence of a deep forest," saying, "It almost hurts one's ears. You are more likely to hear the strange rushing sound of your own blood, as if somebody was shaking tiny bells, like kernels of mist." He concludes that this sound of the "primeval forest" is not heard in Smetana's opera, that elemental voices are absent, unlike his "human" example from Podskalí.

An Example from Podskalí

WRITTEN BY LEOŠ JANÁČEK

I am searching for an example from here, Prague, and also for a guileless human soul. Behold, the frozen Moldau. Its ice rooftop gleams greasily, it is melting.

About thirty wagons in a row, the back wheels already in the river, and a black sea of people rushing to load them.

The first wagon, loaded to the top, begins to move off with difficulty.

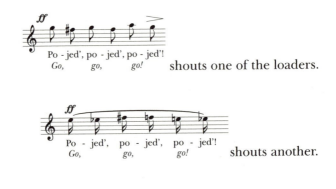

Po - jed', po - jed', po - jed'!
Go,   go,   go!   shouts one of the loaders.

Po - jed', po - jed', po - jed'!
Go,   go,   go!   shouts another.

And from the mouth of the first:

Tak co, po - je - deš ne - bo ne!?
So what, are you going to go or not?!

The heavy, laden wagon now slides over the slippery footing toward the water and lines up at the end of the row.

A long, straight path is cut into the ice; ice floes bump along it with a dull ring and lazily stop at the loading dock under the bridge.

Just like the bare branches of Žofín and Střelecký Islands, the sketched motifs are spiky and stick up in the morning mist. Each tone is sharp, each interval is clear, and their rhythmic portrait is like a fresh tile. To bring out the musicality of the speech motifs, let's reinforce them with the harmonic peace of the winter atmosphere. Something like this:

You will certainly discern in the first motif mere encouragement, in the second an added touch of grouchiness, while in the third a threat cries out.

It is as if these three moods are spread out posterlike over the gray mist, so clearly do we understand them.

And now to the point.

I wish to say that I did not like the performance of *Libuše* at the National Theatre in Prague on January 3, 1909.

Why?

The harvest! The sickles ring along the crickets' tremolo, the highly piled wagons sink into the soft earth and sway from side to side; the load bangs against the planks.

The sweaty team yanks the wagon, and how many worn-out exclamations descend on the pair with the whip!

Only the harvesters' song can come to us unchanged, now from afar, now from near by. The wings of a viable motif grow with every breath. It doesn't settle down in a nest after a while, nor would it fit into it: it cannot be repeated except in a child's play, i.e. just as a little game, as music.

It is painful to listen to scenes 3 and 4 in Act II of Smetana's *Libuše*.

Heya, heya, aaah!

Why for the duration of 4 x 30 bars in moderato and allegro do the harvesters loudly jubilate in exactly the same way, nicely arranged for four voices, from the same place, with the same intensity?

One little word in the Podskalí example and over a period of a few seconds it changes three times! There is no proof that our folk, while absorbed in the hard work of harvesting, would become spiritless.

Only the harvesters' song could be heard a while ago and then again—it alone in its lapidary style, grown right into the earth, sinks deeply even into one's soul—but all the fleeting cries of joy of the early morning that settled in its crown will not last through noon. By scene 4 these cries of joy have already matured into rotten fruit!

Art cannot be unnatural.

Noontime stillness; stagnant hot air everywhere, both in the shade of the linden trees and in the golden sunlight.

Why is the orchestra made to sound as dense as a downpour? Why is it playing to the point of storming? Yet, the linden trees are merely exhaling fragrance, the wind whispers legends.

I understand: the orchestra joins up with the force of longing and passion; yet at the same time here lies the relief of sound in nature; the faint clippity-clop of horse hooves is measured out—we hear it with our ear to the ground—and the rustle of linden trees, but their character, loftiness, nuance, does not find its way into the orchestra.

We desire a softer breath of fragrance, legends whispered more softly than the sound of hoof beats.

In our example the shouts of the loaders were freezing in the silence of the morning mist.

Are you familiar with the dead silence of a deep forest? It almost hurts one's ears. You are more likely to hear the strange rushing sound of your own blood, as if somebody was shaking tiny bells, like kernels of mist. The silence and coolness descend on your thoughts, on your steps, on your words. You have time to think, your thoughts are not racing, you stand here and there, your speech is sparse.

This power of expressiveness is required by the dramatic quality in music, so that it can either compress motifs to fit between narrow walls, or lean them against hundred-year-old trees; so that the motif can crawl through wet mountain grass or crumble and break in the dust of a room, so that the hushed whisper of love would be afraid to resonate, so that anger would seek support in an echo.

The tone of the sinister primeval forest is not heard at the beginning of Act II in *Libuše*. There is no trace of its influence. It doesn't shimmer in the singing of Krasava, Lutobor or even Chrudoš. They all succumb only to their own passions.

The sinister tone is absent even from the orchestra. The thick orchestral colors are used for a different painting. Noise is added to noise, resonance to soft moods. The primeval forest, which swallows human speech, has no voice, nor does the earth, the air or the sun!

That kind of voice has no place here. It is in the way and forces upon us the certainty that the century-old trees are merely painted.

It is from this shortcoming that a mistrust of the stage is born; it compresses the characters into theater heroes. Puppets on strings that are being yanked about.

A strange style in these operas!

Additional harm can be inflicted by the conductor—

The baton keeps everything accurate to a T; a forte is even exaggerated and a pianissimo subdued—a caricature.

My Podskalí example says it all.

The loader shouted:

Tak co, po - je - deš ne - bo ne!?
So what, are you going to go or not?!

But the motif stuck fast in the dead morning silence. No echo.

I felt the urge to peer over the railing to see who was shouting thus? A human being! A human being in a coat, unbuttoned as if it were summer, with ruddy cheeks.

"Whitsunday 1910 in Prague" (1910)

"Whitsunday 1910 in Prague" is another broad portrait in place and time, animated by speech melodies. Here Janáček expresses his desire to take down enough melodies "to fill the largest Czech book, enough for a dictionary of the living Czech language." Once again he seeks to find balance between "mysteries" and "theoretical formalism" and concludes that "he who is concerned with only one or the other is in the position of producing either dry descriptions or clichés."

We may remember that during this period Janáček was in a kind of nether world. His *Jenůfa* had been successfully produced in Brno in 1904, but was not welcome on the boards in Prague. The consequences of this were dire: success in Brno meant nothing; the path to international repute lay through Prague, and only through Prague. But Janáček's natural progress had been stopped, stifled. Thus his somewhat bitter and ironic discussion of coming upon a man carrying a piano score of *Jenůfa*. "How can anyone be carrying it around Prague so openly!" Here the speech melodies fly like sparks from Janáček's unhappiness and anger, fastening on the persona of Kovařovic, director of the Prague National Theatre, the man responsible for keeping *Jenůfa* off the stage. Are these truly heard melodies? Imagined by the composer? Surely the comments recorded stating that the opera "aims for formalism" and leans on a "bad theory of song" were the kinds of things being trotted out against the opera in Prague circles at the time.

The last pages of the article, published as an appendix, are a description, with equal bitterness, of a lecture delivered by Zdeněk Nejedlý on May 27, 1910. Nejedlý, for better or worse, is the father of Czech musicology, a viciously partisan Smetanian, a lifelong disparager of Dvořák, and someone who dismissed Janáček totally. A man with a decided gift for polemic, he polarized the Prague musical community around him, a kind of powerful prickly magnet for controversy. Indeed, Nejedlý and his cronies created such a toxic atmosphere in Prague musical circles that perhaps it is not coincidence that the only two composers who rose to international prominence, Janáček and Martinů, both managed to make their careers outside the capital city. Nejedlý continued his divisive polemic for decades, ending his career as Minister of Culture under the Communist government.

In his rant, Janáček draws a distinction between Smetana, who was "as close to the living source of speech motifs as any true composer, any genuine dramatic composer," and Nejedlý himself, who was not "capable of following Smetana into this realm" and who "has not uttered a single original thought."

Whitsunday 1910 in Prague

WRITTEN BY LEOŠ JANÁČEK

The St. John's rapids are spraying white foam. They have risen after the incessant rains and their waters have swelled over a meter above their usual level. Afraid of getting into the little boat. We are the first to allow ourselves to be carried away from here on the spring currents. No people from Prague have been here yet. Will the little boat manage to carry us?

Nic ne-bu-de, Vaš - no - sto!
Not to worry, sir!

the skipper assures us.

The hillsides have grown younger; they are covered with dark green moss and yellow flowers! Wherever bare rock is exposed, there it glistens with bottom water. Behold, what a slim torrent cascades down from the heights. One can catch it in one's palms. Now it forces its way through the gravel and disappears among the stones. It is certainly sorry not to have leapt directly into the Moldau River.

Ja - rov!
Ja - rov!

The skipper gestures with his head.

The cliff appears, jutting out; for a while nothing else is visible.

Ta - dy se me - nu - je Lín, ta ská - la,
Here they call it Lín, this cliff,

came the voice of our steersman from behind. I looked back; veins and muscles popping; the splashed-on water trickling down the groove between them.

An air of melancholy set in among all of us. Now Štěchovice is back in sight again. Soon they'll have a church.

—jak je tam to vo-ra-ny po-le—
Over there, where you see that plowed field is where it will stand.

The oars dip deeply. Is that Davle on the horizon?

The skipper:

Už by to mo-hlo sko-ro bejt!
By now it could well be!

We landed. The skipper, Mr. Souček, asks that we recommend him in Prague. We are happy to.

Another traveler-entrepreneur got on the train with us. Talkative. First the youth distributed the wares and then he ran around

po pe-ně-zich za-seje.
Sowing money.

Indeed, how could one get through the holidays without it! Then just before getting to Prague, I think it was in the tunnel underneath Vinohrady, in the pitch darkness, it was as if the train got blocked; it didn't move for a good long while. Suddenly, through the palpable darkness, rang out:

Je - dou, je - dou!
It's moving! It's moving!

I am sure that each one of our faces lit up with a smile. We walked out with it into the scrubbed Prague streets.

Prague streets! I would love to walk through your every intersection.

In search of speech motifs. Haven't they become tiresome yet?

I would like to note down enough to fill the largest Czech book, enough for a dictionary of the living Czech language.

What one could learn from such a book!

From it I know that one and the same law of rhythmical combinations applies to speech, song and folksong, and that a rhythmic relief, which is the image of the progress and development of thought, emerges from words, and not from a word.

In examples taken from this living book, who would not discern the strength of mood in the even beat into which a word blurts forth? Who wouldn't be convinced that the relief of rhythmical combinations, with the same strength of mood quality of tones of even beats, has an effect, even in the present moment, that is harmonic?

Let's make this first bond of harmony even tighter, namely let's even add a heavier-lighter beat and we will hear the harmony (the nuance of the resulting harmony), like so

A mere change in tempo prompts the way in which the staked out harmonic impressions merge, in the cumulative example,

the first flitting across like a mere shadow, the last already resistant to finding a connection in our mind, i.e. how III and II shimmer through I.

And to try furthermore to illustrate the direction harmonic analysis, which does not recognize any mysteries even in the works of B. Smetana, R. Wagner, not even Regner *[sic]* or R. Strauss, is to follow? We are talking about theoretical formalism, but a kind that always and continuously counts on a causative animation of the forms.

He who is concerned with only one or the other is in the position of producing either dry descriptions or clichés.

So on through the streets!

the worker struggles with the hoist, which drops into a cellar. He drowned out even the bell of the passing streetcar, the unyielding bell:

In Celetná Street, a light rustle of a silk dress; a fiery glance and a sigh like gossamer

m - m!
m - m

There, the freedom of a purely instrumental motif; just a simple octave. It initiated from a carefree mind; I imbued it with impudence.

Ba - bi - č - ko!
Grandma!

A child is sprawling in a baby carriage. Grandma left him feeling very anxious near the sidewalk at the end of Liliová Street. She is picking out and buying a change purse in a little shop. Careless woman!

They are tearing up the tracks along the edge of the Francis embankment. One of the workers is giving someone a simple answer:

Je tam už.
He's there already.

Vem si to!
Take this!   an approaching horse-cart driver calls out.

Ah, such a breathtaking picture! A boat is being pulled against the current through the gate of the lock. A raft is moving along with the current. With a great effort three people are trying to hold back the raft that is as long as a monstrous python; they also need to get through the gate. Here and there passers-by stop to anxiously watch the scene.

Vi - dě - jí, že jim to špat - ně do - pa - dá,
See,   it's not   looking   good   for them,

comments an elderly gentleman to his lady companion.

The raft is twisted to the point of breaking. But the timing is perfect.

They have pulled the boat through the gate and the raft is already rocking through the freed gate, dipping deeply.

I am waited on with charming salesmanship in the publishing house near the National Theatre:

jest - li si rá - čí - te přát, já vám to po - šlu.
If you like, I would be happy to send it to you.

It was a piano score of substantial thickness.

A pair of youths with hampers on their backs is striding toward Vyšehrad. One is counting up the change in the palm of his hand:

a já sem u - tra - til tři - a - dva - cet no-vejch!
And I spent twenty - three new ones!

The wind is swirling in Charles Square. It blew a fierce gust down the little street called Na Morani. Something flitting by like a blown-away butterfly. A doll's hat. A slight little girl clutches her doll tighter and runs after the hat.

Vi - díš, jak si o - pa - tr - ná!
See how careful you are!   her mother's chiding flies after her.

I don't even feel like I am walking alone through the Prague streets. At my back I can still hear the worker's voice at the hoist, the rustling of the silk dress, the youths counting change. It is as though a throng is growing behind me like a tail. The doll's hat up front like a star.

Now the flow of people has increased and is spilling out the far end of the street toward the Královské Vinohrady [the Royal Vineyards]. One frozen thought on everyone's face. How close and heavy at the entrance. All file under the high vaults in a secretive silence. The emanating vapors carry one right up the stairs. The flow of people fans out in all directions. At least one's glance can glide over a whole person now.

One pulls out a notebook and starts sharpening several pencils. His neighbor carries a pile of books under his arm. The top one looks familiar. It's a piano score—of *Jenůfa!* How can anyone be carrying it around

Prague so openly! It's practically offensive. Hurry to get away from it. In the dusk, one hardly knows where to turn.

Eyes adjusting to the darkness, they stop at the sight of a bright wall, on which is reflected a white puff. It must be a pale face, thickly, darkly framed. You are sitting opposite it.

It takes me a moment to understand the word: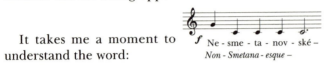

A voice woven only of a few cloudy fibers, slaked with water and not blood. Each consonant stretched into a perfectly grammatical duration, coiffed and glued together according to an outmoded fashion. Demigods speak like this. Mortals imitate them adapting each word to the prototype stating, "that a one-syllable word like 'zvlášť' requires a duration of 1½ seconds, while a two-syllable word like 'a-le' is satisfied with a third of that amount of time." I have most likely landed in the sanctuary of science and art. O let but not the minutest word escape you!

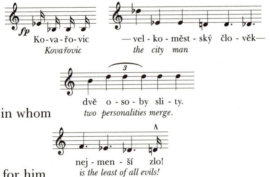

in whom

Eclecticism for him

The bandleader doesn't hear many things in life either!
As if art did not mean putting everything through one's own grinder.

did wonders for Kovařovic.

is still being questioned.

As one can see, lightning bolts of rage seek out Kovařovic's head.

How can one compose a "grandmother"? If she's old, she doesn't sing; so of what use is she in an opera? A sort of choked laughter, low, without vowels, rocked through the space. Impossible to jot down. Suddenly even I am seized with anxiety. The white puff, I'm not sure if others are noticing—is fighting with a specter. He has cleverly slipped out. The first round is a victory: likeness recognized in Kovařovic's sextet (in *Psohlavci* [The Dog Headed Ones]) and in the sextet from *The Bartered Bride!*

Now to quickly groom the wild-haired Kovařovic into a conductor

na - pro - sto bez kon - ku - ren - ce,
Absolutely   no   competition,

who must be preserved for the theater

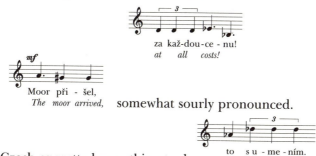

za kaž-dou-ce - nu!
at   all   costs!

Moor při - šel,
The moor arrived,   somewhat sourly pronounced.

to s u - me - ním.
with   art.

Czech operetta has nothing to do

But listening now is anxiety-provoking; the words slip out like sweat. I can see quite clearly now: the apparition is growing in all directions, even the mental one, and the white puff is shrinking before the Tone to the edge of the pulpit. Suddenly it flies up and they are in each other's faces. He is trying to force a kind of comedy, using a funeral march for two voices—why, even in polyphonic majesty he seeks the mask of comedy.

The tones ring out with a laughter that is so natural, yet the attack on them moves one

k plá - či než k smí - chu.
to tears rather than to laughter.

* * *

Abruptly the title falls as if into deep water.

—mo - rav - ské   o - pe - ry!
Movarian   *operas!*

I hadn't even dreamt of it, and here it is already, out with a splat, making ripples.

There's no time to spare in considering it. The tempered bullets are just colliding in the air. They sound:

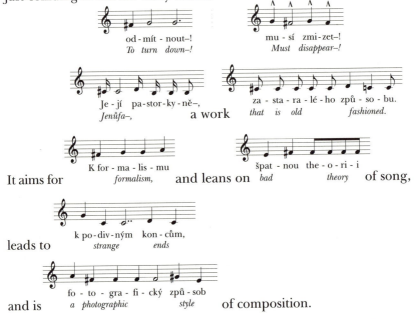

It aims for   *formalism,*   and leans on   *bad   theory*   of song,

leads to   *strange   ends*

and is   *a photographic   style*   of composition.

The white puff flits past; summoned forth with lightly veiled reluctance, he is absorbed into the piano score and makes some kind of a music box resound.

A handful of shaky, sleepy tones sticks to the motifs

sta - řen - ko
Grandmother

Three measures can sum up, what was clumsily played.

Where have I actually fallen? I'm ashamed to look around. Who is saying that I compose my choruses differently than I did *Jenůfa*? Why, he would have to be speaking only in my name.

Who claims that at one point in the composition I soak myself in a photographic bath and next perhaps in ambergris? Who here is spouting off about my supposedly poor and unscientific exposition of the origins of national Moravian songs?

Who here in Prague dares to openly reproduce operatic excerpts on a miserable piano so abominably? To shout out into the ungraceful playing mere text instead of singing?

I scrutinize this scientific forum with astonishment. I am searching all my pockets for my ticket—I feel so embarrassed—ah, here it is: number 79. Could I have been last in line and here in this order? Can all the others have disappeared through other doors?

On May 27, 1910, Dr. Zdeněk Nejedlý, a university professor, was giving a lecture in the theatrical hall in Královské Vinohrady. Don't judge a person by one little word. But then again sometimes, when looking through a crevice, one overlooks a desert. Dr. Zdeněk Nejedlý's musical reticence is such a crevice.

Let us consider for example the torrent of words with which he discusses the masterpieces of B. Smetana. What does he mention that is musical? What sum total of musical thinking is this?

We stake out this musical horizon in the lecture

about *The Brandenburgs in Bohemia* (the musical flow, closed scenes, harmonic daring, leading of voices),

about *The Bartered Bride* (the technical achievements of modern music)

about *Dalibor* (the flight and uniformity of musical invention, declamatory style),

about *Libuše* (great progress, symphonic flow, singular character: pathos, peace, dignity)

about the cycles *Má vlast, From my life* (themes, motifs that are different musically, illustrating genius, as well as formally),

about *Czech Dances* (nothing)

about *The Kiss* (nothing), about *The Secret* (relates it directly to *The Kiss*, the collection of music and drama is more varied, more plastic, thematic unity heightened by mechanism, musical individuality, most Smetana-esque).

"Syntax, the nature of music, musical originality; Smetana was a genius in harmony, in the art of counterpoint, he was a master of polyphonic art without limits."

Simply stated: Smetana-esque melodies, rhythm, harmonies, the artificial forms of counterpoint; declamatory style, working out particular motifs, lapidary architecture, the Czech words consciously and consistently declaimed along a natural cadence.

In discussing *The Two Widows,* in musical terms: national character of music,

about *The Devil's War:* stylistically he didn't transcend *The Secret,* three augmented triads, one above the other, illustrate the freshness of Smetana's harmonies, the artificial contrapuntal fabric, from Rarach's motif with the forms of ecclesiastical music,

about the *Second Quartet* in D-minor (nothing),

about *Viola* and *Carneval* (nothing)

"Smetana's oeuvre is an amalgam of modern demands with national demands."

"He introduced the national style into the realm of symphonic poems and musical drama,—the founder of Czech music. Sunny musical nature—his style."

Dr. Zdeněk Nejedlý, judging by his history of music, thus has not advanced, in his understanding of B. Smetana, even one inch beyond the 1850s! He has not uttered a single original thought. Had he singled out one Smetana-esque element, identified its indisputable expression! But not a peep!

The same phrases can apply to Gluck or Mozart or Wagner or even R. Strauss.

But all (at the very least) fit even Dr. Antonín Dvořák, who in the eyes of Dr. Zdeněk Nejedlý, never ever made it.

We read, however:

Dr. Zdeněk Nejedlý says, about this place in *Libuše:* "This place cannot be explained by any harmonic 'laws.' Here Smetana is creating, if one can say so about music, using pure intuition, by means of which he bonds elements without regard for the dissonances, which arise from the logic of this process."

Dr. Zdeněk Nejedlý thinks that the composer creates intuitively only sometimes. He is wrong. He thereby degrades not only Dr. Ant. Dvořák and others, but also B. Smetana.

Dr. Zdeněk Nejedlý and those whom he questioned (he speaks in the plural), states that this place falls outside of harmonic law. For certain, then, he is not aware of the harmonic law that rules here. Dr. Zdeněk Nejedlý got snagged in the mesh of notes in his next speech: "Rarach's motif itself is an ingenious example of harmonic intuition. Its use in the hellish dance in the third act presents to us a master at the pinnacle of his harmonic art both in daring as well as in the logic of harmonic connections."

Of course, here as always, the rules of "music theory" will not do for Smetana, because here Smetana creates his harmonic beauties by directly striking at the very root of all musical logic. It's enough to quote chords, seemingly unrelated to devilishness and yet harmonically so organic:

Dr. Zdeněk Nejedlý is hiding something here using the logic of harmonic connections, using devilishness, which has already been stated long ago more clearly. He refers to even the simple application of harmonic law, which has ruled from the days of the very beginnings of harmonic composition, as novelty, daring, logic, psychology of harmonic perception, intuition. Thus he is talking about a "novelty" that is several hundred years old.

Pronouncements, defined by these terms as if framed, have at least some degree of focus. The reader can thus at least wander along the edges.

Should Dr. Zdeněk Nejedlý step out of these boundaries, it becomes pointless to follow him. With a torrent of words he forces B. Smetana into the mere developing line of declamatory style, which is, needless to say, but a tiny fragment of full dramatic quality.

Dr. Hostinský has, by use of examples, all too clearly defined and documented the motif in such a way that it is impossible not to be able to distinguish between a motif based on declamatory style from a motif based on raw speech. Dr. Nejedlý, in one breath, applies one and the other interchangeably, referring to both the spoken word as well as the melody of a word* as the principle of declamation.

B. Smetana's motifs move within a much more lapidary breadth than within the declamatory stencil. Thus there is no dearth of examples of speech motifs analogical to this example of Milada's "O heaven, heaven give. . . ."

B. Smetana is as close to the living source of speech motifs as any true composer, any genuine dramatic composer.

Dr. Nejedlý is no longer capable of following B. Smetana into this realm.

The white puff hovers by the gate to artistic creation, but Providence won't let it in.

It assumes that those outside the gate are playing dice.

They have arrived at the foot of the throne with a bagful of little figurines.

"Behold, O Lord, that one is Malice."

(One of those gathered, a slight one, brandishes a little motif:

—mo - rav - ské   o - pe - ry.)
    Movarian   *Operas.*)

"The photographic likeness is good!"

(He places it into the score of *The Excursion of Mr. Brouček to the Moon.*)

That will be Conceit, that Vanity, that Ignorance. (He carves little Prague street motifs out of words and again places the peels into *The Excursion of Mr. Brouček to the Moon.*)

The Creator is blinking in astonishment.

"Yes, this is how I compose by the rules of inedible [nejedlý = inedible] earthlings."

God started catching lightning bolts.

* Dr. Nejedlý, *Smetanas Operas*, pp. 106, 117.

"Stage Direction" (1918)

What follows is a translation of an article by Eva Drlíková published in *Opus Musicum* (No. 4, 1994, pp. 173–82) reconstructing Janáček's notes on stage direction. Dr. Drlíková is administrator of the Janáček Center and has been the editor of *Opus Musicum* for more than twenty years. The article is a remarkable document showing the vitality of Janáček's engagement with the stage. Although Janáček was never considered a Wagnerian, it is difficult to imagine a composer who has thought more deeply about the connection between a broad range of staging issues and the musical flow of a work. He asks potently how stage direction can illuminate the dramatic pace of a work and bring the "printed word" to life. As usual with Janáček's feuilleton style, there are more questions than answers, but he wonders when gestures should be used—before, after, or during a speech. He makes it clear that a dramatic work is flawed if a "human brain in its clearest consciousness cannot grasp it."

Particularly brilliant and instructive is his description of the climax of Act 3 of *Jenůfa*: "The stage as if in a blizzard; the bare, hard floor and in a moment an avalanche of people confronting each other. Jano comes running in with a red baby bonnet, a throng of people behind him. There Kostelnička is crouching like a knot that won't give, there Karolka is throwing herself at her mother, there Barena's anger permeates Laca. Everybody screaming, shrieking. Laca like a column about to collapse." He continues to describe Maria Jeritza's performance as Jenůfa with gratitude, and in the process of telling the story of his own opera, he reveals an astonishing ability to create dramatic conflict. It is this sense of carefully modulated tension, simultaneously intuitive and honed, that more than anything accounts for Janáček's growing appeal for new generations of audiences.

Fragment of Janáček's Feuilleton on Stage Direction

Reconstruction of autograph
Edited by Eva Drlíková

In the Janáček Archive of the Moravian Regional Museum under Section 92 are found fifty pages of an autograph entry entitled "Stage Direction." It is the draft of a study, feuilleton, or lecture that Janáček dated, on the reverse side of a used quarter-sheet of paper, 27 August 1918, which actually corresponds to the mention in the text of his appreciation of the dramatic creation of Jenůfa's character as portrayed in the famous premiere in Vienna by Maria Jeritza.

The manuscript is made up of three parts, of which the first exhibits the greatest number of cuts, and from which Janáček drew for the second and third parts, titled "Ridiculous Addendum" and "Factual Addendum." The autograph is not preserved in its entirety; many pages, especially in the first part, are missing; even some musical examples referred to are missing and cannot be guessed at or deduced from the text—at least for now. The cuts are of three types: An entire page or passage may be marked with a cross or struck with a pen stroke from right to left. This does not mean, however, that Janáček rejects this part of his text in principle, rather that, at a given moment, it did not suit his purpose and served only as a draft for his ideas. Second are the cuts where one expression or part of verbalized thinking is replaced with a more concise or more fitting expression. Finally, there are the sometimes easily legible, sometimes less legible cuts, where Janáček abandons the direction of his prior thinking for a detour he has begun to explore (see example on p. 284).

I tried to open up cuts of the second and third type where they were legible (a thick black spot remains indecipherable even under a magnifying glass), especially where Janáček expresses an interesting idea for how to complete the text or where a direction of thought is indicated. Passages cut in the manner of the first type—entirely crossed out—are noted. Otherwise I present the text in its original form, filling in only punctuation. The word *cut* in brackets indicates Janáček's rejection of a given text; if *cut* is followed by a colon, what follows is deciphered text written by Janáček. In the autograph some passages are underlined once (rendered as bold here), or even twice (bold and underlined). Addenda that originated during Janáček's writing or subsequent revisions also appear, accompanied by an appropriate note concerning their placement. Asterisks indicating the end of a section as well as those used to refer to a note are original markings. The letter X indicates an illegible word.

Janáček did not bring this study to a state where it could have been published or used for a lecture. This feuilleton, then, belongs among incomplete and unfinished literary works. I believe it should be published as it was preserved. Much of it was formulated at other times and in different ways by the author, in a more forcible and perhaps more precise way. Beside that, however, the reflection yields a genuine Janáčekian pearl, worthy of a keen and innate dramatist.

1
Stage Direction

WRITTEN BY LEOŠ JANÁČEK

Everything the eye [cut] **has ever noticed, or captured, everything that has ever touched the body, the emotional response to all that—the abstract relations to all that—is my consciousness.**

[cut: **Beneath it there can be nothing else**] [alongside in small type:] **self-consciousness**

[entire page crossed out]

7

Only in the whole melody and in the full chord is its life cause revealed.

Which part of life binds these components of expression together?

What is their sequence?

[on the right side in small type:] (difficult to answer, the example is X a different speech melody? Affect is eclipsed by it, that is certain. The expression is not constructed just from what the consciousness has absorbed. Not every expression reaches the threshold of clearest consciousness, speech melodies! The key to stage direction: in first consciousness)

8

I would classify stage direction according to expressive density. Is ever a word, be it spoken, be it sung, a unique expression? When is it a part of the whole component of the whole expressive chord?

[Use one or the other in stage directing blindly, and the manifestation will be monstrous: either]

[cut: An idle chatterbox, a static female singer, both will get tired of mere musicality since harshness of expression takes us aback.]

19

There is a certain **relationship** between a word and a gesture that precedes, accompanies or follows it. **But there is also a dependency between a melody, [cut] the *"scǎsování"* of a spoken word [cut] and the accompanying gesture.**

II.

Ten examples carefully observed. [cut: indisputable stage direction]

But what if stage direction is to bring to life merely the printed word, singing? To guide the threads of expressive writing that is not its own? Here it cannot [cut] be extracted from disputes.

[entire II crossed out]

[in verso:]

II. Stage direction, however, not necessary anymore! 27 August 1918

20

[cut: Doesn't know the starting point when assessing gestures and does not know their measure. It is disputable:]

[cut] The manner of a gesture itself! But when and where to append it to a verbal expression? When speaking is finished? Before speaking began? [cut] It seems that a gesture appended at the end of speaking tastes of humor, of ridicule. **During speaking?** Here we are often of two minds. To pay attention to gesture or speech?

[entire page struck right to left]

[in verso:]

more than six incidents being represented simultaneously [cut] have converged [cut] the clearest ones in a time plane of one second of consciousness [cut: of the same clarity]—our brain cannot cope

21

As an introduction to speech a gesture certainly arouses the greatest interest and how should it mature? Beckoning with one's finger is sufficient, or Kecal's famous: "Hey, Vašek!" How to pace oneself? A glance? [cut]

22

[cut] Of greatest significance is the **verbal** expression. One has to know it. [cut] Not just in general: that we speak, perhaps loudly, perhaps in a whisper, perhaps rapidly or in a drawl. No, **what a loss that would be**

22

The starting point of this dependency is **the clearest content of our consciousness.**

If I can ascertain its musical-verbal substantiality, in as great detail as possible, I will also know how, if at all, and when a gesture might be appended to the word.

[entire page crossed out]

23

The starting point of this expressive dependency is our consciousness. If I can ascertain in as great detail as possible its musical substantiality and the degree of clarity of the dependency [cut: even within the interval of one second], it is then a simple feeling of being able to allow this expressiveness to mature into even another expressive mode. If I know it musically—verbal expression and its physical manifestation in the course of one second,

24a

then I already also know **when it would be possible** [cut] to append a gesture to the spoken word. * **

24b————————————————

I read in a work by some Russian writer: expressiveness of sounds changes and completes the expressiveness of words!"

24c————————————————

** *in* Voyage *magazine from 9 August 1918 I read in an article "A Year in the Slavic South" by Josef Pelíšek: Professor Sondfeld-Jensen of Copenhagen wrote: "If a nation left us no monuments, not even the slightest records, and only its entire language* *were preserved somewhere—from that language we would be able to learn the history of the disappeared nation."*

"To get to know the language of a certain group of people means to get to know their soul stripped bare."

24a [conclusion]

Disputes can be settled in a scientific way.

We get to the truth of expression by careful observation of life. From among the given examples the sixth is the most instructive one.

In it, not only the melody of speech is established in detail,

* _____

25

The gesture cuts wedgelike the sturdy, logical union of the sentence. [cut]

26

A pause is a torrent of tones—in a dramatic composition!

[cut: a gesture of such expressive force] It is like zigzag lightning only after which the thunder roars. Dramatic singing—the composition counts on gesture. It has a **pause** for it [cut], but the bottom of the sea still remains land that rises up nearby to form an island. Thus a melody lowers itself to a dramatic pause, thus does it rise from it.

[entire page crossed out]

26

The helplessness of stage direction not based on scientific research [cut: of phenomena is **most evident in ensembles.**] It puts them together where it is not necessary (the scene at the inn in *The Bartered Bride* . . .) every corner of the stage ostentatiously alive easily becomes stencil-like. A supposedly realistic rendering that meanwhile stifles expression, expression. Actors whisper barely audibly, but are furthermore lazy in movement. And they persist in joining both together in their interpretation.

The sung melody resonates by the order of self-sufficiency, but in addition, the banging of chairs is thrust into it.

[entire page struck right to left]

[in verso:]

A gesture?

1. A well of expression: the entire consciousness

2. Before it is made: "Do you love sunshine?"

3. Manifestation of consciousness: expression.

(reproduction)   4.) Its presentation, not of its own,
just to direct: the task of **<u>stage direction</u>**.

[page struck with three lines]

26 [cut: 27]

Faces merge into a brightened canvas, singing sinks, begins to disappear, and flies up again with a lark, the hundred-voice orchestra rises like the vault of a faraway horizon against which we can clearly see the twigs [cut] of a tree that [cut] "skipped out of the forest."

A dramatic work is **faulty**—not as a whole, not in part—but perhaps in a second-long moment if a human brain in its clearest consciousness cannot grasp it.

28

A work—either in its whole—or perhaps in one act—but even in a fleeting second should grip us, captivate us. It is a mistake when the mind turns away from the work as a whole: when we hear an opera as if there were no orchestra in it, [cut] when the ear follows the orchestra's melody [cut] off stage [cut].

A faulty opera—perhaps as a whole—or in part, but also in a moment lasting only a second—if it kills the brain's perception.

28a

To only see children at play but with no sun shining upon them, no general bustle—**how shallow the expression would be,** what a composition with stunted roots!

the deeper, more truthful its tonal expression would be, the more force-ful and more varied the affects of tone. [a dense cut]

29

We are unable to listen—revulsion grows into discomfort. You want to scream: "Stop already!" In vain! But—the lady next to me—dozed off.

**

The action in [cut] Act III of *Jenůfa* surges through three converging ravines. The stage as if in a blizzard; the bare, hard floor and in a moment an avalanche of people confronting each other. [cut] **Jano** comes running in with a red

30

baby bonnet, a throng of people behind him. There **Kostelnička** is crouching like a knot that won't give, there Karolka is throwing her-self at her mother, there **Barena's** anger permeates Laca. Everybody screaming, shrieking. Laca like a column about to collapse. **Madame Jeritza! It is, in my work, your most famous piece of acting. Like a fury you run through the throng to the opposite end of the room, you clench the fingers of your white hands into collapsed Laca. You drag**

31a

him like a carcass and fling him away, so that there would be no eyes left that would not see the cause of all the misfortune. [cut] The musi-cal symphony carries a whole symphony of gestures. **"Look, this is your doing!" Hundreds of sounds roll through the narrow room, its air misting with motion, the walls wavering as if to fall and you, famous artist, with your tone carry live fire,** [cut] **which triumphantly floods the whole stage. The souls of all who see and hear you in this moment are trembling!**

31b

If the words: "Look, this is your doing" do not achieve this expressive exultation, [cut] **Jenůfa** remains a shrub that does not grow into a crown, a cloud that does not bring forth lightning, a soul, a soul that has not been hardened by will.

This is why I remember your performance with gratitude.

*

32

Direction of such scenes! Direction of a work that inevitably requires the truth of life! Its preparation will grow into a book, the dramatic coaching will spread over months!

32

[cut] Let it be anchored so deep that nothing else can be found anymore at the bottom of the human soul. Only through it can one cry, through it laugh [cut], just perish and be born. When it stands upon these markers, it can be the colonnade upon which the dramatic vault safely rests. Otherwise it is rubble that chokes and buries.

[entire page crossed out]

33

The absolute master of delivering gestures [cut] is actually the actor himself, the opera singer himself. But to bring together the overall picture of all participants among themselves and in space [cut], **to have in the mirror a well of expressions, living consciousness, both onstage and in the house:** there stage direction is on its own. **<u>It is above all those interpreting a work.</u>**

***

34
Ridiculous Addendum

"She doesn't know what to do with her hands"—onstage! No wonder.

He—she was barely born and already the midwife [cut] wraps him—her up, binding his—her arms to his—her sides.

"Hands on your desk," the teacher, pedant orders every minute. During all "object teaching": hands on your desk!

35

Saying numbers "by heart": [cut] "How happy the child would be to be able to count on his fingers! But: hands on your desk!

Geography: [cut] She would cram the image of Moravia into her palm, press it to her heart, carry it around with her, but: hands on your desk!

Hats off to historical gestures.

Hands folded, "making the sign of the cross" and for a soldier: hands on your seams!

36

What then in life, in that sweet, beautiful, free life, what is one to do with one's hands! [cut]. In Auntie's family they at least teach you not to "put your fingers in your mouth," "not to pick your nose," "scratch your head," etc. They teach a little girl to "sit nicely"; boys never get used to it. "Sit nicely" but in their heads they are rushing, swarming! **Hypocrisy stretches across a face and slips off a tongue.** [cut] A fawning [cut] personality grows.

36

An irrelevant gesture, that is, feeble, inappropriate, is foreign, **destroys its musical complement. It ruins** [cut] **the dramatic work** [cut].

[entire page struck right to left]

37

We perceive through our whole body, therefore it is natural not to stifle, [cut] **not to cut off its expressiveness anywhere.** [cut] **Excessive expressiveness will limit itself through the full mastery of language,** [cut] **factual education, one's vocation in life.**[cut]

38

Even though a boy is in appearance a boy—he will be a real man.

The trait of character evolves sharply, we again meet **typical people:** a farmer will be a farmer, a farrier a blacksmith from Lešetín, a scholar a scholar. [cut: "Acting will be harder, but better] And for those who [cut] "make faces" on stage—all sorts, there will be examples. The stumbling block of "what should I do with my hands?" will disappear.

***

39b

In all six examples we observe that [cut] their clusters of affects, their clusters of expressions, [cut] combine into a whole.

When there is a gesture being made **simultaneously** with the speech melody (4th, 5th examples), when the melody embraces it (6th, 7th examples), this [cut] wholeness is the most apparent.

If the gesture is hidden (3rd example), if it is present only in the glint of an eye, if it merely is extinguished within it or is prolonged (3rd, 7th, 8th, 9th examples), i.e. [cut: if we don't catch it] if it lacks vehemence,

39c

In order to be applied to one's consciousness, [cut] it is because a verbal expression conceals it.

A verbal expression has its preparation: **a subject is present in one's mind, the thought** and its clarification is still discernible in its utterance—it runs across it through an accent.

As soon as the subject—thought already takes hold in this form of a body, of senses, it gives birth to a gesture.

The play of gestures always runs through the body; if it indicates

39d

the same subject, thought, as a verbal-musical expression, it stands out most clearly. This is the case in the 4th and 6th examples. The gesture carries out and prompts what is substantiated by the word.

[cut: The same emotional basis as well as its course in the heat of the moment is the reason why **it is impossible to compose musical drama using only musical thoughts.**]

39e

And the "subject," which aroused a whole expressive component!

The delightful song of a blackbird. You walk down the little steps from the cottage into the "small courtyard" with the shed on the right, the pigsty with a snow white pig and sixteen little rabbits milling around in a cluster behind the fence; on the left a stable [cut: stall], in which you see through the gate a ruminating cow. [cut] A dovecote tucked under the eaves. Dark red hair, lively eyes—as though they too glowed red—

A hodgepodge—

An unnecessary question—The memory of a particular event—A populated, measured space—Sugar in the mud—Shiny convergent tracks —.

39f

And the phenomenon, upon which the gesture [cut: expression] grew, the phenomenon, that is now spreading [cut] through a resounding word?

Here baby blackbirds, here again a crested hen, there a person—a child—little Mary, a saucy middle-class woman, a country girl, a worn-out soldier, a brewery worker, a market woman, a quiet observer—and already a human is "falling short of God's image."

Such simple cases!

But woe, if the villain himself is the plotter of horrific events and mankind in its state of dulled expression under his sway.

41
III.

The most complex, most significant expression is the **verbal**-musical one.

It is necessary to know it not just in general; "that one speaks" perhaps loudly, perhaps in a whisper, perhaps quickly or perhaps in a drawl.

42

This is **not even enough for directing a play.** One must know how to capture not only the general "speaking tone," **but even in a definite manner the melody of the motifs of words and sentences, their rhythmic quality and the modulation of even lengthy speeches. It is from this purely musical image, which one can fortunately measure in as little as a second or a fraction thereof, from which not only the limiting of** [cut] **gestures follows, but also the manner of gestures and how they are adjoined to verbal expression.**

*

43

Every manner of expression—gestures as well as verbally musical expression—mutually limits one another. The stage for this action is our consciousness and the final expressive picture is in our **clearest** consciousness. I went after the picture of consciousness and even its clearest content by visiting the blackbird family (1st example).

43

There is a certain **relationship and dependency** between a word, its melody, its "*sčasování*" and the gestures that accompany it.

49

[cut: If a work of art with an immediate expression] From the noted-down speech melody, we can infer what remains apart from it **in each**

second for additional psychological breadth. **The speech melody is a testimony to the speaker's psychological potency.**

I read in the work of a Russian author: "expressiveness of sounds changes and completes the expressiveness of words."

50

However, Professor **Sandfeld-Jansen** from Copenhagen to my delight [cut] expresses himself more specifically:

"To get to know the language of certain people means to get to know those people themselves, to get to know undisguised their soul."

> * "If a nation left us no monuments, not even the slightest records, and **only its entire language** were preserved some-where—from that language we would be able to learn the history of the disappeared nation."

* Josef Pelíšek, *Cesta*, 9 August 1918

51

W. Wundt sized up the "game of gestures" in the regimentation of the steps; when **J. Goncharov's** Oblomov inhaled, it was present.

*

Would there be a pause in the melody:

 (sixth example)

and a rest in the melody:

 (seventh example)

if it were not for a gesture, the turn of a hand, a questioning glance?

52

Would the melodies be articulated thus only while thinking in tones?

Would that thinking suffice for a musically dramatic composition?

Reproduction of two pages of Janáček's manuscript, from the first part.

***

1/a
Factual Addendum

The most beautiful form of expression is the word, is our language.

The most pleasant: an inviting smile on a face.
We extol the expression of love.

It does not matter if the expression is the means of communication, if we pursue nourishment with it, if we carry it on our backs like an unnoticed self-portrait.

[The last paragraph struck right to left]

1/b
It does not matter if its course, inspiring so much scientific attention passes into a **mechanical** motion—**into sheer labor**

[paragraph struck right to left]

It always **affects us,** is a part of our life, **satiates its picture.**

In an artistic representation, we cannot even leave out **sheer labor.**

> "Scraping with a pin
> calling for Mommy"—

As if it were opening up new sources!

1/c
R. Wagner went as far as the **instrument** of sheer labor ("poison" motif, "sword" motif, etc.). The apple of his artistic contemplation rolled as far as that.

2
[cut]

The harvester was hammering the blade of his scythe. Each blow aimed at its edge made it ring out; he wasn't in the mood to talk, but felt like singing.

Sheer labor channels life energy productively, uses it, devours expressiveness in gesture and word. It is life's expression of hard striving.

I don't know if the ultimate reason for all labor is **nourishment**: in that case it is certainly an inconsiderate expression and [cut] an essential ingredient in the picture of life. [cut]

3

If it becomes a dramatic motif, [cut] be it the slash of a sharp knife, or the mixing of greenish poison, then the verbal or even gestural expression sits on it like fire on lightning.

[cut: But appropriate work is a fitting filler in other ways as well. Without it, the picture of life is impossible, fragmentary. However, the picture of life was dying in Wagner's poison motif, in the sword motif].

4

Work as a pretext. Jenůfa sorts through the "bouquets" of corn spread out on the drying rack, **not to give the impression that she has only one thing on her mind, Laca.** She pulls a sack of grain a little away from the porch; but how! So as not to give the impression—.

Work as a filler, that direction can add to or take away from. After all, does one return from working in the fields as if coming back from a walk?

5

If you want to hammer to death the room of one in childbirth confinement, hang diapers out around the stove? [cut] To put "sheer labor" out on display, [cut: cover it up to that extent] is bad taste on the part of the direction as well as the composer. [cut] The composition dies on the instrument of labor, on Wagner's "poison motif," "the sword motif"!

"Janáček on Naturalism" (1924–1925)

"Janáček on Naturalism" is a translation of an article published by Miloš Štědroň in the journal *Opus Musicum* (no. 6, 1995, pp. 281–92). Štědroň has been a leading Janáček scholar for decades, whose work is most brilliantly summed up in his *Leoš Janáček a hudba 20. století (Leoš Janáček and Twentieth Century Music)*, a virtual compendium of Janáček's connections to the various artistic movements of his time. Štědroň's comments, included as an editor's note at the end of the study, explain the layout of the piece. Simply, the LJ numbers refer to the pages of Janáček's own notes.

As jottings for an unwritten article, this torso appears as a kind of hyperfeuilleton, more lapidary than even the composer's most flightly attempts. It is filled with wonderful questions: "How can the splendid spatial rhythm of Hradčany Castle—which takes up several kilometers—be condensed into the space of a few measures? How shall the amazing stature of the human body sound tonally?" It is surprising to find that Janáček, like his younger contemporaries Debussy and Bartók, was occupied with the question of the golden mean. His discussion of it takes us from Plato through the formalist thinkers Robert Zimmermann and Josef Durdík, on to Wilhelm Wundt, his favored arsenal of philosphers and scientists. Written around the time of his seventieth birthday, the article reveals an increasing revision of his views about Smetana—perhaps as he began to realize how similar he was to the older composer. It is filled with the wondrous musings of a composer who has just penned an animal opera, *The Cunning Little Vixen*: "And why should the toilsome tread of a beetle not awaken at least a compositional smile, or butterfly kisses at least a tonal longing?" and argues that neglecting concrete reality results in emotional weakness and artistic "untruthfulness."

Janáček on Naturalism

EDITED BY MILOŠ ŠTĚDROŇ

LJ: 1
Outdoor surroundings

The silhouette of Hradčany Castle—the flow of the Moldau River:
rhythm, lying there for centuries now
Eye movement "time"
When the ice was rising—murmur, crash
   How long—evenly thick—like an outside wall!
A field of space and colors and sounds spreading through living
beings
The screech of seagulls—black and white flecks—the lines of their
flight.
Broaden the fields—even through a person
Through his appearance "a golden mean"! (through his laugh-
ter—crying—speech.)
And within ourselves
through bodily sensations—heartbeat, lungs rising and falling,
breath
freezing—sweating—heat
Some thousand rhythms are here! (in German time-space)
And the emotions that accompany them! Five white splotches on a
green hillside. Of Ondřejník. Are those geese? <u>And the eye sizes
them up with suspense.</u> No. Little sheep? No. Little goats.
The emotional accompaniment is a certain bridge across which
the stimulus travels towards the combination with tone—to
composition.

LJ: 2
Never mind the stimulus!   (reality)   (individuality)
                             (Realism —   concreteness)
B. Smetana's: Moldau—Vyšehrad
Suk's: Praga
But the adherence of adapted tonal rhythms and even melodic
figures!

Moldau:  (wavelets)

Vyšehrad  (emotional ecstasy)

> The adherence of involuntary combinations—the union in
> which I lose this awareness
>
> ("Natura"—nature) from here—
> Up to actual use—the detached emotional flow
>   Do I know how a mother giving birth feels as she agonizes
>
> Both are called naturalism in art

LJ: missing
If space goes up—the tone goes up;
    —as a result of the same emotion
if it falls, the tone falls
Ornamental rhythms taken in at one glance, in the blink of an
eye, demand:

I can run through the groove of time in the blink of an eye, 1/10",
or slower or slowly: then (10" for ex.) a new life insinuates itself
into one's consciousness, a new tonal world.

<u>Underlying motifs:</u> a chord—key, orchestral color

LJ: 3a
Understand:
The groove of time of a certain length—whether within it I go
between the horizon and silhouette of Hradčany Castle, or along
the black rim of a little yellow flower in green grass, or if I run
through it with a tone—<u>it is the result of the proportion of ideas
inside the clearest consciousness.</u>
Nothing of <u>that proportion</u> changes in consciousness, not even
much emotionally (color—shading—tone) when <u>tone</u> instead of
color skips over into that groove.

This is why it is so easy for a tone to settle into spatial and colorful time grooves and why it easily assumes rhythms that are spatial—colorful—provided the proportion of what is inside the consciousness does not change.

The dimension of these rhythms.

LJ: 3b
How can the splendid spatial rhythm of Hradčany Castle—which takes up several kilometers—be condensed into the space of a few measures?
How shall the amazing stature of a human body sound tonally? And it did sound, and it fits!
There is always a decisive moment in which the entire spatial rhythm is taken in by the eye.
If it is the time period of 1"—then a tonal expression to 9 suffices!
It will be a blinding bursting into flame—I can't find the words—and in that instant—not even a spellbinding tonal exclamation.

LJ: 4
I go back to Smetana's image of Vyšehrad. It did not stay in his mind for just 1"— the flaming up of emotion, the historical vision, lasted longer: the musical expression floats along for 48" (16 measures in 3/4 time)
In short: In spatial—colorful rhythms I have the power to condense or extend my temporal basis: it is the work of my consciousness.

There are enough examples. I recall the sunrise in Smetana's *The Devil's Wall*.
And spatial rhythms are always highlighted by either the shading of light and—by the influence of the marginal contrast of colors—in particular colorful ones.
The eye travels precisely along this margin.

LJ: 5
You know how in Smetana's *The Devil's Wall,* behind the packed together picture of *Rarach*, black through cunning, a musical expression lashes out in the split of a second (on p. 9),

over a longer time (on p. 12), in a bar of 3/4 time (p. 10), and in a bar of C time (p. 77). The space of falling into bottomless darkness and then again it being lit up by the fiery symbol of a cross in time (p. 169)

In the recalled sunrise, we notice even the pale glow of the moon (p. 82)

and the impact of this combination occurring within 10"!

LJ: 6

The growing capacity of the tonal rhythms ♪♪♩ or ♩ ♪♪ is outright precarious, as if it were feeding on the life sap of human growth according to the ratio of the so-called <u>golden mean</u>!

And that *sčasovka* in human form!
<u>Why is this sort of naturalism not easy to comprehend?</u>

If in a C chord of....." length, in an F sharp chord of 10" length, in a ♩♩ ♪ rhythm, etc., there is no reason to discern the sunrise, the moon's glow, the waves of the Moldau, the grandeur of Vyšehrad—it is first and foremost a result of the variety and mobility in the spatial—colorful measure of rhythms and the measure that is tonal, personal, narrowed down by the composer's consciousness!
<u>The listener draws comparisons differently still</u>—should he pull away in his emotional and other thoughts, he will not hear, in C . . .", the sunrise, etc., etc.

LJ: 6a

The liveliest appearance with which a tone settles into the temporal groove of an articulated space is through the

<u>Golden mean</u>

We can see this spatial rhythm in the human body. <u>Hands.</u>
In those calloused hands: how many times do one's eyes rest painfully on them?
In soft hands: how many times do one's eyes seep into them with a kiss!
No wonder that a tone rests there, where articulated space exists
No wonder that this rhythm of tones grew in folk songs
Plato already recalled it. (*The History of Aesthetics* by Dr. Zimmerman, p. 18)
He states in *Timaeus*: "a certain ratio

in which the "middle" acts as the first and the last
and "the last"
and first are the middle   b:c = a:b.
Dr. Durdík speaks of it.
W. Wundt proves it.
Carelessly put into notes. It is the counterbalance to cool symmetry.

LJ: 6b
<u>The limits of spatial understanding in compositional naturalism</u>

The circle I perceive in 1″ is condensed into a chord if the eye wanders along its groove over a longer bar, and in the following bar already a melodic wave is born

they have only the time wave in common
the spatial and melodic figures already differ.
Hence the unintelligibility of musical expression—and the end of pure naturalism.
The zigzag of a lightning bolt.
And without a <u>sign</u> to help us—<u>we cannot guess</u>.
Joke: a wrong sign. Without a sign—off the path. A self-sufficient composition—mature, fully developed thinking.

LJ: 7

On the other hand the agreement of the golden mean proportion

with the mysterious rhythms of folk songs ♩ ♪ ♪ would
attest to the fact that it is easy to get to it along the groove of
spatial rhythm—somewhere at the crossroads that exist in our
brain:

Note. This kind of compositional naturalism that we are subject to,
as we are to a dark night, which binds us to sleep, and to the light
of day, which gives us work, does not impair creative freedom.

How many nocturnes have already been composed, how many
more Pragas there can still be! How many Tatra Mountains, sunsets
and sunrises, pale moons! Which regions of our country would not
contain natural wonders that could stir us to awakening.
And why should the toilsome tread of a beetle not awake at least a
compositional smile, or butterfly kisses at least a tonal longing?

LJ: 7b

The immediate model of materialism

The motif is born <u>while gazing</u> at Vyšehrad, while a stream is
rushing, <u>during</u> gale and thunderstorm.
It is transformed in the inner environment—but perhaps <u>not too
much!</u>

*

<u>I read</u> about Vyšehrad, about the rushing of the stream, about a
gale and a thunderstorm.
<u>I see</u> the picture "————," I see the picture of a stream rushing
away, of the lightning and the bending trees.

Surely the tonal expression runs out only through the inner envi-
ronment
Its furnace will change it—<u>perhaps a lot</u>!
Can this expression count as naturalism?

I think it can. I must have at some earlier point experienced the "model" it is fashioned from.
I couldn't represent a "lark's song" had I not previously heard a lark's piping.

LJ: 7c
And if a composer were to neglect these literary suggestions, the mediated models of naturalism? If he didn't react to a "black-bird," darkness, light, a rose, the greenness of grass, the majesty of mountains, the flood of sunlight, the paleness of the moon? Alongside the neglect of the concrete a significant emotional component would be lost, too. Untruthfulness.

*

And if those concrete subjects were not present in the text?
a) there remains an emotional paleness, dependent on manners of thought
b) there remain sequences of marvelous richness of melody and speech rhythms: transformed by inner environment—I am not stealing. Plato.

*

And when the work comes into being in a state of ecstasy and a forgetting of the self? The little threads of naturalism are lost in the mist. Do not think, however, that tones are born merely from tones!

LJ: 8
March

Bare pure naturalism
Of things and living beings—

Beethoven's storm in the Pastoral Symphony; although the din of timpani is torpid it is possible to discern in the density of tones the impact of shrieks as well as the rumble of thunder.

The creaking of the hinges in Dalibor's cell in length, melody and even coloring recalls reality.

In Smetana's *The Secret*, the thresher's flails beat sounds out of the threshing house floor, whose tonal position is faithful (in rhythm?) to the rushing of a brook. The voice of bells must take from the bells even their rhythmic remoteness.

LJ: 9

The fluttering tones of jingle bells to be awakened again only by using jingle bells.
The "wailing wind" plays the piccolo. The clatter of the mill—the xylophone.
And what a task to come close to the babbling of a brook using orchestral colors (Fibich), and what "musical instruments" get wedged into the orchestra in the process! (Strauss—Mahler)

*

The sound expressions of communication among living creatures acquire the significance—duration, tonal modulation, *sčasování* — of motifs.
(!) Saint-Saëns' little cock (Danse Macabre)

LJ: 10

sings a well-known melody.

The owl mourns at night with its hollow:

How many times does Smetana capture the lark's singing, even the lark's song!

Don't believe that a dog simply has a bark; even he whines when he is lonely, and pleads ▆▆▆▆▆▆ and expresses anger by growling.

That the cock knows only ▆▆▆▆▆▆ he has an expression even for astonishment, and warning, and summoning, and distributing.

LJ: 11

The blackbird's heart overflows with so many ardent melodies,
but he takes off screeching when he spies a creeping cat;

and

of <u>M a n</u> ?

Why should he be left out of compositional naturalism? Why
should he be presented through inept recitative? Why should he
be deluded by the excessively sweet scent of song? Finally
through R. Wagner the flame of individual accenting re-sparked,
the word warmed by its own heat.
It did not thaw. Just by the warmth of a chord. A merit as well as
a mistake. Dr. Hostinský's—Smetana's. Why wipe it clean of
childish playfulness, adolescent ardor, a grown man's wisdom, an
old man's weariness?

LJ: 12

Why the robustness of health and the faintness of illness? Why all
this stretched even in the realm of gender across soprano—mezzo
—alto—tenor—baritone—bass?
Why wipe away character and type?
   Now (?) I exempt the classical example of Vašek in *The Bartered
Bride*.

A <u>nightingale's</u> song requires the closeness of his mate, the fresh
green of springtime, warm nocturnal vapors: from there it pours
forth and is nourished.
Why don't we capture the atmosphere of humans? Why is
historical distance disappearing? And the way of thinking? How
far away man is from himself when placing himself into a
compositional work!
And yet he is easier to fathom than the shy lark, the pensive
rooster, and the atrophied fidelity of a dog.
Bare naturalism fails here. We want to hear the lark—but to hear
man—that freak!

LJ: missing
A lark's song captured—speech melody unnoticed?
And yet already Plato says: . . .

Examples of bare naturalism in composition have the effect of a
burning torch: they illuminate clearly, unfailingly <u>the situation</u>
and the composer's relation to it.

L.J.: 13
4 March

In a compositional work I want to learn about man from his
language—speech—song—from his appearance—when he is not
speaking from his actions—to discern his emotions from his
work—to get to know his thinking—even the sparkling of an idea.
Naturalism in composition reaches for all that.

1. Do not have (?) a chord in your mind—and only then try to
construct the speech melody of the word within that chord's
emotional cloud.
The source of this speech melody is more complex, deeper than
the pale emotional cluster of a chord.
The path goes the opposite way—every now and then it carries
things away into the waves of music.
2. The musical expression for a miser, a begging child, an ascetic
or even a profligate, a philosopher, or a chatterbox is born.

LJ: 14
How many typical characters are found in our nation—only the
Germans in Schumann's *Carnival* present a similar photograph.
I was standing on the bank of the Moldau. A hole cut into the ice.
Near it, a fisherman with bait in his hand stands out against the
white snow. Dusk around 4 P.M. Bone-chilling cold, snow-covered
ice and <u>expectation</u>.
So much going through my mind—that I don't know where the
spark of a new tone will flare up!
<u>In this field there are not too many eager ones among us.</u>

LJ: 15
But it is the thought and its functions in art that we are hunting
for, in our case, the <u>thinking of a composer</u>.

Plato himself advised . . . The psychological process of composing.

LJ: 16
Rest assured that if today there was published a work <u>containing</u> <u>something unheard of</u>—in the name of compositional development, educational progress, or whatever other term—it will be devoured tomorrow.
<u>That's not just happening today</u>, but has been going on for ages. <u>Why does this manner of "putting the human appearance to use"</u> <u>not count as naturalism?</u>
In it I see the nature of naturalism in general, and of this ingenious one in particular.
One takes the first chord, the first architectonic construction, everything new, everything unusual, even Hába's 1/4 tone, without hesitation.
I would say <u>destruction!</u>—if times were not so bad. There exists in each of us an <u>inner environment</u>.

LJ: 17
Inner environment

By this Professor Dr. Nachtikal means <u>the functioning of inner</u> <u>organs</u>. I add to that <u>the sequences of all cognitive processes</u>, in general: <u>all consciousness</u>.
All that has fallen into it—even perhaps unnoticed—disintegrates, collects, crisscrosses, pushes through, <u>disappears—but never</u> <u>vanishes</u>. What is important for us are the rhythmical pictures engendered by all senses and—emotional accompaniment.

Illustrative example:

LJ: 18

I recalled the fisherman on the frozen Moldau:

And immediately in my mind there appeared a pond from my childhood, and we boys out catching frogs on Good Friday Night:

and immediately thereafter

a ship in the bay in Carskoje sělo

and immediately
after that

the mountain lake
Štrbské pleso.

The images followed one after another in time in my life, their
rhythms settling one atop the next, here muffled emotionally with
tranquility, there with childish wildness, there with wonder, there
with suspense.

LJ: 19

Their crisscrossing, seeping, becomes even more pronounced
<u>when we think them into the time frame of 1"</u>. This seeping—
whether conscious or unconscious—is that inner environment.
We see through it, we hear through it—through it we more or
less even exist.
Each in his own way—each differently.
Every impression proceeds through it, penetrates through—and
spontaneously changes a little—as long as I don't make a conscious
effort to resist.
Should I apply bare naturalism to something—Each of
us composes a skylark's singing differently. Each differently.
A rooster's call. Each storms, wails, rejoices differently.

LJ: 20

Each of us in his creative soul—i.e., with a strong inner environment—
projects differently either an augmented triad, or this or that,
Each of us will realize—even though he will be bound by the laws
of "ingenious" naturalism—the architectonic sequence of his work
differently

Beethoven—Smetana
Adagio from *The Devil's Wall*

<u>Not to fear naturalism,</u>

And I think that in this inner environment—teeming even with ideas—the concept of idealism is born and shines through.

LJ: 21

Naturalism is developmental.

I exempt those notations of pure naturalism (a lark's song, creaking, a storm)?
whose image wanders through a work like a water lily in a pond.
It captures something that has already often been glimpsed in the inner environment.
Examples of ingenious naturalism (architect.) made
R. Wagner, Debussy, Liszt.
   of fizzled out chords
they turn the modernism of Schrecker, and Hába's 1/4 tones,
practically into a sanction of clusters of tones one can only become aware of, into a chord.
To recognize—to overcome. He moves on and reaches for something new.

LJ: 22

Modernism
Subjects of naturalism

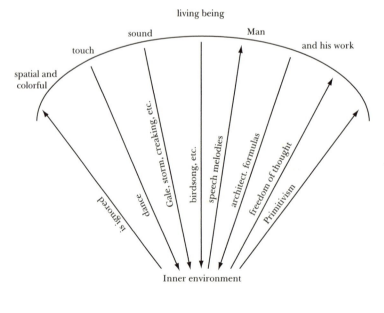

• 300 •

I think that naturalism <u>is not refuted</u> by idealism but by <u>ignorance</u>; this leads to primitivism. Rebikov went off into Asian deserts to sever his ties. He never returned.

LJ: 23

Afterword

The composer of *From Bohemian Fields and Groves*
The Moldau
Šárka

the composer <u>of the terrible tone</u> in the quartet *From My Life*—the composer breathing with the joy of life in the beautiful Czech world—should he shut himself out of it?
I could present examples from all <u>his</u> operas, examples of fresh, eternally young naturalism—and that weight would be equivalent to that of all his oeuvre.

Editor's Note

The text published here is deposited in the music department of the Moravian Regional Museum in Brno, JA S 72 and 73. The study can be chronologically placed in the year 1925, but it may have been written as early as 1924. The dates are not quite clear, but the Smetana accent is substantial, which would attest to the influence of the 100th anniversary of Bedřich Smetana's birth.

The most expressive passages in this generally still unknown study have been analyzed in my dissertation *Leoš Janáček and Twentieth Century Music*, typescript, Brno 1970, especially passages on pp. 94–101. Examples, as long as they contribute significantly to a greater understanding of the text, are reproduced as the composer's facsimiles. We also include parts of a sentence and word connections that were crossed out.

In the text we preserve Janáček's articulation of words as well as his orthographic peculiarities. In cases where this does not apply, it is a matter of correcting evident mistakes. We graphically separate individual pages of Janáček's manuscripts, and preserve the author's numbering in the following way: LJ:1

Next to this indication we sometimes add in parentheses the number indicating which page number of Janáček's manuscript it actually is. We do this because Janáček was often in the habit of adding to the single page of text and continuing to use the original page number: 6, 6a, 6b.

Janáček and Naturalism

This text will not resolve the many year-old questions of numerous musicologists, namely to what degree it is possible, in the context of Czech musical and cultural thinking, to categorize Janáček's artistic contribution after the year 1900 as naturalism. In any case, it will document something: after more than a quarter of a century of the composer's efforts, it will bring into view his long-term interest in naturalism, and will present several authentic explanations. We know that the creator's self-analysis is often a dependable deformation of viewing the work, which is almost always wiser than the author.

In spite of it, however, we read with excitement Janáček's visions of naturalism or of that which he considers as such. The greatest manifestation of naturalism is the existence of speech melodies. This form of a "natural" object caught out in the open is one we have already marked several times as the basic "meta style" starting point for Janáček's "impressionism," "expressionism," "verismo," etc. One can as well note stylistic and directional indications without using quotation marks.

Speech melodies are, despite their overall primary naturalism, a form that has gone through a considerable amount of stylizing. For example, only a rather approximate choice of intervals is used (which reflects the composer's preferences), and also rhythms are conceived in considerable detail. Janáček bases the authority for capturing these objects on his hearing (it's not that we don't trust him, but we rightly surmise that totally subjective points of view and the choice of preferred intervals took the upper hand). The whole manipulation of Hipp's chronoscope and its share in forming the rhythms of speech melodies is more than problematic. Vladimír Helfert's generation and his students either ignored these "authentic" fragments of music or even acted as if they were, in a way, scientific research into the melody and rhythm of human speech. Janáček considered these to be part of his scientific and professional activity, and he tried to keep them strictly separate from his artistic creativity. However, one cannot rule out the seeping of these auto-stylizations of speech expressions into operatic and vocal creation of all types.

Janáček's "natural" speech melodies became a supply house of situations that could be newly particularized. We consider the speech melodies in themselves a method of viewing speech communication and its variously exposed positions. The contexts of these speech melodies can lead, according to contexts of space, color, sonic quality, chords, etc., to positions such as "impressionism," "expressionism," "verismo," etc.

It is certainly worthwhile to point out two moments, that are directly related to questions of Janáček's so-called naturalism:

1. The use of speech melody situations in the whole extensive sphere of Janáček's chamber, piano, symphonic and other works—
   the impossibility of repeating Janáček's method of carrying over "speechiness" and "speech melodies" into an instrumental dimension.
2. Janáček's late attempt to use "natural" objects and his refusal to substitute other sounds for them. Thus, for example, in the violin concerto "A Little Soul's Journey" he uses shackles,

whose evolution leads to a work directly connected with the violin concerto—to the opera *From the House of the Dead*. We do not know how Janáček imagined creating the sound—banging the shackles together, amplifying the bang by hitting the shackles against the better resonating surface of tympani, and so on—this example, however, together with some additional ones, we consider an instance of naturalism "from objects."

INDEX AND CONTRIBUTORS

Index

Notes on the Contributors

Michael Beckerman is Professor of Music at New York University. His books include *Janáček as Theorist* (Pendragon), *Janáček and Czech Music* (Pendragon), *Dvořák and His World* (Princeton), and *New Worlds of Dvořák* (Norton). He has received the Janáček Medal from the Czech Ministry of Culture and was Laureate of the Czech Music Council in 2001. He writes regularly for the *New York Times* and is a founding member of the Czech and Slovak Music Society. He is currently writing a book on musical representations of the idyllic.

Leon Botstein is President and Leon Levy Professor in the Arts and Humanities at Bard College. He is the author of *Judentum und Modernität* (Vienna, 1991) and *Jefferson's Children: Education and the Promise of American Culture* (New York, 1997). He is also the editor of *The Compleat Brahms* (New York, 1999) and *The Musical Quarterly*, as well as music director of the American Symphony Orchestra. He has recorded works by, among others, Szymanowski, Hartmann, Bruch, Toch, Dohnányi, Bruckner, Richard Strauss, and Mendelssohn for Telarc, CRI, Koch, Arabesque, and New World Records.

Geoffrey Chew is Senior Lecturer in Music at Royal Holloway, University of London. His research interests range from Czech and Slovak music to music analysis, music of the Renaissance and Baroque, and the relationships between music and literature. His publications, which include studies on Janáček and Dostoevksy, on Czech musicology after World War II, and on pastoral elements in Austrian music, have appeared in several books and journals.

Tatiana Firkušný was born in Czechoslovakia and lives in the United States where she followed her husband, the concert pianist Rudolf Firkušný, in 1965. A graduate of New York University, she has worked on translations from Czech and German for a number of publishers and institutions, including Sony Classical, BMG Classics, Lincoln Center for the Performing Arts, Princeton University Press, Catbird Press, and Farrar, Straus & Giroux.

Véronique Firkušný-Callegari was born of Czech parents in Switzerland and grew up trilingual in Czech, French, and English. She has a degree from Barnard College and, apart from collaborating with her mother on translations from Czech, also translates from French, German, and Italian, and works with opera singers as a Czech language coach. She lives in New York City with her husband, two children, and a corgi.

Derek Katz is Assistant Professor of Music at Lawrence University, in Appleton, Wisconsin. He has published articles about Czech music in *Musical Quarterly* and *Hudební věda,* and also writes about music for the *New York Times*. He has contributed to program books for the San Francisco Opera and Lincoln Center, and presented pre-concert lectures at Lincoln Center and Carnegie Hall.

Diane M. Paige is currently Assistant Professor of Music at Hartwick College in upstate New York. Her dissertation, entitled "Women in the Operas of Leoš Janáček," examined both real and imagined feminine figures in the creative output of the composer. She has presented and published work on *Dvořák* and related Czech topics in the United States and Europe. She is currently at work on a study of the use of the female image in Czech national opera.

John Tyrrell is Professorial Research Fellow at Cardiff University. His books include *Czech Opera* (1988), *Janáček's Operas: A Documentary Account* (1992), translations of Janáček's letters to Kamila Stösslová (1994) and Zdenka Janáčková's memoirs (1998), and, with Nigel Simeone and Alena Němcová, *Janáček's Works* (1997). He is also the editor, with Sir Charles Mackeras, of the Brno 1908 version of Janáček's *Jenůfa*.

Paul Wingfield studied music at King's College, Cambridge, where he wrote his doctoral thesis on Leoš Janáček. He was a Research Fellow at the University of Sydney in 1987–1988, and at Gonville and Caius College, Cambridge, in 1988–1990. Since 1990 he has been a lecturer at Trinity College, Cambridge. He is the author/editor of two books, *Janáček's Glagolitic Mass* and *Janáček Studies*, for Cambridge University Press, and has also edited the *Glagolitic Mass* for Universal Edition. He is currently working on two major projects: sonata form in the first half of the nineteenth century and a critique of musical biography.